The Ethics of Mourning

The Ethics of Mourning

Grief and Responsibility
in Elegiac Literature

R. Clifton Spargo

The Johns Hopkins University Press
Baltimore and London

The Johns Hopkins University Press
2715 North Charles Street
Baltimore, Maryland 21218-4363
www.press.jhu.edu

Library of Congress Cataloging-in-Publication Data

Spargo, R. Clifton.
    The ethics of mourning : grief and responsibility in elegiac literature /
R. Clifton Spargo.
        p.   cm.
    Includes bibliographical references and index.
    ISBN 0-8018-7977-9 (hardcover : alk. paper)
        1. English literature—History and criticism. 2. Mourning customs
in literature. 3. Elegiac poetry, American—History and criticism.
4. Elegiac poetry, English—History and criticism. 5. American literature—History and criticism. 6. Holocaust, Jewish (1939–1945), in
literature. 7. Loss (Psychology) in literature. 8. Ethics in literature.
9. Grief in literature. 10. Death in literature. I. Title.
PR408.M7S68 2004
820.9'3559—dc22   2004000150

A catalog record for this book is available from the British Library.

For my parents

Contents

Acknowledgments

I am grateful to the many teachers who have contributed to the making of this book, inspiring and clarifying my thought over the years. When this book was still a dissertation, seeming, at least from this point in time, more like an Ur-text than an early version of the work here presented, Richard Brodhead provided unwavering encouragement, his enthusiasm as an adviser as remarkable as his generous insights into a wide range of elegiac texts. I wish especially to thank, among other early influential interlocutors, Harriet Scott Chessman, Harold Bloom, and Lynn Enterline. Thanks also to the readers of my dissertation—Paul Fry, Margaret Homans, and Linda Peterson—whose feedback helped me begin to reconceive the project as a book. I am grateful in memory also to Michael G. Cooke, whose untimely death meant for me the loss of a mentor and friend.

In the years during which the project was reinvented, I have been the beneficiary of generous support from Cathy Caruth, Geoffrey Hartman, Vera Kutzinski, and Jahan Ramazani. A number of friends and colleagues helped hone my theoretical thought on mourning and my literary critical readings of particular poetic texts, and I am grateful to Ed Duffy (specifically, for his thorough response to chapter 4), George Justice, Christine Krueger, Peggy Reid, and Leon Waldoff. I am thankful also for the tireless generosity of friends and family for moral, technological, and even financial support, especially my parents, Robert and Joan Spargo, my sister Jennifer Spargo Mitchell, and Anne Kathryn Ream, whose influence on my life and work is profound and, as Levinas would say, immemorial.

Research for this book was supported at an early stage at Yale University by the Mrs. Giles Whiting Dissertation Fellowship. In the final stages of its composition, I spent a year in residence at the Center for Advanced Holocaust Studies of the United States Holocaust Memorial Museum as the Pearl Resnick Fellow for 2000–2001, and I owe special gratitude to Robert Ehrenreich, Wendy Lower, and Paul Shapiro. I wish to acknowledge my two readers at the

Johns Hopkins University Press and my copy-editor Dennis Marshall, and special thanks go to the two editors, Trevor Lipscombe and Michael Lonegro, who have been instrumental in bringing this book to light.

Three close friends have had the most sustained (and perhaps from their perspective also the most taxing) engagement with this book in its evolution. From our earliest collaboration in graduate school through the countless conversations related to our respective projects and parallel intellectual interests, Kevis Goodman has been a truly remarkable interlocutor at each stage, and I feel fortunate in every respect to be able to chart the development of this project at least in part as a consequence of our ongoing intellectual conversation. Amelia Zurcher's insightful advice about interpretive readings as well as her countless suggestions for clarifying both stylistic and conceptual issues have been as invaluable as they are finally immeasurable. She has read the book in its entirety at least twice, and I know, however it may hereafter be received, it would be a far lesser work without her contributions. Finally, Leslie Brisman has overseen this project (first as an adviser and later as an always ethically interested reader) for longer than a decade now. If indeed the ethical questions posed implicitly by literature are not simply derived from, but also inspiring of ethical engagement in the real world, then Leslie's scrupulously conscientious practice of reading each entirely new section of this book shortly after it was composed and offering each time precise, yet deeply insightful criticisms seems to me an argument, at least, for the ethics of reading literarily.

The Ethics of Mourning

Introduction

In the opening chapter of *The Vulnerable Observer: Anthropology That Breaks Your Heart* (1996), Ruth Behar retells a short story by Isabel Allende in which a young girl lies trapped by a catastrophic avalanche, her body pinned by rubble invisible beneath the surface, her head held afloat (with the aid of a rubber tire) on the quicksand-like mud. As the international media transforms the girl into a symbol of a national tragedy that has claimed twenty thousand lives, one reporter in particular is frustrated, as Behar sees it, by his own detachment from the event and decides he can no longer "document tragedy as an innocent bystander."[1] Though the action he takes is ultimately futile, by story's end he has cast aside his camera and his documentary objectivity. After three days and two nights, when he realizes there is nothing to be done for the girl, he flings his arms around her and removes the tire as the girl dies, sinking into the mud. Embodying the dilemma of the contemporary ethnographer who would take a stand against the modes of alienated, voyeuristic, and objectively useless witness that pervade so much of our Western cultural apprehension of suffering and death, Allende's reporter has overcome professional scruples and permitted himself instead to become, in Behar's phrase, a "vulnerable observer." Nevertheless, the skeptical reader may wonder whether such a story does not subvert its own sentimentalism and with it the moral Behar would derive—not because the man's sudden vulnerability to the connotations of witness seems so great, but precisely because his real vulnerability is so slight.

Though I wish to draw attention to the contrivance of Allende's scene, I am not unsympathetic to the hermeneutic Behar would deduce from it. Ultimately, Behar imagines, we must construe our acts of listening such that they might be at the same time vulnerable and interlocutive, as if those aspects of her life in which a witness is similarly vulnerable to the one who suffers could render a challenge to the entire field of empirical, objective investigation. It is not at all clear how different this solution really is from traditional constructs of sympathy, be they formulated by Adam Smith or Jeremy Bentham, and at least one of the dangers of such a model is that it operates by means of a self-reflexive mechanism in which the other's suffering functions as if it were always also about one's own. This would seem to be, at least in part, the point of Allende's story, over the course of which the sympathetic reporter, through his compassion, comes to confront his own traumatic past (as a child he had witnessed the concentration camps and suffered the tyrannies of an abusive Austrian father), crying finally for himself more than for the girl.[2] The reporter keeps the girl company during her prolonged suffering, while also imploring his television station, his government, and members of the international media to procure a pump to drain the mud surrounding the girl and allow rescuers to get at the rubble and free her body. But the man's final compassion seems conveniently timed with the girl's death, evoked at a moment in which he can do nothing. It may be precisely the contrivance of Allende's fiction that attracts Behar to it: the young girl dies as sympathy, if not real help, arrives. In strictly utilitarian terms, such emotion is wasteful. It accomplishes nothing on behalf of the other. Moreover, since at a basic level what the man suffers is instantaneously converted into a thought for himself, it seems that as soon as one declares and symbolically performs one's own emotional vulnerability, one also deflects it. To be truly vulnerable—literally, to be capable of being wounded— is to occupy a position one would rather not occupy; it is to move toward that position reluctantly (at best), involuntarily (at worst), perhaps even to be taken there by force.

Still, there is the peculiar pathos of a subject's felt need to act in a situation that is, seemingly, beyond his control. According to the hypothesis of movement at the etymological center of *emotion*, whether one conceives of emotion's movement as a substitute for real action or as the imaginative stirring (or motivation) of action itself, the pathos of any scene of dying derives from the vague apprehension on the part of the observer (or the reader who is a witness by proxy) that something might still be done to spare the one who is dying. The sympathy of such scenes turns on the tension between the hypothetical action we are willing to take (if aided by an author) to spare the victim her fate and our desire to spare ourselves the perceived lack of control over what happens to her. Our imaginative vulnerability is real to the extent that we can do nothing to alter what we are witnessing. Allende's reporter is only one in a long series of self-reflexive figures for the reader as a limited witness to real life. From the archetypal shipwreck scenes of Lucretius through those contrived images of distanced suffering that proliferate in seventeenth- and eighteenth-century literature, the overly staged scene of sympathy has drawn attention to literature's limited capacity to approach the core of human suffering. According to the basic contrivance of literary scenes of suffering, the reader stands in the place of a witness in order to be moved by the suffering of another, all the while fortunately aware that the representative scene is a fictive one. Yet few among us, except perhaps the most rarefied of literary readers, could pretend that these scenes have nothing to do with real life and the basic interpersonal problem of whether one can be present in any real way to the other in her moment of suffering, in her moment of dying. Indeed, if we reverse the burden of contrivance, directing our concerns to the real-life situations upon which the literary conventions are modeled, instead of the artifice of the conventions themselves (which is also to say, if we insist upon the premise of realism that makes Allende's story seem familiar to us, an example of what could happen or has happened similarly in other real-life situations), we might well conclude that such literary contrivance is oddly proportionate to the real-life contrivances of the ethical imagination addressing itself to a world of suffering. It is in this sense that we might begin to say of Allende's reporter that he represents a fantasy of intervention that is not only ethical but may be the very basis for ethics itself.

At least part of what may bother us about the reporter's demonstrative sympathy is that it seems a form of premature mourning—an act of surrendering the dying one, through a useless expression of grief, before she has died. There is, however, a basic truth about mourning concealed in such useless actions, for insofar as mourning serves ethics, it necessarily depends upon the less-than-realistic hypothesis whereby one treats the dead other as though she were still living (thus Allende's story may seem a fantasy scenario of mourning in which a grief-stricken subject longs for the deceased while still in her actual presence). So many of our examples of poignant literary mourning insist upon the newness of grief as a symptom of this very ambiguity, almost as if the mourner were unsure whether the one he mourns is yet or still dead. Mourning frequently deploys a psychological trick of time, treating its retrospective concern for the other as if it were anticipatory or potentially preventive of loss.

As mourning begins in impractical defense—in the simple sense that one defends another who has already been irrevocably harmed—it may proceed against realism and our predominant cultural norms to a point where the mourner starts to doubt the verity of the prevailing structures of her existence. Having identified herself with the outrage of a brother's alienated, unburied dead body, Antigone famously declares, "my life has long been dead, so as to help the dead" (559–60).[3] Of course, the immediate help she would offer is the rather minimal service of burying the body, and one might well remark that it is only the result of violated burial rites (specifically, the brother's body before her eyes) that produces in Antigone this somewhat unnatural allegiance to the dead. Yet it will be a working hypothesis of this book that to represent a crisis in the norms of mourning entails a concern for the inadequate praxis of the moment (say, the fact that a brother's body remains unburied), but also for an injustice that inheres in every situation of mourning. There is an ethical crux to all mourning, according to which the injustice potentially perpetrated by the mourner against the dead as a failure of memory stands for the injustice that may be done to the living other at any given moment.

Often, mourning promotes a temporal confusion whereby the question of memory is treated as though the remembered dead stood within range of an imminent threat of violence to a living person. According to a further ambiguity in mourning's perception of injustice, there is an interrelation implied between the general injustice of death as the end to which any life must come and the particular occasion of the unjust death as a socially determined event. Just as we would contend that it matters ethically whether Allende's reporter starts grieving for a dying woman before she has died (having perhaps won the right to do so by exhausting all resources that might be brought to bear to aid her rescue), we would want to insist that it matters which deaths one perceives as unjust. We might find highly suspect the mourner who weeps at the grave of his one-hundred-year-old grandfather, crying, "It's not fair," but less suspect the brother who leaps into the grave of his sister, a young woman who has committed suicide after being overthrown in love by a melancholic prince. We do well to suspect any too-easy conflation of the existential fact of death with the untimely or violent death, yet there can be little doubt that the literary tradition of mourning frequently treats these two terms as dialectically intertwined. For instance, in *Hamlet* the relative interchangeability between the hero's objection to his father's death qua death and the murderous fate the father suffered provides much of the symbolic momentum of the prince's complaint against his country's customs of mourning. In Shakespeare's play, we get to have it both ways: the hero's melancholic complaint with the conventions of mourning intuits the history of a perpetrated injustice lurking beneath the surface of such cultural attitudes. If *Hamlet* teaches us nothing else, it makes us ever aware that an imaginative opposition to even the most ordinary of deaths can be suddenly turned toward an interrogation of the predicative conditions of the unjustly perpetrated death.

Though it may be imaginatively convenient to configure a stubborn act of mourning with the report of an injustice done to the one who is being mourned, a mourner's willingness to oppose those cultural norms that preside over his society's attitude toward death is what gives to mourning its ethical connotation. When mourning sides with the impossible as though it were standing against the injustice of the death of the other, it demands from its society a re-configuration of the very idea of ethics itself. Much of the limit placed upon mourning as an ethical act comes from those who stand outside of its perspective, and almost every literary work of mourning develops a dialectic between those who are outside (those, for example, who have mourned inadequately) and the mourner who is truly dedicated to the memory of the other she laments. Thus in Sophocles's play, it is Ismene who tells Antigone, "you are in love with the impossible [*amēkhanōn*, literally, what is beyond help, what is impracticable]," as if the heroine might relent from her aggrieved dedication to the memory of her brother if only she were a little more realistic about what is possible (Loeb, 90). Solidarity with the dead is an impossible standard; yet Antigone's ethically oppositional mourning is also a complaint ridden with political connotations, not least of all because Creon's associating the rites of mourning with the favor of the state interprets Antigone's willingness to mourn beyond civilly prescribed bounds as an act of dissent.

Throughout this book I will be concerned with an aspect of dissent that is proper to mourning. Mourning's symbolic actions function as a belated protection of the dead, and therefore this retrospective effort always pertains to a question about the place the other still holds in the world. There is something fundamentally unrealistic about such a stance, in which one is vigilant on behalf of the other past the point of being useful to her, but it is the peculiar quality of mournful memory to proffer a value separate from use—what we might call a kind of negative idealism. By focusing especially on a resistant strain of mourning, in which there is opposition to psychological resolution and to the status quo of cultural memory, I wish to suggest that it is precisely because our cultural modes of memory so often neglect the other whom they would remember that unresolved mourning becomes a dissenting act, a sign of an irremissible ethical meaning.

Ethics versus Morality

The argument of this book proceeds, then, along two ultimately complementary trajectories—offering both a theoretical elaboration of what we might mean by an ethics of mourning and a critical exploration of the deeply ethical plaintiveness of literary works of mourning. My interpretive intervention in contemporary ethics focuses especially on Emmanuel Levinas and Bernard Williams, in whose work I discern the extent to which ethics itself is defined extraordinarily and mournfully. As mourning becomes a figure for memory, loss is always also the means of a surprising mode of valuation in which the past relationship is preserved, even in its painfulness. This problem centers any cultural or poetic ethics of mourning: whether we are to appreciate the other by imaginatively elaborating those meanings designated in and through our feelings of loss; or whether we are to interpret that loss as having signified responsibility, not only by identifying the other's finally unalterable alterity but by placing us upon the threshold moment of responsibility's conception, when another who was vulnerable and about to die called for our protection even though he or she had not yet asked for it directly.

Throughout this book (but especially in chapter 1) I chart a theoretical course that depends on contemporary distinctions between ethics and morality, according to which the former might be interpreted as designating a responsibility that not only precedes morality, but perhaps more fundamentally also questions whether the conventions of morality are ever adequately ethical. By reading the assignation of responsibility described by Levinas in conjunction with Williams's persistently antimoralistic critique of moral philosophy, I mean to emphasize how each philosopher implicitly develops an ethics of emergency, according to which the extreme or extraordinary situation becomes the conditional ground for ethics. Unmasking ordinary moral knowledge, the emergency situation ultimately places the subject on the threshold of an incapability or impossibility from which ethics arises. I take this connotation of impossibility to be not only descriptive of the mournful cast of ethics, but also constitutive of the fundamentally ethical thought inscribed in every act of mourning.

Since I have already begun speaking of the ethical situation that arises through mourning, I need to offer at this point a brief account of what I mean by ethics. Most basically, I use *ethics* to denote the primordial facticity of the other. This is to invert our ordinary expectation about ethics as a language of obligation (the realm of *ought*) into a claim about a relation that is always already and necessarily in place. By this emphasis, ethics is not the study of the imperatives through which we privilege relationship or some aspects of relationship; rather, it is the inevitable and persistent fact of finding oneself in relation to the other. More specifically, I contend that ethics is as often signified negatively as it is positively; it is a structure of relationship articulated through critique or in impossibility as fully as it is in the realized forms of our moral consciousness. Levinas has done perhaps more than any other contemporary figure to develop the connotation of ethics as relationship given over already to the meanings of alterity or, more specifically, to the particular of alterity that the other always signifies. Jacques Derrida has called Levinas's project an "ethics of ethics," by which phrase he points to Levinas's attempt to find the constitutive structural basis of ethics itself and also identifies a doubleness within ethics.[4] So too Williams glimpses this doubleness when he argues in *Ethics and the Limits of Philosophy* (1985) that the traditional distinction upon which ethics had been maintained—between the "ethical" and the "meta-ethical," or between prescriptive or substantive claims about how one should live and descriptive or theoretical evaluations of those same claims—no longer holds.[5] For, as Williams insists, it is always the case that how one thinks meta-ethically must determine the questions one asks about ethics in the first place.[6]

As Geoffrey Galt Harpham has put it, ethics is by definition a language symptomatic of the difficulty we have maintaining boundaries between our descriptive and prescriptive modes.[7] Ever since David Hume first suggested that the prescriptive *ought* of morality could not find its way back to its descriptive

is, moral philosophy has been open to the suspicion that our language of pre-
scription is either too arbitrary or too overdetermined to enter effectively into
the lived reality and everyday decision-making process of the modern person.
In the twentieth century, spurred by Saussurean linguistics and the poststructuralist thought of theorists such as Derrida, Jacques Lacan, and Jean-François
Lyotard, a further suspicion has arisen that all descriptive and referential language depends upon an element of arbitrariness traditionally veiled by metaphysical and idealist superstructures, so that the language of *ought* has become
ever more suspect.

In light of the cultural and theoretical pressures placed upon our prescriptive codes, a number of contemporary philosophers, from Levinas to Williams
to Paul Ricoeur, have sought to separate the more complex meaning of ethics
from its implication in the (often flawed) historical developments of morality as
a field of applied knowledge or a normative system of regulations. Williams and
Ricoeur adopt the separation of ethics from morality as a matter of discursive
convention, in order to permit our contemporary thought about ethical agency
to take seriously the criticisms that have been brought to bear on morality.[8]
Morality, in this view, can refer to the normative field of ethics, articulating but
just as often limiting the "ethical aim" that directs moral action (Ricoeur's
view); or it might prescribe a set of moral principles and associated social expectations that greatly reduce the complexity of ethical decision making
(Williams's view). In this book, I employ the term *moral* (or *morality*) most
often when referring to the conventions, regulations, or parameters of knowledge that determine behavior, and I use the term *ethics* to refer to more basic
structures of relationship as well as to the critique that motivates and conditions
"all" moral knowledge.

By attempting to bring a contemporary revaluation of ethics into dialogue
with literary mourning's own vocabulary of ethical protest, part of what I hope
to suggest is that mourning's sense of impossibility does not merely arise in the
difficulty posed to memory by the lapsing significance of the dead, but also
positions a subject on the threshold of an irredeemable failure (in, say, the conventions of morality or the socially constructed terms of our responsibility) crucial to our sense of what ethics, in any context, can possibly mean. Focusing
specifically on the intersection between mourning and ethics, I contend that
our revaluation of mourning should begin with the mourner's objection to an
injustice inherent in every death. Mourning's tendency to treat each death as,
at least potentially, an injustice refers us to—and thus exposes—our cultural ten-

dency to conflate morally and socially normative attitudes about death with the philosophical acceptance of injustice. As Freud had insisted, there is something fundamentally unrealistic about mourning, but perhaps that quality of wishfulness, inscribed in any mourner's refusal to relent his grief, signifies a movement toward ethics. By interpreting, for example, Niobe's belated protection of her last child or Derrida's elegiac remembrance of Paul de Man as a species of such ethical wishfulness, I devolve a hermeneutics in which mourning might be interpretively positioned as that which is about more than its necessary implication in self-concern. Might not the mourner's wishful revisioning of the past, through which she unrealistically sustains relationship, also signify profoundly as an ethical openness to the other? Or more specifically, to put this idea in mourning's own terms, how does a vulnerability to the other, an imaginative proximity to her suffering and death, also define what it means to be ethical? As I discern the extraordinary ethical connotations of Levinas's and Williams's philosophies, I assess what it means for Levinas to discern responsibility precisely as a vulnerability to the other's fate, and chart in turn, through a reading of Williams's essay "Moral Luck" (1976), the imaginative hypothesis of mournful agency at the heart of responsibility itself.

From Literature to Ethics, and Back Again

Although the present discussion of the ethics of mourning might well be applied to questions of responsibility in the everyday world, it is still the case that the examples of mourning I treat in this book are taken from the long tradition of literary mourning, which means at least two things: (1) there is, as a result of the pressures of literary representation and generic convention, a deflected, oblique, or self-conscious dimension to the question of mourning posed by the literary text; and (2) there is similarly a tendency to treat the ethical dilemma or problem as if it were properly a matter for aesthetic resolution.

The inevitable sway of stylized representation accounts for much of Levinas's own deeply Platonic suspicions of the literary text as a realm of pure hypothesis, obliquity, and finally of irresponsibility. Worrying that when a text is most persuasive, when it functions as a substitute sphere of relations successfully supplanting the literal ethical situation of the face-to-face relation, then literature will be least ethical, Levinas does not believe ethics fits all that well with the imaginative capacities of literature.[9] My way of answering Levinas's objection to literature would be, first, to join ranks with an array of postmodern critics from Nietzsche to Derrida and Foucault in insisting upon the prevalence of representation in even the most ordinary of ethical scenarios from the everyday world. I would also emphasize literature's capacity for irresolutions that challenge the normative, often reductive capacities of the social rules presiding over representation, so that habits of self-consciousness, the impulse to interrogate the generic conventions an author inherits, or the strategies of formal incompletion already mark the realm of the aesthetic by patterns of thought readily bridged to the realm of ethics. Finally, I would give priority to the qualities of ethical thought that derive from the eloquence of the aesthetic text. As J. Hillis Miller has maintained for a long time, the movement from literature into ethics can be a profound one, even when—or especially when—it is not based in the effort to establish a set of moral norms, virtues, or values upon which a reader might straightforwardly model herself.[10] This is not only because, as deconstruction has long insisted, so much of our reality is textual, but also because the aesthetic realm promotes modes of reflection that pertain to our ideas about ourselves and others.

Among its other capabilities, literature is perhaps especially suited to foreground the problem of alterity that troubles the ordinary capacity of language as representation, if only because in everyday speech, as a philosopher such as John Searle has tried to show, we must always assume a certain amount of socially constructed context and a degree of reliable, institutionally signified meaning.[11] Having suspended the immediate requirements of communicative discourse, literature offers the opportunity to interrogate the premises, strategies, and conventions of language and to discern the ways in which ordinary language becomes irresponsible to its greater calling. Such questioning is ethical in a basic sense, but it might also be debilitating if applied too rigorously to the everyday situation. Perhaps the only thing more absurdly self-indulgent than a journalist who finally intervenes in the fate of a girl buried under an avalanche by throwing his arms around her dying body would be one who stands to the side questioning whether there is really ever anything one can do for the other. In ordinary speech we cannot interrogate our premises as consistently or relentlessly as we do in the realm of literature. Literature, then, provides the occasion for an ethical reflectiveness about the limits of our language. Though there is not necessarily a determinative relation between literary thoughts and the world of everyday ethical action, it is possible that the relaxed reflective space of literature can pattern, to a greater or lesser extent, our reflectiveness about language and thus influence our ordinary ethical deliberations, especially inasmuch as our situatedness in language presumes a relationship between representation and any action we might take on behalf of ourselves or other people.

At least one way of conceiving of ethics as it pertains to the realm of ordinary language would be to advocate language's capacity to repair continuity—between representation and the real, between the indicative realm of action and the symbolic realm of motive, between presence and absence. It is often supposed that since mourning traces the gaps, aporias, or chasms of language, the real cultural work of literary grief is to mend the rift between language and meaning that develops from the perspective of one who experiences a great loss. For Peter Sacks, for example, this means that poetry itself is a vehicle of a compensatory psychological work, and mourning—as part of a quasi-mythic task that makes poetry serve the substitutive needs of the psyche and the requirements of a symbolic sphere in which loss is necessary to the progress of representation and civilization—becomes the very sign of our capability within language. Jahan Ramazani, on the other hand, has given greater emphasis to mourning's signs of discontinuity and resistance, presuming that the modern elegy reflects a larger cultural collapse of the social idealisms whereby mourners traditionally found meaning through loss.[12] Yet although Ramazani suggests that the turn against conventions might intimate an ethical dimension to mourning, he shows that negative strains of mourning must become the engine of proximate resolution, intervening where much of the cultural language for grief has failed and playing a cultural role that, if it does not fully restore an otherwise incapable mourner, still serves the psychic need for symbolic expression.

Both Sacks and Ramazani refer to the melancholic potential in all mourning, an asocial extreme in which the mourner might become alienated from those structures of symbolism or idealism that nourish identity and maintain the social order, yet neither perceives melancholia as evocative of an ethical concern for the other elaborated by the mourner's objections to the cultural practices presiding over grief. That is precisely how in this study I interpret melancholia —as the elegy's most persistent sign of a dissent from conventional meanings and as its similarly persistent sign of a dedication to the time and realm of the other. Even when it seems to emanate from the esoteric subjective grievances of a specific mourner, melancholia interrogates the symbolic social structures that contain and reduce the meaning of the other who is being lamented. Thus it is on the threshold of symbolic meaning that every melancholic mourner stands again as for the first time when she refuses the consolations of language.

The melancholic's characteristic lament—identified not only by Freud, but so often in the literary tradition of mourning (most palpably, through the conceits of the pathetic fallacy)—is that the surviving world has become poorer and even perhaps worthless as a result of the other's death. The melancholic person turns against the compensatory mechanisms of idealization and mythic resolution by imagining an impossible recovery of the dead, sometimes quite literally a retrieval of the dead body. As she protests her inherited reality, the mourner may remind us of Freud's description of the artist as one who adheres more closely to the pleasure principle than the rest of us and, as a result, often perpetuates the neurosis of fantasy "without following the long roundabout path of making alterations in the external world."[13] For no other reason than that a symbiotic relation exists between the poetic imagination and the psyche focused on loss—indeed, it is this very play between creativity and depressiveness of which Julia Kristeva speaks so eloquently in *Black Sun* (1987)—elegists might afford us a uniquely privileged lens for viewing cultural attitudes about death.[14] If it is true, as Harold Bloom contends, that the "poet begins (however 'unconsciously') by rebelling more strongly against the consciousness of death's necessity than all other men and women do," our studying those cultural views of death that poets would overthrow might allow us to articulate a contrary ethics of mourning and to obtain a clear-sightedness about the costs, as measured against the potential gains, of such a rebellion.[15] Insofar as I propose reading the ethical dimension of mourning and its divergent cultural expressions through the literary lens of elegy, I assume that the literary tradition has incorporated over time many of the implicit norms and larger cultural attitudes toward death that define the responsibilities proper to mourning, but I also credit many of the literary texts I read with resistant attitudes toward our predominant cultural models for grief.

Perhaps it is the fictive claim of the literary text that permits elegy to view our cultural mores as having become too comfortably immersed in narratives that require further testing and reformulation, and it may be, for example, that the artifice of the literary tradition of mourning is what allows for the expression of a concomitant critical trajectory in these mournful works. Whatever the reason, in the elegiac tradition the dialectic created between represented or accepted truths and resistant phenomena such as unpleasure, failure, and melancholia promotes a greater turn to poetic or narrative facts unredeemed by the mythic structures of our cultural order, by the symbolic structures of meaning, or even by the aesthetic and figurative patternings of moral, emotional, or intellectual sensibility. Such literality is, at a basic level, merely an alterity within figurative language, but it also points us beyond what is claimed as true and complete toward that which is outside the text and the province of ordinary representation. When resisting cultural and psychological narratives of resolution, our mourning refuses the substitutive nexus between grief and representation that inheres in a consolatory, symbolic valuation of the dead, so that in the language of literary mourning, the depressive meanings of melancholia insist upon the other's uncancellable and unassimilable value, much as though the anticonsolatory forms of literary grief could preserve the other as an implicit value beyond our immediate capacity for relationship.

Thus as I describe herein a strain of melancholic or anti-elegiac lyric that foresees no end to mourning—in neither the social sphere of commemoration nor the symbolic conventions and utilitarian principles by which it is organized—I attribute ethical meaning to the elegy's resistances to elegiac convention, to social commemoration, and even to the mourner's own wishfulness. Though the primary form of its ethical argument is negative, a resistant and incomplete mourning stands for an ethical acknowledgment of—or perhaps a ceding to—the radical alterity of the other whom one mourns. Presuming that mourning is ethical insofar as it supposes an imaginative protection of the other who has already been lost, I will argue over the long course of this book for the elegy's persistent habit of figuring the ethical imagination as though it were determined precisely by such a mission of impossible protectiveness, as I argue simultaneously, if implicitly, on behalf of literature's fundamental capacity to include and advance ethical inquiry.

CHAPTER ONE

Toward an Ethics of Mourning

According to our most familiar moral philosophical models, ethical deliberation is recollective in cast. The process of looking backwards confers authority
on that which is conceptually prior to the present moment of decision, so that
an agent deliberates a course of action by referring the self to what it has already
promised or, in social contract theory, to that which it has been promised.[1] Yet
this leads to a problem: for if the moral law is objective in such a way that it
cannot conceive of anything outside of itself or the relatively unitary history of
concepts through which it has been defined, then the subject who operates from
within this model, Bernard Williams worries, has to confront the moment of
ethical decision as though she were empty of psychological motives or competing ethical concerns. If the particular responsibility to be enacted is largely an
application of the abstract or universal moral paradigm, a subject's decision has
already been made for her. The psychological form or situational complexity of
her considerations can only distort the objective demand.

Sharing Williams's suspicion of the recollective forms of moral knowledge, Levinas offers a more radical critique, pursuing the matter all the way back to the philosophical properties of knowledge itself. For Levinas the problem is not that there might be a divergence between the psychological forms of our self-understanding and the objective sphere of truth, but rather that the conventional plot of cognition—which entails both the pole of subjective experience and the totality of thought in which it is included—necessarily limits the alterity of the other and the alterity of the subjectivity it signifies by returning each term to the flow of knowledge. Cognition refers the fact of alterity to an origin in thought itself. Any disruption or difference subjectivity meets with is already to be found and eventually included in the conventions of representation, which may be dialectically expanded, but never withstood from the outside. In other words, as Levinas says in *Otherwise Than Being* (1974), the conceptual truth of cognition coincides with the reductive or containing properties of representation:

> Truth is rediscovery, recall, reminiscence, reuniting under the unity of apperception. There is remission of time and tension of the recapture, relaxation and tension without a break, without a gap. There is not a pure distancing from the present, but precisely re-presentation, that is, a distancing in which the present of truth *is* already or *still is;* for a representation is a recommencement of the present which in its "first time" is for the second time; it is a retention and a protention, between forgetting and expecting, between memory and project.[2]

This would mean that the subject can recognize his obligation only to that which is truthful, and since that which is truthful is already a principle, concept, or potential datum of received knowledge, a subject encounters the obligating event only by representing it through familiar forms of obligation. In such a view, responsibility originates prima facie in prescribed, intelligible commitments: one takes responsibility for a particular situation or for the welfare of another person according to identifications one has developed with the cultural and moral norms that define the *good* of a society. When ethics functions straightforwardly as a matter of cognition, a failure of responsibility can occur only because one has insufficiently learned what it is good to do, or perhaps because a subject who can recognize the good has allowed unreflective desires or inordinate self-interest to take precedence over his rationally mediated desire.[3]

One of the central problems with a model of ethics in which responsibility is always the measure of the concepts by which it has already been defined is that a moral agent who acts responsibly by esteeming himself for fulfilling culturally defined moral expectations necessarily forsakes that other motivating principle of moral action—the benefit of another.[4] Morality acted upon as an external code or priorly conceived obligation stands always in jeopardy of losing its focus on the other. For Levinas, this slippage within morality—in which the person to whom one would respond becomes an object of thought that falls already into the past tense—occurs as a necessary result of any obligation perceived strictly as a matter of knowledge and pursued faithfully as a matter of choice. Responsibility, in the Levinasian sense, exists on the hitherside of knowledge, "a modality not of a knowing, but of an obsession, a shuddering of the human quite different from cognition" (*OTB* 87). As the subject is taken up by that which is beyond her control and knowledge, greater even than the idea of herself as agent, responsibility is assigned anterior to any instance of moral consciousness. To be ethically motivated beyond moral intentions is to be put in order by the other apart from the cultural structures of identification that construct the self and its responsibilities, apart from all those conceptual properties that by referring to a prior history of represented truth would determine identity and its obligations.

If we were to arrive at such a critique through the eyes of Levinas alone, it would be hard to decide how far we should attribute it to the politics and cultural transformations of the twentieth century. But Williams is convinced that much of what makes moral obligation obsolete as conceived by the tradition of Western philosophy has to do with a historical narrative that involves, as he says, the "coming and departure of Christianity" and "the failures of the Enlightenment," both of which failed narratives make it plausible that we might draw closer to conceptions of morality reappropriated from the ancient world (*ELP* 98). Like Williams, Levinas suggests that the construct of identity presumed by moral philosophy has been betrayed by the Enlightenment's inability to deliver its promise, but he attributes at least some of the failure of the modern moment to the failure of philosophy itself—to its preference for modes of thought positioned on the side of systemic totality and to a cognitive rationality that for all its effort to bring a unity to the self and its concepts has neglected the history of the other inscribed upon the very possibility of subjectivity. As humanism reveals its complicity with a metaphysics that abstracts the self toward principle, universal reason, and the totality of systems, it fails to privilege the humanity of the other person as the radical of philosophy. Identity owes itself to a signification that deposes the intentional structure of action as the expression of an agent's commitment. Before every attempt to locate the self and the other through the descriptions and representations of the knowledgeable subject, Levinasian ethics pronounces an impossibility within identity, specifically the ethical structure whereby the subject finds that it is for-the-other before it can be for itself.

Thus through Levinas and Williams we arrive at a paradox, which I state here as a principle: *Emerging as a disruption of consciousness, responsibility means to be obligated beyond even the thoughts and actions of which we are capable; and yet despite the fact that it is always in excess of our capability, without the event of responsibility we would be less than ourselves, less than fully human.* Since it always exceeds the bounds by which we would choose to characterize it, responsibility so conceived is set against the liberal construct of rights. Understanding obligations through the construct of rights foresees an end to obligation at the very point where the language of rights also ends. I cannot be responsible for that which is not defined as an obligation, nor for that which I cannot have reasonably known to be my responsibility. Williams reminds us that the conception of obligation in the discourse of rights is negative, having to do with "what we should not do," but that there also exists a positive sort of obligation that, in the situation of immediacy, will demand and inspire deliberation (*ELP* 185). It is of no small importance that these situations of immediacy are imbricated in Williams's account with the exceptional circumstance of emergency, a situation in which the vital interests of people force themselves upon a subject who has a potential to act—that is to say, to act specifically in a manner that does not refer to a generalized obligation. Interpreting this gap between practical necessity and moral obligation, Williams suggests that in the case of a subject who responds to an emergency by performing a heroic action, his reasoning may share the structure of obligation and he may even experience his motivation in the form of a demand (say, as something he had to do), but his response necessarily departs from those expectations that have been defined through moral obligation. Simply put, even the one who has acted heroically realizes, if only in retrospect, that this same course of action "would not be a demand on others" (*ELP* 189).

If Williams turns to the act of heroism precisely because it represents an exceptional demand and is not therefore a pattern of deliberation for all agents, Levinas reads this heroic proportion into ethics as if it were there from the start. Employing conceits that demand emergency connotations—when he signifies responsibility in the question of the other's persecution, in his wretchedness, nakedness, or exposure to wounding, in his poverty, pain, and imminent death—Levinas nevertheless does not expound the practical dimensions of intervention.[5]

An ethics signified as though it were simultaneous to emergency must be meaningful beyond any action taken on behalf of the other. Whereas according to the deliberative model of moral philosophy, a self must always be left the choice whether or not to intervene, in Levinas's account responsibility precedes and is larger than the choice or the perception of it. All the vestiges of voluntarism in Levinas's language—as, for example, when he speaks for the ethical subject by saying ". . . I am obedient as though to an order addressed to me" (*OTB* 91)— refer the instance of command, as it were metaphorically, to the anterior significance of the other herself.

What is connoted through the emergency situation of ethics, then, is the diminution of the free and voluntary deliberation of the moral subject. To have time enough to choose one's obligations is already to ignore the plight and untimeliness of the other. Any subject's capacity to act—to be capable in the face of what he recognizes as obligation—may be (as Williams has insisted) no more than a matter of moral luck, or those conditions, whether extrinsic or intrinsic, that influence the subject's ability to perceive the moral matter purely.[6] Levinas suspects the capability (or *pouvoir*) and voluntariness of morality's subject: "I am obliged without this obligation having begun in me, as though an order slipped into my consciousness like a thief. . . ." (*OTB* 13).[7] But whereas Williams argues for a persistent gap between moral obligation and ethical deliberation such that morality fails the reality of the subject, for Levinas the failure is more absolute and works in reverse: it is the subject who must fail—or at least fail to apprehend the full extent of—obligation. Not only is it the case that the other imposes obligation before the subject chooses it, but obligation itself is, as it were, an alterity in relation to subjective consciousness. In the subject's paradoxical debt to an alterity without remission, the ethical life of the subject is pronounced. Indeed, I would like to suggest that the other who is perceived in the ethical encounter is characterized by the fact that our responsibility for him can never be completed or fulfilled, so that his obligating alterity also predicts a failure in the moral subject's definitive capabilities. Thus a paradoxical value attaches to the failure of any particular act of responsibility, since it is always as such also a sign of ethics' larger calling.

When Mourning Is Ethical

In trying to discern an ethics of mourning, one might proceed either from mourning to ethics or from ethics to mourning. Clearly, the latter is more familiar—to proceed from an intact system of morality to a reading of the often aberrant situation of mourning. To the extent that there is an ethics implicit in the psychoanalytic work of mourning, for example, it would emerge, as Paul Ricoeur has aptly perceived, as a practical, therapeutic hermeneutic offering to restore the mourner to right relation with her world and to the conditions in and from which she can make decisions and perform actions aiming toward just relations among the living.[8] Not only would it seem too much a commonplace to bear remarking that no good could come of excessive grief, but, according to the largely utilitarian rationale of psychoanalysis, the good of attaching our- selves to objects of this world is a far greater good than a perversely prolonged attachment to the deceased from which the surviving party can derive no prac- tical benefit. The ego, Freud says, "confronted as it were with the question whether it shall share this fate, is persuaded by the sum of the narcissistic satis- factions it derives from being alive to sever its attachment to the object that has been abolished."[9] In this view, ethics might be expressed as the necessary opposition to grief, with the mourner called upon to resume cooperation with those social narratives privileging utility and the functional autonomy of the self in culture. To mourn ethically would be to mourn in such a way that the mem- ory of the dead might serve the living, and in such a way that the survivor's grief, already beginning to be consoled by the practical, utilitarian functions attach- ing to memory, would extend only to the point where grief does not prevent the resumption of normal relationships among the living or to the point where the work of mourning can be conceived as a useful act of commemoration, putting the memory of the other in service of the general good, of morality.

Yet the very fact that mourning is such work suggests that it operates on re- sistant, formidable material. Finally, for Freud, it is the economic rationale that wins out: since reality has proven too painful—has revealed itself quite literally, through the evidence of the other's death, to be opposed to our pleasure—a mourner must overcome his state of being attached to the dead as though to an- other, more wishful reality. It is in part this imbrication of wishfulness with an- other reality in mourning that I want to elaborate as central to a subtler account of the ethics of mourning. Significantly, in the Freudian account a mourner's initial resistance to the fact of death and his stubborn loyalty to the dead are characterized as though they stood for a potentiality—indeed, a pathology—in every one of us. By such a logic, grief, even in its temporary expression, would oppose the necessity of death, causing the subject to adhere unrealistically to her attachment to the other and eventually to fall out of the time of the living.

Viewed simply from the outside, a description of mourning's ethical complaint may not be all that different from a summary of its seeming pathology: in either case, as mourning prolongs an attachment to the other it is in explicit tension with any pragmatically conceived notion of possibility.

Even as mourning seems a straying from the cultural status quo and from a mode of representation ruled by more ordinary possibility, there is a quality of ethical wishfulness in it, reminiscent perhaps of idealism, but perhaps more properly referred to the moment before any idealism forms an image or an idea of the other it would commemorate. This stance is based upon the crudely phrased insight that an opposition to death, which is also an opposition to political forms of death bearing directly upon our philosophical attitudes toward death, may function as the predicate of justice. From a strictly psychoanalytic or therapeutic standpoint, the wishful state of mind is taken to be that which the work of mourning must overthrow. When extended unnaturally—that is, beyond a certain culturally determined time frame—the unrealistic wish for the other unfits the mourner for the world and also unfits him for any service he might still do on behalf of the other's memory in the world. An ethics of mourning positioned on the horizon of a more general ethic of therapy must therefore negotiate the uncomfortable tension between real and wishful idealisms, while advocating that the mourner progress beyond impossible attachment. By revisiting mourning's wishfulness, however, I aim to challenge the possibility of separating ethics from the perspective inside mourning precisely because such a view seems to insist upon realism as though it were inherently an act of overthrowing the other's persistent meaning.

How are we to know when the acceptance of death, which necessarily means relinquishing the other to death, might also mean tolerating unjust deaths and those who perpetrate them? As an ethical attitude, accepting death means turning to what is at hand and cooperating with the very evidence of reality as we find it. Thus the acceptance of one's own or another's death may develop into a cultural ideology that increases the practice and use of death as a cultural weapon in much the same way that Socrates' drinking hemlock ratifies the right of the state to continue itself through its death-dealing actions. In his 1959 essay "The Ideology of Death," Herbert Marcuse proposes this very conceit, arguing against an exaggerated cultural focus on death because it steers us away from what is culturally useful, doable, or valuable. Yet Marcuse thereafter fails to examine particular instances in which death is culturally produced versus those in which it is a natural and unavoidable fact, and so never distinguishes between practices indebted to an ideological manipulation of death and those attitudes tracing a general, ontological understanding of mortality.[10] The reason for this, I hold, is simple: Marcuse assumes that we become capable of recognizing the social practices of unnecessary death once and only once we free ourselves from seeing in death a redemption from or triumph over life. By protesting our participation in the ideology of death, Marcuse calls for a break with the imaginative hold of death on our lives and a refutation of the deathly morbidities that reify the broader cultural practices of death enacted by our political systems. If we run Marcuse's logic back against his assumption, however, the impulse to protest and undo the unjust death would extend to a much larger ethical protest of the ontological fact of death. Just as the acceptance of death can produce a cultural ideology that is truly pathological—that is, one in which individuals ratify the state's practice of power through the production of death— might not the seemingly pathological and unrealistic response of the mourner who refuses to accept the other's death stand for an ethical protest against a dominant cultural pathology that trivializes death? Whether we refer to Freud's condemnation of the mourner's unrealism or Marcuse's explication of a cultural ideology of death that makes us treat the living world as if it were less real, what gets called realistic or unrealistic in any system of thought will always bear traces of ideology.

Mourning, especially in its most extreme cases, brings our assumptions about reality into question. Loss always threatens *in potentia* and against the demands of utilitarian, pragmatic, or contractual realisms to create a competing reality. To the extent that the Freudian work of mourning has become interwoven with other historical, religious, and philosophical conceptions of grief, a psychoanalytic interpretation seems nowhere more prevalent than in our larger cultural preference for utilitarian relationship.[11] Utilitarianism shares with psychoanalysis the view that any thought about the other can be distilled to a thought or care for the self. According to a strictly utilitarian rationale, sympathy and antipathy are already by definition aberrant states of mind, symptomatic of a resistance to reason because they refer to strictly private states and so unrealistically convert the ordinary relation to the world of real things into an interior, affective state.[12] Then too, according to the utilitarian perspective of psychoanalysis, sympathy for the dead seems an especially ridiculous phenomenon because such prolonged sympathy depends on leftover feelings for the dead as if they were still living and so can only produce an identification threatening the well-being of a self. In the effort to conform the other to the ego, a mourner's sympathy is opposed by a doubly resistant reality—because other human beings as objects of desire do not cooperate with our wishes in the first place, and because they do so even less once they are dead.[13]

Put another way, the problem that every death presents to the ego is precisely its own implication in the death of the other. Witnessing the other's death and finding itself "confronted as it were with the question whether it shall share this fate," the ego, Freud suggests, is motivated to begin the work of mourning, a work of severing its attachments to the lost object, which is necessarily a work of self-preservation.[14] It is as though to think (for too long) of another's death must lead one to consider taking one's own life—hardly an obvious or pragmatic conclusion, but one any cursory reading of *Hamlet* or "Adonais" will have made quite familiar.

In *On Death and Dying* (1969), in which Elisabeth Kübler-Ross ostensibly proffers an itinerary for sympathetic listening to the voices of the dying, she remains confident that such narcissistic fear is often the concealed content of manifestly excessive grief: "A husband and wife may have been fighting for years, but when the partner dies, the survivor will pull his hair, whine, and cry louder and beat his chest in regret, fear, and anguish, and will hence fear his own death more than before, still believing in the law of talion—an eye for an eye, a tooth for a tooth—'I am responsible for her death, I will have to die a pitiful death in retribution.'"[15] Though intended as anecdotal narrative, Kübler-Ross's example exploits the spectral connotations of a case history, garnering its rhetorical power from the author's implicitly scientific demeanor and authority. Imagining years of past fighting, we intuit not only that the husband's exaggerated grief resulted from his guilt about past failures of relationship, but that all exaggerated or prolonged grief traces a similar etiology. Any concern for the other, as signified in the inarticulate gestures of excessive grief, seems in reality an only too articulate expression of self-concern.

Notably, when the husband pulls his hair, cries all the louder, and beats his chest, his show of grief imitates the harm that might yet be done to him and thus offers an imaginary satisfaction to the deity (or fortune) who intends retribution. Grief as such may be traced to a religious logic of repentance. In the ancient Greek and Roman world, for instance, the story of Niobe and her children directly associates grief and repentance. Having boasted of her beauty and a fortune that surpasses even the glory of the goddess Latona, Niobe imagines herself immune from harm in proportion to the bounty of her fourteen children, proclaiming, in Ovid's rendering, "Suppose she takes much from me; there is

more / She will have to leave me still."[16] As the story unfolds and Latona strikes
down each of Niobe's children, her grief grows as a substitute for her repentance, the tale drawing much of its pathos from the fact that, as it signifies
retrospectively a moral attitude of humility, grief comes too late to recover the
virtuous mind that could have prevented such suffering in the first place. By way
of comparison, consider how grief functions in the prophetic writings of
Jeremiah, where God, speaking through his prophet, foretells the punishment
of the people's waywardness and forbids any rites of mourning for those who
will die under his afflicting hand:

> For thus saith the Lord, Enter not into the house of mourning, neither go to
> lament nor bemoan them. . . . Both the great and the small shall die in this land:
> they shall not be buried, neither shall men lament for them, nor cut themselves,
> nor make themselves bald for them: neither shall men tear themselves for them in
> mourning, to comfort them for the dead; neither shall men give them the cup of
> consolation to drink for their father or for their mother. (KJV 16:5–7)

This prediction of mourning interprets both the violent will of God (who desires the grief as a consequence of his punishing actions) and the actions of the
people themselves (who have knowingly acted in such a way as to produce this
effect). If mourning functions as a figure for future regret, there is also an implicit assumption that the retrospective cast of mourning is to be distinguished
from true repentance, which would occur before judgment has descended. As is
also the case in Ovid's account of Niobe, Jeremiah's narrative portrays mourning as futile precisely because it is consistent with the primitive defensiveness
Kübler-Ross perceives in chest beating and pulling one's hair. Still, each of
these ancient texts retrospectively restores an appearance of causality, suggesting that what is experienced within the moment as arbitrary fits finally into a
moral narrative about actions and consequences. It is highly significant, for example, that in the Jeremiah account grief explicitly occupies the place of repentance, since the potential for grief to signify otherwise—that is, otherwise than
in proportion to wrongdoing—intimates an ethical attitude to be recovered in
the realm of human actions.

Part of the problem grief always poses in a religious context is that it marks
a resistance to mythic purposiveness, and if the more orthodox religious solution would be to contain grief and show it submitting to piety, much of the proleptic humanism of both Ovid and Jeremiah is that the expression of grief
remains unaccommodated. In each case, grief enacts a useless defense against

harm, a futility that is proclaimed by Jeremiah's God if only to enhance the glory of his covenantal mercy and a futility dramatically enacted by Niobe as she utters her loudest lament while trying, haplessly, to protect her last daughter's body with her own. According to the Niobe story, we are most vulnerable to harm through our attachments, and if grief will not appease the wrath of the deity, it emerges nevertheless as an attitude of defensiveness against misfortune.

But to what does such defensiveness refer? Does grief primarily concern the ego as if our every expression of sympathy were merely a matter of extending the ego's narcissistic satisfactions to the realm of the other? Niobe's story seems to require a moral. Perhaps Niobe is supposed to have understood that others, even one's own children, are never merely subjective hypotheses to be submitted to one's own egotistical satisfactions. Or perhaps all Niobe can be expected to have learned is that one cannot have it both ways—the other cannot be an extension of the ego and also a site of vulnerability. By the logic of much modern psychology, which even as it breaks with psychoanalytic assumptions continues to uphold the basic premise that social attachments reinforce self-interest, ethical consideration must translate, at least in part, into a defensiveness on behalf of the self. Through attachment, the ego's boundaries might be extended to include the other, grief functioning then as the vestigial show of the sympathy one voluntarily invests in others, and thus always also as an expression of self-interest.

But I want to pose a naïve question: must this be so? If Niobe's grief is not merely an extension of her egoism, but a reversal of all she had previously been until this last desperate moment, it is possible that this scene of mourning, which depends upon a bodily intervention between fate and her daughter, comprises both a defense of the other surpassing self-interest and perhaps the first moment in her life in which she apprehends her children as others. Similarly, the pathos of elegiac rhetoric, even when recognizably determined by compensatory mechanisms, may express a more fundamental ethical wish—the revisionary wish that events had been and might still be otherwise. Since death is the literal occasion of a failure in relationship, the mourner would enact a fantasy of care in which grief functions as a belated act of protection, expressing an ethic exceeding self-concern. Though it may proceed under the aspect of fantasy, this imagined protection recalls or introduces a willingness to risk oneself imaginatively for another, the very narrative effect attained by Niobe's cumulative grief. When Niobe futilely shelters her final, dying child, it is quite as though she could participate in the moment in which another is truly vulnerable to death. Much as Milton fantastically attributes to the nymphs of his pastoral apparatus a power he lacked to keep Lycidas from harm, we glimpse in Niobe's action what I want to call a *wishful intervention.*

Even though mournful realism insists upon the failure of such ethical wishfulness ("Where were ye nymphs . . . ?"), the fantasy persists in the call for a revision of the all too human attitudes that have permitted death's reign. The mourner who finds herself unable to effect any change in the real world turns to a revisionary seeing of the event of death. As the mourner contemplates an event she might have anticipated, her failure to be on guard against the possibility of the other's death gives rise belatedly to a fantasy about agency, albeit a dramatically failing agency: if the mourner had only possessed knowledge of the other's death and achieved a proper state of preparedness, harm might never have come to the other. Inscribed in such wishfulness there is an answering concern for the other, even at the very moment when concern appears to lose all practical possibility.

The impracticality of mourning is what is so often stressed by Derrida when in his 1984 lectures for Paul de Man and in more recent work such as *The Gift of Death* he speaks of death as the occasion that tells us what or who our memory is for.[17] At the very moment in which Derrida seems most implicated in an act of mourning—which is to say, in the 1984 lectures for his late friend—he refers to the paradox of an "impossible mourning." Much to the point here is Derrida's rhetorical self-implication in de Man's articulation of memory as an impossible but relentless performance of itself. With a sense of exposure less desperate than what we see, for example, in Niobe's mourning, Derrida nevertheless permits the play of his pathos to become crucial to our remembrance of de Man. Indeed, Derrida's appeals to pathos seem finally less incidental (even when tossed off as digressions) than instrumental to his argument: "I would never manage to prepare these lectures," he recalls, "I would have neither the strength nor the desire to do so, unless they left or gave the last word to my friend" (19). This passage works by way of an elegiac conceit: in speaking for his departed friend, much as Milton speaks for Lycidas or Shelley for Adonais, Derrida imagines that his friend also speaks for him. Elegiac speaking begins in weakness (a "strength" Derrida has lacked) and quickly becomes a hypothesis of intervention—the only action of which the mournful Derrida is still capable. And the crucial figure in all of this is finally one so central to the de Manian enterprise—namely, prosopopeia, which is literally a making or conferring of the face. As memory's central trope, prosopopeia is the figure of all autobiography and in this elegiac context a sign of what de Man still says to us about himself.

By emphasizing the fictionality (in the original sense of making) of all address, de Man identifies the threshold moment in which what we make of the other is a tension between an impossible presence and a permanent absence, as if memory were always an act of inventing the conditions for our invention of the other.

I use *in-venting* here to speak not only of memory's role of place-holding but of its act of reception, the permission it gives the other to approach. In mourning, everything remains, as Derrida says, "in me" or "in us" or "between us," but since the other is literally no longer, memory is all that is left to us of him, the vestigial sign of relationship. In effect, Derrida has foregrounded his own wishfulness, most notably when he asks, "is it desirable to think of and to pass beyond this hallucination, beyond a prosopopeia of prosopopeia?" (28). This question precipitates the further observation that death brings about a moment in which there is no longer any choice "except that between memory and hallucination," where the interaction of these two terms seems less about distinguishing, say, between the former as ethical and the latter as delusional than in suggesting the imbrication of hallucination with memory, as if hallucination were added to memory's possibility almost from its inception.

Derrida's account of mournful memory intersects with the themes of Freudian mourning. As Derrida admits that all we might still say of the friend has been situated and can only take place "in us," he anticipates the objection that this might seem merely a narcissistic resolution (one that psychoanalysis terms *incorporation*). He meets the objection only by refusing to accept a simplifying definition of narcissism, by gesturing instead toward a rereading of narcissism as a mode of speculation that succeeds only by "supposing the other" (32); and he continues undauntedly from there to define mourning's necessary movement into interiority. One of the immediate checks on any note of self-satisfaction in Derrida's account of mourning comes as a result of a pathetic emphasis he gives to the mourner's solitariness. The mourner recognizes sorrowfully that he has become the only resource of the other's meaning. Ever since he has been capable of a "relationship to self," simultaneously constructed as singular, corporate, or interpersonal, this "possibility of the death of the other" has influenced all relationship to others, his awareness of memory's finitude seeming directly proportional to the other's alterity. "We weep," Derrida says, "*precisely* over what happens to us when everything is entrusted to the sole memory that is 'in me' or 'in us'" (33). With this note of pathos Derrida undoes the resolution of the Freudian work of mourning, the mourner's solitariness seeming no longer a sign of functional autonomy but an existential deprivation of the possibilities memory might suggest. There is something admirable about Derrida's refusal to renounce tears and his willingness to embrace a mourning that is, paradoxically, both wishful and realistic. From the standpoint of cultural utility, since all of mourning's language-acts fail to produce anything measurably effectual in the way of action, mourning must seem aberrant, characterized by nothing so much as its resistance to the cognitive and recuperative structures of identity that might gather the other into the self as a resource for symbolic meaning.

Yet the failure inscribed in every work of mourning reminds us that mourning is the state in which all that is possible has become impossible; it is, Derrida tells us, "[w]here *success fails*" (35). I take this moment to be a direct allusion to the Freudian paradigm and the so-called successful work of mourning, where success is predicated upon the psychological work of substitution. For Derrida, as mourning fails even in the midst of its continued attachment, it seems (rather than, say, an assertion of the ego's autonomous will or of the utility that determines psychic resolution) the sign of a longing to preserve what is obviously impossible. This is also mourning's only possible success. For, as Derrida says, the "*failure succeeds.*" The incomplete interiorization of mourning, signified by the mourner's loneliness and those vestiges of alterity that trouble memory, yields "a respect for the other as other" (35). When Derrida also alludes to the short-comings of the "interiorizing idealization," of that largely Freudian "*ideally and quasi-literally devouring* [of the other]" (34), we might consider that in elegy, for example, there is in every apotheosis, every personification of the other as a virtue or abstract principle, already an intimation of the more difficult relation to the other in her alterity. The elegy's installation of a protective principle (say, of Lycidas as the one who overlooks those who travel in the "perilous flood") is always also a sign of what it risks—the other who is recognized, admitted, or protected too late for any practical advantage to either party. Idealization is a fiction restoring the promise of mutual benefit. But it does not require a deconstructive reading so much as a faithful reading of the elegy's own internal resistances to its resolutions for us to suggest how often and consistently elegies doubt their own apparent resolutions and idealisms.

The Ethical Imagination and the Defense of the Other

What I find lacking most significantly in Derrida's account is the sense of peril that informs elegiac address. Though Derrida helps us attribute ethical weight to mourning's wishfulness, to its oftentimes hallucinatory pathos, he continues to put his trust in the mourner's interiority, thus always considering the other from the perspective of the one to whom he or she has been lost. For the most part, I wish to leave aside the objection that Derrida's mourning for de Man is innocent of that historical moment (a few years later) in which the memory of Paul de Man became compromised by the controversy arising from the discovery of his wartime writings, except to make the single point that what history has since added to our knowledge now makes the refuge Derrida takes in the mourner's interiority seem a naïve reading of the memory de Man's writings bequeath us. To mourn interpersonally in the space of subjectivity may not take us far enough unto the other—all the way to a historicized view of the political consequences of our purportedly ethical mourning.[18] As Derrida recuperates mourning's ethical significance through the peculiar sympathies of its figures and modes of address, he fails to give enough emphasis to the way mourning also means to remember at our peril, the sense in which ethics is put at peril by every death of the other. If the valuation of the other is put at risk through the event of death, we also perceive the other's alterity because she is one who suffers death, because she is one who has been closed off from ordinary moral relationship, challenging both its meaning and efficacy. Elegy always sets itself the task of discerning an ethics through a specific case of ruptured relationship. It seems both a matter of course and at the same time a remarkable fact that a language open to the risk of the other is not easy to come by.

A sense of peril, however, may be the very point upon which a Levinasian account of ethics hangs. In an essay entitled "Dying For . . ." (1988), Levinas ventures beyond the conception of relationship as care for the other based upon work or what human beings can accomplish together to a point where "worry over the death of the other comes before care for self."[19] Levinas calls this attitude "dying for the other" and says it gives the very meaning of "love in its responsibility for one's fellowman" (216).[20] What seems most surprising about the mournful cast of Levinasian ethics is that it not only figures ethics as a responsibility for the death of the other, but insists that the imperative of responsibility is not diminished by the apparent end of relation. In fact the death of the other demands a renewal of responsibility—on the other side of loss, as it were, in a beyond that structurally resembles the obligation that precedes the event of death. What mourning imparts to ethics is a view in which the subject is signified precisely as one who is answerable to the unjustness of the other's death, as the very being chosen by the other for responsibility. Opening oneself to the death of the other would mean both a receptivity to the other who is dangerously on the threshold of death and, perhaps more significantly, a receptivity to the other beyond the point at which such a receptivity seems literally possible, a responsibility designated even before it can be conceived and enacted in the world.

Much of any vocabulary for ethics must necessarily be figurative or anecdotal, and frequently a figurative vocabulary reaches a critical mass after which it starts to characterize the topic in question by way of its illustrative examples. In the writings of Levinas, such a concatenation of figurative thought is glimpsed in his habit of evoking those moments in which the other dies or of invoking the historical specter of the unjust death in order to trace an ethical significance that inheres in every relation to another person. With metaphoric vigor, the imaginative stance of protecting the other from death is implicitly inscribed, perhaps as the necessary corollary to the situation of peril, in what Jill Robbins has described as Levinas's "ethicofigural" descriptions.[21] As he attempts in *Otherwise Than Being* to define sensibility through vulnerability, Levinas refers to the fact that every self is exposed to the other as also to the other's vulnerability: "In the having been offered without any holding back, it is as though the sensibility were precisely what all protection and all absence of protection already presuppose: vulnerability itself" (75). Protection is at once a conceptual repetition of the ethical condition of vulnerability and, at the same time, according to Levinas's reversal, an a priori proof of vulnerability itself; which is to say, just as one can only protect what is vulnerable, that which is vulnerable requires and demands the posture of protectiveness.

Almost from the start, certainly as early as *Totality and Infinity* (1961), Levinas oddly predicates the transcendence of the other, which should be that which exempts him from harm, upon the fact of his defenselessness. The other occurs to the self "in the total nudity of his defenceless eyes [*la nudité totale de ses yeux, sans défense*], in the nudity of the absolute openness of the Transcendent."[22] When Levinas further declares absolute alterity to be "the resistance of what has no resistance—the ethical resistance," he attributes a positive power to that which is, in simply realistic terms, without power. For the negation of the other's powers of defense already refers to those who are always on the threshold of encountering the defenseless other, those in whom, I would argue, the prospect of an ethical defense has already been written. However, this ethical posture is not oriented toward a refutation of the facts of defenselessness, as if one could render the other invulnerable. One cannot wishfully exempt the other from harm by taking up arms or perceiving in him a virtue imbued with the Socratic confidence that the good man cannot come to harm. Rather, we are closer to an ethical insight to be gleaned from Niobe's defense of her last and dying child—that a defense of the other signifies finally a risk to self. The other is, by definition, one from whom I cannot—and would not, if I could—be defended, and this promotes the ethical requirement of approximating her fate. For Levinas, the defenselessness of the other signifies a responsibility that must yield power precisely to that which is existentially or pragmatically separate from the structures of power, and one is implicated in what we might call the ethical imagination of defense anterior to being implicated, politically, in structures of power. All vulnerability runs toward the significance of death, the point at which an injustice done to the other becomes irrevocable.

If a psychoanalytically inflected ethics of mourning insists on both psychological and social closure for fear that the self and the very meaning of the symbolic structure will be undone, such a model of *healthy* mourning also requires that the survivor defend herself against the other's defenselessness, symbolized and proven in his death, if only so as to prevent herself from becoming similarly defenseless. For his part, Levinas insists on the risk psychoanalysis would suppress, while also insisting that it is only by neglecting her defenses to a point where she is wounded by the other that a subject realizes the meaning of subjectivity as responsibility. This meaning of subjectivity, he proposes in a 1986 interview, pertains to the possibility of becoming responsible for all that may happen to the other: "I have the order to answer for the life of the other person. I do not have the right to leave him alone to his death."[23] Similarly, when a mourner's ethical fantasy of protection fails (as it must), the sense in which she has been called to responsibility is not diminished by what she has been unable to accomplish.

As I delineate the extent to which ethics intersects with the situation of emergency, it is important to chart the dialectical relation between accident and intention—by which the phenomenality of the accident reverts to the possibility of the intention (in the Husserlian structural sense), and any perception of moral intentionality also averts, or converts, the circumstances of contingency. This may be part of the reason Levinas's implicit scenarios of emergency are never given the full status of story. By suppressing the narrative dimension of his anecdotal figures for responsibility, Levinas empties the scene of emergency of a dramatic quality it would require to hypothesize a moral intervention. The point is not that the subject might be exempted from a response of nearly heroic proportions, but rather that the requirement of responsibility is never met by the agent's self-conception or by her singularly heroic actions. Answering to an immediate exigency as if obligation could be fulfilled by a particular action only defeats the signification of responsibility itself. Even if an intervention succeeds in returning the other to safety, the requirement of intervention permits of no relief. The ethical relation is characterized, as it were, through the persistence of emergency, as if any particular ethical response could only increase the demands of responsibility.

There is, however, a danger that these figurative transpositions of the dangerous situation onto the structure of ethical signification itself would make emergency appear to be normative.[24] To name ethics as though it were tantamount to the emergency situation might intimate the ruination of agency. It is only a partial answer to this objection to argue that, whereas Levinas seems to ruin moral agency for the concept of an irremissible, even unanswerable responsibility, he also intimates a critique of moral agency as that which might conceive of its motivating responsibility as something added to a self's autonomy. What I would like to suggest is that this critique of morality inscribed within ethics needs to be appreciated for what it says about the deliberate shortsightedness of our constructs of obligation and also for what it says about the positive possibility of agency. A focus on responsibility even in the moment of failed agency necessarily pronounces responsibility (and the agency it continues to require) as greater than the self-limitation of the agent or the limited circumstances of a singularly obliging event. By this logic, critique—as the measure of the shortcomings of morality's history of rational deliberations—is brought back into line with the very possibility of agency.

For its part, the tradition of elegy offers an analogous site for an inquiry into the sense in which ethics is always in part an unanswerable relation. Since the plot of the elegy depicts an emergency that has been fulfilled tragically, the possibility it permits to agency seems merely hypothetical or unreal. When the elegy explores the subject's wounded agency as part of his response to the death of the other, it apparently delineates what has commonly been understood, through the Freudian conception of mourning, to be a recovery of the prospect of practical agency. The ethical problem here is that one would move toward the practical possibility of moral action only by foregoing or forgetting the other who is the occasion of ethics. In mourning, the specter of failed agency is redoubled by every possible lapse in a mourner's retrospective attention. Mourning comes too late to the question of agency—too late, that is, to effect real action. As such, retrospection is always a hypothesis of agency, a reaching back in time to another possibility as though to a cause. Intriguingly, Williams has positioned responsibility at just such an intersection between the failure of agency and the imaginative task of retrospection. Not only does he offer a powerful critique of the conventionally conceived moral agent, but he also provides us with a vocabulary for thinking about how much the language of moral agency may be dependent upon imaginative acts of retrospective justification. While his skepticism about moral agency proceeds from a different set of philosophical questions, Williams shares with Levinas a penchant for thinking the ethical situation of obligation at the limit of its possibility—what Williams calls the "obligations of emergency," those scenarios in which the suffering, harm, or wrong that might be avoided is already realized in extremity.

A fascinating such instance of the emergency situation arises in Williams's essay "Moral Luck," an anecdote in which an unlucky lorry driver accidentally strikes and kills a child and then attempts to understand his responsibility for the incident.[25] As Williams studies the relation of responsibility to the extraordinary effects of contingency in a situation that is already defined as mournful, he draws near to a Levinasian construct in which responsibility is by definition that which cannot be properly fulfilled. From a reading of Williams, then, I wish to deduce a further relation between the hypothesis of agency operative in the elegy and the properly ethical possibilities of agency in the everyday world, elaborating the sense in which mourning's capacity to dwell in failure always also signals the task of responsiveness.

Revising Impossibility

Before I come to Williams's anecdote, I need to take some account of its place in his essay's larger argument. The category of "moral luck," which Martha Nussbaum would more fully explore in *The Fragility of Goodness* (1986), refers to those conditions, both extrinsic and intrinsic to the self, that determine our actions in addition or in contradiction to our motivations, intentions, and moral agency.[26] Though, as Williams points out, this idea of an immunity to luck has not prevailed in Western culture, it remains vestigially strong in some of our most basic suppositions about moral agency. When we insist that it is motive that counts more than power or style and that the capacity for moral agency is a talent present to all rational agents, we attach a special importance to moral value, which would assert not only "morality's immunity to luck" but the agent's "partial immunity to luck through morality" (21). Almost from the start, morality offers the thought of justice functioning as a "solace to a sense of the world's unfairness," so that, in Williams's view, our systems of morality already compensate for luck and the "bitter truth" that morality is itself subject to luck (21). This question of a compensation for the world's unfairness looms large in my reading of Williams, for it not only prompts us to examine the role that psychological justification plays in any agent's conception of the choices she has made, but it also points to an oblique exploration of mourning evident in the anecdote of the lorry driver.[27]

One of the ways in which the tension between extrinsic versus intrinsic luck gets represented as a mode of moral thought is in the distinction Williams makes between regret and agent-regret. The constitutive thought of regret is "how much better if it had been otherwise," but as such it always refers to a state of affairs with regard to which any person who gained knowledge of the situation might be equally regretful (27). With *agent-regret*, a person feels regret for her own actions, supposing that if only she had acted otherwise, the event might never have occurred. Regret and agent-regret can be viewed as poles of moral accountability: just as one might be unable to perceive any extrinsic determination of an action (the extreme attitude of self-accusation or self-sacrificiality), one might err in the other direction and be unable to find oneself the cause of any event whatsoever (the extreme attitude of blaming in order to claim innocence). Still, for Williams there is an even more surprising dimension to agent-regret. At quite a distance from the question of voluntary causation, the subject may evaluate herself as though she were causally responsible for that which she has not done intentionally. In expanding the notion of agent-regret beyond the parameters of voluntary agency to cover the idea of anything "for which one was causally responsible in virtue of something one intentionally did," Williams introduces the story of his lorry driver:

> The lorry driver who, through no fault of his, runs over a child, will feel differently from any spectator, even a spectator next to him in the cab, except perhaps to the extent that the spectator takes on the thought that he himself might have prevented it, an agent's thought. Doubtless, and rightly, people will try, in comforting him, to move the driver from this state of feeling, move him indeed from where he is to something more like the place of a spectator, but it is important that this is seen as something that should need to be done, and indeed some doubt would be felt about a driver who too blandly or readily moved to that position. We feel sorry for the

driver, but that sentiment co-exists with, indeed presupposes, that there is something special about his relation to this happening, something which cannot merely
be eliminated by the consideration that it was not his fault. (28)

Simply by driving the truck, an endeavor he undertook voluntarily, the lorry
driver has assumed a relation to these unforeseen consequences. Williams
might easily have added an element of error here, perhaps imagining a lorry
driver who looked away from the road for an instant or had been driving a few
kilometers per hour over the posted speed limit, actions in which an intention
or negligence would implicate the truck driver more overtly. Without such
elements of objective fault, however, the driver's response seems both proper
and excessive. There is always an excess in responsibility—beyond the pro-
scriptive obligations of law that limit desire in order to protect the rights of
others, beyond also the positive obligations of immediacy in which one apprehends a responsibility not predefined by categories.

Williams's anecdote is also implicitly a scene of mourning. Williams's lorry
driver imaginatively applies himself to an already accomplished tragedy, and in
light of his failed agency the specific attitude of agent-regret emerges. As the
anecdote conflates the ethics of emergency with the retrospective attitude of
mourning, the lorry driver gives himself over to the premise of a belated and
therefore impossible intervention. This is how we arrive at the connotation of
"something special about [the driver's] relation to this happening," and though
it is only sensible that the driver eventually extract himself from his peculiar
implication in the child's death, Williams insists we would most likely doubt the
humanity of a driver who too readily accepted such consolations. Indeed,
Williams's speculation on this point could almost be an allegorical gloss on the
work of mourning, and much as Freud is capable of surprisingly identifying
himself at times with the melancholics he calls pathological, Williams overtly
approves of the lorry driver's recalcitrant guilt and implicitly approves his
resistance to strictly reasonable definitions of responsibility.

Imagining thereafter that the lorry driver might act in some way to symbol-
ize recompense, Williams maintains that if an insurance payment could satisfy
the driver's unease, then he is not truly experiencing agent-regret. By its very
nature, agent-regret inclines the lorry driver to excessive impulses—whether to
offer financial compensation beyond the insurance payment or to wish to proffer
another appropriate action while yet being afflicted "with the painful consciousness that nothing can be done about it" (29). Grief—which is here a sign

of his responsibility—instills in him the thought of further action, even though it be futile, compensatory, after the fact. This is not unlike what Levinas means by the ethical demand to answer for the other in the moment of his death, to answer as if "all relationship to the other person were not undone."[28] Ethics demands a responsiveness to the other at all costs, even if it is premised on an imaginative and impossible defense of the other against a death that has already occurred.

Filtered through the lens of mourning and its ethical implications, Williams's anecdote of the lorry driver suggests that a fundamental dimension of moral agency always arises after the fact, as we are forced to account for actions belatedly and not only in light of what we had intended or what we wanted to have happen. It also helps us articulate the spectral agency that arises in mourning— that hypothesis of intervention troubling most elegies. One of the fundamental conceits of elegiac voice is the division between the indifferent spectators who have witnessed a death and the mourner who bears the burden of a kind of agent-regret. When the natural world is indicted by Bion, when the mythic world is blamed by Milton, and when the indifferent world of humanity is condemned by Pope or Shelley, it is the spectator who is often used as a gauge of moral failure. These elegists suppose not only that the spectator might have intervened, but that the spectator's failure to be moved to a position akin to agent-regret signifies his willingness for the death to have occurred in the first place. By contrast, the true and stubborn mourner, as one who perceives agency where it is no longer possible, is faced with such impossibility as the sign of an actual responsibility, even to the point where she pursues the other's value through a self-accusation that refuses to spare her the memory of her own ethical incapability.

It is perhaps not surprising that as Williams treats the question of agent-regret through an exceptional case in which an intentional or directly causal relation to the event is lacking, he must also consider how agent-regret veers toward pathology. When the need for reparative action arises even in one who has not directly caused a misfortune, Williams admits, "there is room . . . for irrational and self-punitive excess" (29). Yet even if such extreme behavior can be reasonably identified and checked (Williams does not say how), a person not at all inclined "to experience sentiments of this kind towards anyone" would be upholding an "insane concept of rationality," a codified absurdity wherein one surrenders all moral matters to merely objective terms of causation (29).[29] For Williams, not to attach ourselves to the "unintentional aspects of our actions" is to reach a point where rationality must entirely diminish the identity and character of the agent as a human being who is located in and influenced by a web of relationships (29). To charge reason with its own potential for pathology is an insight running straight to the core of ethics—or at the very least to the core of an ethics of mourning.

Even in Freud, who is divided between the inclination to pathologize extreme grief and a sympathetic response to mourning's enduring, if useless, attachment to the other, mourning's status as pathology is thrown into doubt. Though I would avoid Foucault's perhaps overly dichotomous characterization of a good and bad Freud—the Freud who with Nietzsche conducts a "dialogue with unreason" versus the Freud who is the thaumaturgical representative of severe medical and institutional protocols—I share Foucault's intuitive sense that the Freudian response to occluded or pathological behaviors often recedes from the strength of its own larger admissions.[30] For Freud, as for Foucault, there is an intimate relation between reason and pathology, the latter of which seems latent in every individual psyche. Such a set of assumptions also informs Peter Sacks's strangely compassionate reading in *The English Elegy* (1985) of the mourner's aggressive tendencies, where the complex of aggressive instincts and thwarted eros elicits a demand for language's substitutive praxis as a means of displacing violent responses to—or defenses against—the other.[31] Put most severely, Sacks might almost lead us to conclude that mourners are by nature inclined to pathology: it is lucky for us our poets become people who grieve through language, since otherwise they might become murderers.

Still, whatever the psychological reasons for violent grief, a mourner's apparent anger may have far less to do with any preternatural constitution of the psyche through aggressive instincts than with a subject's difficult-to-express opposition to the violence about to be done (perhaps already done) to another. The melancholic mourner whom Freud describes as taking the burden of loss into the very space of his ego, who perhaps cries aloud, "I did it, it's my fault," may mistakenly express her responsibility as though it were a perpetrated action, when all she really means to express is the existential fact of having been at fault insofar as she was unable to prevent harm from befalling another. It is part of the pathology of ethics, as well as the pathology of grief, to treat matters of ostensibly extrinsic luck as if they were matters of intrinsic luck—or we might say, bringing these two together, to announce an ethical agency past realistic possibility. Far from being an abdication of agency, such unrealistic agent-regret is a kind of hyperagency conditioning the interventionist possibilities of all moral agency.

Since mourning depends on a hypothesis of defense, howsoever wishful, Williams helps us see that an agent is humanized in proportion to his capacity to regret what he has done and to perceive what he has not done as if that too were a form of moral action. Responsibility is almost apprehended (even if it is never quite ready to hand) as that which lies just beyond what a subject as agent can enact. Though an elegiac fantasy of care emerges even, or especially, in the midst of pragmatic failure, the point is not (as a cruder reading might suggest) to find fault with others and thus exempt oneself from responsibility and its pathologies. In the event of the other's death, the mourner apprehends a failure of relationship, whether she is its cause or not, and in no way does the perception of responsibility's extraordinary, even its impossible, connotations lessen the requirement of action. Rather, the specter of failure, the incapability of agency, inspires the future of action.

In elegy, the language of defensiveness, hovering always close to the specters of self-interest and the attempt to protect a self from the other, competes with a hypothesis to which it is always also related—an impossibly vigilant protection of the other. Even in its more traditional consolatory function, the elegy tries to master the arbitrariness and injustice of death, but more often than not what we witness in the most enduring elegies is a lapsing of the premises of protection. Embedded in mourning is a requirement to interrogate our cultural expressions of grief and to be on guard against the movement toward consolation—as a matter not just of time, but of ethical disposition. For consolation always involves a relenting of the hypothesis of agency, a humbling recognition that there is nothing more one could have done or might still do for the other. What Williams says about agent-regret in general is especially true of mourners: "Whatever feelings these agents had after their decision, but before the declaration of their success or failure, lacked the fully-developed wish to have acted otherwise—that wish comes only when failure is declared" (31). In this nexus of wish and failure, we hear grief's wishfulness as ethical, even as we are reminded of the ethical disposition that inflects any genuine possibility of agency. Though the failure of agency produces the impulse for a moral accounting, it also projects the possibility of actions that might yet dissent from fatalism or the status quo.

In this respect, grief is an emotion always dismantling morality and those conventions of consolation dependent upon a perceptible moral order, while also intimating the very condition under which moral agency might arise—which is to say, particularly as a response to the need of another. Here I think we find ourselves on the cusp of an insight that Levinas at least partly intuited. An ethics of mourning need not refer to those cultural practices that curb and contain mourning as if it were instinctively and perhaps primitively inclined to retreat from culture toward pathology, as though mourning could only become ethical by moving beyond the affective relation to the other and finding once again ethical norms by which to regulate itself. Perhaps an ethics of mourning should turn instead on the crucial and paradoxical tautology we derive by reading the term *ethics of mourning* as a subjective genitive, by seeing ethics less as that set of regulations or normative practices that interprets mourning than as a connotation of responsibility already characterized by mournfulness. By such a logic, it might be less the case that ethics applies itself to mourning and curtails the aberrant symptoms of mourning than it is the case that ethics is already an egress of mourning. At the very least, it is the peculiar claim of the resistant strain of literary mourning treated in this book (as is also much the case for Levinas and Williams) that mourning is already ethical.

CHAPTER TWO

Mourning and Substitution in *Hamlet*

As our archetypal melancholic, Hamlet has often stood for mourning's pathology, as if he represented too closely our cultural discomfort with persistent grief. We could come up with a short list of literature's most influential mourners—figures such as Orpheus, Niobe, Antigone—but none of them has been so enduring, so persuasive, or so troubling as Hamlet. To my mind, much of our contemporary response to Hamlet has been characterized by a deepseated cultural inability to permit Hamlet's grudge to have its full ethical validity. What the psychoanalytically derived readings of *Hamlet* reveal, for example, is a cultural bias informing the history of interpreting Shakespeare's play—namely, a tendency to underestimate the ethical dimension of Hamlet's mourning as a resistance to prevalent cultural modes of commemoration. To read *Hamlet* therapeutically is to discount its critique of the cultural model whereby mourning, insofar as it commemorates the dead, aims to put an end to our responsibility for the dead and the injustices they may have suffered.

Perceiving Hamlet's protest as though it anticipated and objected to the central insight of Freudian mourning—which is, specifically, to glimpse the substitutive praxis whereby our emotional attachments to the dead are completed and our attentions fixed elsewhere—I argue that it is not merely coincidental that a figure such as Claudius presents the arguments for a ritual and formal resolution of the dead father's meaning. For, as Hamlet intuits, what we witness in Claudius's self-serving rhetoric even before it has been exposed as murderous is the fundamental failure of commemorative mourning in regard to the dead. Ironically, the ghost, who might suggest an opposing model of memory, is also governed by an adherence to a substitutive, symbolic mode of valuation— namely, the superficial form of cultural memory that is revenge. In Hamlet's melancholia there is a rejection of two social alternatives, each of which is posed as a way of coping with the loss of a father. A first alternative is cultural forgetting, the process whereby the survivor participates in institutions and rituals that would dictate the cultural acceptability, say, of conflating funerals and marriages or of permitting the death of the other to coincide with a utilitarian loss in value. In Hamlet's case, this would mean permitting Claudius to occupy the place of the "father" precisely because as a cultural function fatherhood is a role that another can fill. A second alternative is the revenge code, which is implicated in what Terry Eagleton describes as the traditional model of society and would offer Hamlet the opportunity to cling to aristocratic privilege and patrilinear preference. But Hamlet intuits the relative obsolescence of this traditional paradigm, perceiving that revenge is, as Peter Sacks has suggested, fiercely substitutive, and therefore altogether lacks any prospect of restoring the father's presence.[1] Each of the two cultural alternatives available to Hamlet turns upon an act of representation and an exaggeratedly formal act of commemorative mourning.[2] Whereas the first alternative requires submitting dumbly to survival as an ethic consistent with the ritual and formal dimensions of society, as if culture were not also about preserving the value and idea of otherness, the second reads the relation to the dead only through the symbolic constructs of identity, through falsifying idealizations of the dead. In each model, the value of the other is premised on exchange, on the possibility that esteem can be transferred to another object or substitutively fulfilled through a violent action that effectively symbolizes and stabilizes it.

Against the modes of cultural memory available to the hero in the world of *Hamlet* and against many predominant modern interpretations of the play, I here position the recalcitrant stance of a melancholic Hamlet and his negative social perspective and praxis as already ethical. When Hamlet dedicates himself to delay in acts 2 and 3 or to the strategies of artistic representation in "The Murder of Gonzago" or to the tactics of rhetorical persuasion in the closet scene, he implicitly opposes modes of representation that reduce the abiding ethical significance of the other to a usable political commodity. According to the play's deep implication in its hero's mode of mourning, the crisis of the father's posthumous meaning brings into question the very possibility of ethical relationship itself. If this is true, Hamlet's delay should also be read as an attempt to deflect murderous obligation toward a more ethical end—that is, to enact for Claudius and Gertrude a recognition of their respective ethical failures and thus to preserve a meaning of ethical relationship that depends largely on the enduring value of the dead.

The Emergence of a Norm

From the 1950s through the 1970s, a mode of psychoanalytic interpretation that veered toward sociological theory came into prominence, as authors such as Norman O. Brown and Herbert Marcuse cast searchingly to define the healthy individual who could speak honestly about the cultural illusions simultaneously shaping and distorting identity. Employing Freud and his followers on behalf of socially progressive stances for increased sexual and civil liberty and against the politics of war, these psychoanalytically influenced critics promised the liberation of life from the throes of deathly cultural morbidities canonized by state and church. How sanguine the prospects of a cultural defeat of death actually were might have been foretold by William James, not himself inclined to a highly morbid view of human nature: "Let sanguine healthy-mindedness do its best with its strange power of living in the moment and ignoring and forgetting, still the evil background is really there to bethought of, and the skull will grin in at the banquet."[3]

In *The Denial of Death* (1973), Ernest Becker had taken James's memento mori to heart and offered what he thought of as a more sober account of the light that psychoanalysis promised to shed on death. As he argued that the driving force behind the production of cultural meaning was repression, which was not simply "a negative force opposing life energies" but a force using those life energies "creatively," Becker saw reality and fear coming together naturally.[4] Not only is the fear of death an ineluctable and determinatively structuring component of the human psyche, Becker maintains, it is necessary to our very existence, organizing the human organism and preparing it for the task of self-preservation. Since fear would make us unable to function, it cannot be constantly present to the mind, and so repression—or the forgetting of which James speaks—enables human beings to construct a world of cultural meaning and to evolve a symbolic identity that, in point of fact, "brings [man] sharply out of his nature" (26). Everything we do in the symbolic world seeks to overcome our nature and what Becker calls our "grotesque fate," which is to be bodies governed by animal instinct and death. In order that we might better cope with death, Becker argues, the life of each individual enacts the cultural disappearance of death, as every self, on the road to maturation, claims authorship of itself through the "vital lie" of character. By way of an initial confrontation with and then swerve from death, character lays claim to a heroic autonomy and participates in the cultural production of symbolic meaning, but such autonomy is also always a disguise against limitation and the material facts of our existence.

Becker's critique of death coincided with the emergence of the new field of thanatology pioneered by such authors as Elisabeth Kübler-Ross (1969), who turned an eye and ear to the way people die in modern society, and the social historian Philippe Ariès (1974), who offered an important historical account of Western attitudes toward death.[5] Ariès accounted for the modern avoidance of death through the straightforward thesis that death contradicts our Western optimism about the progress of culture and life, derived largely from the Enlightenment and persisting in the modern world through the configuration of reason with the pleasurable imperatives of the contemporary moment. As Ariès and others would suggest, the evolution of mourning rites and funereal practices cooperated with modern society's increased ability to disguise death or, at the very least, to remove it to the back rooms of consciousness. What is not so easy to decide is whether the elaborate critical machinery that developed in Western cultural history to criticize both the contemporary moment and the entire history of death should be viewed as a phenomenon concomitant with—or perhaps merely as the byproduct of—a social fact that the psychoanalysts, thanatologists, and social historians of death were alike agreed upon: the erosion of religion as a persuasive cultural narrative, and thus the erosion of consolation itself. For if the moment of mourning quite literally arises as a problem about where and how to place the dead—and it is precisely this obsession about what happens to the physical body that the elegiac tradition, from Moschus to Milton to Shelley and beyond, so often traces—the loss of religious narrative meant that the dead had either lost their place or perhaps, as corpses, gained too much place in our world.

One of the results of this suddenly large critical apparatus for interpreting our attitudes toward death, I want to suggest, was a greater confusion about what constitutes a pathological response to loss. So many of the elegies born in the modern era, and especially those engaged with the cultural shift in paradigms of mourning, seem divided as to whether pathology would consist in a morbid focus on the dead (reminiscent of the traditional Christian prohibition against excessive mourning) or in the psychological and cultural avoidance of the dead (a denial more blanketing than had ever been necessary within religious systems). If Ariès, Becker, and their progeny have made it hard to imagine the healthy mind as one so openly dedicated to ignoring or forgetting the fact of death, our cultural optimism—though now lacking much of its mythic superstructure—continues to have its say, reminding us that to think of death is not to choose life and to choose life means not to think of death, or, more specifically, the dead. As the structures of consolation were loosened and a greater skepticism about the ideological claims governing the cultural practice of mourning was introduced into our consciousness, many cultural critics, when not calling nostalgically for a return to traditional religious frameworks for accommodating death, suggested that the healthy response to death would be characterized by an honest acceptance of our fate.[6] Of course, this solution only proposes to give a new name to an old philosophical attitude—namely, stoicism—and, as Marcuse has suggested, this stoicist turn of mind may be similarly implicated in our cultural "ideology of death."

In the "The Ideology of Death" (1959), Marcuse had argued that the Western ideological construction of death reconciles two apparently contrasting ethics—the stoical acceptance of death coinciding and eventually getting imbricated with a glorification of death as the very thing that bestows meaning on life. The virtuous stance of Plato's Socrates may put his judges in the wrong, Marcuse contends, but his stoical acceptance of his fate simultaneously embraces their right to judge (and, finally, to execute) him, however wrong they may have been. Following close upon this model, Christ's willing death became an even more compelling example of the meaningful death, and over time the philosophical mind (Marcuse focuses specifically on Hegel's contribution) comes to be characterized by its ready embrace of the inevitable event of death and the belief that death bestows meaning on life itself. Though we may wish to interpret human nature as though it were in contradistinction to the facts of natural necessity, an "ontological inversion" informs almost all of our philosophical interpretations of death: we reify the ontological necessity of the natural death and make a virtue of such necessity. If, for Becker, the insidious, though also necessary, lie of culture results in the production of human character as a denial of death, for Marcuse (as also for Brown and Robert Jay Lifton) what seems most insidious in our Western attitude toward death is that a teleological, narratological rationalization of death leads all too easily to an inverted relation to reality in which one views the event of death as constituting a "necessary entrance into real life because man's factual life is essentially unreal."[7] In other words, our cultural narratives of death instill a dangerous social conformity. Not wanting to overvalue life, we cooperate with the existing social order resignedly, heroically, or even with the unquestioning acceptance that we must be punished for our sins—our focus on death as the "ultimate cause of all anxiety" thus developing and sustaining conditions of unfreedom. Persuaded that we are powerless to alter the facts of death in our world ("If it be not now, yet it will come" [5.2.159–60]), each of us stoically accepts his fate as Hamlet does in the play's final scenes, rationalizing his relative powerlessness in the name of "moral duty, virtue, or honor" (75). Or, as Jonathan Dollimore puts it, summarizing Marcuse, Western culture's "ideology of death implies acceptance of an existing repressive political order, and marks the birth of a philosophical morality which rationalizes it" (221).

To read the hero's stoical acceptance of death at the end of *Hamlet* as a sign of his having been further reconciled to the symbolic structures of meaning in his society would depend entirely on muting the questions raised by his resistant mourning. For the Hamlet of the first four acts of Shakespeare's play might well be imagined as one of the first of death's social critics, one who in demanding from us a confrontation with the grim facts of death anticipates Becker and exposes the cultural mindset that denies the dead. A survey of *Hamlet* criticism, however, would quickly yield the impression that Hamlet's death obsession and the behaviors arising from it are simply pathological, since in seeking unnaturally to extend the meaning of the dead Hamlet must finally oppose himself to all that is natural and continuous and life-affirming (for all three words, read *sexual*) in his world.[8] Even as many critical readings mute the question of injustice posed by Hamlet's mournful complaint, they intuit the extent to which mourning must set the subject apart from the ordinary sphere of moral action, putting him at odds with his world and its predominant cultural language.

Such is the point of the two scenes juxtaposed at the opening of *Hamlet*, in which the ghost's appearance signifies a symbolic indictment of the present social order, while Hamlet's melancholic demeanor indicates a psyche still seeking a name for its suspicion. Each scene represents the precarious status of a disfranchised identity or a culturally dislocated consciousness (the ghost of the father or the ghostly attachment to the impossible idea of the father) that symbolically resists the ordinary flow of cultural memory. The rhetorical effect of this juxtaposition should not be underestimated, for taken together these two scenes already attribute a meaning to Hamlet's mourning, before the hero himself has begun to understand the history in which he is implicated. Put into analogy with the ghost's own disruptive relation to cultural memory, Hamlet's mourning is dedicated to a specter of injustice before the injustice itself is subject to memory. The truly remarkable claim of the first act of *Hamlet* is that the hero's unextraordinary mourning witnesses to an extraordinary injustice—an injustice that, like the father whom Hamlet laments, might otherwise have been lost to the cultural memory of Danish society. Indeed, the point bears repeating, if only because it has so often been lost on readers of the play, that Hamlet's mourning is quite unextraordinary in these opening scenes. From what we can plausibly deduce, there is every reason to believe that all of Hamlet's prior actions—before Gertrude and Claudius try to persuade him to forsake his mourning, and before he learns later on that same night that his father has indeed been murdered— have been perfectly consistent with his society's codes of mourning.

Whether Claudius inquires about the source of Hamlet's "distemper" naïvely or dishonestly, the matter seems quite plain to Gertrude, for one: "I doubt it is no other but the main— / His father's death and our o'er-hasty marriage" (2.2.56–57).[9] Searching for direct causes as if they were first principles, Gertrude's explanation seems deliberately reductive—her perception of a motive "no other" than the simplest one seeming to abrogate the ethical complexity of her son's mourning, as if she would offer a demystifying account of moral conscience and suggest that what we are really talking about at this moment is mere custom. In mentioning the king's death and her remarriage in the same breath, Gertrude offers what has become a publicly acceptable view of the matter: the two events, even in such close proximity, need bear no interdependent relation to each other. As the play opens, it is only in Hamlet's mind that the conjunction of the two events seems more than coincidental. Though Gertrude has acknowledged that the rites of mourning have been violated, her actions suggest that perhaps mourning itself is a bit archaic. Gertrude's willingness to side with haste, which is precisely what draws Hamlet's complaint, suggests a progressive consciousness in the most casual sense. If she is not a conspirator in her husband's murder and not especially committed to a war against her husband's memory (each of which I assume she is not), Gertrude has less to fear at this point in the play from a deliberately repressed past than she does from the claim that mourning is in and of itself an ethical act.

Well over forty years ago, Jacques Lacan suggested that the central dramatic problem in *Hamlet* had to do with truncated mourning rites and that Hamlet's complaint devolved from the rather ordinary ambition of making sure that the dead are properly buried. It is somewhat remarkable, then, that insofar as an implicit ethics of mourning has been addressed by readers of this play, mourning has often been deemed either incidental to the dramatic occasion of revenge or a symptom of Hamlet's own interior pathological tendencies. Even those who have argued for a reading that moves mourning to the center of our understanding of the play (from Lacan to Sacks or Alexander Welsh) have by and large accepted the view made popular by psychoanalysis that, when the play opens, Hamlet's mourning is already aberrant, or, at the very least, egotistical.[10] Following Freud, Lacan had been willing to give Hamlet his philosophical due, arguing that this much-celebrated and much-maligned hero embodies a psychic state of crisis in which the subject compensates for the loss of the object of desire through neurosis, since the neurotic is by definition temporally dislocated in his attachments, a subject out of time, one who is "charged with the significance sought in . . . the hour of truth," but is at the same time "always at another hour, fast or slow, early or late" (17).

There is little doubt that literary mourning, even without the explanatory rubric of psychoanalysis, is similarly characterized by a temporal dislocatedness or a persistent sense of belatedness, and Lacan seems merely an astute reader of mourning's centrality in *Hamlet* when he suggests that the much-besieged prince seems, as the play opens, a subjectivity suspended in the "time of the Other." For Lacan, however, this dedication to the time of the other means that subjectivity cannot return to itself and to its proper cultural function, so that although the opening scene of the play signifies a problem of mourning, it also asks what it might mean for the dead to survive too long in cultural memory, having been improperly put to rest.[11] What Lacan never quite lends his ear to is the play's more radical critique of mourning, a critique that would focus Hamlet's complaint less on a particular case of hastily aborted mourning rites than on a larger cultural malaise encouraging all mourners to mourn efficiently, briefly, and thus—in ethical terms—insufficiently.

Articulated, though sometimes obliquely, as an ethical sensitivity, Hamlet's melancholic mourning directs itself against a cultural logic calling for an almost immediate erasure of his dead father. Almost by necessity—and precisely because an ethics of mourning is at odds with necessity—Hamlet meets with limited success. And this is true whether one defines success, with Freud, as working to overcome the unpleasure resulting from an enduring attachment to the lost object, or whether one imagines, with Hamlet, success as the capacity to distinguish the other from the cultural economics of value that determine the significance of the dead. In the Freudian view, mourning is a wish less to preserve the dead than to be released from the other's abiding significance, so that any too severe departure from the realism and economic considerations that orient the psyche would be not only aberrant, but pathological. Hamlet appears to prove the point only too well. He not only fails to accept the psychic necessity of a mourning that gradually renounces the other, but as he rejects the predominant cultural logic of mourning, he casts himself outside the practical possibilities of social meaning. What's more, there is a failure already inscribed in Hamlet's project, since his resistant mourning would preserve the other as if he were still alive and bestow a value upon the father he has never entirely possessed. Susceptible to the overestimation by which Freud characterized all loving relationship, Hamlet forces us to consider whether the idea of the other that a subject preserves is merely a compensatory defense against reality or whether it pertains to an ethical reality of the other surpassing the appearances of cultural esteem.

Contra Freud

Much of Hamlet's protest depends on his mother's seeming indifference to the temporal conflation of the father's death and her remarriage. As it is modeled more sincerely by Gertrude than by Claudius (and practiced implicitly by the rest of an obedient Denmark society), mourning seems an intention that the lost other should be diminished, as quickly as possible, in value. Ordinarily, according to Freud, when a mourner tests the world for the absent other and finds his libido still cathected onto the irretrievable object, his ego is persuaded to relinquish the attachment precisely because it is damaging. In response to its own woundedness, the ego seeks to restore the balance of relationship by reattaching to a substitute object. Without these steps of decathexis and substitution, mourning must remain incomplete.[12] Gertrude, in her willingness to practice substitution, exemplifies the Freudian work of mourning; and Hamlet, by contrast, seems the very model of incomplete mourning, melancholically extending his grief and altogether refusing to reconstitute his emotional cathexis. Trans-fixed by or on that which is no longer (his sense of what it is "to be" turning almost necessarily upon the question of "not to be"), Hamlet measures circum-stances and custom, as well as all people, by what they are not. Insofar as this attitude of looking in the dust for meaning seems to her inherently pathologi-cal, unseemly, or perhaps only metaphysical, Gertrude seems to offer a model for the great majority of our literary critical explanations for Hamlet's melan-cholia when she decides that Hamlet's distemper must be a product of his own inability.

In *The Interpretation of Dreams*, Freud had read *Hamlet* not all that imagina-tively as a case-in-point example of the Oedipal paradigm. When he turned again, though more obliquely, to *Hamlet* in "Mourning and Melancholia," Freud offered a more reflective reading of Shakespeare's play, one implicitly troubling some of the basic premises of his own method. Perhaps what is most surprising about this essay, which (along with *Hamlet* itself) has become so cru-cial to our modern critical vocabulary for the work of mourning, are the occasions therein in which Freud registers a discordant sympathy with the pathological mourning of the melancholic. Hardly a rhetorical device, Freud's sympathy oc-curs as an inconvenience to his plausible therapeutic goals. In these exceptional moments, Freud shows himself to be a sympathetic reader of *Hamlet* and a com-passionate witness to both mourning and melancholia, even perhaps at heart something of an elegist. His astute sensitivity, paired with an intellectual sin-cerity that is also Hamlet's best characteristic, enables Freud to make observa-tions that subtly undermine his own overarching paradigm. A first instance of such potentially unproductive sympathy occurs when he tries to account for the reluctance of the mourner to abandon his attachment to the lost other:

> Reality-testing has shown that the loved object no longer exists, and it proceeds to demand that all libido shall be withdrawn from its attachments to that object. This demand rouses *understandable* opposition [*begreifliches Strauben*]—it is a mat-ter of general observation that people never willingly abandon a libidinal position, not even, indeed, when a substitute is already beckoning to them. This opposition can be so intense that a turning away from reality takes place and a clinging to the object through the medium of a hallucinatory wishful psychosis. (*SE* 14: 244, emphasis added)

It is possible that *understandable* here refers to the extent to which the mourner's opposition can be scientifically or naturally explained according to a psychic economy governing all attachment, but I suspect that *begreiflich* is a much more personally reflective gloss, indicating sympathy for the mourner's unrealistic impulses to cling to the other. Though he cannot ultimately condone such an unrealistic orientation, Freud *understands* the impulse to challenge the demands of reality-testing, to oppose substitution, and to maintain relationship with the other even after she or he has disappeared.

With his passing citation of Hamlet serving as an example of the self-critical mechanism in melancholia, Freud traces a deeper debt, one that becomes clear in his subsequent summary of the melancholic's self-description as "petty, egoistic, dishonest, lacking in independence, one whose sole aim has been to hide the weaknesses of his own nature." What Freud remarks upon here is the melancholic's tendency to read loss back toward a poverty of self and so also to conflate a criticism of the world with a pervasive, corrosive self-criticism.[13] He might well be describing Hamlet, whose diminished self-regard and inward-turning critical faculty—"I am myself indifferent honest. . . . I am very proud, revengeful, ambitious, with more offences at my beck than I have thoughts to put them in, imagination to give them shape, or time to act them in" (3.1.123–27)—seem especially resonant here. Much like the melancholic he describes and like Hamlet before him, Freud advocates a project of radical deidealization and so must hear at least some truth in Hamlet's reproach of human honesty. Still, for Freud, the search for "truth" can be a pathological quest. Even though the psychoanalyst must be prepared to uncover all the illusory mechanisms and cultural meanings that govern the ego, when Freud encounters the severity of his own critical method transposed onto the situation of the patient, it quickly becomes evident that one can pursue some truths too far. In other words, the melancholic's fault is mostly a matter of degree. To pursue the idea of oneself as an object in the world, subject to a complex of petty desires and bereft of an idealizing project, might lead one to enter a state of abjection altogether opposed to participation in the present and future of society.

Such a rejection of the world is modeled at times by Hamlet, who overextends his melancholic suspicion of all motive into a ruthlessly anti-idealistic view of human sexuality.[14] As the symbolic site at which a basic affirmation of humanity would be located, sexuality bears the burden of Hamlet's loathing of his present reality. Yet even read this way, Hamlet's rejection of the world through his deflated conception of desire and motive calls attention to itself precisely as a sign of society's injustice. In claiming that he is "indifferent honest," Hamlet refers to his own inconsistent sexual mores, but also to an even more overt sense of *honesty:* he cannot preserve his honesty in a dishonest (or unchaste) world because the integrity of personhood seems jeopardized by the evidence of desire's casual acquaintance with death. In such a world, melancholic indifference might make one a truthsayer, yet the melancholic's paradoxical rejection of the world, the anti-idealistic rigor through which he accesses a truth of some kind, is always a feigned detachment: the melancholic closes himself out of human relationship, while at the same time wishing, negatively, for a highly integrated and meaningful reality. As the melancholic's characteristic attack on self becomes a question posed to the very form of expressiveness, his contemplation of the self's falsity reflects the formal falsity of society. Or, to quote Freud more extensively,

> When in his heightened self-criticism he describes himself as petty, egoistic, dishonest, lacking in independence, one whose sole aim has been to hide the weaknesses of his own nature, it may be, so far as we know, that he has come pretty near to understanding himself; we only wonder why a man has to be ill before he can be accessible to a truth of this kind. For there can be no doubt that if anyone holds and expresses to others an opinion of himself such as this [*wer eine solche Selbsteinschatzung gefunden hat und sie vor anderen außert*] (an opinion which Hamlet held both of himself and of everyone else), he is ill, whether he is speaking the truth or whether he is being more or less unfair to himself. (246–47)

By insisting that to hold *and* express opinions of this nature is illness, Freud altogether diverts the question of psychological wellness away from the question of truth.

In the footnote that accompanies his allusion, Freud cites Hamlet's witty rejoinder to Rosencrantz and Guildenstern in the second act that none of us should escape whipping if we got only what we deserved; but the overall emphasis of Freud's argument, concentrated as it is on the tension between holding and expressing a view, would seem also to allude to Hamlet's remark that he has "that within which passeth show" (1.2.85).[15] The melancholic exists always under the burden of a "within" that defies expression, and when Freud openly muses as to "whether [the melancholic man] is speaking the truth or whether he is . . . unfair to himself," it is, presumably, the conjunction of holding such opinions and expressing them to others that creates a problem because such expression violates cultural norms that encourage us to forget in order to function. What is most peculiar about this as a reading of *Hamlet* is that so much of Hamlet's dissent is silent, and yet in his silence he remains every bit as threatening to the present social order—the reason for which can only be that Hamlet's silent delay threatens the continuity and good conscience of a society ready to move forward, as it were, on the basis of an injustice already lost to memory.[16]

In the challenge that the melancholic poses to expression, in his characteristic turning toward the "within which passeth show," there is dissent and hesitation, the meaning of which is a deflation of the conventions and norms governing expression. Though melancholic distrust of language can arrive at a state of fallenness, or what Julia Kristeva calls *asymbolia*, in the depressive mood there is also a questioning of the cultural forms of communication, of language's very capacity to show forth either the genuine interiority of self or the self's necessary ethical relation to another.[17] Pronouncing upon the lack that inheres in all language, melancholia admits the inadequacy of language to restore a relationship interrupted by death, drawing out the antisymbolic potential of all mourning. Melancholia confronts an aporia in language that arises, ironically as it were, as a consequence of an ethical focus on the value of the other. Though language reverts to the memory of its ethical inspiration only imperfectly, melancholia may suggest that as the death of the other, or the situation of suffering, exerts a strain on language, it opens up a gap in the symbolic structure in order to question the present order. Through melancholia, a self might except itself from participation in language, denoting its own radical dissent from what are most often poorly perceived injustices. In short, the melancholic's truthfulness is negative; it is critique.[18] When Claudius and Gertrude, for their part, demonstrate an adherence to enjoyment altogether opposed to the memory of the other, not only do they embody a cultural propensity to prefer the pleasurable assertions of representation (which supposes useful or usable knowledge) to the radical challenge the other always poses to our present pleasures, but their dramatic persuasiveness likewise emphasizes the extent to which they reflect ordinary, quasi-utilitarian virtue.[19]

Although Gertrude is just barely faithful to her husband, if not to his memory, and although Claudius has secretly murdered his own brother, they are in every other way seemingly ordinary and rational, which accounts at least partly for their ability to enlist so many of the play's readers to their perspective. I think we gravely misunderstand the opening scenes of *Hamlet* if we put too much emphasis on the relative secrecy or hypocrisy of either character, since the dramatic point is that they must seem in large measure convinced by their concern for Hamlet. Even Claudius need not be entirely in bad faith in the opening scenes: he is persuasive because self-persuaded, and insofar as we also find some of his words persuasive, our own complicity in patterns of cultural forgetting is, by means of the play's deeply melancholic logic, revealed to us. In hearing Claudius sympathetically, we accept the tacit facts of injustice possibly because it is easier to get on with things as they are than to adhere to the memory of what seems inalterable. As for Gertrude, though it has been remarked upon by critics ranging from T. S. Eliot to Jacqueline Rose that she receives an undue portion of Hamlet's blame, this fact is perhaps less mysterious if we take her to be the sign of a larger cultural complicity in—or of an unconscious adherence to—injustice. By such a logic, Gertrude becomes (contrary to Eliot's famous charge) worthy of ethical attention precisely because she represents the more ordinary foil to Hamlet's mournful memory.

The Argument against Substitution

Part of the reason the ethical protest in Hamlet's mourning may be hard to perceive is that it so often takes the form of brooding antagonism—directed initially toward Gertrude, Claudius, and the kingdom of Denmark, then more generally toward the suffering condition of humanity, and, later in the play, emerging in the violence done to Rosencrantz and Guildenstern, Ophelia, and Polonius. The conflation of anger and grief most certainly owes a formal debt, as Sacks, Welsh, and Philip Fisher have all remarked, to the revenge tragedy—specifically, to the Ur-text *Amlet* and perhaps also Thomas Kyd's lost *Hamlet*. Fisher tells us that anger and grief "cannot occupy the same place; that is, the same soul at the same time," but that in *Hamlet* the normal "humane progression" from anger to grief has been situationally inverted, as the hero is asked to move from grief to anger.[20] For his part, Welsh would argue that a proper reading of revenge tragedy makes this movement from grief to anger, from mourning to revenge, less of a surprise. Despite all our humanistic inclinations to read revenge as the more primitive sentiment (or, as Sacks proposes, to discern vestigial elements of the cultural plot of revenge and the primitive aggressivity it traces as displaced by the language of mourning), Welsh suggests that, when we read the play in its cultural and literary context, a separation of the two modes seems less enticing, if not altogether impossible. Since at least part of my purpose here is to read *Hamlet* forward in time as an archetype for the posture of resistant mourning in the elegy, let me perform a prolepsis and look ahead briefly to an example from the post-*Hamlet* elegiac tradition in which anger and grief are thus associated, even permitted to occupy the same place and stand one for the other.

To emphasize an elegiac convention that also elaborates a sociopsychological phenomenality of grief, I employ the term *elegiac blaming* to describe a specific literary habit of mind in which a mourner blames the world for revealing the absence of the beloved and specifically denounces those survivors who seem to offer themselves as potential substitutes for the dead. For the sake of simplicity and because it is such an archetypal example, let me refer here only to Milton's "Lycidas" (though any cursory reading of elegies by figures as diverse as Alexander Pope, Thomas Hardy, and Sylvia Plath would uphold the long life of this conceit in the elegiac tradition), where a number of characters are blamed simply for having survived the poet's loss. For instance, as a figure for the poet's personal grievance, Milton's Saint Peter angrily disparages the shepherds who must inherit Lycidas's role and yet are inadequate to it:

> How well could I have spar'd for thee, young swain,
> Enough of such as for their bellies' sake,
> Creep and intrude and climb into the fold?
> Of other care they little reck'ning make,
> Than how to scramble at the shearers' feast,
> And shove away the worthy bidden guest;
> Blind mouths! that scarce themselves know how to hold
> A Sheep-hook, or have learn'd aught else the least
> That to the faithful Herdman's art belongs! (113–21)[21]

Even if we take it on faith that the shepherds really are a faithless and corrupt lot, according to the conceit governing these allegorically besieged clergymen they still fail in direct and inverse proportion ("The hungry Sheep look up, and are not fed" [125]) to a duty that Lycidas would have well performed had he lived. It is quite as if the neglect of their duties were a second assault on Lycidas, insulting the honor of his vocation and usurping a social place he alone should occupy.

All of this turns on an economy of moral evaluation. Even if the value attributed to Lycidas is retrospective, fanciful, and contrafactual, it is in light of his standard that those who come after must necessarily fail. There can be little question that the severity of moral judgment is produced through the economic stinginess of the poet's heart, a sentiment evident in Milton's harshly ironic play on the verb *to spare*. One begins to read this verb according to the more ordinary connotation of permitting someone to be free of or exempt from a particular task (*OED* 1c), as if Milton had said, "How well could I have spared thee." Yet the *for* of Milton's phrase *spar'd for thee* alters the transitive sense of *to spare*, thus heightening the connotation of exemption. Milton's use of the verb floats somewhere between two additional connotations—between a withholding of violence (typically with a connotation of divine power) and a hoarding for the sake of frugality. When Milton fulfills the transitive property of *sparing* with the vaguely defined *enough* (of those "such" who will stand for Lycidas as shepherds of the Christian flock), he insists upon a more severe economy of exchange, as though estimating the comparative worth of Lycidas has forced the poet to reckon a difficult ratio and decide just how many it might take to fill his shoes. To spare the others for Lycidas might well be honorific (Saint Peter declares that he spares them "for thy sake"), but such an imaginative exemption depends upon a harsher possibility inscribed in sparing—namely, a violence withheld. Since even this kinder reading depends upon the principle of exchange informing all sacrifice, with Lycidas made a sacrificial object akin to Christ, one to whom violence is done in order that it should not be done to others, there must come a moment in our attempt to understand the act that remains unenacted: we imagine a Saint Peter who restrains himself from murdering the usurping clergy only by referring his actions to Lycidas's gentler example.

What I want to stress, however, is that the hypothesis of a violence that might be done to the other is much less an unconscious dimension of Saint Peter's meaning than it is the economic corollary of his wish to exempt Lycidas from his fate. In other words, the wish to spare Lycidas cooperates neatly with Milton's own attempt to identify an appropriate procession of mourners, those who might mourn Lycidas properly and so perpetuate the idea of him in the world. All the negative examples of attentiveness to Lycidas's death—whether of neglectful nymphs who fail to notice him drowning or of shepherds who neglect his pastoral legacy—prove a discrepancy between the virtue of the survivors and of the deceased. Although the principle of sacrificial death has allowed Lycidas to stand for virtue, it also seems that for virtue to be protected against misuse Lycidas would have to be restored to the world in exchange for those who are far less virtuous. In a state of emotional confusion that leads him to utter an angrily mixed-up phrase such as "[b]lind mouths," Saint Peter attacks the cultural logic of substitution, in which the shepherds take up the place and role of one who has come before them, by reading the sacrificial principle that supports such substitution, as it were, in reverse. It is as though Saint Peter would arrest substitution by doing violence to those who would enact it in the world—his wish to hoard the survivors to himself seeming a euphemism for killing them or taking them from this world. Such imaginative killing may not be murderous in an ordinary sense (if only because it involves a moral rhetoric, rather than a pragmatic intent), yet there is little doubt that the economic logic of Saint Peter's angry denunciation is to speculate vengefully on the lives of the survivors. As he hypothetically prefers Lycidas to those survivors, he expresses an ungenerous aspect of our grief, in which we might wish to rid ourselves of "such" as are expendable and save the one (Lycidas) who was not (114). Indeed, even more innocent versions of this comparative fantasy—for example, the clichéd sentiment that it is the good who have died young and been taken from us—depend on a latent hostility toward survivors.

Typically, a mourner who employs elegiac blaming exempts himself from the unworthy survivors by his appreciative recognition of the deceased other's worth, but it is also possible that a mourner's appreciation for the other may be evidenced by his aggression toward the rest of the world. When anger infuses mourning in this way, it often involves a deflection of the work of mourning and the associated work of relationship, since in such a state the subject quickly loses sight of the relationship it seeks to preserve and simultaneously exonerates the mourning subject from the painful responsibility for the lost other. By projecting responsibility for the other elsewhere, elegiac blaming might employ anger as a resolution to loss. This is the sense Fisher makes of the relation between mourning and anger (or revenge), where the latter presents itself as a public display of "innocence"—a simplifying resolution that Hamlet refuses to accept. Instead, Fisher argues, Shakespeare's play insists on presenting the "inescapable feeling of responsibility" at the heart of all grief (66). Similarly, even as it deflects the overbearing specter of guilty obligation, elegiac blaming inscribes responsibility in a negative form, glimpsing an obligation implicitly structured as an accusation against the self. In other words, when elegiac blaming describes the occasion of loss as a moment of impossible responsibility, it simultaneously denotes (if only unwittingly) the mourner's own complicity in an ethical question of responsibility.

Such is the case with Hamlet. As his anger protests the condition of the surviving world and opposes the survivors who offer themselves as substitute objects for the deceased, he also turns his anger on himself. This is not merely a self-destructive sign of a dispositional pathology (as a psychoanalytic reading might suggest), but an implicit acknowledgment of a responsibility for the other, even though—or perhaps especially because—the other's death has made practical responsibility for the other finally impossible. Mournful protest is Hamlet's first and most directed activity in the play, and it is developed in response to a cultural praxis of substitution for which Gertrude stands and of which Claudius is the play's most eloquent spokesperson—a praxis diminishing the importance of the dead father. As Claudius advocates a substitution that rationalizes his murderous action and also acts as a prospective sign of his intention to be rid of one who stands in the way of his desires, he makes the ordinary work of mourning seem a willful assault on the meaning of the other. Consider, for instance, Hamlet's famous *kin/kind* quip:

KING CLAUDIUS	But now, my cousin Hamlet, and my son—
HAMLET	A little more than kin and less than kind.
KING CLAUDIUS	How is it that the clouds still hang on you?
HAMLET	Not so, my lord, I am too much i'th' sun. (1.2.64–67)

Since it is Hamlet through whom we most often perceive the extravagances of the Oedipal plot, it is easy to understand why many critics read the text as if it were merely a subjective, projective play of Hamlet's desires. Yet Hamlet's Oedipal keenness has been cued in this scene by Claudius's quasi-incestuous language, his conflation of the relational terms of *cousin* and *son*. Drawing out the incestuous connotations of such rhetorical obfuscation by emphasizing the excess of relation ("more than kin"), Hamlet points to the extravagance of the substitution that Claudius proposes.

It is easy to be drawn in by Claudius's declarations of rationality—for instance, by his observation as Laertes begins his suit to return to Paris that "[y]ou cannot speak of reason to the Dane / And lose your voice" (1.2.44–45), or, half a scene later, his identification of Hamlet's grief as a "peevish opposition" and a state of mind that is to "reason most absurd" (1.2.100, 103).[22] Claudius would have us believe that he has suppressed his own impulse to grieve only through long consultation with a rational conscience:

> Yet so far hath discretion fought with nature
> That we with wisest sorrow think on him
> Together with remembrance of ourselves. (1.2.5–7)

Through Claudius, Shakespeare locates the impetus for a rational mourning in an ethos of self-concern, so that when Hamlet arrives on stage to protest Claudius's mourning, he will imply that such "remembrance of ourselves" opposes remembrance of the other. On Claudius's tongue "[w]isest sorrow" seems oxymoronic, but all contradiction is soon resolved as he steers a course of action having little to do with sorrow or remembrance.[23]

As though anticipating the audience's accusation (for in addressing the court, Claudius also serves as an unreliable chorus, providing the play's prehistory and staging the occasion of dramatic concern), this player of a king here argues he has obeyed the forms of mourning and felt a proper grief for the brother. With increasingly oxymoronic flair and self-consciously apologetic language, he turns from the hypothetical tension of "wisest sorrow" toward the patent absurdity and insincerity of a self-effacing rhetoric, claiming to have married Gertrude "as 'twere with a defeated joy" (1.2.10). Claudius would like to achieve the impression of both public duty and private grief, and his cock-eyed posturing ("With one auspicious and one dropping eye, / With mirth in funeral and with dirge in marriage" [1.2.11–12]) argues that he is merely a servant to a strange twist of fate by which his grief was conflated with his joy. Yet the "mirth" he attaches to the funereal moment reveals the silliness of his self-effacing strategy and further elaborates the confused temporality of "defeated joy" by presuming a preexistent, perhaps even anticipatory "joy" through which Claudius held himself an heir to Gertrude's heart even prior to the king's death. One does not have to read this as a cryptic allusion to a previous affair or an unconscious slippage in which he confesses his substitutive wishes (or murderous contrivances) to see that "defeated joy" is most significantly a figure to Claudius—a hypothesis of mourning that is entirely about keeping up appearances. In the balance, his claim to have grieved for his brother is proven false by a show of "sorrow" that is so obviously and casually unabiding.

To the extent, then, that Claudius's rhetoric depends on suppressed memory, there emerges a logical consistency between his advice (substitution) and his past action (murder). In arguing for an acceptance of the status quo that simultaneously conceals the memory of injustice and for an acceptance of loss conveniently concealing his murderous act, Claudius belittles the remembrance of the dead. By contrast, Hamlet's sense of being in the light of the *sun/son* involves an ethical clear-sightedness that will not let the obligations of relationship be obstructed or obscured by their usage. It is fitting that Claudius should metaphorically attach clouds to Hamlet's appearance, for the proffered relationship of substitute fatherhood that would restore Hamlet to a sunny disposition is an obfuscating rationalization of the way he "clouds"—and has historically prevented—Hamlet's anterior relationship to the father. Rather than moving toward the fact of the murder as a revelation contradicting Claudius's apparent reasonableness, the plot guarantees the falsity of the king's language by letting the murder prove a will to substitute inherent in the act:

> GHOST   But know, thou noble youth,
> The serpent that did sting thy father's life
> Now wears his crown.
> HAMLET   O my prophetic soul! Mine uncle? (1.5.38–41)

According to the temporal inversion of *prophetic*, in which Hamlet sees into the past as if this present were its only possible fulfillment, the point is not that Hamlet has suspected his uncle to be a murderer. Rather, his "prophetic soul" has recognized the consistency between what he has now learned and his prior suspicions of Claudius's efforts to substitute himself as the object of Hamlet's esteem (1.2.106–17). In other words, it is Hamlet's protest, not his knowledge, that predicts the uncle as murderer.[24]

"Good Hamlet" and the Absent Father

Hamlet's argument with substitution ought to be read, I am contending, as a desire for continued relation to the dead father. Having responded with either perfect cynicism or ironic obliviousness to Hamlet's quip that he is "more than kin and less than kind," Claudius urges Hamlet to "think of us / As of a father" (1.2.107–8), perhaps conceding in the stilted formality of this simile a ground he can never absolutely obtain, even as he also demands that kingship be understood as if it were synonymous with fatherhood. If only by contrast to Claudius's example, Hamlet intuits the extent to which the father's usefulness as the source of cultural identity (since the term *father* is equivalent to the symbolic dimension of culture qua language) deemphasizes the ethical sense of a father as a valued other, one who is not merely a symbolic authority or a cultural idea. As Hamlet strives to preserve the father's otherness as a significance in Denmark's culture and language, not only does Claudius oppose his ethical quest, but the father-like ghost himself worries that Hamlet's efforts to interpret the father through mourning may run awry of revenge. Functioning especially as a representation of the father's kingly status, the ghost demands that Hamlet act in the political realm to restore or achieve a symbolic measure of his father's interrupted life, a purpose that, although diametrically opposed to Claudius's usurpation of the role of king and father, is nevertheless closer in spirit to Claudius's political economy of value than it is to Hamlet's own ethical revision of the father's meaning.

In the opening two scenes, Hamlet and the ghost seem initially united as the two characters immediately and symbolically opposed to Claudius's reign. In symbolic solidarity, father and son each bode opposition to the state, their respective stances marked sartorially. It is probably not overly speculative to assume that King Hamlet was not wearing armor while taking the nap during which he was murdered, but the ghost Horatio sees in the first scene is dressed for battle ("Such was the very armour he had on / When he th'ambitious Norway combated" [1.1.59–60]), almost as though he had fitted himself in some divine dressing room to challenge the usurping Claudius. So too, when we first see young Hamlet, his "nighted color" is a sign of his sincerity in relation to the father and of his opposition to Claudius's and his mother's truncated mourning.[25] The ghost of the father characterizes a split between the rhetorical uses of language and its underlying ethical significances, as all of the ghost's speeches seem to reduce ethical relationship to political meaning. Proposing a world that would remain meaningful through the present political system, the ghost demands from Hamlet only a symbolic recuperation of his status in the world of Denmark, insisting that the restoration of the father's identity is necessary to the son's—this patrilinear passing of names being tantamount to the cultural politics of identity.[26]

Any symbolic treatment of the lapsing meaning of the father as such evokes the famous debate about the status of the ghost, whose potential unreliability persists in my account, if only through Hamlet's steadfast doubting of his manifestly vengeful urgings.[27] Read largely as a remnant of an Ur-text, perhaps Kyd's *Hamlet*—in other words, as a souvenir of revenge tragedy, with its formal patterning of grief though the ritual requirements of vengeance—the ghost fosters a dialectical tension between its own public rhetoric and Hamlet's interior recalcitrance, a dialectic figuring the distance between the inherited form of the Ur-text's plot and Shakespeare's understanding of that same material. Indeed, Hamlet's moments of condescension ("Ay, thou poor ghost, while memory holds a seat / In this distracted globe" [1.5.96–97]) may refer to the forgetful and revisionary nature of Shakespeare's own memory, which has relied upon the audience's fading memory of Kyd and his ghost. The metadramatic dimension is important here, for the influence of revenge derives more significantly through the stylized emotional catharsis of the Elizabethan conventions of the revenge tragedy than through any real-life Elizabethan code of personal revenge.[28] According to Shakespeare's revisionary and highly literary use of the ghost and the filial task he sets Hamlet, revenge becomes a trope for—and, at the same time, the vehicle enabling his implicit critique of—commemorative mourning itself. Just as commemorative mourning refers to the symbolic value of the other, which can be resolved through adequately appreciative cultural expressions of grief, the ghost as a trace of the revenge code refers to the public, symbolic logic of the idea of father. If Adam Smith would later argue in *The Theory of Moral Sentiments* that the dead provide a ground for value in the economy of sentiments, what the ghost of *Hamlet* advocates is precisely a kind of mourning that may (in Freudian terms) be completed, with the revenge code substituting for the aborted proprieties of stately commemoration.[29]

In almost every respect, then, Hamlet's delay and interpretive struggle run contrary to the form of cultural memory that the ghost would promote. The ghost's precarious dependence on memory has been established at the beginning of the play when Horatio demands to know,

> What art thou that usurp'st this time of night,
> Together with that fair and warlike form
> In which the majesty of buried Denmark
> Did sometimes march? (1.1.44–47)

According to the ironic resonance of "usurp'st," the ghost who here commemorates the victim of usurpation returns as a usurper, as one who occupies a space improperly or abnormally. Unwittingly alluding to the ghost's symbolic purpose—to steal back or "usurp" from the usurper his proper place—Horatio anticipates a struggle over a public valuation of the other that is expressly political, underscoring the point that symbolic places can be usurped. Observing the "fair and warlike form" in which the ghost resembles the dead king, Horatio deems the ghost an interpretation of the dead king's public meaning, already mistrustful of the ghost's ominously commemorative costume. Though Horatio cannot have anticipated the scope to be given later to his own suspicion by his friend's objections, it is highly significant that he is unable to equate the ghost to the person of the dead king and must instead read him as a stately sign:

> In what particular thought to work I know not,
> But in the gross and scope of my opinion,
> This bodes some strange eruption to our state. (1.1.66–68)

Much as Barnardo had observed that the ghost bears "the same figure like the King that's dead" (1.1.39), Horatio views the ghost as a social phenomenon.

What Horatio's uncertainty about the specific public connotation of the ghost means is that we cannot interpret this ghost as a straightforward emanation of collective memory symbolizing a violated public norm, but rather must view him as a sign of estranged public memory.[30] It is not so much that Hamlet's protest relies upon a lost form of memory (say, abandoned funeral rites) as it is perhaps that his personal objection to the public meaning of the court intuits the unknowable dimensions of memory itself or of any public meaning built primarily on symbolic terrain. Demanding a mode of interpretation that denotes political meaning as derived through ethical forms of memory, Hamlet seeks to preserve and, if necessary, create a unique value for the father that emerges at the level of personal connotation in order that both son and father may remain remarkable and distinguishable amidst the laws of nature, which otherwise equate the person to corporeal matter, making each of us *commonly* indistinguishable. As Gertrude warns Hamlet, "Do not for ever with thy vailèd lids / Seek for thy noble father in the dust. / Thou know'st 'tis common—all that lives must die" (1.2.70–72). As long as Gertrude speaks literally of death in order to be reconciled to the symbolic realm, where significance is negotiated among the survivors, the father can no longer be distinguished from dust. Though Gertrude believes in the father's one time nobility, the uniqueness of his personhood is ironically eclipsed because she fully expects (and why shouldn't she?) that nobility is transferable from one king to another. By contrast, Hamlet's particularized mourning ("Why seems it so particular with thee?" [1.2.75], his mother asks) opposes a commemorative logic based in the interchangeability of public value with the "common" corruptible estimation of a father's worth. Ironically, therefore, when he opposes Claudius and his state, intuiting that it is Claudius who represents the true logic of the state, Hamlet also opposes the kingly dimension of his father. Though Horatio praises King Hamlet as a "goodly king," Hamlet specifically rejects the political and ceremonial language of idealization: "A was a man. Take him for all in all, / I shall not look upon his like again" (1.2.186–87).

In order to refuse substitution, Hamlet must refuse the commodification of the father's value that occurs when one makes kingship an adequate expression of the person. Thus Hamlet exercises a degree of creative license in responding to the ghost:

> I'll call thee Hamlet,
> King, father, royal Dane. O answer me!
> Let me not burst in ignorance, but tell

> Why thy canonized bones, hearsèd in death,
> Have burst their cerements, why the sepulchre
> Wherein we saw thee quietly enurned
> Hath oped his ponderous and marble jaws
> To cast thee up again. What may this mean,
> That thou, dead corpse, again in complete steel,
> Revisitst thus the glimpses of the moon,
> Making night hideous, and we fools of nature
> So horridly to shake our disposition
> With thoughts beyond the reaches of our souls? (1.4.25–37)

After he has named the ghost and called him father, Hamlet reverts to apostrophic negation, which is to say, to calling the ghost a corpse ("dead corpse") rather than a father. Unlike Gertrude's recollection of death, which focuses on the collective condition of mortality and thus refers as much to the survivor's fate as to the other's demise, Hamlet's melancholic glee over the corpse's return credits the father's bones with a personifying agency that has "burst their cerements" and "oped" the tomb's "marble jaws."[31] As an objective datum surpassing its social repression, the corpse erupts into the symbolic structures that order Elsinore, and the melancholic attention paid to the corpse suggests the perverse need to play, both after Polonius's death and in the graveyard scene, upon the antisymbolism of death, almost as though the mourner were striving to interpret the world in which a father dies by referring that world again to the bodily evidence of the father's death.

The emphasis on the corpse is the grisly counterpart to Hamlet's obsession with the particular person of the father, and in this sense it is diametrically opposed to the too symbolic meanings the ghost elaborates each time he speaks to Hamlet as king to his subject or even with the authority a father commands over a son in society. Intuiting Hamlet's resistance, the ghost denounces a form of forgetting that is tantamount to inaction:

> I find thee apt,
> And duller shouldst thou be than the fat weed
> That rots itself in ease on Lethe wharf
> Wouldst thou not stir in this. (1.5.31–34)

Fearing that Hamlet might adhere to the (new) symbolic order and let his father's public reputation be tarnished, the ghost interprets forgetting as a son's disobedience to patriarchal meaning. In the midst of this expressed anxiety, there is sounded an ethical note—since the vulnerability of the conditional mood ("Wouldst thou not stir in this") suggests just how much the father as other depends on an elegiacally and personally connoted memory ("if thou didst ever thy dear father love"), rather than on any symbolic value that would be ritually preserved.

Yet the ghost's rhetoric remains thoroughly nostalgic, revealing the deeply conservative dimension of commemorative mourning, which too simply restores the symbolic order and preserves identity as a function of already established structures of justice. Insofar as the ghost argues that the failure to restore the father's status disqualifies their past relationship, and perhaps more importantly Hamlet's present identity, this narrative of identity appeals to Hamlet's vulnerability as a son, projecting the anxieties about his fatherly status onto Hamlet as an anxiety about bastardy. According to a cultural narrative of identity in which bastardy might disenchant the mythic history through which Hamlet fosters his own identity, he can take for granted his point of origin from the father only by relying, with mythic and cultural confidence, on the mother's "honest" relationship to the father:

> Ay, that incestuous, that adulterate beast . . .
>   . . . won to his shameful lust
> The will of my most seeming-virtuous queen.
> O Hamlet, what a falling off was there!—
> From me, whose love was of that dignity
> That it went hand-in-hand even with the vow
> I made to her in marriage, and to decline
> Upon a wretch whose natural gifts were poor
> To those of mine. (1.5.42–52)

As the ghost retrospectively imagines a son's bastardy, Hamlet's identity may not only be questioned, but literally dis-placed by Claudius's wrongful occupation of a father's place.

The retrospective charge of adultery violates the mythic positioning of personal identity within cultural identity by drawing into suspicion the very way one depends on an account of one's origin, but it also calls for the preservation of those places and signs of symbolic value through which identity is derived, even to the point where a violation after the fact might upset bloodlines. Although Elizabethan culture did for the most part understand marrying

a brother's wife as incestuous, it is important to recognize the mournful premise of such a cultural logic: the wife remains the brother's relative and therefore
unavailable to him only by her continued relationship to the husband beyond
his death. The incestuous violation pertains to a cultural immortality given to
the deceased husband, and it is according to this logic that the ghost threatens
Hamlet's identity, for fatherhood and the patriarchal system are subverted by
any lapse in this symbolic ordering. By the logic of the incest taboo, Claudius's
sleeping with Gertrude during the time of mourning is "adulterate."[32]

This brings us to a question often posed to this play: if the time of mourning preserves the place of the spouse through a retrospective valuation of his
worth, is not the accusation of adultery more than metaphoric? Has not the
ghost actually accused Claudius of sleeping with Gertrude before King
Hamlet's death? I opt here for a metaphoric reading of the charge of adultery
largely because the matter is not finally decidable from the dramatic evidence,
but also because it seems to me that, according to the retrospective reach of the
ghost's logic, the charge aptly characterizes the play's obsession with the symbolic work of substitution as a function of mourning. Whether or not an act
of adultery predated the murder, the metaphoric charge of adultery traces an
anxiety about the diminishing significance of any original object and tropes the
lapsing form of faithfulness necessary for any survivor to move beyond his
mournful attachment. When, in his thoroughly retrospective imagination, the
ghost speaks of the "falling-off" from himself to Claudius, he adopts the voice
of a storyteller who employs the fictive time of the preterite ("what a falling off
was there" [1.5.47]) and speaks of all events as part of the same past. The most
peculiar connotation arising from this failure to distinguish between the past
and present occurs when the ghost describes Gertrude's choice under the hypothesis of simultaneity ("to decline / Upon a wretch whose natural gifts were
poor / To those of mine" [1.5.50–51]), supposing Claudius's natural gifts might
be immediately contrasted to his own, quite as though Gertrude had her first
husband's gifts still before her when she made her deplorable choice. By this
strange reversal of the logic of metaphor, the very possibility of comparison
cancels the real separation in time enacted by death, as though memory could
literally preserve the thing it remembered.

According to the conservative mournful logic expressed by revenge, the
ghost would preserve the purity of his own former identity and make Hamlet
dependent on it, but already the appeal to emotion has begun to qualify his
fatherly authority. Rather like the Player Queen whom Gertrude accuses of

protesting too much, the ghostly father exposes a deep cultural anxiety about patrilinearly derived identity. Perceiving the paradoxical inversion whereby the father's authority is now subject to the son's interpretation, Hamlet seems almost willfully to redirect the conversation toward his own more personal focus. By parroting the ghost's words ("Adieu, adieu, remember me" [1.5.113]), Hamlet parodically alters the ghost's meaning, his repetition standing not so much for obedience to the duty of revenge as for the difficulty of remembrance:

> Remember thee?
> Ay, thou poor ghost, while memory holds a seat
> In this distracted globe. Remember thee?
> Yea, from the table of my memory
> I'll wipe away all trivial fond records,
> All saws of books, all forms, all pressures past,
> That youth and observation copied there,
> And thy commandment all alone shall live
> Within the book and volume of my brain
> Unmixed with baser matter. (1.5.95–104)

Interpreting the ghost as though he were an authoritative and fatherly form not to be remembered personally, Hamlet reveals his ambivalence toward the father's command by noting that were the ghost to be remembered on its own terms, Hamlet would have to assault all the ordinary capacities of memory. And if proper receptivity also means that he must "wipe away" all his former lessons in order that the father's "commandment" might take place in the "book and volume of [his] brain," the mixed metaphoric conceit of a record keeping tending toward oblivion makes it clear to us that the ghost's task contradicts the son's acculturated habits and ideas.

Another way of understanding all of this is to see Hamlet's response as indicative of a necessary vacillation between personal and public memory. Since his own thought must be in dialectical tension with the public meanings by which it is cued, Hamlet charts for us the limited agency of individual memory as a reflex of cultural memory. As he promises to remember the ghost "while memory holds a seat / In this distracted globe," Hamlet's qualification plays on *globe* by referring ambiguously to the ghost's status in the world at large and in the mind of Hamlet himself. Though Hamlet indicates in the rest of the speech that he is converting the precarious memory of the ghost in the larger "globe" to a dependence on the seat of his own memory, he simultaneously serves notice that the promise he makes is a weak one, since the standard for remembrance must be set by cultural norms. The public standard for memory in Denmark is such that Hamlet sees little value in the father's being reconciled to it. As he speaks condescendingly to the "poor ghost," Hamlet seems unable to decide whether the ghost is worse off being remembered by Denmark or by its mal-contented prince. In this sense, all his puns on *globe* depend entirely on the epithet *distracted*, which denotes the privilege of personal memory, its neces-sary location in the symbolic context, and therefore also its complicity with prevalent social norms. If we are to judge from the distractions presented by society—whether those distractions be thought of as the demands of survival, in which reality-testing measures the incompatibility of attachment to the dead and relationship to the living, or, more cynically, as the forgetting that serves the political concerns of Claudius and Gertrude—the ghost will not be re-membered for very long.

It might be said that the revenge code is the greatest of Hamlet's distrac-tions. Since the ghost is metadramatically a vestige of inherited plots that Shakespeare revises, Hamlet can never fully break with the form first given to his remembrance of the father, and in the world of this play he must address himself to erasing or revising a revenge code that presents itself as the foremost ground for relationship to the father. With the relation between personal and public memory ruled by a theatrical conceit in which holding a "seat" stands for the very possibility of memory in the world of the Globe theater, the ghost's imperative is subjected to an additional irony presiding over his exit: he is force-ful only so long as the extended audience or Hamlet's own theatrically con-ceived mind recalls him. Though our memory of the ghostly father only re-cently departed from the stage is still strong, Hamlet insists upon the specter of our forgetting as also of his own—on our mutual ability to be distracted, on the world's necessarily distracting assault upon memory's fixedness. As the scene closes, Hamlet echoes the ghost's words before he also leaves the stage: "Now to my word: / It is 'Adieu, adieu, remember me.' / I have sworn't" (1.5.111–13). One hears the emphasis that falls to the doubled "adieu" as though Hamlet were punning on the appositional relation between parting ("adieu") and re-tentive memory ("remember me"). Even the ambiguous referent of the pro-noun *it* in "I have sworn't" creates a question as to whether Hamlet has sworn obedience to his own version of memory or to the father's task of vengeance. As audience, we participate in the business of forgetting, which has just been staged through the visual disappearance of the ghost, and even though Hamlet protests this rule of forgetting, once the metadramatic conceit chastises us and suggests the fragility of theatrical memory, we have been implicated in the larger failure of commemorative mourning.

"Look you now what follows"

Despite all his distrust for theatricality, Hamlet eventually brings about his only overtly ethical actions through the theatrical performances of act 3—in his redaction of "The Murder of Gonzago" and in his performed speech to Gertrude in the closet—quite as though his belief in the receptive potentialities of audience were to give his resistant, mournful desire its special ethical calling. Over the course of the play, it is Gertrude who becomes the symbolic and ethical center of Hamlet's contentious struggle to prove the father's value. As Hamlet attempts to disparage Claudius in the court and theater of his mother's opinion, he probably inserts lines into the play-within-a-play that intimate his first overtly ethical action. Reading revenge tragedy as though it were as much about an interior drama focused in the speeches of the Player Queen as about the naming of murderous crime, Hamlet implicates all those who would endure through consent to the substitutive practices of culture, censuring Gertrude's refusal to mourn appropriately as an ethical failure seemingly inseparable from Claudius's crime. Though "The Murder of Gonzago" is ostensibly a revenge tragedy, it seems, under Hamlet's revisionary influence, more properly an exercise in mourning, staged as much to catch the conscience of the queen as that of the king. As the Player Queen voices Hamlet's complaint for him, it is likely that the audience should recognize the following lines as among those that Hamlet told the players he wished to insert into the play:

> In second husband let me be accurst;
> None wed the second but who killed the first.
>
> . . . .
>
> A second time I kill my husband dead
> When second husband kisses me in bed. (3.2.161–62, 166–67)[33]

Perhaps indicating the voice of Hamlet as elegist, the repeating of *second* four times in these four lines insists upon a metadramatic reference (moving outward, as it does, from the play-within-a-play to its assembled audience) to the secondness of Gertrude's marriage to Claudius. Since "The Murder of Gonzago" begins with a dumbshow that establishes the plot of murder and makes the Player

Queen's complicity part of the viewing audience's memory, there is a temporal ethical irony created when the Player Queen speaks hypothetically of a future action the audience has already witnessed. The assembled audience must hear these lines as if they inclined toward an inevitable meaning; namely, the murder of the Player King. The effect of this foreknowledge is to shift the ethical responsibility from the decision to murder onto the hypothetical willingness to consider remarriage, as though the substitutive propensity of sexual desire designated an ethical proclivity for substitutively forgetting the other and the slippery slope running from there to murder.

To the extent that the dumbshow offers a mimesis of events in the real world of Denmark, its meaning hits home a while later when Claudius interrupts the play because he finds it too difficult to watch. Oddly, however, little of the moral action we see staged has much to do with Claudius. The focus is almost entirely on the Player Queen's dilemma, which has provided Gertrude with an ethically ideal language that her stand-in in the play-within-a-play too obviously and hypocritically fails. By imagining an ethically ideal course of action that preserves the memory and value of the husband/father, Hamlet reconfigures the mother's estimation of the father as though it were also strong enough to refuse substitution in advance. By this logic, the Player Queen is not merely a blaming representation of a Gertrude who hypocritically fails her own potential ideal, but rather a projection of Hamlet's unrealistic memory of the father, one he wishes Gertrude might still share. Thus, when Gertrude dismisses the melodramatic performance before her ("The lady protests too much, methinks" [3.2.210]), she characteristically and pragmatically opposes reality to fiction, perhaps even recognizing that this is Hamlet's fiction of a perfectly preserved relationship with the father. As yet unconverted to Hamlet's perspective—that state of self-accusing ethical responsibility she will take on, if only momentarily, in the closet scene—she is nevertheless capable of identifying the whole exchange as an excessive *protest* against substitution, perhaps intuiting that such a perspective must imitate a contrafactual innocence that denies the subject's own ethical complicity in the patterns of cultural forgetting.

In the closet scene, called by William Kerrigan the greatest scene in all of Shakespeare, Hamlet's ethical appeal to his mother moves to the very center of Shakespeare's larger revision of the revenge plot.[34] Despite the scene's ostensibly ethical purposiveness it also presents Hamlet's most ethically culpable action, his callous murder of Polonius. Perhaps even more alarming is Hamlet's behavior after the murder, when our too strident mourner-cum-accidental-murderer

refuses to deem Polonius an object worthy of his grief. There is something bru-
tally comic about a Hamlet who steps over the dead body of Polonius and might
even be standing directly above his victim as he tries to persuade his mother to
think more dearly of the play's original and most significant dead body. So intent is he on the ethical task of persuading the mother to acknowledge a value
she has denied the father that Hamlet fails to acknowledge what he has done;
so concentrated is he on a singularly cathected object that he insults and indeed
assaults the ethical value of others who would be complicitous merely through
bystanding, eventually sacrificing all of Polonius's family to his protest. The
irrelevance of Polonius has been foreshadowed in act 2 scene 2, where Polonius,
eager to ascertain whether Hamlet is really insane, indulges the hero's mad
interpretations of cloud formations. The comedy resulting from Polonius's
responses is less a result of his deceitfulness than of his innocent adherence to
etiquette. Even in spying on Hamlet, Polonius remains sincerely solicitous of
the perspective of his better, and his death illustrates the uselessness of blind
obedience to the status quo. In symbolic terms, Polonius serves as a dramaturgical scapegoat to the objective, but largely concealed, problem of Claudius's
guilt. When Hamlet dismisses the sacrificial Polonius, he says rather cursorily,
"I took thee for thy better" (3.4.31), apparently interpreting his own possibly
self-defensive violence as though it had been a planned action, or, perhaps we
could say, as though it were symptomatic of another intention—that of murdering his uncle the false king.

What this illustrates is that Hamlet can name his revenge as an intention
only in retrospect, and since this happens only accidentally—contingently, in
Renaissance terms—it is quite as though revenge were the forgotten occasion
of his ethically revisionary plot of mourning. In other words, the revenge plot
that determines the play happens even without intention, so much so that it
appears in the closet scene to have been absorbed symbolically into the hero's
and play's unconscious, as if Shakespeare's newer Hamlet carried with him at
all times the memory of his more primitive theatrical forbears. According to
the play's many turns from revenge toward mourning, from the ethics signified by mourning back toward the politics signified by revenge, the closet
scene marks a return of the revenge logic Hamlet has so long held out against.
Since the violence that Hamlet is able to perform as a revenger is always ironically (or perhaps retrospectively) related to his intentions, ethical purpose
accidentally fulfills itself through the displacement of revenge, with the dramatic assault on a substitute for the substitute king standing for the mourner's

radical opposition to substitutive praxis as a principle ordering the symbolics of culture. Having already mistaken Polonius as a substitute for Claudius (who is the referent of "I took thee for thy better"), Hamlet accuses him further of behaving like Claudius by taking the place of his betters. It should not be lost on us that the speech Hamlet makes over Polonius's body is itself a stand-in for the one he might have made over Claudius's dead body had Hamlet followed orders and taken the usurping king's life in the name of one who was his better.

It is obvious that Hamlet cannot murder directly: he murders substitutes, and concealed substitutes at that. All his actions are thus pitched in a symbolic key. Anticipating Milton's Saint Peter, Hamlet acts as though he meant to suggest that all survivors are substitutes—Polonius, Gertrude, and Ophelia seeming, no less than Claudius, objects that merit the attention of elegiac blaming. When we consider the dramaturgical urgencies of the closet scene, it is even likely that Polonius's murder has inspired Hamlet's eloquence, that this accidental murder of Claudius's substitute has proved to Hamlet that substitute objects can be refused.[35] As he thereafter adopts the comparative strategy I have associated with elegiac blaming, Hamlet finds the proper pitch of mournful eloquence and forces his mother to listen to him while he compares her two husbands ("Look here upon this picture, and on this, / The counterfeit presentment of two brothers" [3.4.52–53]) and attributes godlike qualities to Hamlet Senior, the original of her desire. His newfound capacity for idealizing the dead father depends in part on the recent defeat of Polonius as substitute, and as Hamlet now slips into the eulogizing, heroic rhetoric he associates with the idea of his father, he insists on a father who is not merely "for all in all . . . a man," but one who "give[s] the world assurance of a man" (3.4.61).

Revising his formerly modest estimation of his father in the first act, Hamlet's later language resembles Brutus's elegiac tribute to Caesar—"the elements / So mix'd in him that nature might stand up / And say to all the world 'This was a man'" (*Julius Caesar*, 5.5.72–74). Much as Brutus asserts Caesar's value by tearing him from the past tense of remembrance and offering a present tense idealization of the dead that is much to the detriment of all the lesser surviving men who hear these mournful words, Hamlet's remembrance renders the father an object of the mother's present emotional cathexis. Though the evidence of the father's worthiness depends upon circular reasoning (since only the overvaluation of love proves the object's worthiness), Hamlet proceeds as if the father's value were self-evident, to be discerned as much through the object of inappropriate substitution as in the idealized original:

> This *was* your husband. Look you now what follows.
> Here *is* your husband, like a mildewed ear
> Blasting his wholesome brother. Have you eyes?
> Could you on this fair mountain leave to feed
> And batten on this moor? Ha, have you eyes? (3.4.62–66)

"Look you now what follows" refers, first of all, to the staged order of Hamlet's presentation of the two pictures and the chronology of his mother's substitution. But the relative passivity called for in the phrase, through which Gertrude is asked to consider only the order of the events and not the reasons behind them, also permits her a temporary reprieve in intentionality—a space in which she may contemplate the unworthiness of the second object to which she is now attached and long for the original. When Hamlet resumes even more accusingly, he interrogates her adherence to substitutive praxis, demanding to know "what judgment / Would step from this to this?" (3.4.69–70).

Whether his speech employs a rhetorical stratagem or is perhaps motivated by delusional attachment to the father, Hamlet presents the two pictorial representations as if the men were truly comparable in the present, as if Gertrude might at that moment choose either kingly brother for her lover. Supposing that esteem for the father might be equivalent to his endurance, Hamlet expects his mother to accept his metaphoric idealization of the father as if the representation referred to a real possibility in the world. It is difficult to overemphasize just how aberrant this moment is in the play, not so much because it is a departure from our ordinary expectations about how to honor the dead (for Claudius has already perverted the ordinary world of love and remembrance), but because it is crucially atypical of Hamlet himself. In succumbing here to the pathos of pure emotional attachment, Hamlet indulges a ridiculous naïveté about representation. Not only is Hamlet's description of the two portraits unlikely because, as René Girard has emphasized, two brothers are not often so physically disparate,[36] but it is highly unusual that a Hamlet who has been skeptical of the ghost's command, of the entire code of revenge as a vehicle for commemoration, and of the very capacity of all representational memory should here treat the portraits as if they were evidence. Throughout much of the play, Hamlet tests the limits of evidence—can he trust the mother's advice? can he trust Claudius's proffer of friendship? can he trust the testimony of the ghost, or must he find other evidence? and then, in the graveyard scene, what should he make of the evidence of death?—but he employs the portraits as if they were, oddly, the only evidence needed to make his case before the mother.

Though Hamlet's naïveté about representation in this moment may limit his final efficacy, it is not often enough noted that his rhetorical urgency temporarily works its spell on his mother and that he becomes most persuasive precisely when he confronts the limits of his own estimation of the father's merit. At the height of his encomium for the father, Hamlet pauses and seems to doubt the power of the portraits qua representation. Repeatedly questioning his mother's vision ("have you eyes?"), Hamlet implicitly realizes that he cannot make her see what she cannot see on her own. One might argue that his proof has been flawed because his comparative conceit is itself indebted to an economy of cultural valuation and commodification in which one object or person can be exchanged for another and thus is, in a certain sense, already a falsification of the irreducible ethical value of the other. Yet mourning's protest must work from what representation affords it, and despite the obvious limits of Hamlet's speech, the mother is temporarily converted. Perhaps it is Hamlet's rhetorical vulnerability—his inability to prove his point—that makes his speech all the more effective, for in her response Gertrude confesses for the first time the value of her own perspective, "Thou turn'st mine eyes into my very soul" (3.4.79), thus drawing our attention to the maieutic device whereby the portraits stand for the estimation of each brother in the queen's eyes as those eyes have been guided, or turned, by Hamlet's.

With a mind dedicated alike to passion and pragmatism, Gertrude thereafter confesses her returning focus on the material world and soon reverts, at least ostensibly, to her loyalty to Claudius and the unjust status quo he represents. It seems this is the only way she can imagine coping with her compromised reality. Gertrude knows too well that there is no pragmatic benefit to being loyal to a corpse. It is she who in the play's second scene focuses us on the dead body's literality and associates Hamlet's downcast demeanor with the act of looking for his dead father in the dust. To remind herself of the dangerous consequences of Hamlet's persuasive and affective state of mind here in the closet, Gertrude need only look to the body of Polonius that lies at Hamlet's feet or, if she requires still further proof that her son's protest is unrealistic and unmanageable, to the air above her, which Hamlet, with auspicious timing, is about to address.

It is an almost perfect dramatic irony that Hamlet's efficacy on behalf of the father should dissipate at the very moment the ghost reenters the play and distracts Hamlet's attention from the mother. It is also an apt comment on how great an obstacle the revenge code poses to Hamlet's ethical endeavor in the play. As the ghost returns to remind Hamlet of his "almost blunted purpose" (3.4.101)—in other words, to recall once more the vestiges of a revenge plot Hamlet has been trying to escape—he ends up providing Gertrude with all the proof she needs to decide that Hamlet's devotion to his father is unreasonable, delusional, and dangerous. In his reappearance in the closet scene, the ghost is a private ghost, and this might lead us to interpret him, as we would, for example, the ghost of Duncan in *Macbeth*, as the sign of an interior psychological conflict. But though it is true that King Hamlet's ghost is no longer publicly significant (he cannot be seen by Gertrude), in his private meaning for Hamlet he is a mere redundancy, a reminder of what Hamlet already knows:

> Do you not come your tardy son to chide,
> That, lapsed in time and passion, lets go by
> Th' important acting of your dread command? (3.4.97–99)

Though one could read these lines as an example of self-recrimination, Hamlet's preemptive move creates an ironic distance between the father's command and the son's obedience. Referring to his own lapse in "time and passion" as if his delay were the measure of just how contrary he is to the task assigned him, Hamlet may even pronounce *important*—which in Elizabethan connotation bears a temporal emphasis closer to our sense of "urgent" or "importunate"— with a slightly sarcastic intonation. Indeed, the fact that Hamlet never lets the ghost reiterate the revenge itinerary only further emphasizes the obsolescence of the revenge code, which has little to do with what is ethically on Hamlet's mind.

Oddly, the ghost comes to reprove Hamlet at the very moment in which the bloodletting of revenge tragedy has begun, as Polonius's death signals a return to the Elizabethan and Jacobean stage conventions determining vengeful violence. Unless, perhaps, it is Hamlet's ethical focus on the mother, his psychological alienation from vengeful purpose, that brings the ghost back. Since by immediately charging himself with tardiness Hamlet has beaten the ghost to his reprimand and so preempted his dramatic purpose, the spectral father seems a bit confused, finally observing what the audience should already have noticed: "But look, amazement on thy mother sits. / O, step between her and her fighting soul" (3.4.102–3). Even as the ghost reports an effect that he is in part creating, he remembers an affect entirely of Hamlet's making—which is to say, Gertrude's "amazement" as a sign of her rekindled conscience, her "fighting soul."

Upon first appearing in the play, the ghost had urged single-purposed revenge, advising Hamlet to "[l]eave [his mother] to heaven, / And to those thorns that in her bosom lodge / To prick and sting her" (1.5.86–88)—advice that might seem intended to spare Gertrude her son's accusation, but which I would interpret rather as a sign of the father's basic indifference to nuanced ethical distinctions. It is nothing less than amazing, therefore, that in the closet scene the ghost is struck by the importance of Gertrude's potentially converted heart, almost as if the scene entailed a momentary conversion (dare we say, a revision) of the ghost to Hamlet's purpose. Not only does the ghost seem suddenly impressed by the son's revisionary purposes, he encourages them: "Conceit in weakest bodies strongest works. / Speak to her, Hamlet" (3.4.104–5). Though his words reveal his warrior's bias that language is the weaker form of action, as he disparages those who are susceptible to such influence the ghost at the same time contradicts his primary dramatic purpose of advocating revenge, conceding both work and strength ("strongest works") to the affective realm in which Hamlet would prefer to operate.

Even as he recognizes the ethical validity of Hamlet's mournful persuasion, the ghost proves to be the dramatic vehicle for dissipating the effect of Hamlet's words and finally for defeating his own significance in Gertrude's eyes. There is just a hint of Orphean pathos here. As the father is brought back within range of Gertrude's moral vision, his dramatic resurfacing from the underworld proves to be the occasion of a more final departure, as though he were witnessing the moment in which he is finally dispelled. Once Gertrude perceives Hamlet's distraction, the patently unrealistic dimension of his ethical project becomes clear to her, and her son thereafter can draw her attention only to the empty place of the father:

> Look you how pale he glares.
> His form and cause conjoined, preaching to stones,
> Would make them capable. Do not look upon me,
> Lest with this piteous action you convert
> My stern effects. Then what I have to do
> Will want true colour—tears perchance for blood. (3.4.116–21)

When Gertrude asks, "To whom do you speak this?" (3.4.122), she raises an obvious problem that most editors have tried to solve by suggesting that with the words "Do not look upon me" Hamlet has shifted his address to the ghost. Though this seems an easy way to make sense of the lines, it also presumes that one accepts revenge as Hamlet's consistent purpose. Then too this simpler reading is self-contradictory: the ghost has never been an advocate of "piteous action," even if he has been momentarily struck by Hamlet's moral persuasiveness. The proper place for Hamlet to discern "piteous action" in this scene is in the face of his mother, who is doubly moved by his recent speech as by his present "distemper." This reading is no less puzzling, however: for Hamlet would then address Gertrude as though he had attained the very thing he has hoped for—which is to say, a restoration of her affection and appreciation for the father—but now fears the result. I am not sure the confusion can be completely ironed out.

Having also as a consequence of the ghost's arrival been put back in mind of revenge—as he says, of "what I have to do"—Hamlet ultimately alludes, albeit cryptically, to his assignment when he imagines that the "piteous" look of mother or father might distract him to the point where he would become so focused on grief as to forget revenge, to the point where he might shed "tears perchance for blood," his own tears for the blood of the other whom he must kill. Surely this imagined reversal of intention whereby Hamlet disavows what seems all along to have been his ethical inclination is less than completely sincere, but perhaps oddest of all is that Hamlet's effort to avoid the temptation of mourning carries with it a disparagement of mourning's tears as transparently futile: tears want color, but revenge—whatever else it promises—is colorful, bloody, and picturesque. Polonius's slain body is crucial to the drama of the entire scene. The failure to mourn predicts the sweep of revenge. When Hamlet sheds blood instead of tears and further refuses to offer his tears because he can no longer regret his actions if he is to move forward, his accidentally performed and displaced vengeance sets in motion the stalled revenge plot. Immediately anticipating the return of the ghost, Polonius's slaughtered body, travestied as an object of grief, predicts the revenge tragedy's conventional plot devices—the succession whereby Laertes's seeking to avenge his father provides the opportunity for Hamlet to revenge himself upon Claudius, this entire series of actions having been prompted more by treachery than by intention, which is to say by a social logic that is alien to the hero's own conscience. Despite all his efforts to reverse the trajectory of revenge toward ethical considerations, Hamlet eventually disowns his mourning; and he does this in part because he understands himself to be caught up in a plot or a social logic that cannot be averted, in a world in which, as his confused action against Polonius demonstrates, even ethical purpose remains mired in violently substitutive praxis.

Conclusion

If *Hamlet* teaches us anything about cultural memory, it is that the ritual time of mourning and the forgetful function of commemorative mourning are not readily separable. The question arises, then, as to whether a violation of the temporality of mourning ought to be read as if it were a correctable social flaw or whether it reflects, in a manner symbolically reinforced by the play's anterior murder, a deeper symbolic wrong in commemorative mourning. If, as Lacan proposes, Claudius and Gertrude are inadequate mourners according to the clock of social custom, then why are they so insistent on converting Hamlet to their own foreshortened schedule? Are they trying merely to ease their own conspicuously bad consciences, or does their insistence reflect a more ordinary tendency of cultural memory? It would appear that the reason they are presented as so rational and persuasive is that they have been alert all along to a deep recalcitrance and impracticality in Hamlet, which have to do with his philosophic objection to commemorative mourning.

The Player Queen's remark in the play-within-the-play, "None wed the second but who killed the first" (3.2.162), becomes a kind of poetic proof of a stronger cultural logic in *Hamlet*, suggesting that our cultural modes of continuity may depend upon the anti-ethical praxis of substitution, thereby implicating us in injustices that structure our society even when or largely because they have not been explicitly recollected. One reason to believe Hamlet himself may have originally composed the Player Queen's words is that he echoes them when contrasting his accidental murder of Polonius to Gertrude's deliberate substitution. "A bloody deed," he says, "almost as bad, good-mother, / As kill a king and marry with his brother" (3.4.27–28). I doubt Hamlet fully believes his own accusation, but he imaginatively carries a substitutive, sequential progression to an extreme in which substitutive praxis seems to cancel all responsibility for the past, espousing such a logic either as a cruel travesty of the example set for him by the court or as the necessary by-product of a perhaps less consciously formulated identification with the cultural system he opposes. According to the play's persistent critique of the egocentric logic of substitution, which gives priority to the survivor over any injustice perpetrated against the dead, the social horizon of a failed personal mourning must be the cultural forgetting that Hamlet names (and with the murder of Polonius enacts) as synonymous with the perpetration of injustice. Once one accepts potential injustices in order to keep one's position in the symbolic order, one practices politics as something that is fundamentally anti-ethical in its orientation. When Hamlet equates ethical complicity in injustice with the perpetration of crime itself, he may be rhetorically tendentious or traumatically inspired, but he also claims ethical significance for acts that are not strictly intentional in origin.[37]

The corollary of Hamlet's protest of the cultural logic of substitution is finally a complaint with the time of mourning. For, as Lawrence Danson has remarked, "[i]nexorably moving time is the discreditor of all purpose and action: it is the primary equivocator" (*Tragic Alphabet*, 34). If a next moment always succeeds the present one—in such a way that words are "relegated to a discredited past" or repeatedly substituted for prior words and "original" intentions—the subject cannot maintain sincerity because he or she must lack consistency. We can never fully anticipate the events that will prove our words true or false. As Danson hints, the Player King replies to the Player Queen's dramatic and self-accusing promise of fidelity as though Gertrude's similar ethical failure were inevitable and even necessary: "I do believe you think what now you speak; / But what we do determine oft we break" (3.2.168–69). On the surface, Hamlet accepts the temporal structure that presides over all cultural meaning, but throughout the play he persistently protests the movement of time and its consequences, and he does so, ironically, by imaginatively accelerating what he perceives to be the already rapid flow of time.

Throughout *Hamlet* the temporality of mourning is frequently conflated with the symbolic resolution that brings responsibility for the other to a close. Notably, when Gertrude first addresses Hamlet, she refers not to the time Hamlet has already wasted in mourning, but to an unforeseeable future of mourning, advising that he should not "for ever" look for his father in the dust (1.2.70–71). From Gertrude's passionate perspective, it is possible that Hamlet's two months of mourning seem to have gone on "for ever," but more to her point is the anxiety that mourning, at least along the lines Hamlet has conceived, might have no end. Judging from Gertrude's opinion, Hamlet's "particular" form of mourning would refuse all completion and extend the other's value not through the cultural immortality of symbolic value, but through the persistent incompletion of personal relationship. Conversely,

Hamlet accuses his mother not of having failed to mourn, but of having mourned too quickly:

> . . . and yet within a month—
> Let me not think on't; frailty, thy name is woman—
> A little month, or ere those shoes were old
> With which she followed my poor father's body,
> Like Niobe, all tears, why she, even she—
> O God, a beast that wants discourse of reason
> Would have mourned longer!—married with mine uncle,
> . . . .
> . . . within a month,
> Ere yet the salt of most unrighteous tears
> Had left the flushing of her gallèd eyes,
> She married. (1.2.145–56)

The allusion to Niobe is telling, for if Niobe models endless mourning, Hamlet credits his mother with having successfully imitated Niobe in the first stages of her grief, but also with having somehow managed to condense Niobe's inconsolability into a month's time. In Ovid's rendering of the tale, Niobe's suffering reveals the stubborn dignity of human beings who remain resistant to the facts of their fate, and so (here in Ted Hughes's translation) it is an extraordinary and somewhat belated grief that humanizes Niobe and turns our hearts to her, possibly for the first time:

> Now even those who hated her most
> Pitied her. She bowed
> Over the cooling bodies of her sons.
> She kissed them, as if she could give them
> A lifetime of kisses in these moments.[38]

Both redeemed and destroyed by her grief, Niobe embraces the bodies of her sons almost as though they were alive, and as I have suggested in the preceding chapter, this—along with her desperate attempt to cover her last daughter's body from the arrows of Apollo—is her central ethical act in Ovid's severe morality tale. Obtaining significance through her obdurate, implausible attachment to her children, Niobe becomes finally a monument to an unrealized possibility of relationship ("And there, a monument to herself, / Niobe still weeps" [208]).[39] As miraculously weeping stone, Niobe stands for a human worth on the order of Prometheus's sufferings—which is to say, an opposition to the gods and to the world of seemingly unalterable injustices.

For her part, Gertrude imitates Niobe only in her passionate phase of mourning. Though even by the function of mere appetite (as a "beast that wants the discourse of reason") for that which she has been deprived of, Gertrude's grief might have lasted longer, Hamlet never supposes Gertrude's mourning or her past affection to have been insincere. In recollecting her formerly passionate devotion to the father ("she would hang on him / As if increase of appetite had grown / By what it fed on" [1.2.143–45]), he attributes to her his own high regard for his "noble father" (1.2.71), imagining her esteem as inseparable from the limited animal properties of desire and mortality. Nor does Gertrude's grief in her own mind belie the cultural function of mourning; rather, in her passion she hurries to make of the dead husband a symbolic value. Long before Freud ever put the psychological terms of the work of mourning to us, Gertrude had intuited the aim of mourning to be a completion of past relationship dependent upon the prospects of an erotic substitution, and by this view, the temporal conflation of funeral and marriage is not so much an aberration of mourning rites as an interpretation of their cultural purpose. When Hamlet addresses himself to the temporality presiding over the mother's substitution ("O most wicked speed, to post / With such dexterity to incestuous sheets!" [1.2.156–57]), it is as though the speed would stand in grammatically for the absent subject of the infinitive clause—in other words, as if the speed itself were purposive. He does not imagine Gertrude as having purposed deception, pretending to value his father while adulterously preferring his uncle, but rather reads the purposiveness as a property of mourning itself, which has been fixed by the complementary aims of completing grief and substituting for the lost other.

Such is the logic whereby Hamlet describes to Horatio and Ophelia the recent events at the court of Elsinore. To Horatio, Hamlet even acts mockingly as though he were an advocate of mourning's substitutively progressive plot and the rapidity with which Gertrude remarries Claudius: "Thrift, thrift, Horatio. The funeral baked meats / Did coldly furnish forth the marriage tables" (1.2.179–80). Offering us more than a version of the contemporary commonplace that funerals are for the living, Hamlet here accuses all commemorative ritual of being tantamount to mere symbolism, an effort to advance substitution in order to preserve the present structure of society, regardless of whether there lurks behind the facade of social order any deeper, still recoverable memory of injustice. When Hamlet banters with Ophelia during the performance of "The

Murder of Gonzago," observing, "For look you how cheerfully my mother looks, and my father died within 's two hours" (3.2.114–15), he so ridiculously abbreviates the time of mourning that Ophelia, unwittingly playing straight man to Hamlet's sardonic wit, can only think to remind him that he has the length of time wrong. Of course, the melancholic point Hamlet is making is not that the cultural time of mourning and the ethical valuation of the dead have been violated or abbreviated, but rather that such abbreviation reveals mourning's internal logic. Since we must recall that even Gertrude once wept like a Niobe, the cultural place given to grief proves ultimately to be about the self to the detriment of the other. Any project of mourning that concentrates on the task of substituting a newly valued object for an original, anterior object becomes tantamount to progress and to forgetting. It is against this seemingly inevitable progression that Hamlet has directed his unrealistic protest.

CHAPTER THREE

Lyrical Economy and the Question of Alterity

In the *Eudemian Ethics*, Aristotle supposes that moral goodness exercises a regulatory influence on the emotions and that what is morally good exists at the mean point of pleasures and pain, or excess and lack. Though it is possible to feel too little, most Aristotelian vices are associated with excess, and inordinate feeling generally belongs to the realm of the involuntary.[1] According to Aristotle, the moral philosophical problem posed by involuntary events is not that they are mere fictions; it is that a subject who adheres to such events with the belief that they have been in any way definitive of his rational and moral being is already in excess of both morality and rationality. It is this nexus of rationality and morality that Bernard Williams and Martha Nussbaum interrogate through the concept of "moral luck," which refers in large part to those objects worthy of moral consideration that nevertheless defy the voluntary exercise of reason.[2] Strictly speaking, even Aristotle does not believe that morality, despite all its preference for the voluntary, can refer only to those events produced through deliberation, and in his attempts to account for that which slips beyond deliberation, Aristotle introduces retrospection (as Williams astutely perceives) as a central trope for moral consciousness. A self trying to regulate what it has experienced involuntarily might immediately align such experiences with its voluntary disposition; or it might instead impose retrospective coherence and in this way claim its involuntary experiences as matters of desire or choice.

When a subject looks back to find a coherence that was previously lacking, the task of retrospective reckoning might become by definition an act of omission—either a forgetfulness of that which does not belong to identity or a disregard for the memory of what was unregulated by the psyche and the social order upon which it depends. While Aristotle and Williams concede that a moral subject might altogether exclude involuntary events from morality, each also recognizes that if morality is to remain vital it will need to interpret such events as if they fell properly within its domain. What Williams especially wants to keep alive as a constitutive thought of morality is the notion that moral sensibility exceeds the premises of deliberation and direct causation. Ethics must also treat of a self that is responsible to an involuntary realm, since responsibility is always in excess of the codifications of behavior making up any particular system of morality. Morality depends largely on self-image (the idea that a self formulates of itself as a moral being), which in turn exercises a constitutive influence on the very idea of obligation, and as a result the morally conceived self is often less than responsible to the real network of accidental and intentional obligations in which it finds itself located.[3]

Whereas Williams insists that obligation cannot correspond to the idea a moral subject forms of it, Levinas is less concerned with characterizing the psychological complexity or motivational disposition of the subject than with developing a critique of Kantian obligation by way of the exteriority that obligates any self apart from universal principles.[4] Already assigned by its responsibilities, prior to thoughts both of obligation and of a self that answers to obligation, the Levinasian subject is individuated through its ethical exceptionality. As Levinas says often, there is no one else who can take my place in being responsible for the other.[5] It is this burden of responsibility that systemic morality would attempt to generalize, and thus to disperse and alleviate. Because it both depends on and supports the totality of knowledge and because it also suggests a correspondence between the self and the world as ordered by perceptions of genuine moral imperatives, the Kantian moral system must treat the surprising claim of the other as if it were not at all a surprise, as if all real obligation must be inherently familiar. Moral knowledge, like all other cultural knowledge, would be susceptible to a representation dependent upon universally acknowledged truths that affirm a subject in its identity, and the moral subject would remain bound to its identity through the network of identifications, cognitively ordering its intentions and responsibilities by fitting them into the realm of knowledge, into the world as already given and established.

The turn to exteriority, which in Levinas gets troped as the irremissible facticity of the other and in Williams is figured by the realm of the accidental and involuntary, must always be a turn also to what the moral system ordinarily excludes. As I suggested earlier, both Levinas and Williams are involved in a kind of meta-ethical turn against ethics, which as any well-trained Kantian could point out is already a language given over to the vocabulary of obligation understood as an act of re-turning the self to that which is outside of it. What Levinas and Williams have to imagine, then, is that ethics must always be about the thing that is exterior to thought insofar as it cannot ever finally be included in the selves or moral systems or modes of knowledge it obligates. The constitutive thought of ethics might finally be named as the concern for that which is outside, even for that which has seemingly been left out of all prior consideration. In other words, there is in ethics a constitutively anti-economic relation between the moral subject and that which obligates it.

Still, though we might prefer at times to oppose economy and might be expected to oppose it if we wish to be ethically responsible persons, we can not altogether do without it. If ethics is developed as a set of questions about how one responds to the exteriorly imposed obligation most often made manifest in the other person, economy articulates the structure and system from which the question of ethics arises and into which it always again descends. Economy, as the articulation of a system's internal logic, expresses the self-ordering function of any social or cognitive system. According to the opposition between ethics and morality I emphasized in my introduction, we expect that morality should correspond to economy precisely in ways ethics does not. By the ordinary logic of morality, to be responsible is to operate within a system of discernible rules and precepts and to develop one's identity as an economic function of one's perceived responsibilities. There is an economy of identity, which depends in turn on a system of knowledge according to which any event or instance of alterity returns eventually to a thought of sameness, thus affirming the essential correspondence between self-consciousness and objective phenomena. It was Hegel who brought this line of thinking to its fullest realization, but the interpretation of experience through an economics of knowledge was also part of Aristotle's legacy to Western philosophy.

Closer to the source of Levinas's critique of a morality elaborated as knowledge, Heidegger and Sartre had challenged the epistemological orientation of a Western philosophical tradition that contained being and the existential freedom of the self, arguing for the precedence of existence over essence and for the existential openness in being that would follow from conceiving our humanity along these lines. Part of what was unique about existentialism's revision of ethical questions was that not only were basic metaphysical presuppositions abrogated, but rationality came to depend upon an openness and indetermination that were radically anti-economic. If the need to find a home for alterity in what has come before it has seemed (to Levinas at least) one of the most characteristic thoughts of Western philosophy, not surprisingly it is also a literary preoccupation.[6] It is here, indeed, that the opposition between aesthetics and ethics—between form and the content of thought, between the imaginative realm and action—might almost be said to dissolve. For if ethics is that which signifies the other as though she were someone outside of the moral subject's prior knowledge and preconceptions, it is also by analogy a challenge posed by that which is exterior to the representational capabilities of a literary text.

To be more specific, what social economy and lyric leave out may share an affinity in being excluded from normative affinities, since according to conventional bias the lyric poem cares for what has been already included: if lost, that which lyric still cares for might be regathered or recollected (the basic logic, for example, of the love poem), but it is hard to imagine how poets are to wax lyrical about matters entirely unfamiliar, alien, or excluded from their own premises of identity and experience, from which they would speak representatively for their societies. The lyric's exclusive premises are not merely mimetic, however. There is indeed a tendency in lyric (much as the New Critics had supposed) to limit the world to images concentrated in the personal idiom and to let poetic images seem constituted as sufficient to reality.[7] Thus the language of lyric is economical in the sense that its spareness stands for a kind of purity of language itself. All the same, even the lyric's potential autonomy, its seeming indifference to the world at large, is produced necessarily as a social instance, its apparent lack of bad conscience about its act of individuation (which is also an act of keeping the others at a distance) testifying to its deep immersion in language and in social meaning.[8] This is true, according to Theodor Adorno, because "language is itself something double"—that which assimilates completely into subjective impulses as if it had produced them, and also that which traces and establishes "an inescapable relationship to the universal and to society."[9]

It is my contention that what I call lyrical economy encompasses precisely Adorno's paradox, as the lyric poem seems to gather the contradictory force of language, which exists under the burden of history and ethics, toward a reduced sphere of personal identity constituted through a familiar set of social relations. The conventional way of stating this movement is to speak of the lyrically concentrated voice as a reduction of the responsibilities of the public sphere to a private set of relations, which is then universalized and set back into the public sphere. Such a description speaks to a more general philosophic premise of lyric, which produces the illusion of identity by sustaining it on what almost has the status of a first principle—namely, in this case, the self in relation to a set of clearly defined responsibilities. In such a view, lyric identity reflects and serves cultural constructions privileging a notion of personal identity presumed in advance to have an integrity, an integrity that might be compromised or greatly harmed by severe loss or, for that matter, by the undefinable other with whom one is in relation.

Yet, as Jonathan Culler has noted, the theory of lyric as a personal utterance embodying the speaker's attitude neglects two crucial aspects of the lyric's history: (1) the extent to which lyrics have functioned apart from individualization, most commonly in songs; and (2) the entire bardic tradition that informs the evolution of lyric.[10] To put it in more expansive terms, there is a tendency in much modern theory to reduce lyric to a simple, direct, or naïve mode of speaking and to underestimate severely the layerings and figurations of voice as well as the patterns of self-reflexivity that make lyric significant. When Culler identifies a dimension of lyric voice resisting the reading of poems as fictive representations of personal utterances and discerns the ways in which lyrical voice need not correspond neatly with the attitude of a speaker, he in effect predicts a resistance to economy inscribed within lyric. Although the neglected richness of lyrical voice might lead us to consider how lyrical utterance stands in relation to collectivity and how it stands in history as an instance of rhetoric with a specific audience, an important qualification has to be made here: neither the effort to locate lyric in collective voice nor the perhaps somewhat related endeavor to consider its rhetorical occasionality necessarily brings about a breakup of lyrical economy, if only for the commonsensical reason that most of our cultural thought on identity considers the individual in relation to collective identity and via the question of the speaker's situatedness. The confidence of the speaker as an individual fully representative of himself and at least somewhat representative of others is not shattered by these broader contexts for identity. A more radical critique of lyrical economy requires us to perceive an otherness vying even with that which is sometimes proffered as evidence of externality, as a contextual outside to lyrical limitedness.

A paradox, however, presides over my reading of the lyric throughout this chapter: as I elaborate the lyric's statement of economy, which is often a work of narrowing the field of ethical relevance, I emphasize those resistances to the economic aspect of lyrical voice that are significant and persistent, even as espoused by lyric's own generic trajectory. Much as social economy depends largely upon its acts of exclusion, the lyrical worldview seems regulated by a set of similarly restrictive social imperatives, often treating the challenge and claim of the other as though responsibility were either an already familiar matter for the self or no matter at all. Since this implicit economy of lyric has everything to do with those philosophical constructs of identity guiding both ethics and mourning, I maintain that it is specifically through those moments where lyrical identity is either at a loss or in danger of losing itself that we recognize a resistance that is figuratively excessive and simultaneously ethical—a demand implicitly exerted by the other, not unlike Hamlet's intuition of what he owes the father that transcends a conventional economy of social value and even causes him to fall out of identity in the ordinary sense.

In lyric, what is exterior to the poem and to a speaker's consciousness may seem, paradoxically, far greater than the demands of the world that lyrical economy has deemed possible. In this chapter, then, I read three seemingly divergent, even disparate, economies—the economy of cultural identity, the economy of mourning, and the economy of lyric—as if they could be woven together by what they leave out, which is to say, by their common neglect of alterity. Proceeding from the perspective of ethical alterity, such a critique may often get stated negatively, almost as though what economy has abandoned or exiled were of itself capable of instituting the critique of economy. If as social theory such a contention has the danger of seeming a mere wishful hypothesis, it may nevertheless be the peculiar talent of the lyric to couch the ethical objections to economy within its overt statements or reinstatements of lyrical economy.

Demodocos's Song: The Economic Plot of Lyric

Economy, from the Greek *oikonomia* or more basically *oikos*, refers to matters or contents belonging to the home. *Oiko-nomia*, literally "the law of the
home," includes all that is involved in managing a household, family, or home
(*oikos*), so that there is a redundancy in the very concept of economy inasmuch
as it refers to managing a space that is already, if we recall the Greek verb *oikeo*,
a place to be settled, inhabited, or managed. A fundamental ambiguity haunts
the concept of home, which is already the place in which one is situated, even
as it is also a place that must be occupied. Long before the word *economy* was extended from its etymological definition as the "art or science of managing a
household" to its mid-seventeenth-century connotation of "administrations of
the concerns and resources of any community" and then to its late eighteenth-
century sense of "managing the resources of a nation" or the more recent sense
of "laws that regulate the production and distribution of wealth," economy was
at the same time both self-reflexive and expansive.[11] In the ancient Greek world,
economy was a matter for enfranchised citizens, but could be extended, at least
imaginatively, to include the stranger. Through the ethic of hospitality in which
one treats the stranger as though he were a person of means and property, the
privileges of economy were extended by seeing in the other an emblem of one's
own home and the symbolic apparatus by which it is maintained.[12]

As the hospitality sometimes extended to Odysseus in his travels is meant to
demonstrate, hospitality is a conservative concept, which is to say, an economic
one. Significantly, the crime that earns Penelope's suitors the thorough and
bloody revenge of Odysseus is their having made a mockery of the hospitality
extended to them by a house of mourning. Theirs is a highly poetic crime in the
sense that their every action is a reflection and elaboration of the thematic center of Homer's epic: the plot demands that the suitors violate the laws of hospitality, if only to preserve in our minds, however ironically or negatively, the
idea that the household in Ithaca is Odysseus's home. Were Telemachos to
have put his family's affairs in order, Odysseus might have returned to a place
no longer his own. It is no mere coincidence, but rather a telling one, that
Odysseus returns just as Telemachos has finally set out to seek news of his
father's death and, with that news in hand, to begin the work of taking charge
of the household affairs. Odysseus must return precisely at this moment because
the economic basis of the world to which he belongs is about to shift, and
Homer brings him back in time to postpone the legitimate institution of a home

and law about to be no longer centered on Odysseus, except perhaps as a retro-spective ideal. If Odysseus returns to tell us that the past was a more heroic place, he also tells us that there is still a place for such a past in the present.

Heroism in *The Odyssey*, as Max Horkheimer and Theodor Adorno famously argued in *Dialectic of Enlightenment* (1944, 1947), charts a path in which a self journeys among the preconceptual spaces of the mythic realm in order to bring it under the signification of a rational self-consciousness.[13] Strewn along the path of this self's coming into self-consciousness are adventures that function not so much as a testing ground for the self's capability as distractions from its epic task. Indeed, in Horkheimer and Adorno's view, as Odysseus wanders in the realm of myth, giving rational names to irrational, primeval space, the en-tire mythic world gets construed as a kind of aberrancy that both tempts and succumbs to the hero's task of self-preservation, as he focuses teleologically on "returning to his homeland and fixed property" (38). Positioned along the fault line of epic and mythos, *The Odyssey* presents us with the archetypal hero of ra-tionality, who derives his identity by means of this opposition between epic and myth, his progression into rational identity "so much a function of the non-identical, of disassociated, unarticulated myths, that it must derive itself from them" (39). The highly Hegelian overtones of Horkheimer and Adorno's read-ing of *The Odyssey* do not detract from its sound exegetical insight that Odysseus's adventure is always a function of the alienation of his desire and purpose, so that whether one assumes his journey is symbolically about a re-covery of the privileges of true identity or perhaps about a growth in the self-consciousness of heroism, the fact that "[a]ll the adventures Odysseus survives are dangerous temptations deflecting the self from the path of its logic" (38) also means that most of what Odysseus encounters along the way is so much unnecessary and distracting otherness.

According to a fundamental tension of the plot, Odysseus's cunning and dis-simulation seem necessary attributes of self-preservation. A hero away from home can never be sure he is on safe ground or, for that matter, in a realm where the codes of hospitality provide the stranger with a symbolically substi-tute home. Yet Odysseus's habit of disguise is adopted under an even more basic premise—that one cannot be oneself while away from home. Very much to the point here is the scene in Alcinoos's court immediately prior to Odysseus's only voluntary revelation of his identity during his travels. The result of this announcement will be that, beginning with book 9, Odysseus begins quite literally—since it will be from here on out he who recounts his adventures—to take possession of his story. Yet at the end of book 8, his story still seems, rather like his adventures, to be a property of the larger world of myth. Exactly how tactical Odysseus is being when he implores Demodocos to tell in song the story of Troy is hard to determine, although this has not stopped the great majority of critics from deciding that this is all a rhetorical ploy and that Odysseus knows exactly what he is doing and even knows what the results of the song will be. I would draw attention to two seemingly contradictory details with regard to this question.

In the first place, even if Odysseus cannot foresee that this song will lead him to declare his identity before the court, he attempts to exercise an authority over the song before it has been sung. As he requests that Demodocos tell a story whose center pertains to "the trap that godly Odysseus" prepared for the Trojans, Odysseus refers to himself in the third person, the first time he has done so in his travels (8.494).[14] This self-reference might be read as announcing an intention or at least an unconscious motivation, but I think the simpler psychological explanation is that Odysseus needs to hear a public utterance of his fame and identity, if only to have them affirmed as proof against his years of adventurous wandering, years that might otherwise testify to a loss of self in both a psychological and social sense. Much depends here on our reading of fame as an elaboration of identity. According to the ratio that connects fame to identity, public reputation displaces but also preserves the space of identity whose proper reference is home. When Odysseus assures Demodocos that if he tells the story in its proper form he will be pronounced a "divine singer," the hint of hubris whereby Odysseus equates his own authority with *godly* judgment maintains, if only for the hero himself, an economic balance between true identity and how one is perceived in the world. Odysseus does not lay claim to an authority over the story simply as one who has been a witness to the events or as one who has been personally implicated in them (the conclusion Alcinoos mistakenly arrives at), but rather as one—although the court does not yet know this—who is the heroic agent of the events; which is to say that part of the function of Demodocos's song is to bring about a correspondence between the heroic cunning and knowledge of the Odysseus of legend (whose fate is being described in the ballad) and the Odysseus who stands unrecognized before the court, even now cunningly concealing his identity and declaring that the tale will be judged upon condition of his expert knowledge.

It is even possible Odysseus seeks self-affirmation in the song, and it is easy to see how such a reading slides into an interpretation of the song as rhetorical ploy, since both my own and the more conventional view understand the song as a proof, as it were, of the hero's subjective identity from within the necessary trappings of the objective realm of reputation. What is harder to explain, I would argue, is a second and slightly more dissonant detail. For unless one believes Odysseus to be a rhetorician of truly histrionic and deceptive proportions, the effect the song has upon him gives it a meaning far surpassing its function as a device for revealing himself. Much as Apollodorus's weeping in the *Phaedo* achieves a pathos out of keeping with Plato's rhetorical support for Socrates' philosophical acceptance of death, Odysseus's weeping upon hearing the story of Troy cannot quite coincide with the trajectory of a plot being managed by Odysseus, the arch-rhetorician. It is a matter of no small coincidence that the affect of grief (as is also true in the *Phaedo*) seeks an analogy in the behavior of women, which according to a gendered typology leads to a breakdown in the presidingly masculine model of heroism:

> And Odysseus
> Melted, and a tear from under his eyelids wet his cheeks,
> As a woman weeps embracing her beloved husband
> Who has fallen before his own city and his own people,
> Warding off from city and children the pitiless day,
> And she sees the man dying and breathing heavily,
> And falls down upon him and piercingly shrieks. The enemy
> From behind strike her back and her shoulders with spears
> And lead her off in bonds to have trouble and woe,
> And her cheeks are wasted for her most wretched grief;
> Just so did Odysseus shed a piteous tear under his eyebrows.
>   (Cook trans., 8.521–31)

Under the guise of this elaborate simile, Homer clears room for Odysseus to weep for himself. Yet there is more to it than that.

The simple psychological explanation for what happens here is that the description of the Trojan War reminds Odysseus of the principle of dominion he fought for and also of what he has lost since. As the simile develops the story of a violated home, Odysseus would similarly weep for his lost home. But because the simile also elaborates the subject-position of the weeping woman, its internal narrative stretches beyond the simple containment of the analogy to explore two more difficult modes of identification, each of which disrupts the economy of identity. To begin with, it is easy to imagine the woman who weeps for her fallen husband as an analogy to Penelope. The only problem with this is Penelope knows by legend that Odysseus did not fall at Troy and that if he has been lost to her it has happened since then. What's more, according to a strictly topographical application of the analogy, the woman who weeps for a husband who has died defending his soil would have to be a Trojan woman, in which case the imaginative analogue for Odysseus would also be a Trojan. Even were we to argue that this constitutes only a minor lapse in the narrative logic of the simile, it nevertheless significantly disrupts the nationalistic economy of identity by which Odysseus builds his epic heroism and through which he explores the world as a poor substitute for home. For an instant we might even imagine him as the enemy who carries off the woman as spoils of war, the Achaian as the one who violates home.[15]

By traveling through this rather imperfect analogy to Odysseus's own plight, we arrive at the second identification in the simile; namely, Odysseus's anxiety for his wife. As the simile's internal narrative describes a woman carried off as a result of her husband's ineffective defense of home, the woman's mourning is no longer just for her husband but also for herself. So, by the strange logic of subject-positions in this simile, when the woman as a figure for Penelope weeps for her husband, she is also a device permitting Odysseus to weep for himself. But, likewise, when the woman implicitly weeps for herself, Odysseus laments his fate through his wife's eyes and weeps for her more than himself. In all of this, the woman as a figure for Penelope stands as implicit guardian of the spirit of home, as it were, as an icon of economy. Yet both the specter of the violated home and the very instability that characterizes mourning as a vulnerability to the fate of others make the song testify simultaneously to a possible lapse in economy.

It does not stretch the original function of Demodocos's song too far, then, to employ it as a loose paradigm for a question of economy residing at the heart of lyric. When Alcinoos alone perceives the influence the song has had on Odysseus, he orders Demodocos to break off his "piercing lyre" (8.537, my translation).[16] By the very nature of Odysseus's reaction and Alcinoos's perception, lyric is here given a context greater than its event as personal utterance. Yet Odysseus's response also anticipates a personalizing tendency now especially associated with the modern lyric, as he makes the song his own and hears in it a reference to his own grief. As an emblem for the fate of lyric, Demodocos's song signifies largely through Odysseus's reception of it and thus as the very thought a being has of and for itself, predicting, as it were, the theory of lyric as personal utterance (developed by the New Critics and later such

scholars as Northrop Frye and Barbara Herrnstein Smith) and the more restrictive economy that comes with such a theory.[17] Even though the song relies
upon a larger context, when it functions as a vehicle for Odysseus to tell the
story of his wanderings in alien and mythical places, it economically corresponds to the hero's expressive purpose.

Though Odysseus's remembrances of his wanderings reach ostensibly beyond the immediate economic sphere of home and identity, lyrical thought
always returns to the thought of self as to its home. So greatly has Odysseus's
authoritative utterance become associated with the song the court has just
heard that Alcinoos implores him immediately afterward to say why the song
means so much to him, speculating that his guest must have lost kinsmen in the
conflict of which the song speaks. This is itself a rather economical thought: it
seems reasonable to Alcinoos that one might weep for a family member almost
as for oneself, but there must be some personal involvement, some principle of
identification, for Odysseus's grief to be what it is. And Alcinoos is at least partly
right. Odysseus's weeping gives him away in a crucial if only partial sense, his
excessive grief being finally accounted for as having involved some thought for
himself or his own affairs.

As a consequence of the lyre song (or perhaps because he planned to do so
all along), Odysseus chooses to preside fully over the recognition scene emerging through the song and identifies himself as the hero of the ballad. But even
as it effectively charts the lyric's descent into self, Demodocos's song remembers much of what gets left out of lyrical identity, and it does so according to
the gap that is created—and then bridged—between the contents of his song
and the social occasion of its utterance. This dramatized moment of the lyric as
song recalls not only a range of meaning that Adorno and Culler suggested may
get wrongly excluded from the lyric's meaning, it locates the lyric within an
economically proscribed system of social meanings through which Odysseus
would preserve his identity. Odysseus's invocation of Demodocos's song seems
protective of identity in its final function and demonstrates how often, in fact,
identity gathers strength from the thought that it is not alone in being allowed
to be provisionally for itself.

The Statements of Economy in Renaissance Elegy

In the Freudian conception of grief, mourning would be included, along
with lyric, in a cultural plot whereby individual identity is the privileged site of

a meaning setting itself against incursive or radically exterior aspects of reality. The ethical trajectory of this should be rather evident: according to the substitutive praxis of Freudian mourning, a mourner would account for the energy she expends upon others as though relationship itself were a matter of economy.[18] When a beloved other dies, a portion of the self seems to remain with him. This is because relationship is already a symbolic network of identifications through which the self has been constituted in the world, and thus the damage done to someone on whom the self has depended is fundamentally a damage done to the self. According to Freud's speculation, if the ego were able to withdraw its erotic and self-enhancing attachments, it could hope to regather that expended energy and, by attaching to another object, restore its devastated self-image. For Freud the psychological speculation upon others as symbolic objects is the very reality of the ego, and because this is true, loss always threatens to make the self unreal in and to the world. Thus a basic converse of the Freudian work of mourning follows: insofar as any expression of mourning prolongs the subject's attachment to the dead, this failure to detach oneself from the other becomes itself an anti-economic activity.

In charting the movement from grief to consolation in the tradition of elegy, Peter Sacks deftly conflates the Freudian work of mourning with the raison d'être of lyric elegy, providing us with a sharp insight into the economical workings of the language of a lyric poem.[19] It was Adorno's view that, when lyric poetry presents itself as though it were freely, separately, and subjectively established in the world, it speaks at the height of language's capacity, which is to take itself for granted. By much the same logic, Sacks traces in lyric elegy the function of language as a capacity to produce signs in order to cope with loss (quite as if, according to a Lacanian view of the matter, this coping with loss were the originary function of language), committing himself to a view in which lyric is implicitly and especially social in its private workings. As I turn now to several examples of the Renaissance lyric elegy, there is a predetermining logic to my choices, since an economy of mourning stands always to be transposed in these poems as a screen for lyrical economy, or vice versa. Yet it is precisely my point that these two separate economical imperatives—one interpreted through the lens of modern psychology and the other through the conventions of literary history—are relatively interchangeable when it comes to the challenge of radical alterity pronounced in and by so much of the elegiac tradition. Since the challenge of alterity is magnified in the elegy by the redoubled unknowability of death itself and the other who has been lost, it would be just as easy to decide that the social conventions regulating grief demand a mode of lyrical expression consistent with the economical imperatives of grief as to decide that lyric economy imposes a restriction on how fully and openly grief can respond to the loss of the other. Which economic imperative comes first is not really my concern. I am content to observe that these two economies coincide in the literary work of mourning, each also reminiscent of an overarching economy of identity as self-knowledge that must find in the event of otherness or loss some return to or for identity.

In the Renaissance elegies I consider here, the intersection of an economy of mourning and an economy of lyric is expressed, conveniently as it were, through the figurative conceits of financial economy. This rather overt thematic dimension of lyric may obliquely characterize a more general economic premise of lyrical statement as it also parallels an ethical premise that Levinas phrases through an idiom of bourgeois culture when he insists that ethics is a debt standing without any possibility of remission. One cannot barter, exchange, or buy down the question of responsibility; it transcends every economic metaphor we have for it.[20] Ethics is the asymmetrical relation between self and other, which is not a temporary, situational, or historical question of imbalance to be righted over time, but rather a poverty of self before the other or a poverty of the other before the self—in either case a condition that issues from a gratuitous transaction, from generosity, from goodness. Not surprisingly, then, the tendency of certain Renaissance elegies to render the losses of human relationship in the terms of financial and metaphysical economy predicts a strategy of containment that is directed at the other who is lamented.

The frequent use of financial conceits may be owing in part to the emergent bourgeois ethos of Protestantism, so that the loss of the other, when represented as a type of financial transaction, pertains to matters of both social and metaphysical economy. In one sense, this conflation promotes a metaphysical rationalization of loss that reads the apolitical stoicism of the Matthean Jesus, who accepts the taxes of imperial Rome by saying "Render therefore unto Caesar the things which are Caesar's" (KJV 22:21), through an emergent Protestant work ethic that divines in worldly prosperity or misfortune the will of God. By such a logic, one may interpret even untimely death as if it were a comment on one's overall worldly prosperity; and as the elegy makes sometimes pathetic use of this logic, all loss has the potential to be experienced as reproof. More consistently, however, this conflation of metaphysical and materialistic fortune affirms a larger cosmic order that presides over and indeed superannuates all manifestations of social or financial economy. At its most schematic level, then, as in Edmund Spenser's "Astrophel [The Doleful Lay of Clorinda]" such metaphysical economy can permit no genuine mourning *for* the other precisely because the other now exists in the prosperity of the afterlife:

> But live thou there, still happie, happie spirit,
> And give us leave thee here thus to lament:
> Not thee that doest thy heavens joy inherit,
> But our own selves that here in dole are drent. (91–94)[21]

As the other "inherits" heaven, he progresses—according to the paradoxical meaning of "dole are drent" as "immersed in abundant poverty"—to a richness consistent with his due for living a righteous life, but also for what has always been lacking in earthly existence. By contrast, the surviving self is doubly impoverished by the absence of the other and by having to wait to experience a similar prosperity, the point of deprivation further reinforced by Spenser's pun on *dole*—connoting both the wailing of the mourners and their beggarly dependence upon alms from God. The mourner's state of abandonment is made more poignant by the other's prosperity, and one might almost attribute a proleptic connotation to *dole*, which would come in eighteenth-century usage to signify an act of niggardly distribution. Though it is improbable that Spenser's elegy gives vent to an accusation of God, the stark contrast of the other's prosperity and the mourner's deprivation nevertheless imprints a suspicion within the very statement of the facts of economy.

In this respect, Renaissance elegy anticipates the modern elegy's expressions of ambivalent grief in which a mourner such as Thomas Hardy holds his dead wife imaginatively accountable for his surviving state of deprivation. It is often assumed that the modern elegy permits of a more genuine, or at least more honest, expression of the varied emotions of the mourner, and if we accounted for elegies strictly according to the range of psychological conflict evident in a mourner's attitude, this might seem true.[22] Yet an odd corollary of this seeming progress is that, since so much of modern elegy depends upon the subjective expression of the mourner, the economic imperative of the work of mourning—in which the other must be substituted for psychologically, linguistically, or symbolically, or as Sacks has suggested by some combination of all three—seems more pronounced. According to our modern sensibilities and our waning conviction in the cultural truths of religious consolation, the metaphysical economy employed by Renaissance elegies seems contrived. Yet the paradoxes that inform the Renaissance elegist's move to religious consolation contrast oddly with the resolutions of modern elegists, so few of whom remain as capable of irresolution and its strangely ethical resentments as, say, Hardy, and turn instead to cultural narratives for grief, such as psychoanalysis, that readily exorcise the memory of the dead.[23]

In hindsight, it might even seem that Renaissance elegists, perhaps as a direct result of their statements of metaphysical economy, indulge expressions of grief that are less psychologically redeemed or economically placed than the multifaceted grief of modern elegists. Consider John Donne's sonnet for his dead wife:

> Since she whome I lovd, hath payd her last debt
> To Nature, and to hers, and my good is dead,
> And her Soule early'into heaven ravished,
> Wholy in heavenly things my mind is sett.
> Here the admyring her my mind did whett
> To seeke thee God; so streames do shew the head,
> But though I'have found thee,'and thou my thirst hast fed,
> A holy thirsty dropsy melts mee yett.
> But why should I begg more love, when as thou
> Dost wooe my soule, for hers offring all thine:
> And dost not only feare least I allow
> My love to saints and Angels, things divine,
> But in thy tender jealosy dost doubt
> Least the World, fleshe, yea Devill putt thee out.[24]

All the terms of metaphysical economy are written large here, and they are uttered not as mere conventions or commonplaces, but as truths Donne has fought hard to affirm. Yet within each statement of economy there persists what Kenneth Burke has called the counterstatement of the aesthetic text.[25] For instance, when the poet states that his wife has "payd her last debt / To Nature," his direct invocation of the financial conceit suggests that human beings are mere borrowers of our natural bodies and that we live our lives in a debt to be paid finally with life itself. The potential for complaint is already registered in conceiving of the wife's entire life as an attempt to pay her body's natural debt, but there is also a slight displacement of metaphysical economy operative here as Donne focuses our attention on the anonymity of nature rather than, say, the providence of God.

By the time we arrive at the somewhat surprising use of "ravished" in line 3, the aspect of displaced complaint has been made explicit. To ravish sustains an array of connotations, with the primary meaning of "carrying away by force" distributed equally between the spiritual connotation of "being carried away or transported from the earth" and the military connotation of "taking an item or person away by plunder." The term may even allude to the fate of women as acquired property of war, a meaning for which Helen's abduction stood as the poetic archetype and that Shakespeare, for example, employs as a ready convention when he speaks of "ravished Helen" at the beginning of *Troilus and Cressida* (Prologue, 9). According to the terms of this allusion, Donne has to suppress from the start an impulse to protest the carrying off of his wife.[26] The poet only deflects such a direct criticism by rendering the ordinarily transitive force of the verb *ravish* into a strangely impassive (though not properly passive) construction, the oddity of which is brought home if we ask what it means to "ravish into heaven." Even as Donne appears to offer a more conventional narrative about his wife's spiritual transformation, this slippage in the terms of metaphor suggests that he perceives her death as an abduction by God.

According to the basic movement of this elegy, which follows the wife from earth to heaven and describes the husband's pursuant thoughts, Donne would seem to chart for himself a neo-Platonic Christian progression from an earthly, carnal desire for his wife toward a redirected attention to "heavenly things" or "things divine." The only problem is that as the poet asserts "my good is dead," his wife is the substantive force behind any good that may befall him, with the result that his declaration in line 4 that he is now set "[w]holy in heavenly things" seems either half-hearted or deceptive. By the typical logic of the sonnet form, one expects to find a problem or idea posed in the first half that is resolved either in the final sestet or with the dramatic punch of a final couplet. In this sonnet, Donne pulls the conceptual resolution forward into line 4 and leaves the rest of the poem open for his speculations about why, once he has progressed from thoughts of his wife to God, he should still want more—specifically, of her. The entire structure hints at a dissatisfaction with the proposed resolution, which relies on a precisely stated economy. Indeed, I would propose that the peculiar choice of preposition in the phrase "in heavenly things," where the phrase "on heavenly things" might make plainer sense, expresses the poet's feeling of having been enclosed in a metaphysical economy.[27] As his mind pursues his wife in her heavenly state, he arrives at a place in which God's grace is offered to him as a more proper home, and all of this seems quite ordained, as if the wife's death had been intended as a catalyst for him to "seeke" God.

The poet's implicit dissatisfaction coincides, then, with his perception of just how neatly his loss fits into metaphysical economy, both in the sense that the wife's body has been ordained to a natural fate and in the sense that there is a point to his loss—namely, to point him toward God. Still, one hears little resignation when Donne asks, "But why should I begg more love, when as thou / Dost wooe my soule, for hers offring all thine" (9–10). Remarking that we never do get to hear Donne begging, Arnold Stein has suggested that the poem's silence on this point resides among its many other silences, "like the felt grief allowed no immediacy of expression but allowed only a bare, absolute declaration and a few taut signs."[28] It would seem, however, at least according to Stein, that God has anticipated the poet's increased desire for his wife and so set himself in her place as a difficult to obtain but nevertheless adequate substitute. Though Stein's reading squares with the bare facts of the poem, it still cannot be taken for granted, since the muteness of the poem's crisis in lines 9–10 in no way suggests that Donne gives up his line of questioning.

It is not as though Donne refers merely to a hypothetical moral state— asking, *why would I beg more love?*—he then rejects. Rather, Donne hypothesizes a present course of his own thought and action, better paraphrased as, *why should it be that I continue to beg more love?* This reading is reinforced by—even as it also heightens the force of—the temporal clause that follows: "when as thou / Dost wooe my soule for hers; offring all thine." God's wooing is an enduring action, and Donne's slightly revisionary reading of a Protestant grace, which has often been personally conceived (as in his own Holy Sonnet 14, "Batter my heart, three-person'd God"), makes God's pursuit a direct response to the poet's enduring reluctance to accept the offer. This is so much the case that in the poem's last four lines Donne attributes to God himself the anxiety that Donne's abiding desire for his wife may put God out of mind. By such a projected reversal of anxiety, Donne masks his own resistance, which instead occurs as the speculation of an overly attentive God. There is of course biblical precedent for such godly attention, as the God of Ezekiel or Hosea lets his zealousness function as a substitute for the faithfulness of the feminized Israel to whom he gives his attention, and Donne cannot have missed the irony whereby the "tender jealosy" of God would describe the poet as sinfully resistant to salvific economy.

Donne thus offers a doubly oblique account of his own resistance—first in the muted question and then through the speculative anxiety of a too-attentive God. For a God who woos the poet's soul has reciprocatingly responded to the poet's muted act of begging for "more love." Imitating the poet's earthly supplication, God here pleads to be accepted as an adequate substitute, begging in his own right for the poet to accept the scripted plot of substitution in which God woos his "soule, for hers" (10). In his act of supplication, according to which wooing is metaphorically interchangeable with a providential intention, Donne's God seems slightly ridiculous. The extravagance of the entire scenario is suggested by the further detail wherein God offers all of himself ("wooe my soule, for hers offring all thine"), his offer seeming finally both too much and not enough—not enough because in his resistant attachment to his wife the poet refuses to accept a metaphysical economy that would reconcile him to his loss as if it were gain; and too much because the offer adds to metaphysical economy as if it required justification. The excess of God's offer literalizes a conceit operative in this poem and in much of Donne's poetry: God's love competes with the poet's rival love for earthly things, in this case, his extreme erotic attachment to his dead wife, and the poem's unstated—or counterstated—resentment resides in the perception of a metaphysical order that cannot quite permit these two forms of love (devotion and eros) to coexist. In his grief Donne exists somewhere outside of economy, never at home among heavenly things, unable to accept the demand that he sacrifice his wife, as it were, to another good.

No matter how resistant we decide Donne's relation to metaphysical economy finally is, it is important that in first observing that his wife "hath payd her last debt / To Nature" before considering her new function among "heavenly things," he makes the facts of metaphysical economy complicitous with the natural fate of the body. A similar structure is operative in Ben Jonson's "On My First Son" (1616), where yet again, as the poem's opening suggests, a statement of metaphysical economy may mask the poet's true feelings:

> Farewell, thou child of my right hand, and ioy;
>   My sinne was too much hope of thee, lou'd boy,
> Seuen yeeres tho'wert lent to me, and I thee pay,
>   Exacted by thy fate, on the iust day. (1–4)[29]

More overt than Donne in accusing himself of a sinful attachment, Jonson may be in bad faith in the charge he brings against himself. Through the language of financial economy in lines 3–4 ("lent to me," "I thee pay," "[e]xacted by thy fate"), he reads his fatherly sin as a kind of speculation on the boy's future, as if he had invested too much of himself in the boy's prospects. Yet there seems to be little proportion here between the metaphoric self-accusation and the boy's tragic fate. As Jonson fails to list the specifics of his hope, we are left to intuit the ordinariness of any father's hope that his son might survive long enough to confront and possibly face down the high expectations so often placed by fathers upon their sons. Since hope by definition must be in excess of material circumstances and present reality, Jonson exploits a redundancy implicit in his expression of "too much" hope. In the famous "spot of time" in which Wordsworth reproves his own youthful expectations as if they were the cause of his father's death, much is made of a similarly vague and open hope as both the condition and measure of loss. Wandering too loosely into the future, detached from all definite knowledge, hope is the very extravagance of human attachment. Thus when Jonson repeats the charge of excess against himself at the end of the poem, vowing never again to "like too much" what he loves, his devotion to his son seems a sign of pure extravagance.

The statement of economy in Jonson's poem is set against the form of hopeful love that dies with his son. If Jonson employs the financial conceit in the spirit of renunciation, there can be little doubt that the economics he describes come off as stingy. One hears, for example, a world of difference between this poem's conceit of financial economy and Jonson's employment of a similar conceit in the elegy for his daughter who died at six months ("Yet, all heauens gifts, being heauens due, / It makes the father, lesse, to rue" [3–4]).[30] The difference may derive largely from his having come to see time in the elegy for his son as a function of expectation and attachment. In announcing that the boy has been lent him seven years, Jonson speaks as though the time he had with his boy were a partial generosity when in fact the extra time has led him to take his attachment for granted, with the result that his loss seems more ironic and severe. Though Jonson agrees to pay a debt, his payment—rather like Spenser's emphasis on a mourner left "here in dole" or Donne's incautious impulse to beg "more love"—is shadowed by resentment. Any idea of paying a life as debt is necessarily sacrificial and connotes, according to a Christian supersessionist typology, the crude justice of an Old Testament God. Indeed, Jonson's phrase "I thee pay" echoes the trial scene near the end of *The Merchant of Venice*, when Antonio tells Bassanio that he will pay off a Shylock who is the very embodiment of a relentlessly, yet outmoded version of biblical justice:

> Repent but you that you shall lose your friend,
> And he repents not that he pays your debt;
> For if the Jew do cut but deep enough,
> I'll pay it instantly, with all my heart. (4.1.273–76)[31]

Asserting not once but twice that he will pay the debt, with his second declaration ("I'll pay it instantly") Antonio interprets the financial metaphor with a
fiercely transformative literality. While the first mention of payment is merely
a punning metaphor in which the literal fact of Antonio's willingness to pay
a financial debt stands for his sacrificial willingness to yield his life for his
friend's benefit, the second use of *pay* functions as a euphemism for this same
sacrificial death, while altogether canceling the resonance of the financial conceit. The temporal insistence on paying instantly keeps us focused on how
Antonio's life will expire, rather than what it will stand for. The wordplay
points to the severity of payment as to the severity of the one who exacts payment. With a similar connotation, Jonson speaks of his son as having been
"[e]xacted" on the "iust day," an ironic note descending upon both *exacted* and
just, as if godly justice had become too exacting, as if God were indulging an
overly literal application of his right much as Shylock had also intended to do
(4). Like Antonio's declaration of his own generosity, Jonson's statement of
strict economy takes back through resentment much of what it concedes in
piety.

"Adventure most unto itself": Dickinson, the Home, and Identity

By tracing a resentment lurking in the economic conceits of Renaissance elegies by Spenser, Donne, and Jonson, I seek to emphasize that, even when it is
accepted as necessary and as the way things are, economy remembers a relation
to what it excludes or to that for which it fails to account. One of the consolations we may derive through a declaration of economy is an emphasis on what
remains to the self in the way of significance or, perhaps more basically, what
resources a self has for affirming itself in the face of adversity. To illustrate this
point further, I want to examine the poetry of Emily Dickinson, which sometimes employs conceits of financial economy, but refers more generally to an
economic tension between the risk and managing of experience (as if inspired

by, say, the exorbitance of beauty or the terror of death and transcendence).[32]
In Dickinson, the guardedness of self is often conceived through the idiom
of domesticity, and her verse keeps ever before us an aspect of economy quite
distinct from the thematic representations and content of poetry—namely, the
economic spareness of lyrical poetic language.[33] It has sometimes seemed also
as though Dickinson's lyrical power is immersed in history in proportion to the
measured strains of economy we discern there.

Dickinson's peculiar insight is that for the soul to remain healthy and sane
it must subject itself to a rule of "strict economy" (Superiority to Fate, 7).[34]
The concerns of economy in Dickinson are many; they include the difficult
regulation of secular versus religious desire, of life versus death, of home versus adventure, experience, or untamed alterity. For instance, a poem such as
"Superiority to Fate" (1043) offers the economical sentiment that the teleological focusing of life on a religious end should proceed "[a] pittance at a
time" (5)—not in order to arrive at eternity, but only so that "The soul with
strict economy / Subsist till Paradise" (7–8). It is the implicit excess of immortality that creates the impetus for conceiving of one's life as an act of economical subsistence directed teleologically, if ironically, toward its fulfillment.[35] In
a poem such as "Because I could not stop for Death" (479), death is the oddly
irregular force violating the speaker's ordinary routine, and so intent is the
speaker on seeing the world in her own habitual way that she must narrate her
death in a familiar conceit, much as if she each day repeated the funereal procession for herself as yet another predictable event in her life. Only in the
poem's final lines is there a suggestion that the chariot pointing toward "eternity" (24) signals a shifting in the ground of identity that will not allow the
speaker's tone of familiarity to persist. Economy has been threatened without
yet having been interrupted.

If it is true, as Sharon Cameron has observed, that in Dickinson's poetry
death is often credited with the potentially positive significance of dissolving
the boundaries between subject and object, we should note how often Dickinson's poetry nevertheless insists upon a language of boundaries—and not
merely as proof of an impoverished subjectivity that longs especially for what it
lacks.[36] Though Dickinson often represents humanity in terms of a lack that is
at the same time a relatedness to the excesses of immortality and experience,
economical compromise always imparts the capacity to tolerate the multiplicity
of experience. The requirement of psychological balancing may recall notions
of Aristotelian temperance, but it bears an even closer if also anticipatory affin-

ity to the Freudian psychic economy (which itself traces certain Aristotelian constructs of virtue). Much as the Freudian ego deflects the excesses of reality that might otherwise devastate the self, the Dickinsonian soul concentrates its attention in order to preserve its integrity.

Fittingly, one of the central conceits Dickinson uses for such an economic management of experience is the home. Employing the idiom of the domestic situation variously and often ironically, Dickinson reminds us that the family itself is a threshold concept, the apparatus by which the public world enters the private domain and by which the private realm is returned to a larger construct of social meaning. What is most significant about the family is that it elaborates the private sphere by extending the construct of identity, even as it also reduces the social by delimiting those relations deemed crucial to identity. In other words, family is a concept negotiating between that which falls within or into significance and that which gets pushed outside of significance. Insofar as home is the situating trope of family, Dickinson can one minute advocate the province of home in a primordial sense of domesticating or making endurable the natural world and then, almost in the next, portray the home as that which has so well protected a self that it has lost a sense of the world from which it lives. For instance, in a minor poem from early 1860, " 'Houses' - so the Wise men tell me" (139), Dickinson restates the sentiments of wise men who have told her an all-too-obvious fact—that "Mansions must be warm! / Mansions cannot let the tears in - / Mansions must exclude the storm!" (2–4). With the conception of home seeming here an especially masculine protection against a natural feminized world, the "tears" might function only as a metaphoric anticipation of rain, so that the inside world of home would articulate an exclusion that is hardly regrettable. But if these "tears" connote a feminine principle internal to a rigid masculine economy, the poem's exclusion seems more vexed and self-defeating. The second stanza builds on this tension:

'Many Mansions,' by 'his Father' -
I dont know him; snugly built!
Could the children find the way there -
Some, would even trudge tonight! (5–8)

The evidence of a fatherly hand suggests that we might be reading about a forbiddingly masculine, lost ancestral home.[37] These children, who seem allegorically imprinted with Israel's status as God's wandering children, stray from the very home that should protect them, and whether we imagine they have been neglected, forgotten, or cast out by the implicit masculine economy, they bear witness to the severity of economy and its failure to serve those to whom it is ostensibly dedicated.

In another poem, a better-known one from roughly the same time, "Bring me the sunset in a cup" (140), Dickinson turns from reflections on natural economy to a contemplation of home as a deflection of experience and nature's overwhelming wonder. The rhythm of "Bring me the sunset in a cup" is ecstatic, the poet's sentiments racing to keep pace with nature:

> Bring me the sunset in a cup -
> Reckon the morning's flagons up
> And say how many Dew - (1–3)

Though the opening supposes a domestication of nature, it does so entirely without conviction. The plain impossibility of gathering the sunset into a cup predicts the failure of the speaker's project and testifies ironically to an excess that is synonymous with nature and the very pulse of life the speaker would imbibe. Dickinson pokes fun at the speaker's impulse to concentrate her own enthusiasms and to possess them, as it were, through containment. The playful spirit of Dickinson's voice yields the wonderful nonsense of the phrase "how many Dew" (which is meaningful only by way of a proleptic, homonymnic pun on *due* [18]), as she pushes the poem forward into similarly preposterous images of counting or measuring—such as "Tell me how far the morning leaps - " (4) and "Write me how many notes there be / In the new Robin's extasy / Among astonished boughs - " (7–9) and finally "Who counts the wampum of the night / To see that none is due?" (17–18). Given the absurdity of any one of these figures, it is easy to see how the cumulative effect of such images tends toward what we might call a mathematical sublime (the kind of divinely ordained counting we get from the God of Job), even as it travesties providential economy. A commonsensical approach to these conceits must eventually prove their futility. Dickinson plays here with the economic dimension of all knowledge and with the theoretical premise that representation could ever be adequate to the idea, content, or referent to which it refers. Language simply cannot catch up here with what it seeks to represent, so that the poet's every act of imaginative containment necessarily misses its mark.

The fourth stanza begins with the kind of statement that has led so many readers of Dickinson over the years to perceive in her writings a reduction of scope pertaining specifically to the facts of her life:

> Who built this little Alban house
> And shut the windows down so close
> My spirit cannot see? (19–21)

The arrival of a sudden claustrophobia is unmistakable, and just as suddenly the spell cast by a natural world too great for the speaker's imaginative containments is shattered. Part of the cognitive difficulty of this moment is that the speaker seems the victim of an act of containment by another's hand that is both prior to her own imaginative wanderings and consistent with the acts of imaginative containment she has been experimenting with. If anything, the one who built the house (perhaps some fatherly builder of mansions, as in " 'Houses' - so the Wise men tell me") offers only a more absolute and effective version of containment, so that we might even be inclined to read the speaker's imaginative tendency as an extension of her preconstituted situation. Despite the notes of economic measure in the first three stanzas, the abundance of nature would defy these imaginative acts of counting and measuring— unless they are finally to be attributed to the providence of God. If it is God who can "say how many Dew" (4) or count "the wampum of the night / To see that none is due" (17–18), such divine attention, when placed in juxtaposition with the confining house, bespeaks an oppressive watchfulness that reminds us not a little of Job's complaint as he struggles to square his sufferings with God's remembrance:

> What is man, that thou shouldest magnify him?
> and that thou shouldest set thine heart upon him?
> and that thou shouldest visit him every morning,
> and try him every moment? (KJV 7:17–18)

So too the Dickinsonian speaker delineates a principle of watchfulness that swerves suddenly at the end of the poem into a thought about the oppressive confinement of her own situation.

It is hard to say which comes first—whether the attempt to reckon the natural world as part of God's economy issues in the all too human response of self-protection to be achieved by narrowing the social sphere upon which identity is built, or whether instead the urgings of the narrowed self are extended toward and into the natural world, if only via the idiom of domestication. Either way, one economy comments on the other; there is no simple opposition between the natural world's freedom and the home's confinement. All of the external world is subject to the imaginative or representational hubris of human reckoning, to conceits of counting and measuring that conform experience to inherited notions of identity. The principle of economy has been lurking, if only as a negative measure, in the poem's every description of nature. Either as a presupposition or derivative manifestation of the claim of representation, the Dickinsonian God implicitly cooperates with the economy of knowledge. Though Dickinson's speaker might long at the poem's end "to fly away, / Passing Pomposity" (23–24), such a final transgression of economy seems merely wishful and there is little reason to believe she can again attain her rapturous state once she has yielded it to the reality of economy.

Quite possibly, the ending of "Bring me the sunset in a cup" is meant as a critique of the economy that produces such pathos. Yet this reading would compete with a stoical sensibility in Dickinson's poetry, which suggests that the economic management of experience, of expectation, of God, nature, or other human beings is what makes life possible. If humanity, as opposed to so much else in the natural and larger world, is that which can be contained, Dickinson is far from suggesting that since such an economic management of the world seems vaguely unnatural we should yield ourselves to nature as if to a lost affinity, finding again a proper home for identity.[38] In her most famous nature poems, such as "A Bird, came down the Walk" (359) or "A narrow Fellow in the Grass" (1096), there seems little possibility that human consciousness could return to its natural element. Each poem depends upon the startling effects of an encounter (with bird or snake), the situational conceit of watchfulness suggesting the general problem of interrelatedness. If the speaker could watch without intruding, as is sometimes the case in Wordsworth's nature lyrics, then we might expect that human consciousness could, at least hypothetically, return to or participate in the natural economy. But in Dickinson's view this can never happen. There is no retreat from self-consciousness, and even the bird the speaker observes seems inspired by self-consciousness to take anxious flight. The final effect on the speaker's consciousness is in each case disruptive, isolating a psychic economy as set apart from—and only reluctantly permitting the intrusions of—the natural world.

Isolation also seems the primary effect of a poem such as "The Soul selects her own Society" (409), which opens with the soul's choosing to shut itself in, however selectively:

> The Soul selects her own Society -
> Then - shuts the Door -
> To her divine Majority -
> Present no more - (1–4)

The conceit of home becomes here a figure for the soul's receptivity or lack thereof, as the soul takes these facts of economy to heart, seemingly self-satisfied and content with a choice that will make her "[p]resent no more" to most of the world. But to whom or what exactly has the soul shut her door? The phrase "her divine Majority" involves an odd conflation of two separate referents—God and society—requiring us to pause for a moment to unfold their mutual implication. Though we may be inclined to read "divine" strictly as a qualifying epithet intimating the soul's relation to her divinely ordained company, a more general connotation of the "divine Majority" as transcendent and diverse experience soon suggests itself. Read alongside one another, the two meanings emphasize an act of economy that shuts down both relationship and experience. When in the next stanza the soul is said to remain "[u]nmoved" (5) by chariots at her gate as by emperors at her feet, the queenly conceit ascribes to the soul a posture of self-importance, as if identity depended especially on a capacity to find oneself important and to admit others only selectively to a like importance. As the conceit retrospectively reads the "majority" as the implicitly inferior masses who could become significant only in being selected, it is hard to hear much dissent on Dickinson's part from the terms of such exclusive economy.

Though we might democratize Dickinson's conceit by arguing that each of us constitutes his or her world with more or less the same presumption of arrogant self-worth, throughout the poem the royalist conception of soul competes with the contrary force of democratization, as the third stanza makes clear:

> I've known her - from an ample nation -
> Choose One -
> Then - close the Valves of her attention -
> Like Stone - (9–12)

By beginning the third stanza with "I've known her," the speaker of the poem appears to step back from direct implication in the selective economy she has been observing, as if she has received her information secondhand. Yet the ironic result of this objectifying or self-objectifying stance is to make economy seem all the more natural, if not altogether inevitable. The assertion that the soul can and has in the past chosen "from an ample nation" does not so much emphasize a loss of abundant company and possibility as it pronounces the good fortune that the soul has had so many from among whom to choose. Dickinson here measures worth by the disproportion between what has been admitted to significance and what has been left out.

Selection is finally an act of hard exclusion. When Dickinson's soul closes the "[v]alves of her attention," it is not clear what the costs of such closure might be. If we suppose there are indeed costs, much depends on what it means for the soul's attention to have closed "[l]ike Stone." According to Dickinson's highly elliptical syntax, the closing line supports equally well both objective and subjective attributions of the simile. In the objective sense, the ending would refer severely to those who encounter the soul from outside its economic selectivity, coming up against the soul's inattention as if against stone, representing a challenge silenced before it ever had a chance to be articulated. Yet there is little evidence to suggest that Dickinson here concerns herself with the perspective of those who have been excluded. Rather, she proceeds entirely from within the stated economy, her idiom seeming nationalist or communitarian in the restrictive sense of either term. More immediately, Dickinson's privileged selectiveness resembles the inexplicable principle of election by which Israel is favored or the mystery through which the Christian is saved by grace, through no fault or virtue of her own. In the Gospel of Mark Jesus speaks in parables in order to maintain the position of privilege held by those to whom he addresses himself:

> Unto you it is given to know the mystery of the kingdom of God: but unto them
> that are without, all these things are done in parables,
>> that seeing they may see, and not perceive;
>> and hearing they may hear, and not understand;
>> lest at any time they should be converted,
>> and their sins should be forgiven them. (KJV 4:11–12)[39]

Though an ironic reading of Mark's rhetoric of salvation is possible, Dickinson would have found ample evidence for the straightforward, less-generous reading of this economy of salvation in the largely Calvinist sensibility of her family and the town of Amherst on the whole. Cofounded by her grandfather and made successful in part by her father's astute financial management, Amherst

College had positioned itself as a bulwark against the liberalizing strains of Unitarianism so prominent at Harvard University, and one of the primary tenets of any viable Calvinism was that piety was precisely the appreciative response to an already predetermined economy. To suggest otherwise—to suggest, for example, that one might alter the facts of election and move from outside of grace to become its privileged subject according to the merit of one's own behavior—was to appropriate a privilege of choice belonging only to God. Though Dickinson's poetry is hardly pious in a conventional sense, she often employs the idiom of providential force and like-minded stinginess, as though the psyche's existence in the world would be thrown into chaos—perhaps a democratic chaos—if it could not also live by way of exclusions. Howsoever we choose to hear a poem that closes "[l]ike Stone," the connotations of entombment put us within range of a conclusion that reads the poem's selective economy as producing a loss experienced finally as spiritual death.

Come Again, Odysseus

In shifting to the elegiac connotations of Dickinsonian economy, it is perhaps not surprising, after the emphasis I have placed on Demodocos's song as an emblem of lyric economy, that I should now turn to the use Dickinson makes in two poems of Odysseus as a figure desperate to find himself again included in economy. If any statement of economy must impress upon us an awareness of our finiteness and mortality and further promote the impulse to limit our sphere of choices, this is precisely the Odyssean logic of a poem such as "This Consciousness that is aware" (817):

This Consciousness that is aware
Of Neighbors and the Sun
Will be the one aware of Death
And that itself alone

Is traversing the interval
Experience between
And most profound experiment
Appointed unto Men -

How adequate unto itself
It's properties shall be
Itself unto itself and None

Shall make discovery -

Adventure most unto itself
The Soul condemned to be -
Attended by a single Hound
It's own identity.

As is often the case with Dickinson's poetry, the first stanza makes the most difficult cognitive move. We are never quite sure why the awareness of neighbors
and the sun should lead to an awareness of death. Is there a logical or associative flow here? Or is Dickinson only stating that consciousness includes the
awareness of both realities, so that the person who is aware of one will also be
aware of the other? Either way, the conjoining of the two makes it seem as
though the movement toward exteriority transports the self back unto the shores
of its own identity, as though encountering others only proves the essential
enclosedness of identity.

"This Consciousness that is aware" depends upon the turning inward of the
adventurous spirit, which tests itself against death not by what it braves in the
world but by how it endures its own identity. Thus, the vaguely allusive texture of the poem puts us in mind of Odysseus, as Dickinson ironically reduces
the scope of epic adventure to a question of self-possession. The real test of self
becomes not how much company (as in "Neighbors" [2]), how much beauty (as
of "the Sun" [2]), or how much adversity or perhaps exteriority it can stand, but
"[h]ow adequate" (9) a self is unto itself. As Dickinson asserts the tautological
logic of self ("Itself unto itself" [11]), she asserts cryptically that "None / Shall
make discovery" (12), a phrase seeming to forbid the experience of the world
as newness. Discovery, as the cognitive corollary to adventure, would stray
from identity to find meanings that are given exteriorly, and Dickinson quickly
deflates the typical quest of mythic personality to find a ground for itself elsewhere. Such a demystifying logic, as Horkheimer and Adorno have suggested,
is more consistent with *The Odyssey* than we might be inclined to think, since
Odysseus wanders among the distant and mythic world only as one who must
concede the foreignness of nature to subjectivity as though enduring an adventure.[40] The fact is that all of his wanderings yield no genuine discovery.
Rather, by coyly and strategically withholding his name, Odysseus preserves
himself because he never quite submits to the claims made by any exteriority,
mythic or human. In her final stanza, Dickinson comes to the all too Odyssean
conclusion that adventure is really only an attending to self. Reversing slightly

the fate of an Odysseus condemned to wander so long from his home—
"Adventure most unto itself / The Soul condemned to be -" (13–14)—Dickinson
makes it seem as though the achieved state of being at home with oneself were not
the resolution of a bad fate, but a continuation of the gods' adverse judgment. Although Dickinson again insists upon economy, she ends the poem on a vaguely re-
sentful note, objecting perhaps to the isolation that is identity's requirement.

In an earlier poem, "Tho' I get home how late - how late" (199), Dickinson
relies even more heavily upon an Odyssean conceit as she configures *The
Odyssey*'s economic plot with a question of mourning. At first she makes the
thought of home coincide with the plot of identity charted as a movement into
self-knowledge. Indeed, the speaker of "Tho' I get home how late - how late"
might be thought of as an emanation of Odysseus's nostalgia. As someone long
away from home, he lives upon the thought of a return to home in which he will
again become truly himself:

> Tho' I get home how late - how late -
> So I get home - 'twill compensate -
> Better will be the Extasy
> That they have done expecting me -
> When night - descending - dumb - and dark -
> They hear my unexpected knock -
> Transporting must the moment be -
> Brewed from decades of Agony!
>
> To think just how the fire will burn -
> Just how long-cheated eyes will turn -
> To wonder what myself will say,
> And what itself, will say to me -
> Beguiles the Centuries of way!

This is Dickinson at the height of her powers, seducing the reader through the
speaker's enthusiasm and deceiving us by way of his simplicity. The reference
to "decades of Agony" (8) forces us to imagine a situation much like Odysseus's
preposterously long separation from his family. Even if we cannot attribute to
Dickinson's speaker the precise intention of deceiving his audience (in the same
way Homer's Odysseus maintains a distance between his true self and his acts
of self-representation), he does share Odysseus's capacity for scheming and
self-dramatization.

The antecedents from Homer's text are too numerous to list, but Odysseus's cautious delay in his reunion with Penelope may be the central model both for the scheming imagination of Dickinson's speaker and for the plot of reunion the poem foresees. When Odysseus returns, he reveals himself to his father Laertes, to his son Telemachos, and even to the maid Eurycleia, and yet he withholds his identity from Penelope. So extraordinary is his delay that even after Odysseus has slaughtered the suitors and Eurycleia wants to run to tell Penelope the news, Odysseus postpones her yet once more (22.482–83), the effect of which is that when Eurycleia does at last, at the beginning of book 23, bring Penelope the news that the suitors have been slaughtered by the recently arrived stranger and that the stranger is none other than her returned husband, Penelope will not believe her.[41] As Penelope remains adamant in her skepticism and her maid reprimands her, "Child, you always were mistrustful" (Fitzgerald, 23.80), Homer ironically illustrates the Greek principle of *homophrosunē*, or "harmony of minds," that binds Penelope and Odysseus.[42] For throughout book 23 Penelope is every bit Odysseus's match in guile and mistrust; her behavior, a dramatic return on Odysseus's deception of her. With an intention rooted in doubt and quite possibly reproach, Penelope tests the man she still insists on perceiving as a stranger by declaring that she will accept him as her husband only if he can bring her marriage bed into another room. Since the real Odysseus will know that their bed has been built into a tree trunk and is impossible to move, what is important about Odysseus's response to the test, as Ralph Hexter has remarked, is not so much whether he has the right information, but how he responds to her demand.[43]

Much as he had responded to Demodocos's second song by weeping, Odysseus here reacts spontaneously, with an exasperation that reveals his vulnerability. In the midst of his emotional outburst Penelope says, "Do not rage at me, Odysseus" (Fitzgerald, 23.236), using his name and acknowledging him in his true identity for the first time. Penelope's off-handedness is at once subtle and commanding, for even as she deflates Odysseus's expectation of a dramatic and grand recognition scene, her tone recaptures instantly—though it has been twenty years in abeyance—all the tenderness and presumption that belong to intimacy. One has to conclude that Odysseus entirely loses the upper hand in a human interaction for the first time in the epic. In his hesitation to reveal himself to Penelope and in his effort to stage his self-presentation, Odysseus has ironically made himself absolutely dependent upon Penelope's reception and recognition of him.

With *The Odyssey*'s emotional reunion in the background, Dickinson's poem portrays an Odyssean character who similarly sets his mind to the drama of his return. According to the speaker's expectation, his return home will "compensate" (2) for prior absence, for the long separation he has endured. Significantly, this economic premise of compensation focuses on a question of reception, with the speaker's sufferings and expectations to be repaid in the "long-cheated eyes" (10) of the others who greet him. As is also the case with Odysseus, Dickinson's speaker seems most concerned about the impression he will make, which is to say, about the status he has retained—or gained—through absence. When he imagines in the seventh line how "[t]ransporting must the moment be" (7) when he returns home, he renders the literal question of movement that activates and perpetuates the plot of *The Odyssey* entirely metaphorical and subjective, the issue of transportation now converted into a conceit through which the speaker imagines himself emotionally or cognitively received. It is almost as if the separation had been intended to achieve this very effect, a possibility that gathers force from the fantasizing tone with which he imagines the ecstatic response of those who have awaited him, which will be "[b]etter" (3) the later he arrives. The poem's entire language of anticipation becomes a descriptive language of wishfulness wherein everything the speaker imagines is precisely how he would have the scene of reunion unfold.

The pathos of Dickinson's poem is enhanced but perhaps also mitigated by the fact that what is being described is all part of an internal or private adventure. It is for this reason that the return can be thought in terms that seem, on first impression, to be so efficiently economic, as if the delay that corresponds to absence were not externally imposed as it is in Homer's epic, but rather a purposeful withholding of the self for effect. In *The Odyssey* the question of return is largely a formal matter, with Odysseus's intentions produced as strategy, corresponding more or less to the epic's dramatic problem of reintroducing its hero into the society of Ithaca. Only in the more personal scenes with his father and with Penelope, in which Odysseus postpones and contrives his self-presentation, does this formal concern find a ground that seems properly psychological, as if Odysseus's contrivances sought to conjure personal affect and not just social effect. Taking her cue from this rarer, more subjective emphasis of Odysseus's character, Dickinson makes her speaker imagine the question of his return home almost entirely at the psychological and emotional level. It is good, the speaker thinks, that "they have done expecting me - " (4).

As *Hamlet* teaches us, the time of grief has everything to do with its ethical dimension: grief is organized by the very possibility of a time in which the other remains meaningful. At the end of Homer's epic, for instance, it is significant that Odysseus's journey home coincides with Telemachos's attempt to declare his father dead and that his arrival comes immediately prior to Penelope's declaration that she will accept the hand of the suitor who can shoot Odysseus's bow. Though Penelope's test is meant to emphasize Odysseus's irreplaceability (since only Odysseus in disguise will be able to string and shoot the monumental bow), it has also created the demand for Odysseus in the present, bringing him back dramatically from the world of legend and death. By contrast, when Dickinson's speaker pushes just beyond that time of grief or plausible expectation, he risks the moment in which he might be no longer significant. This seems a deliberate, perhaps slightly parodic overextension of the plot of reunion on Dickinson's part. Perhaps she is poking gentle fun at the most basic implausibility of *The Odyssey*, which is not Odysseus's heroic endurance but Penelope's extraordinary waiting. Dickinson's speaker gives expression to a thought that seems oddly enough never to have crossed Odysseus's mind—the thought that Penelope might be done expecting him. Dickinson's Odyssean speaker realizes, perhaps two years into his delayed return, after all the other Achaians have returned or died, that he exists in his every moment beyond the ordinary time of grief and the plausible time of his expected return. Though he remains obdurate in his expectation of a glorious return, by confessing (and perhaps even desiring) that his arrival might occur past the point of plausibility, he simultaneously draws attention to the fact that his value at home and in the world is no longer assured. Such is the point of an extraordinary return as it is also of extraordinary waiting: neither can be reasonably expected and neither can remain, in any sense, economical.

It is on this note, then, that I draw our attention to a subtler drama of "Tho' I get home how late—how late." While it is true one can read much of the poem as a fantasy of return in which the descriptions of the speaker's reception are ruled by his imagination's narrow economy of identity, there is another sense in which fantasy is always uncertain of itself:

> They hear my unexpected knock -
> Transporting must the moment be -
> Brewed from decades of Agony! (6–8)

Above I read these lines, implicitly, as if "[t]ransporting" referred to the emotions experienced by those who receive the speaker, but according to the syntactical ambiguity of the participle, the speaker could just as well be referring to his own imagined rapture. (Indeed, even if we adhere to a reading that attributes the transported feeling to those who have waited for him, the logic of fantasy requires that the imagined emotion should be, if only by projection, also the speaker's own). The emotional risk he runs is rather poorly concealed by his insistent imagining of what the future *must* be like, and the reference to "decades of Agony" leaves a lot of pain to be compensated for by this single moment of return. If this seems an intentional staging of an emotional drama, we see now that the drama readily pertains to the requirements of the speaker's own emotion.

Much as Odysseus unwittingly plotted his vulnerability before Penelope by withholding his identity past the point of any plausible necessity, Dickinson's speaker has delayed, intentionally it seems, in order to cultivate his own emotional vulnerability. A first explanation of this rather odd intention is that the speaker is engaged in an elaborate rationalization of his vulnerable condition, a reading consistent with the poem's fantasy logic. If Odysseus himself never indulges the anxiety that Penelope has forgotten him and moved on, Homer's use of minor counterplots such as Agamemnon's story (which Odysseus hears while in Hades) makes the point for us. Thus it is altogether possible that when Odysseus withholds himself from his wife, he seeks a mastery over his fate he has previously lacked. The fact that Homer's epic hero ends up plotting his own vulnerability is an irony worthy of Dickinson, and it is therefore not surprising that as her Odyssean speaker strives to become master of his fate, he exposes a vulnerability within the plot of identity.

Especially as the poem moves into the second stanza, the speaker's voice is modulated by a wish for control that veers ever closer to a prospective loss of control. I would suggest that those moments in which the speaker stands to lose his control of the situation correspond to the poem's fall into anti-economic excess, and, as it so happens, this crisis in the economic plot of identity has been brought about by a thought of death. Even before Dickinson lays hold of it, *The Odyssey* is already an aberrant or displaced plot of mourning, wherein the time of grief is constantly converted back into a hope for the return of the absent other, who should by all realistic accounts have been given up for dead. Part of the sleight of hand employed in *The Odyssey*, as well as in "Tho' I get home how late - how late," where Dickinson revisits the Homeric scenario of return as potentially a scene of mourning, is to consider the crisis mourning occasions in the value of the other from his perspective. The one who has been hypothetically lost to the world speaks from the situation of alterity to give a new connotation to survival, which is not simply an alignment with a social order that endures past death, but a challenge to it. This is the symbolic significance of Odysseus's brutal campaign against the suitors: they represent the usurping or surviving order with which his heroic survival must now compete. According to this same basic inversion, we are made to consider in Dickinson's poem the conflict between an economically efficient work of mourning that calls for the surrender of any expectation of the other's return and an economy of identity that must account for his absence and for lost time as if they were already implicit in the plot of identity. The elaborate fantasy of reception maintains the possibility that the one who has been absent past the time of reasonable expectation can return and still be part of the cultural plot of identity—which is to say, can still be identified by way of his role and participation in the culture he left behind.

Following in the wake of *The Odyssey*, there is a long history to this plot of fantastic return—from Shakespeare's *The Winter's Tale*, to the legendary true story of Martin Guerre, to Balzac's *Colonel Chabert*, to name only a few examples. Putting an especially modern and legalistic twist on the plot of return, Balzac tells, for example, the story of a hero who has been pronounced dead during the days of the Napoleonic War.[44] Rising from his untimely mass grave and spending several years recovering, the colonel returns to Parisian society to find that his wife has remarried and that he has been entirely disfranchised: he has neither property nor name. Denied his rightful place in society, he descends into beggary as into a second identity, and the whole story might be read as a parable about the implicit legal equation of identity to property. To be disfranchised is to be without identity, and this is a logic that goes at least as far back as the legend of Odysseus, who must kill the suitors precisely because they have laid claim to his property and thus to his very identity.

If this plot of propertied identity seems remote from Dickinson's Odyssean speaker, its resolution strikes closer to the heart of her poem. For if the right to property both objectively and symbolically maintains one's position in the present cultural order, it is the work of retrospection, which so often coincides with the cultural logic of nostalgia, to mend the potential divide between the hero and his possessions. It is only in looking back to the past as if it still ruled the present that Odysseus and Colonel Chabert come into conflict with the world unto which they return. In its most conservative function, then, retrospection would establish a perfect continuity between what one has been and what one must be in the present, or between who the other was and what she may still be.

As such, retrospection is an economic concept related to, but also in competition with, the progressive flow of society, which would depend upon more flexible economic concepts such as those that derive identity through property. In Dickinson's poem, the compensation the speaker imagines for his absence will come as a direct consequence of the recollection of identity into the sphere of home. A spectral doubleness—much in the spirit of Odysseus who lurks too long in disguise and gets tested by Penelope as though he were a stranger—still troubles every plot of return.

Though Dickinson's speaker maintains his identity through a kind of retrospective fantasy, he also encounters, as it were, a doubleness in himself:

> To wonder what myself will say,
> And what itself, will say to me -
> Beguiles the Centuries of way! (11–13)

At the center of the imagined reunion, there is always this slight estrangement of the self from itself. According to a point we have taken for granted and then almost forgotten—that the entire poem is pure wish, a projection into the future—we have to remember that whereas previously the future had been fully imagined according to the familiar trajectory and stated economy of identity, the speaker now draws up short of the future moment and suddenly admits a disjuncture between present imaginings and future reality. This happens in the transition from line 11 to line 12 where the speculative thought of wondering what the speaker's self might say suddenly gives way to a self-objectifying logic in which the foreignness of that future self is confessed by converting "myself" into an "itself" and by imagining this slightly estranged "itself" as having something peculiar to say to the speaking "me."[45] The speculation of line 11 is premised on a continuity of identity in which a self imagines what it might say in the future to others. But once that self seems foreign enough to speak as though it were an interlocutor to the speaker's present self, then the mysterious, even perhaps future interiority of identity is suddenly also an intimation of that which can still be added to present identity. The future always has this function of announcing itself as that which remains by definition unknown and so challenging the self-presence of identity.[46] Here, in Dickinson's poem, the future articulates a vulnerability in the self, as it speaks of a place and time in which identity cannot be assured of remaining the same. It is this very excess of the future that belies the poem's economic logic of return, since identity has been alienated from itself and from its habitual cultural logic.

If the plot of return is troubled by an unknowable future, the ending of Dickinson's poem adds a temporal twist that renders this fantasy of the future at one and the same time a nostalgic thought of the past. Dickinson might almost have ended her poem at line 12 and not added the cryptically reductive turn of line 13, as she might also be expected, in this poem resembling a sonnet, to have given us one more line. Apart from the question of grammatical requirements, line 13 is either too much or too little of a surprise. Rhetorically, it functions as a trick, suddenly converting a projective fantasy into a self-deceptive form of retrospection. Much as in "Because I could not stop for death" (479) where the representation of a speaker who looks back across "centuries" ("Since then - 'tis Centuries - " [21]) taunts us with the impossibility of a posthumous narrative perspective, Dickinson suddenly revises in the final line of "Tho' I get home how late - how late" the wishful longing of her Odyssean character and interprets him as one who never returned from his Hades. Suddenly here is death, introduced into the economy of identity with its plot of return. The powerful longing of the speaker's voice is abruptly qualified by our recognition of the impossibility of his ever achieving what he desires, and it is quite as if his death has surprised him as much as us. Initially a stranded self who yet sees his place in economy, the speaker has come suddenly up against the fact of his own death, the most severe of anti-economic thoughts. Though the posthumous voice of Dickinson's speaker may seem to cooperate with his economic fantasy of return, I think we have to hear the entire fantasy as a resistance to his death. If the speaker's fantasy of home had aligned with a recognition of death's dominion, then perhaps we could see death as the completion or final statement of an identity ruled by economy. But the emphasis here is rather on the impossible coincidence of the fact of death and the rule of economy.

A similar dynamic is at work in "The last Night that She lived" (1100), where Dickinson, while portraying a scene of mourning, contrasts the economic thoughts of the living to a time coinciding with the death of the other. Beginning with a wry use of litotes—"It was a Common Night / Except the Dying" (2–3)—"The last Night that She lived" focuses on the smallness of the perspective of the living, but not in order to suggest how life finds fulfillment in the largeness of perspective about to be bequeathed to the one who is dying. To survive the death of the other is starkly accounted as blameworthy in this poem:

> As We went out and in
> Between Her final Room
> And Rooms where Those to be alive
> Tomorrow, were, a Blame

That others could exist
While She must finish quite
A Jealousy for Her arose
So nearly infinite - (9–16)

Most likely the speaker discerns "[b]lame" by inferring the resentment of the one who dies, but it is through the authority of that dying perspective that she characterizes the entire scene of mourning according to a claustrophobic economy. The rooms of the living and the room of the dead are confined spaces, the thought that belongs to one realm excluding the thought that belongs to the other. It is this mutual exclusion that explains the somewhat surprising move of lines 15–16, in which we switch from an implicit resentment of the dead for the living to the jealousy the living feel for the dead. As the speaker says of the dead woman, "while She passed - / It was a narrow time - " (17–18), she refers to the stagnant incapability of the mourner who survives the other, emphasizing here the restrictive sphere of attachment almost as though she envied the dead woman her larger world of experience. Since it is impossible to respond to the dead precisely because the idiom of living has no place for them, in mourning's narrowing focus she becomes conscious of the exclusion she enacts. The narrow time of grief eventually yields to a laxness in time ("an awful leisure was / Belief to regulate - " [27–28]), a leisurely excess of time that remains to the living alone, and it is "awful," at least in part, because it has nothing to do with the dead. If religious belief is supposed to "regulate" such atheistic thoughts about the irrelevance of the dead, we cannot help but see such regulation as an attempt to serve the economy of the living—the encounter with death having proved our smallness of aspiration and the narrowness of the ordinary realm of existence.

Whereas in "The last Night that She lived" we get intimations of a deathly consciousness that comments on the world of the living, in the Odyssean poem "Tho' I get home how late - how late" it is only by a slippage in the speaker's consciousness that death enters his mind, even as he holds to thoughts that would keep the fact of his own death far from him. Dickinson plays perhaps on the Greek conception of Hades where the dead long for news from among the living as if such news might temporarily relieve their longing to be alive. There is, for example, the case of Agamemnon, who overidentifies with Odysseus's return and extols Penelope as a compensatory fantasy for the fate he has suffered at the hands of his wife and her lover (Cook, 11.378–466). An imaginative world in which the dead long to be living is subject to a cultural logic that reads one's

death as the final comment on one's life. It is especially, then, the unjust or untimely death that occasions such longing, as the dead perhaps resent that they
were not better favored by the gods. Yet Dickinson's Odyssean persona shows
no specific resentment about his fate, and we must surmise that his state of mind
stands for a more general resistance to death. The knowledge that the speaker
is dead grants us an ironic perspective on that difference he imagines in himself
upon his return. It almost amounts to a ghastly joke at his expense: he does not
know he is dead and therefore cannot imagine what he will say because he must
remain forever silent. Insofar as he has been persuasive in his longing, however,
his nostalgia takes on a surprising and subversive force. It expresses the implicit
demand—expressed, as it were, by the other who has died—that the dead not
be excluded from the contents of economy. That such a demand seems practically impossible has been made to coincide ironically with his impossible fantasy of return. As a result of this retrospection entirely in excess of reality—or
perhaps a reality that is in excess of retrospection—death becomes the sign of
what an economics of identity cannot include. Dickinson suggests not only that
the others who die must be left out of the mutual economies of mourning and
cultural identity, but that on the threshold of death lyrical voice is at a complete
loss. To continue speaking the language of economy at this point suggests an
incapacity in our very concept of identity, which can account for neither the
radical unknowability of death, nor the real temporal and ethical alterity that
challenges the lyrical self and its economic fantasy of knowable identity.

The Dissatisfactions of Economy

According to the example set by the Renaissance elegies and Dickinson
poems I have considered, lyrical economy intersects with a theory of psychic
identity by deriving the significance of the outside world, the other, or the
varieties of experience that constitute exteriority as hypotheses of an already
coherent and self-sufficient system. Insofar as the claim of exteriority does not
cooperate with identity, it posits a surplus of meaning, an element of unpleasure, or simply a reality that is discordant with the realism expounded through
the system of identity. In other words, faced with the claim of exteriority, identity becomes subject to an unease. In considering the relation of pain or difficulty
to the rhetorical ease of Renaissance elegies, Arnold Stein has argued that a grief
turning too readily to consolation may seem suspect because the consolation
seems unearned. Pain becomes a credential of authenticity, but in deploying pain

in the service of rhetorical persuasiveness, the elegist runs the risk of making pain merely a temporary departure from the poem's originating and concluding premise of consolatory pleasure or pleasurable consolation (148–49).

Similarly remarking upon the elegy's economical proficiency for turning sorrow into fortunate loss, but espousing a Freudian view of representation inflected by Lacanian theory and so perceiving in poetry's work a condensation of language's symbolic properties, Peter Sacks argues that the lyric elegy proves the premise of language as that which is necessarily elaborated as a relation to loss determining us all.[47] By referring the elegiac occasion of loss back to a primordial condition of language as loss, Sacks recapitulates an ethical weakness of the Freudian project, which must interpret the alienation of identity that occurs in loss as though it were a further comment upon the original Oedipal determination of the psyche. The result of this determining model is that the poignance of loss as a response to particular subsequent occasions stands already diminished by the peculiar impossibility that our latest, newest loss could ever be other than an extension or elaboration of original grief. We might pause at this point to ask an all too pragmatic question: can it really be that the death of the other depends for its significance upon an original dissatisfaction of desire that involved loss of an esteemed object (specifically, the mother), but yet no final disappearance of her person? If this were the case, there would be an economy even in loss, and the Freudian family romance would draw much of its persuasive power from the fact that loss is already familiar to us and has from the start rendered a paradoxical service to identity. Without the original loss of the mother, Freud supposes, the ego could never have imagined those boundaries, however fictional and provisional they may be, through which identity was first established and subsequently maintained. This is the peculiar insight of the anecdote of the fort-da game: the child who throws the toy away with the cry of "fort" (or "there") is imitating the mother's frequent departures; and if he resorts less and less to the cry of "da" (or "here"), the game seems no longer about demanding the mother's return, but about mastering her departure.[48] The problem with using this game or any similarly Oedipal story as a model for mourning (as psychoanalytically informed criticism has so often done) is that the child's mastery depends upon a hypothesis that the mother will sometimes return, since otherwise the game would not be pleasurable. The mother can be renounced provisionally only because she has not fully absented herself or been made absent by fate. There is no death in this plot of absence.

Even if we loosen the determining mythic structure of the Oedipal paradigm, psychoanalysis typically treats the present occasion of loss as the symptom of a former determination. In this respect, however, psychoanalysis is not at all atypical of the Western philosophical tradition's construct of identity. What Freud as Hegel before him accepted as a natural fact, consistent with bourgeois ideology but having its origins long before, is that loss—even when read as a point of a hypothetical alterity—will pertain to identity as if it were a comment upon that which is already familiar. Hegel seems to offer the most pointed expression of a dialectical habit of mind in which the hypothetical antithesis or alterity presented by any new event refers back to a prior thesis of identity, yet it is surely telling that he turns at a significant point in the *Phenomenology* to the archetypal plot of familial loyalty in *Antigone* in order to make his case.[49] In Sophocles's famous tragedy, the unburied body of Antigone's brother becomes the site for a debate about whether the symbolic actions and language of mourning are most significantly public or private in their connotation. The wrongheaded and politically willful Creon answers the question for us negatively if also a little too simply: his denial of the rites of burial means that the family has to enact and preserve its grief privately and that the private esteem for the brother must become alienated from public meaning. It is through familiarity, *Antigone* teaches us, that one claims the other who dies.

According to such a well entrenched cultural pattern for formulating grief, the turn to the personal idiom fosters the very possibility of identification. It is surely more than coincidence that Stein argues (by way of Renaissance elegies) that public elegies are most susceptible to the charge of being inauthentic, since they turn more often to pat resolutions—which may be only to say, to well-worn or public habits of mind. Let me offer a more contemporary and non-literary example of this preference for personal grief in order to illustrate the persistence of a cultural habit of mind that may have been strengthened, but was certainly not invented by Freudian theory. In January of 1991 I took a trip to El Salvador with a group that was studying liberation theology and the popular resistance movement. One day we visited the University of Central America and had recounted to us, on the site where the violence had taken place, the story of the brutal November 1989 murder of the six Jesuits and their house-keeper and her daughter. Later that evening, when our group had remained unusually silent, one of the members offered us an interpretation. "I know what we're doing," she said. "We're grieving." Moreover, in her view we were each of us grieving in our own way, through losses that were already familiar to us—

the death of a father, a grandmother, whatever that first and most significant death in each of our lives had been. This explanation was not meant to downplay the significance of the story we had heard earlier in the day; rather the point was that each of us was reliant upon forms and habits developed through past grief in order to confront new losses and to make sense of them. According to such a view, grief exists in some necessary proportion to identity and the cultural plot of identification that make up the history of any self mourning in a particular moment.

My point in relating this story is that according to our cultural narratives for mourning, as Freud saw only too well, the fact of loss will tend to promote our participation in symbolic meaning and turn us to those personal narratives that are derived in cooperation with larger cultural narratives enabling our existence even in the face of adversity. Identity posited through the reign of the symbol must conceive of itself through those predominant cultural narratives that read loss as constructive. Since our psychological predisposition to loss has constituted us in advance as defensively related to future loss, we deflect the harsh realities of a future that must further diminish the other who has just been lost, and we are able to do this because we have always known that every other to whom we attach ourselves must eventually be lost to us.

What this might lead us to conclude is that mourning in its most basic function always poses a question about what our psyches will allow to become real to us. This is in part what Freud addresses in the notion of the reality principle, which is less about the psychic system's admission of external reality than the psyche's realistic estimation of its desire and how the often uncooperative sign of the real can be made to conform to desire. As Paul Ricoeur has emphasized, Freud developed the concept of reality in stages, revising it most remarkably in the metapsychological papers of 1915–17.[50] This revision was not so much a change as an enlargement, and a key step in the process lay in moving beyond the definition of reality as self-evident statement toward a sense of reality as the interplay and perceptible opposition (so often glimpsed in dreams and neuroses) between the external phenomena of life and the wishfulness of the psyche. In the end, Freud arrived at his highly economic conception whereby reality becomes, as Ricoeur says, "the correlate of the function of consciousness" (261). When the reality principle replaces the pleasure principle and deploys the strategic postponement of satisfaction in order to align desire with perception, the representations of reality become its function. How a self, as an emanation of its cultural milieu, constructs the real determines at every point what it will call reality.

As early as 1911, in the essay "Formulations on the Two Principles of Mental Functioning," Freud had begun to elaborate the representational economics of reality:

> . . . the state of psychical rest was originally disturbed by the peremptory demands of internal needs. When this happened, whatever was thought of (wished for) was simply presented in a hallucinatory manner, just as still happens to-day with our dream-thoughts every night. It was only the non-occurrence of the expected satisfaction, the disappointment experienced, that led to the abandonment of this attempt at satisfaction by means of hallucination. Instead of it, the psychical apparatus had to decide to form a conception of the real circumstances in the external world and to endeavour to make a real alteration in them. A new principle of mental functioning was thus introduced; what was presented in the mind was no longer what was agreeable but what was real, even if it happened to be disagreeable.[51]

According to Freud's speculations, an ambiguity has been introduced into the real as a consequence of the pleasure principle's relative failure. Overcoming an initial instinct to deny reality through hallucination, the reality principle instead modifies the real in such a way that a formerly naïve or more literal real datum, an impossibly unmediated relation to exteriority, no longer poses the threat it once posed to self-worth and satisfaction. Freud's rhetorical move from "real circumstances in the external world" to the attempt "to make a real alteration in them" marks a progress in consciousness, which is itself a principle that both revises and yields the very meaning of reality. Thus, the emphasis here on "real alteration" is probably close to what Freud elsewhere calls the "action" of the psychic apparatus, and his point is clearly that the real world is always that which is imaginatively acted upon, so that representation seems, by definition, the faculty for psychically altering and composing the real. Also notable—and more in keeping with Ricoeur's timeline—is the paradoxical fact that Freud's account of reality has not yet submitted to the psychic alteration or definition of the real, functioning here as a trace concept of a cruder idea of reality that is not strictly economic by definition.

In other words, Freud's early understanding of the real as an intrusive exteriority is never quite contained by his later theoretical definitions of an economical relation between the ego and the objects it finds in the real world.[52] By a similar logic, even as it extends the reign of the pleasure principle, the reality principle traces a relation to the other—if only because the other is forever a resistant object in the real world. To the extent that the Freudian system of consciousness in both its unconscious and realistically conscious phases is ruled by the pleasure principle, it demands a satisfaction of desire to which the real alterity of the other is almost entirely irrelevant. So when in an essay such as "On Narcissism" (1914) Freud finds that all loving attachment turns on a potential loss in self-regard, this is so because a self always proceeds toward the other without any initial assurance of a return of affection—that is, without the guarantee of economic compensation. Consciousness is the system assuaging the real physical and emotional vulnerability of a self that must function in a world prepared to do it damage, if only by way of the damage that stands to be done to those others whom the psyche has chosen as significant in order to sustain itself in the world. What this means for the situation of mourning, as Freud explains in "Mourning and Melancholia" (1917), is that once reality pronounces the hard verdict that an "object no longer exists," a mourner is "persuaded by the sum of the narcissistic satisfactions it derives from being alive" to abandon its prior anti-economic attachments (*SE*, 14:255). The early stages of mourning, like the early hazards of love, put the self at risk before the other. But since it has been constitutively dedicated to an economic conception of relationship, the psyche recovers itself through a grudging economics of identity, as the ego refuses the connotations of risk and deflects a reality that might otherwise be too severe.

One might well wonder, then, whether the Freudian worldview permits of any critique of this basic psychological selfishness so firmly rooted in an esteem for the self's present tense privileges and possibilities. For Ricoeur and (with a slightly different emphasis) for Althusser also, it is, oddly, the unruly reign of the unconscious that enables the very possibility of critique.[53] Since the unconscious remains a desire never fully incorporated into consciousness, it forges a psychic space always departing, at least potentially, from desires that are too consistent with the present cultural or ideological order. Spurred somewhat mysteriously by a gap between those conditions of consciousness anterior to self and the vicissitudes of self-perception, the subject finds, in Althusser's view, an impetus for critique in its fundamental distance from the fount of its motivations. For my purposes, I would amend these sound insights about the space of critique psychoanalysis permits within its own theory of consciousness to include what seems a constitutive intersection between critique and disappointment. In every seeming disappointment of a particular desire we find announced a dissatisfaction that troubles the definition of identity. It is the trajectory of unsatisfied desire that fosters a critique of the status quo of the psyche and the world in which it operates.[54] By introducing the entire revisionary project of the reality principle, Freud had already admitted a paradox: it is dissatisfaction, or the failure of original satisfaction, that produces the thought of reality as an alterity to the self's desire. Accordingly, the ordinary maturation of the individual psyche—from a being guided instinctually by the pleasure principle to a being regulated by the basic temperance of the reality principle—means that, at least in part, an original myth of self-sufficiency has failed.

Though reality is the name we give to our commonsensical apprehensions of a real world we must inherit, even as it is also a measured standard of that toward which any normal, healthy person ought to strive, it is produced in disappointment. In the parallel between the structural workings of the unconscious and the incursive function of reality with regard to the psychic system, we might be inclined to perceive a resemblance between that alterity in self preserved by the workings of the unconscious and that greater alterity to self which is reality, but even more basic here is the structural fact that each of these aspects of self-insufficiency or noncorrespondence opens a self to what lies beyond its immediate ken. Late in his career, specifically in *Beyond the Pleasure Principle* (1921), Freud would try to formulate a theoretical account of the sources of unpleasure with the hope of finding a more economical source for what troubles the psyche, as though exterior disturbances of the psychic system might be traced to an origin as speculatively vague as the death drive and thus attributed to interiorly motivated causes. What has proved most memorable over time about that late text has been Freud's statement of the problem of trauma as a challenge to his psychic system; much less persuasive is his somewhat mythic-minded theoretical solution.[55]

All I want to emphasize here is that it seems to have been the experientially anti-economic nature of unpleasure that made Freud's theoretical speculation necessary. For if trauma poses the most dramatic challenge to Freud's formulation of a psyche pleasurably oriented by its internally regulated stimuli, it also illustrates yet again the same basic structure whereby a disturbance to the psychic system is marked as a potentially threatening space of alterity. In this basic sense, the Freudian psychic system works similarly to lyrical economy as I have described it: the economic statements of a system of identity are most insistent in the face of that which opposes the system by its resistant alterity. In response to apparent otherness, economy vacillates between acts of appropriative inclusion that read the object as already familiar and acts of stubborn exclusion that deny the object's claim upon the regulatory principles and responsibilities of the system. Any incursion of the real upon the psychic system of identity potentially yields an ethical connotation, even if Freud never quite names it as such and even if it is depicted only as recalcitrant and unsatisfactory evidence of an unregulated reality. So too, the dissatisfaction of desire marks at every turn a lurking dissatisfaction in economy, reminding us that the statement of economy may be constituted and reaffirmed as a neglect of the other.

CHAPTER FOUR

The Ethical Rhetoric of Anti-Elegy

Any elegy's turn against grief may eventually be put in the service of its own consolatory purposes. Nevertheless, to the extent that such turns are revisionary—that is, to the extent that they also function as anti-elegiac turns against the history of consolation and the strategies of commemoration implicit in the very conventions of the elegy—they make an ethical demand on us. It is precisely this insistent and sometimes excessive ethical demand of a mourning that refuses to accept the precedent and custom of mourning that I seek to explore in this chapter. Anti-elegy, I argue, alerts us to a continuum of economic relations—from the substitutive economics of the psychical work of mourning, to the related economy of the elegy itself, which in Jahan Ramazani's estimation frequently deploys the language of psychic wounds as poetic capital, and finally to an elegiac ethics of reciprocity, which in responding to the crisis posed by the lost other, seeks to protect and contain the connotations of alterity brought to light by the other's death. In the process anti-elegy traces the horizon of dissatisfaction, from its status as the sign of alterity within the system of lyrical economy to a more open mode of ethical complaint. As I set out to elaborate the import of a set of dialectical resistances embedded in the elegiac tradition, I here consider three figures that denote an anti-elegiac resistance to the idealist norms of the traditional elegy—belatedness, the remembrance of failed intimacy, and the ambivalent wish for reciprocity—in order to articulate the special quality of an ethical discourse that either produces or is produced by anti-elegiac sensibility.

As perhaps the most overt gesture that poets employ to challenge the end of mourning, *belatedness* is a figure that disrupts the temporal flow of tradition and the basic assumptions about continuous identity so central to an idealistic evaluation of the lost other. Frequently elegies imagine a mourning that begins after other survivors have already mourned. Functioning as an anti-elegiac version of the elegy's conventional renewal of grief, the figure of belatedness is indebted to a more traditional hermeneutic, yet it often turns severely and ironically against its derivative status. Simply put, belatedness signifies an element of noncooperation in the mourner, marking him as someone who is, if only accidentally, out of step with the rhythm of his society and its forgetful flow toward the future. Whereas belatedness implicitly opposes all past or completed examples of mourning, the figure of *failed intimacy* discerns a greater paradox at the heart of elegiac address. Faced with a crisis in the symbolic value of esteemed objects and weighted by its own self-reflective interrogations, the elegy must work hard to maintain a claim of intimacy, for the (sometimes fictive) remembrance of intimacy provides assurance that the other was and remains knowable, even as it also protects the cultural identity of both the self and the lost other through an act of commemoration that translates the other as a cultural value with benefit to the surviving community.

Yet when a poet emphasizes her own anti-elegiac distance from the other she mourns or the distance between the many mourners of the past and the often solitary mourners of the present, the elegy must admit more strongly, but also more dangerously, of a crisis in ethics precipitated by loss. Under the exigency of present desires and the demands of her society, the mourner's efforts to distance herself from her culture's ordinary paradigms of grief take on ethical significance. Perhaps no assumption looms larger in the history of grief, as Antigone's story demonstrates only too well, than the idea that there is a privileged space granted to familial or intimate relation. So too Hamlet, melancholia's most famous hero, often protests the public praxis of mourning in

Denmark through personally inflected desires (should not the father mean what Hamlet wants him to mean?). Though private grief, whether modeled by Antigone or Hamlet, can provide an effective means of finding for the other an ethical significance that society might otherwise be unwilling to yield him, in anti-elegy this presumption of personal intimacy most often fails. Private grief, as a mode also determined by the cultural imperatives it resists, can never entirely withstand its own necessarily public significances. As it is shaped by subjective desires that are in turn shaped by culture, private grief with its presumption of intimacy restrictively shapes the other to conform to desire and predetermined cultural meanings.

Ultimately, I contend, the paradox of intimacy forces us to consider the premise of *ethical reciprocity* that governs elegy, a premise that is figured ambivalently in anti-elegy. At the moment in which reciprocity between the self and the other becomes impossible, the elegist casts an eye back on the history of personal relationship and reflects on the degree to which the reciprocity of relationship has been realized, serviceable, or possible in the first place. The defensive response to such reflection will be to (re)establish and strengthen reciprocity as a norm, even to the point of denying the fact that ethics is always also a relation to that which is unknowable, surprising, and quintessentially other. In the history of elegy, again and again we encounter the efforts of poets to meet the demand of the lost other by exaggerating the condition of reciprocity and measuring loss as if it were characteristically a violation of a perfect reciprocity. Clearly, this distortion of relationship has a wishful etiology, but it is also tied more fundamentally to a moral impulse—that is, to a desire to see others as consequent upon the subject's knowledge of them. In mourning, such a tendency may often appear delusive, if only because reciprocity is extended beyond the parameters of a lived interrelationship to include the hypothesis of the other's abiding interest in those who mourn her.

But I want to argue here that it is especially through anti-elegiac turns against elegiac convention that we come to recognize the extravagant claims of reciprocity that preside over the ethical relation to the other, not only after but before death. As they imagine the tremendous burden of an intimacy that cannot be met, elegies typically resort to idealizing the other in order to defend against this burden and to imagine a self-sustaining fiction of intimacy. Attempting to counteract his own sense of vulnerability, which results from being in relation to that which is absolutely other and therefore impossible to desire, the mourner turns to idealization—as is the case with Milton's "Lycidas"

(1637)—to avert the crisis in reciprocity precipitated by the other's death. Even though anti-elegy would question the very premise of reciprocity by reminding us of its sudden impossibility, the wish for reciprocity seems more pronounced in poems such as Shelley's "Adonais" (1821), where the poet admits of a failure in his own protective agency. As Shelley's elegy explores a tension between basic psychic defenses and the poet's defensiveness on behalf of language and ethics, it traces ethics as an impossible preservation of the other's value challenging the cultural diminution of his meaning. Though the elegiac fantasy of reciprocity seems most stable when an elegist is able to declare his elegy an effective means for protecting the one who has died, any failure to achieve this poetic end—and this, I want to insist, is the rich aesthetic connotation Shelley gives to failure—will incline the work toward an irresolution reinscribing the crisis of loss as a matter for ethics.

How Modern Is Your Grief?

Locating *anti-elegy* in the modern moment when the elegy takes a turn against itself and begins to doubt the literary conventions for redeeming grief as well as the broader sociophilosophical possibility of consolation, Jahan Ramazani has nevertheless emphasized how modern literary mourning becomes more than ever a viable, perhaps necessary, resource for our psychic confrontation with death.[1] Though anti-elegiac sentiment—wherein the emphasis falls to the anticonsolatory, nontranscendent perspective of modern grief—resists literary and social conventions, it traces implicitly the survival of grief against a social totality that denies the dead. There is a risk, however, that in characterizing anti-elegy as peculiar to the modern moment, we might underestimate the degree to which anti-elegiac protest is inherent in the tradition of elegy almost from its inception, and also the extent to which modern currents of anti-elegy are indebted to an internal dialectic of elegy with a pointedly ethical trajectory. Indeed, we might argue that elegies are modern to the degree that they are anti-elegiac, rather than vice versa.[2]

At least since *Hamlet*, a radical distrust of the forms of mourning, all those ceremonial trappings and shows of grief, has come to characterize much of our literary—and perhaps, more generally, our cultural—formulation of grief. Though anti-elegiac complaint would sometimes appear to stand apart from elegiac grief, it is perhaps better and more subtly understood as contrapuntal to any movement toward resolution, providing a testing ground for the very possibility of elegiac sincerity. This is so much the case that Samuel Johnson, declaring with regard to "Lycidas" that "where there is leisure for fiction there is little grief," can take it for granted that his readers are modern enough to be offended by the employment of the obsolete machinery of pastoral in the service of genuine mourning.[3] And to whatever extent we might wish to accept Johnson's charge against "Lycidas," our best defense of Milton probably lies not only in conceding Johnson's basic point—that pastoral's conventions are recognizably contrived—but in asserting, as critics from W. H. Auden to Stanley Fish have done, that they are deliberately so. If Milton supposes that only a grief bearing the weight of past, outmoded griefs and the often banal routine of mourning can really place the lost other as culturally significant, it would seem that it is the dead weight of convention that begets his elegy's originating gesture of responsibility. When, for example, Milton's speaker interrogates a mythical world that has failed to sustain Edward King, he seems less committed to a Christian transumption of pagan *figurae*—the strategy more typical of the earlier "Nativity Ode" (1629) and the later *Paradise Lost* (1674)—than to a figural opposition between an outmoded principle of agency (Milton's speaker never believes the nymphs could have protected Lycidas) and a recuperative agency belonging to the speaker's newer, modern, grief. "Lycidas" is by no means consistently a Christian poem, but Milton employs a Christian hermeneutic whereby the interrogation of an older mythic order creates the imperative for the new one, even as he also sustains the truth of the newer mythic principle upon the lapsed requirements and responsibilities it laments.[4]

Milton's elegy opens with a symbolic assault on the ceremonial trappings of the tradition, and it is even possible that this mild violation is countenanced by the tradition itself:

> Yet once more, O ye Laurels, and once more
> Ye Myrtles brown, with Ivy never sere,
> I come to pluck your Berries harsh and crude,
> And with forc'd fingers rude,
> Shatter your leaves before the mellowing year. (1–5)[5]

A temporal ambiguity in the opening words, "Yet once more," immediately draws our attention. Though the vegetation clearly connotes the pastoral tradition, it is unclear whether Milton refers to the past actions of other elegists or to those acts of commemoration previously plucked from the pastoral tradition by his own hands. In either case, once Milton assumes the obsolete responsibil-

ities of a pagan pastoral world (so Fish has argued), his personal anxieties are alleviated as a consequence of having been incorporated into the pastoral world
and the anonymity of elegiac form.[6] Looming either as a figure for his own early
elegiac endeavors or the weight of the tradition itself, or as an allegory for contemporary referents (such as the insincere rites and hypocritical practices of the
Anglican Church), the pagan pastoral machinery has not been made obsolete,
nor has it been adequately transumed by Milton's Christian grief. Rather,
Milton implicates the distant and recent past of ceremonial mourning in the
larger ethical failure of grief itself.

A complaint with mourning often interrogates the intentions of other
mourners, who in wishing for successful acts of mourning perform a temporal
conflation whereby abbreviated (or too brief) remembrance stands for the abbreviation of the other's life. What the revisionary elegist gains by having accused others' grief is a better view of the cultural logic that would intimate the
end of responsibility through the act of symbolic commemoration. Or, to adopt
Hamlet's melancholic logic, we might say that a mourner's willingness to ab-
breviate the value of the other and to equate him retrospectively with a cultural
representation becomes imaginatively an act of second order ethical abbreviation—a completion, as it were, of responsibility. By contrast, the revisionary
elegist perceives a gap between the intentions of the tradition (which seek a resolution of loss and a perpetuation of the social order) and present loss (which
by its very irresolution would stand for the value of the other). According to the
revisionary opposition informing any anti-elegiac turn against elegy, all other
mourners—both those in the elegist's midst who inadequately recall the other
and those elegists of the past who have settled for psychically economic and historically symbolic adequations of the dead—are not only complicitous with obsolete mythic orders, such as those represented by Milton's impotent nymphs,
but remain too satisfied with the elegy's end as the end of the other's value.

Still, the anti-elegy's interrogation of grief is at least in part continuous with
the traditional elegiac task of renewing grief at the very point at which it appears
to be exhausted. According to this convention, the promise of a return of
mourning competes with the end of symbolic commemoration in an ambiguous manner, for even as it enacts a cessation of grief in its immediate exigency,
the elegy refuses to give to this end a permanence that would exhaust the meaning of grief and with it the value of the other who is lyrically maintained
through the phenomenon of grief: "Give over thy wailing for to-day, Cytherea,
and beat not now thy breast any more; thou needs wilt wail again and weep

again, come another year" (Bion, "The Lament for Adonis").[7] The renewal of grief—implicit in Virgil's question in Eclogue X, "Who would refuse verses to Gallus?", as it is in Milton's version of that same question "Who would not sing for Lycidas?"—sets itself against commemorative fulfillment and proposes a progressively dialectical grief made sincere by the hypothesis of its continuation. The impulse against consolation qua fulfillment demands a new (or renewed) work of mourning, yet also requires the cancellation of the present honorific effort. It is in this sense that Bion's "The Lament for Adonis" can only end by promising not to end, refusing a symbolic catharsis of emotion that would diminish the other who is the object of the poet's emotion. For elegy typically negotiates an ending governed by ironic consolation. The future of grief permits the mourner to be consoled by grief's temporary cessation precisely because it gives what is only the appearance of an end—an ending to be undone by the sincere mourner's returning grief, by the familiar elegiac imperative to renew the task of mourning.[8]

The traditional hermeneutic treats the newness of grief as always also a renewal, returning the particular occasion of loss to the general history of loss in order to restore in the mourner a capacity for attachment and for subsequent grief. Thus it proffers a temporal continuity that sits less well with an anti-elegiac sensibility. For anti-elegy, though it may take its cues from our desire to renew and preserve grief, identifies a slippage in the new that amounts to a distrust not merely of the old, but of temporality itself. Even at the very beginning of the elegiac tradition, the promise of renewed grief reveals a suspicion that commemoration competes with grief's sincerity, and so exposes grief's limited ability to maintain its original object under the aspect of desire. More particularly, an anti-elegiac crisis in temporality threatens every grief with the recognition that it must fail its most proper object. Each mourner hears an Achilles at his heel, reminding him that even Niobe, most obdurate and bereft of all mourners, had to eat, in order that she could live to grieve again another day. Alerting us to the corporeal frailty of the one who mourns, anti-elegy demands self-conscious awareness of the commemorative task and the doubtful result that the other might be signified as though her or his person were forever extended in history.

As long as our cultural traditions of identity remain in place and the conventions of the genre seem adequate to those social meanings derived and maintained through cultural traditions, the commemorative task has the capacity to resolve itself idealistically, or, in the case of the conventional elegy, to restore ideal meaning through the elegist's ideal(izing) memory. When anti-elegy suggests a rupture in ideal memory, however, it jeopardizes the metonymic transfer whereby the poet's idealized memory, initially dependent upon an idealistic conception of the identity of both self and other, would no longer simply stand for, but would actively install a new form of collective memory. It is for this reason that elegies are so often self-reflective about and defensive on behalf of poetry and language, for one of elegy's central tasks is to maintain idealistic premises that, in turn, maintain the value of the other beyond his death. Conversely, anti-elegiac grief opposes this maintenance of the social order on the ethical grounds that, if the other can be too easily recollected and made part of collective meaning, the social forms of commemoration would seem only to repeat the forgetfulness an elegist would decry. The anti-elegist's unassimilated individual grief stands outside the resolutions of grief precisely because he too well intuits the task of commemoration as a second surrender of the other. Whether we speak of Hamlet's antagonism to all the "trappings" of formal grief or Milton's apparent weariness with the obligation of mourning, of Shelley's necessary revisioning of his own reception of Keats's poetry or Hardy's self-blaming figuration of his past relationship with his wife, anti-elegiac mourners perceive in themselves a lateness that comes after grief, and so arrive at a point where they no longer trust themselves to grieve as others have—that is, to renew or add to previous grief in a manner that embellishes grief itself.

Belated Mourners

Belatedness, though so often determined accidentally, begets ethics as a paradoxical inability. And this is so if for no other reason than that a mourner's ability has always to do with an efficacy in the social world that demands, according to the claims of progressive knowledge, a diminution of relationship for the sake of the practical, political uses to which the other can be put. From the perspective of the one who remembers the other, to insert oneself into the elegiac tradition as if grief were about accumulated history and progress is to accept what Martin Buber sees as the deceptive "dogma of immutable process," which is itself an abdication of the personal value of a human being to the rule of the objectifying principle of the "I-It" relation.[9] Or, to put it in terms inherent to the elegiac tradition, the renewal of mourning would occur as a comforting familiarity in which one's grief is like the grief of one's precursors, but in which the other is also like so many who have previously died. Since *similitude* is only another word for *exchangeability* or *interchangeability*, since the other has been made familiar, objective, and knowable by being put in relation to a history of others like him or to the mourner's historical memory of her, she would become someone who no longer troubles us with the event of her alterity. Anti-elegy opposes itself to this, the ordinary progress of our grief. According to a strictly traditional or generic hermeneutic, we might say, paraphrasing Harold Bloom, that belatedness is an anxiety about being modern, specifically, about being too late to be able to say something that will renew grief.[10]

Yet there is also an ethical aspect to belatedness. Divided between the historically realized fact of the other's loss and the poor precedent set by other mourners, the elegist soon finds that the unavailability of the dead retrospectively signifies an alterity having to do with her permanent value as an other. According to the divided loyalty of the anti-elegiac posture, the mourner remains attached, albeit reluctantly, to the historical and contemporary community of mourners that presides over the symbolic possibilities of the other's value, and committed simultaneously to a contrary valuation of the other who has been underestimated in the community's esteem, if only because esteem— whether it is achieved through the more common figure of idealization or put forward as a realistic description of the other—must involve an aspect of reduction enabling symbolic estimation.

I am arguing that literary mourners confess their anti-elegiac resentment as they profess their belatedness. Hamlet as mourner comes always too late to social mourning, or perhaps just late enough. His uncanny lateness informs the series of dramatic ironies that presides over his too late recognition of Ophelia in the graveyard scene. Having observed Laertes's extravagant grief, Hamlet's late arrival and belated response give rise to a mourning steeped in parodic imitation:

> What is *he whose* grief
> Bears such an emphasis, *whose* phrase of sorrow
> Conjures the wand'ring stars and makes them stand
> Like wonder-wounded hearers? *This* is *I,*
> Hamlet the Dane. (5.1.238–42, emphasis added)

Hamlet here extends the moment of mourning through a confused pronominal reference. By the logic of grammatical antecedence and our dramatic witness of him whose grief has just borne such emphasis, we have every reason to believe he initially refers to Laertes. But our reason for believing this lasts only until

Hamlet announces that it is he who must be taken as the referent for the exaggerated show of grief and that we must read his dramatic self-identification, in which imitative action loses the function of protest, as instead a metonymy for the limits of expressiveness within the conventions of grief. Whether or not Hamlet intends to ridicule Laertes's grief, his by now habitual stance as an anticommemorative mourner leads him to interpret the examples of mourning before him as inadequate. In stark contrast to the melancholic reserve that had initially characterized his mourning, he next extends his protest into a manic hyperbole and so professes his own elegiac estimation of Ophelia by way of contrast to Laertes's inadequate love:

> I loved Ophelia. Forty thousand brothers
> Could not, with all their quantity of love,
> Make up my sum.—What wilt thou do for her? (5.1.254–56)

Given his habit of quantifying his mother's love for his father according to the measurable time of her mourning, it would appear that Hamlet's habit of skepticism survives here in his condescending remark that you can add up the love of thousands of brothers without arriving at much love; and yet, an account of Hamlet's own mourning will also arrive, as he himself confesses, at a contrastive and superlative, though not precisely an immeasurable, "sum."

By far the most surprising element in Hamlet's manic speech—and I think he must be imagined here as surprised by his own words—are those last six monosyllabic words: "What wilt thou do for her?" They have an entirely different rhythm from the Ciceronian momentum that culminates with the phrase "make up my sum," where the monosyllables provide a rhetorical emphasis in the service of publicly commemorative speech, much like Antony's famous final words over Brutus's slain body, "This was a man" (5.5.74). The rhetorical mode is not properly Hamlet's, and he has arrived here only by imitation. Though one could read the next few lines as inflected by disdain (added perhaps to his triumphal transumption of Laertes's showy grief), I think it more likely that he speaks here with a bewilderment hinted at in the disrupted meter of his six-syllable question:

ˇ ˇ / / ˇ ˇ
What wilt thou do for her?

If we read Hamlet's interrogative as an anapest followed by a dactyl, with the pronounced pause after "thou" drawing emphasis to "do," his question metrically enfolds upon itself to arrive at the two principals of grief: the mourner and his action on behalf of the dead. It is just possible that, in asking Laertes what he will do, Hamlet asks him to consider the end of his actions and, ultimately, what is to be done for the dead. Or perhaps, since Hamlet's protesting actions have been almost automatically imitative, since he has expected that his mourning requires differentiation from its precedents, he suddenly takes stock here of the purpose of his protest and asks Laertes what *he* would do in mourning Ophelia. By imagining a future action Laertes might perform, Hamlet interprets the question of intention in all of Laertes's actions, as if it had never before occurred to him that Laertes and other commemorative mourners might be thoughtful. As he pauses to consider this possibility, Hamlet's anti-elegiac difference as a mourner is in jeopardy: the danger is that his and Laertes's rival commemorations will amount to the same thing. Shakespeare punctuates the episode by having Claudius interruptively declare Hamlet mad, while Gertrude begs for further tolerance of her son's odd behavior; and after Hamlet again asks Laertes what it is he would do, he offers a list of hypothetical activities, each of which parodies honorific commemoration and draws attention to the distance between heroism and a deliberative account of action. In his disdain for the cultural possibilities of what may be done for the dead, Hamlet arrives finally at a dismissive estimation of Laertes's preposterously Herculean labor of mourning ("Let Hercules himself do what he may, / The cat will mew, and dog will have his day" [5.1.276–77]). Nevertheless, at the moment of his bewildered pause, Hamlet has pursued the ethical implication of Laertes's commemoration and has considered, perhaps for the first time, that those who mourn more conventionally also grieve.

I would like to stress two implications for a theory of anti-elegiac mourning that arise when Hamlet stops to question his own anti-elegiac difference. First, as it announces itself to be after others' mourning, anti-elegiac sentiment characteristically treats its precedents as thoughtless—a view that may be more or less accurate, depending on whether we believe such anti-elegiac protests to be in mimetic proportion to that which they respond, or to be instead an exercise in rhetorical differentiation performed to give an ethical emphasis to elegiac voice. Is the history of anti-elegiac sentiment a reaction to the consistently poor example of other mourners in each and every case? Or is it that, for the elegist to make his point, other mourners (as metonymies for mourning itself) always seem a poor response to the crisis of the other's value revealed by the event of death?

Secondly, since anti-elegiac protest is always dialectically related to that which it interrogates, the anti-elegy is also always in danger of surrendering the ground of its ethical difference. Given the obvious revisionary usefulness of anti-elegiac gestures and their dialectical relation to generic conventions, should we conclude that the trope of lateness, which is so typically an anti-elegiac posture used to denote difference, is merely a contrivance? Consider once more "Lycidas," where the opening depends in large part on pastoral routine, but also on a weariness with such routine:

> Yet once more, O ye Laurels, and once more
> Ye Myrtles brown, with Ivy never sere,
> I come to pluck your Berries harsh and crude,
> And with forc'd fingers rude,
> Shatter your leaves before the mellowing year.
> Bitter constraint, and sad occasion dear,
> Compels me to disturb your season due. . . . (1–7)

Thoughtlessness, as the implicit content of routine, is presumed here, but Milton creates a deliberate ambiguity as to whether the tone of weariness attaches more to the language conventions through which he speaks or to his own obligatory sense that he must speak. Having obscured the question of precedence to a point where his invocation of the convention seems either as foolhardy or as uncertain as Hamlet's mimicry of Laertes in the grave, Milton muses a few lines later, "Who would not sing for *Lycidas*?" alluding perhaps to the commemorative collection *Iusta Edouardo King*, in which Milton's poem was collected with those by other grieving poets and thus seemed to prove that almost anyone would sing through more or less typical acts of commemoration "for Lycidas". As the dative properties of "for" suggest a topicality that mutes the possibility of a dedication rendering the truer agency of service, implicit here is a quieter, less poignant version of Hamlet's question: "What wilt thou do for her?" With Hamlet, Milton worries whether there is to be any revisionary difference in his service to Lycidas, or whether his own song is to be added only as another obligatory act of mourning. Belatedness denotes a threshold for ethical difference.

When Milton later revises the weak dative "for Lycidas" into a dative of real service, "For *Lycidas* your sorrow is not dead" (166), the renewal of Lycidas's value is predicated upon an uncompleted act of mourning wherein the fight against Lycidas's death is translated into a fight against the death of sorrow. A mourning that begins after others have mourned opposes itself to the act of completion and exposes the sense in which mourning *for* the other is also *for* a purpose—namely, to complete the relationship to the other through substitution. Echoing Bion's "The Lament for Adonis," Milton commands the procession of mourners who represent the history of mourning to "Weep no more, woeful Shepherds weep no more" (165), and thus attributes a new value to Lycidas predicated upon the completion of their woeful, less effective mourning. Any reading supposing Lycidas to be ambiguously resurrected in line 166 by being placed in nominal apposition to "your sorrow" must also take "for" to be a logical connective (as if the line were to read, *Thus Lycidas, your sorrow, is not dead*) whereby grief would be completed through symbolic restoration. The shepherds must cease to weep precisely because their sorrow for Lycidas is not dead. Mourning, according to a hypothetically renewable belatedness that designates each time an anti-elegiac refutation of grief itself, finds the truer sign of its ethical purpose in grief's improper timing.

Though the anti-elegiac reading of Milton's elegy seems finally contained by the poet's strategies of ethical displacement and by his turn to a mythically substituted idealization of Lycidas, my greater point is that anti-elegy remains an energizing principle in the poem, an internal tension within its final advocation of consolation, activated in part through Milton's sense of coming late to the scene of mourning. So too, in one of the tradition's most recognizable and severe anti-elegies, "Elegy to the Memory of an Unfortunate Lady" (1717), Alexander Pope presents his act of mourning as a pronouncedly belated reaction to the story of a suicide. Most critical conjecture about the poem, from Samuel Johnson to the present, presumes that the story of the lady in question was passed to Pope secondhand, and Johnson famously complains that the lady is not worth celebrating, that "[p]oetry has not often been worse employed than in dignifying the amorous fury of a raving girl."[11] One almost imagines that Johnson's complaint with "Lycidas" informs his critique of Pope, and that his real gripe is with all excessive displays of grief. The fact that the "girl" is not worth commemorating seems to be acknowledged by Pope through the distant outrage of his persona, the remoteness of a perspective that, rather like the obsolete contrivances of pastoral form in Milton, might prove the elegy insincere. As a mourner who comes late to a work of mourning that is both dramatically incomplete and inadequate, Pope puts himself in analogy to the deliberately neglectful mourners who have come before him:

No friend's complaint, no kind domestic tear
Pleas'd thy pale ghost, or grac'd thy mournful bier;

> By foreign hands thy dying eyes were clos'd,
> By foreign hands thy decent limbs compos'd,
> By foreign hands thy humble grave adorn'd,
> By strangers honour'd, and by strangers mourn'd! (49–54)[12]

The anonymous agents who bury the suicide with a discretion proportionate to her disgrace are ironic substitutes for the intimates who fail to mourn. Perhaps more significantly, they so parody the rites of mourning that they characterize ritual grief as if it were an act of intentional neglect. With a Hamletic scorn for formal mourning, Pope includes himself as the latest among these strangers to approach the task of mourning, but in his belatedness he still seeks to revive exhausted rites. The poem thus hovers between a phenomenology of insincerity, which would coincide with the momentous inertia of the previously enacted examples of mourning, and an anti-elegiac sincerity, which would refer to Pope's present efforts to renew grief.

My point is that Pope's estrangement, his status as yet another stranger, gives him an advantage, setting him apart from a poorer history of mourning. As he seeks to overcome the impersonality implicit in such a distance, he has to renew the possibility of reciprocity that has lapsed with the prior examples of mourning and thus characterizes his own generosity as that which is similarly vulnerable to others' lax remembrance:

> Ev'n he, whose soul now melts in mournful lays,
> Shall shortly want the gen'rous tear he pays;
> Then from his closing eyes thy form shall part,
> And the last pang shall tear thee from his heart,
> Life's idle business at one gasp be o'er,
> The Muse forgot, and thou belov'd no more! (77–82).

The ironically appropriate exclamation point calls attention to the fact that, although this woman was alienated from her family and unknown to the poet himself, she is mourned in these last lines as if she were a woman Pope had loved passionately. It is quite as if Pope has been inspired by her example of passion to take her as an object of his passion, thus revealing the self-interest of so much of our imagined reciprocity. The poem's pathos, though deliberately contrived, depends upon the poet's loyalty to the cause of her remembrance, to the dream of achieving human permanence through perfected memory, even though this form of ideal memory must ultimately be violated by his own death.

Perhaps by coming late to the scene of an original neglect Pope has been inspired to vigilance on behalf of another, but he fully intends his better example to trace a historical failure of intimacy, his new and ultimately lapsing memory recapitulating aspects of the spectacle of inadequate mourning before him. At the poem's end, Pope has set his own compensatory efforts over against the past failure of intimacy, only to find in his own mourning a failure of endurance that traces a fundamental inadequacy in all acts of cultural commemoration.

The Paradox of Intimacy

As anti-elegiac mourning pronounces its own belatedness, it often challenges the presumption of intimacy in the face of death, supplanting examples of failed intimacy with melancholically enduring or ironically impersonal models of grief. The attention paid to a conflicted construct of intimacy may be constitutively ethical, a point that Martin Buber helps us illustrate. For Buber, it is address, the act of speaking "Thou," that "establishes the world of relation" (6). As the "I" masters three spheres of address—the natural world, human beings, and spiritual beings—it develops three levels of consciousness about relational events. If the first sphere initiates the capacity for independence and the second teaches institutional meaning, bequeathing to the person a talent for becoming an object that fits into categories and finds place among the institutional governance of human society, in the third sphere there is a "separation" through which the *I* recognizes itself as an other, an unchanging partner, subject to the apprehension of its own isolation (22–23). Like Levinas after him, Buber does not deny that the turn to objectivity is necessary to social order, but he worries that all institutionalization of knowledge and objective relations by their very nature alienate the true condition of existence. For Buber, the human self occurs in "meeting," not as constructed through nature or things. In an essay written in honor of Buber, Levinas describes the conflicted horizon of what he terms the "between-the-two" dimension of being:

> Man is not a subject who constitutes: he is the very articulation of the meeting. The human self is not a being among beings, but a being who is a category, and who since Nietzsche, according to Buber, has been recognized as such. . . . He is meeting. He is that which puts itself at a distance (and already the anonymous existence of the world and of things that have survived the use we make of them is affirmed in that distancing) and he is at the same time the entering into relations

with that world which is distant—other. Through these two movements, man is at the center of being, and all philosophy is anthropology. He is not at the center by virtue of being a thinking subject, but in his totality, because his totality is the concreteness of his situation.[13]

Posed dialectically between distancing and what I want to call "intimacy," the self, as the core of existence, fluctuates between the impersonality of knowledge and the personal dimension of ethical relationship. By seeing human beings "as the possibility of distance and relation," Buber (at least in Levinas's estimation of him) resists "the notion of a content being, a realized being, a narrated being"—which is to say, a completed or economically contained being (24).

For the elegist who acknowledges the separation that conditions all relationship, the distance that permits alterity finds an awful analogy in the irrevocable distance that separates her in time from the lost other. In order that time may be metaphorically retrieved and the other made to seem present again, the elegist tries to compensate for her loss through a wishful fiction of intimacy, which would retain and contain the lost other. And for this very reason, anti-elegy contests the rhetoric of intimacy an elegist typically adopts. So, for instance, the anti-elegy in a poem such as "Lycidas" coincides with the poem's resistance to the fiction of past intimacy it offers ("we were nurst upon the self-same hill" [23]) as seeming comfort. An anti-elegiac belatedness sets the mourner apart from the traditional cultural economy of identity. Recognizing that the other cannot really be recovered through a mending memory of intimacy, anti-elegiac mourners boldly confront their irrevocable separation in time as a sign of ethical difference. For, as I have already emphasized, timing is the peculiar affect of elegy, and it is precisely because one cannot die with or for another that the position of the belated mourner serves to remind the elegist of the impossible, yet nevertheless persistent vocation of intimacy. One thinks of Edgar's declaration at the end of *King Lear*, "The weight of this sad time we must obey" (5.3.298 [all references are to the Folio text in *The Norton Shakespeare*]), where time's final sadness is the result of awful timing. At the very moment that Lear believes himself to be compensated for his sufferings and on the verge of perpetual forgiveness, as he fantasizes about his renewed intimacy with Cordelia, having declared futilely, but in ironic anticipation of what is to come, "He that parts us shall bring a brand from heaven / And fire us hence like foxes" (5.3.22–23), his daughter suffers her death offstage. As Edmund's good comes too late, so also does Lear's ethical appreciation of Cordelia.

If this is in many ways one of the cruelest scenes in all of literature, it is so in part because, despite the pathos of his gratitude, Lear reveals his kinder self to be yet another version of his original solipsism. In his fantasies of forgiveness, he has raised Cordelia to the stature of a goddess, one who receives the supplications of the penitent because in her perfected generosity she must:

> Come, let's away to prison.
> We two alone will sing like birds i'th' cage.
> When thou dost ask me blessing, I'll kneel down
> And ask of thee forgiveness; so we'll live,
> And pray, and sing, and tell old tales, and laugh
> At gilded butterflies, and hear poor rogues
> Talk of court news. . . . (5.3.8–14)

Ending his speech confident that in a "walled prison" he and Cordelia can outlast all those who play by the politics of the ordinary world, Lear can be comforted by this prospect because imprisonment will enforce the intimacy he has sought all along, demanding from each of them perpetual reciprocity. The fantasy is every bit as confining as the terms of the original ceremony in which the king required each of his daughters to present him with a perfectly reciprocal gratitude for his patriarchal gift of land, and if the terms of Lear's love are not explicitly incestuous, they could at the very least induce claustrophobia in all but the most thoughtlessly derivative children.[14] To put it most harshly, the poetic logic of the scene in which Lear walks back on stage with the dead Cordelia in his arms is less a surprise than an inevitability. Lear's logic is already nostalgic and commemorative ("we'll live, / And pray, and sing, and tell old tales"), valuing the idea of "Cordelia" as a symbolic mediation of his losses. What *King Lear* teaches us is that the idealization of the other may be at once a defense against the burden of intimacy and, at the same time, a presumptuously self-sustaining fiction of intimacy projected in the face of a radical alterity. For it is through idealization, both at the beginning and the end of the play, that Lear proposes dealing with the discomfitures of genuine intimacy. In the beginning he wants his daughters' love to assume the form of praise for his generous paternity, and by the end of the play, as he seemingly challenges and inverts such egotism, his humility seems only an extension of his original pride. Having been fully idealized, one might even say, there is little for Cordelia to do but die. There is no more room in Lear's final vision of intimacy for a dissenting Cordelia than there was at the beginning of the play.

Typically the function of mournful idealization is to solve the crisis in reciprocity provoked by the occasion of death. Through idealization, the other who is no longer subject to the rule of sociality may be elevated to the status of a virtue presiding over other forms of sociality and poetic exchange. With the other's death experienced as a threat to poetic voice, many elegies turn naturally to thoughts of the self and its recuperation, but they do so at least a little uncomfortably. For the gesture of idealization, tending ultimately toward elegiac apotheosization, compensates for a guilt implicit in the mourner's voice, since, as Ramazani has emphasized, the loss of the other has yielded the opportunity for mourning's eloquence and for a song that will enhance the poet's reputation.[15] Thus, in contemplating the other's fate, the elegist anticipates his own death and foresees not only his mortality, but the possibility that he will go unremembered; yet even as he reflects upon his present act of remembrance, a poet defends against this possibility by equating the achievement of his song with the other's value.

In protecting the other from a fate worse than death—the fate of being forgotten—the elegist implicitly protects himself. At the end of "Lycidas," an apotheosized Edward King, much like a deified Cordelia, becomes generous because he is the personification of generosity:

> Now *Lycidas*, the Shepherds weep no more;
> Henceforth thou art the Genius of the shore,
> In thy large recompense, and shalt be good
> To all that wander in that perilous flood. (182–85)

What is suggested here is not a "large recompense" Lycidas bestows after he attains exalted status, but one that is contemporary to his apotheosization, seeming the very reason he has been exalted. With the description of Lycidas's goodness, Milton's "shalt" reverts from a prediction of open-ended, future generosity to the aspect of command. Such promise of "recompense" lays bare the fundamental economic premise of mourning. The crisis in ordinary reciprocity— in which one is esteemed more or less in proportion to the esteem in which one is held, and in which one acts generously or altruistically according to what may be either explicit or concealed compensatory motives, such as gaining reputation or admiration, or sacrificially obtaining virtue—is answered by a restoration of the other to a position worthy of symbolic exchange. In this sense, the elegy's ascription of reciprocity is plainly compensatory, elucidating a fantasy

cooperation between the other and the mourner having more to do with present desire than with the remembrance of relationship.

Toward Reciprocity: Shelley's "Adonais"

Nowhere is the delicate balancing of a compensatory fantasy of reciprocity
more neatly managed than in Shelley's "Adonais," a poem that at the same time
undermines much of the basic economy of grief through its (to borrow Peter
Sacks's phrase) "self-divisive work of mourning." In "Adonais," Shelley offers a
procession of inadequate mourners, who nevertheless, in Sacks's words, "keep
the poem in motion" (151), while constantly threatening to interpose themselves between Shelley and his grief. In the seventeenth stanza, where Shelley
contemplates blighted nature and curses the implicit agents of Keats's death as
having occasioned this crisis in the natural world, his accusation constitutes a
breakthrough in the poem, giving us for the first time the "true ring of Shelley's
voice" (152). Shelley's movement toward consolation, in Sacks's view, depends
upon anger precisely because the anger permits the Shelleyan persona to detach
himself from the "wounded, withered, and annihilated vegetation figures"
(158)—those unproductive and largely feminized versions of a mourning self,
such as the unregenerate Spring or the self-immolating Urania—and celebrate,
however precariously, a Platonic renunciation of the worldly for the ideal realm.

Focusing directly on the Freudian economy that sustains this progression,
Sacks relies at the same time on a long-standing orthodoxy in Shelley studies—
the view that Shelley's idealism embraces a Platonic dualism—and, more particularly, Earl Wasserman's seminal reading of the poem at the end of *The Subtler
Language* (1959). In response to the charge that the poem reverts to "bathetic
self-pity," Wasserman had argued that Shelley's elegiac self-portraiture functions as a necessary preparation for his identification with Keats, an identification that makes the poem's subject finally "neither of them alone, but the
human spirit and its destiny in the 'world divine' beyond the grave."[16] For
Wasserman, as for Sacks, the self-pity of Shelley's grief becomes tolerable once
it also becomes functional, and it is possible that Sacks gives such emphasis to
Shelleyan anger for the precise reason that it implies an intentional relation to
causality—an ability both to perceive the cause of grief and to transcend grief
through the self-empowering gesture of what I have called elegiac blaming.

For both Wasserman and Sacks, the poem's potential solipsism and weakness are defeated once Shelley is able to restore our confidence in language

itself and in poetry as a medium of transcendence. Figuratively speaking, transcendence depends upon a transgression against the natural world: the curse is a central moment in the poem because it signifies (as Sacks suggests) the break and detachment from a myth of the natural world: "Shelley completes the work of mourning by a powerful detachment from the natural man and the natural world and a subsequent reattachment to a transcendent ideal instead" (158). In the myth of the natural world there is inscribed a fantasy of reciprocity. By directing his fundamental narcissism toward a "spiritualized version of itself," an ideal self further connoted as poetic genius, Shelley reequips himself for the world and the project of poetry—but, as Sacks himself must admit, this resolution would be an extension, however transformed, of the central trope of narcissistic identification. It is here, then, that I pick up the discussion of "Adonais," since a large part of Shelley's revisionary contribution to the tradition of elegy, as I see it, is to draw out the crisis in ethical reciprocity suggested in "Lycidas" and to investigate the terms of self-interested mourning—terms whereby the poet's defenses are alerted not only to the other's plight, but to the very cause of poetry itself.

Since the potential death of song is a foreseeable end of grief, the elegist must persuade himself and others that his song succeeds as a fulfillment and replacement of the other's absent voice. In "The Lament for Bion," for instance, this means that with the news of Bion's death comes the observation that "with him dead is music, and gone with him likewise the Dorian poesy," much as, in "Lycidas," Milton's song is predicated upon the fact that Lycidas "knew / Himself to sing, and build the lofty rhyme" (10–11).[17] If Shelley's visionary strain cannot allow such a prospect to obtain fully in "Adonais," he has at least imagined—specifically, through the poem's angry preface on the critics' attacks of Keats's "Endymion"—a time when the poor reception of poetry proves deadly. As he accuses Keats's detractors in *The Quarterly Review* through an act of elegiac blaming, Shelley makes the pastoral allegory of "Lycidas" refer more explicitly to poetic vocation, interpreting reciprocity as a question pertaining to a poem's reception. Having also acknowledged in his preface to "Adonais" his own "known repugnance to the narrow principles of taste on which several of [Keats's] earlier compositions were modelled," Shelley's identification with Keats remains uneasy, fanning the fire of an appreciation that is, throughout the poem, figuratively belated.[18] Proceeding circumspectly, surveying the procession of mourners, and reluctant to add his own voice to theirs, Shelley hesitates not simply because they are inadequate, but because he has yet to establish his own right to mourn. He has first to find his way clear of his own former underappreciation of Keats. For in imagining a restoration of the other, "Adonais" begins almost necessarily from the moment Keats had slipped in the elegist's estimation.

Shelley's idealization soon seems a balancing of his renewed estimation with his former (could we call it anti-elegiac?) underestimation. The central moment in which Shelley negotiates this former ambivalence occurs through his developing self-identification in stanzas 31–35, in the midst of which he requires the mediation of a figure who has from the start appreciated Keats—namely, Leigh Hunt. Before we arrive at Shelley's ambiguous self-identification through Hunt's spectral mediation, however, the poem operates largely under Urania's influence. In at least one influential reading, the poem charts a formal progression beyond the Adonis myth and the presiding grief of Urania who stands, in Ross Woodman's opinion, for "the poet's shaping spirit of imagination." Since Urania represents an imagination that has been directed toward an earthly transformation and a time prior to Shelley's faltering faith in the poet's mythic and creative agency in the world, Woodman contends that as Shelley "abandons the [Adonis] myth, Urania disappears."[19] Although the demise of Urania may pertain to a greater crisis in Shelleyan idealism for which Keats's death has acted as catalyst, it seems to me there is a more elegiacally motivated sense to this crisis. For like the nymphs of "Lycidas," Urania stands for an impossible protection ("where was lorn Urania / When Adonais died?" [12–13]), and her association in Shelley's mind with the "mistress" for whom he told Thomas Peacock he wrote his "Defence of Poetry" only increases what is at stake in her protection of the Keats/Adonais figure. Urania's failure would leave all poets vulnerable, and her failed protection represents the larger failure of all those mythic consolations so integral to the elegiac tradition.

What I wish to make clear here is that Shelley's anti-elegiac separation from the very conventions he employs does not so much ironize inadequate models of mourning in order to achieve a detachment from unproductive mourning and advance a transcendent idealization (which is, roughly, Sacks's argument) as signify an awareness that the reciprocity upon which the conventions of grief depend has suddenly lapsed. Whether we speak of the reciprocity between a mourner and the natural world that signifies enduring grief, or the reciprocity between the natural world and the lost other that preserves his significance, Shelley's anti-elegy makes us aware that the transcendent premise informing any consolatory resolution of grief is really an idealized version of reciprocity. Yet

for Shelley, transcendent vocabularies necessarily mock human fate. Elegiac
song is likewise implicated in this mockery of the mortal body when Shelley depicts one of the Echoes as someone who plays "fading melodies, / With which,
like flowers that mock the corse beneath, / He had adorned and hid the coming
bulk of death" (16–18). Characterizing elegiac song in these "fading melodies,"
Shelley hints that when elegies remain too attached to obsolete conventions they
defeat their own commemorative purpose. Since these songs are signs of transcendent belief, they "mock" the corpse (in the sense that they *tease* it) by referring necessarily to a meaning beyond the corpse's mortal literality. In the midst
of all this, Urania is a figure for the transcendent perspective by which perfect
reciprocity might be maintained. By the time we get to stanza 26, then, Shelley
treats Urania's grief as a parody of Bion's Cytherea, a mere vestige of a former
pathos that further offends by being premised on her implausible immortality:

> And in my heartless breast and burning brain
> That word, that kiss shall all thoughts else survive
> With food of saddest memory kept alive,
> Now thou art dead, as if it were a part
> Of thee, my Adonais! I would give
> All that I am to be as thou now art!
> But I am chained to Time, and cannot thence depart! (228–34)

As a version of what any desperate human mourner might feel, Urania finds
herself separated from the beloved in time, tempted to follow him. But of
course when Urania says she is "chained to Time," she means that because she
is immortal she can never die, so her pity for herself is not only unimaginable
from a human perspective, but necessarily mocks (since death for her is but a
hypothesis with no real bearing on her immortality) the deceased's mortality.

As one not properly subject to time, Urania gives phrase to a melancholic
identification that will characterize Shelley's grief by the end of the poem; as
such she becomes paradoxically irrelevant to her own expression of grief, an
irrelevance signaled in the report of her "heartless breast." A grief that could
endure forever—to be repeated as Cytherea's grief is repeated in Bion's elegy—
requires an impossible, inhuman agency, and it is precisely because Urania's
identification with the dead Adonais is merely hypothetical ("as if it were a
part / Of thee, my Adonais! I would give / All that I am to be as thou now art!")
that it must be, in Shelley's view, "heartless." Not only does the conditional
mark Urania's speculative embrace of her own death as a trick of the imagination

(or put most harshly, as a feigned identity), but according to Shelley's syntax we want to read forward and overextend her phrase of self-reference until it includes, if only for a moment, a future aspect: "[a]ll that I am to be." According to what follows, the line's caesura has to occur immediately before "to be," which means that "to be as thou now art" must refer to Adonais's mortal state—the very condition Urania can imagine but never experience. When Shelley obscures the syntactical flow of Urania's self-reference and gives her an illusory futurity (positioned on the horizon of "to be"), she is momentarily a subject of time, made vulnerable by her capacity to change, her pathos thus imitating a vulnerability that lurks at the center of all melancholic identification. Once this false conclusion is quickly corrected, the acknowledged fact of Urania's permanent separation from Adonais in time seems, in part, a figure for the pathos of any mourner's survival. Shelley assumes that our necessary commitment to an endurance that does not include the lost other would make us similarly heartless. Yet Urania's guaranteed survival, as the figure for any mourner's impossibly extended survival, travesties the teleology of surviving and reveals its most basic function to be an opposition to death and an argument with all mortal vulnerability.

Unlike her precursor Cytherea who ceases her grief in order to renew it at a later time, when Urania ceases to grieve in Shelley's version of the Adonis myth she gives way to examples of poetic mourning that replace her immortal song with more fragile and uncertain examples of mournful voice. Shelley's eventual detachment from Urania does not free him from the spell of her melancholia (as we might expect), but instead he implicitly contrasts himself to her by rendering explicit his own vulnerability. This occurs most dramatically in a section of the poem that "has almost always proved unpleasant reading," in Earl Wasserman's opinion, "because it seems sadly marred by extravagant self-pity and unmanliness" (499). In sections 31–35, after briefly observing the mourning figures of Byron and Thomas Moore, Shelley identifies a "frail Form" that is typically understood as a reference to himself: "of that crew / He came the last, neglected and apart; / A herd-abandoned deer struck by the hunter's dart" (295–97). It is hard not to hear a hint of Byronic separateness in "herd-abandoned deer" (inspired perhaps by Manfred's pronouncement of his separateness from the "mean" as he declares "I disdained to mingle with / A herd, though to be a leader—and of wolves" [3.1.120–22]), as it is also hard not to perceive the Byronic hero's world-weary suffering in the subsequent reference to the figure's Cain-like "branded and ensanguined brow" (305).[20]

Shelley has looked briefly to other poets, as also to Urania, to provide a model for his own mournful posture. He twice emphasizes his own lateness as someone who might have chosen to imitate his precursors but has remained separate from them (the figure arrives "companionless / As the last cloud of an expiring storm" (272–73); and "He came the last, neglected and apart"), and presumably Byron is among the "all" who view Shelley's late and forlorn status with skeptical detachment:

> All stood aloof, and at his partial moan
> Smiled through their tears; well knew that gentle band
> Who in another's fate now wept his own;
> As in the accents of an unknown land,
> He sung new sorrow. . . . (298–302)

It is quite as though Shelley imagines that for sorrow to be new, it has to be estranged from the mourning majority, sung as if "in the accents of an unknown land." Perhaps even more importantly, Urania immediately thereafter fails to recognize him in his grief. To whatever extent she may once have represented Shelley's poetic myth making, his identification with her has entirely lapsed and her failure to recognize him now functions as a sign of his anomalous mourning.

Certainly, I would concede Wasserman's point that there is self-pathos in Shelley's "partial moan," as he admits to seeing his own vulnerability in "another's fate." But the ethical distinctiveness of his mourning resides also in this ability to perceive a threat to one's own identity in the other's fate. Interestingly, it is at this very moment in the elegy that Shelley turns to an ambiguously denoted figure who pays reverence to the corpse:

> Athwart what brow is that dark mantle thrown?
> What form leans sadly o'er the white death-bed,
> In mockery of monumental stone,
> The heavy heart heaving without a moan?
> If it be He, who, gentlest of the wise,
> Taught, soothed, loved, honoured the departed one;
> Let me not vex, with inharmonious sighs
> The silence of that heart's accepted sacrifice. (308–15)

The syntactical placement of "[i]f it be He" makes the clause a fulcrum between an affective state that might be attributed to Shelley and his designation of a newly arriving mourner, and just as Hamlet's famous question to Laertes—

"what is he whose grief / Bears such an emphasis" (5.1.238–9)—seems a description both of the rival's mourning and Hamlet's own borrowed sorrow, Shelley here permits a syntactical confusion of identity to comment on the ethical problem of mourning. For Shelley, like Hamlet, is trying to find his way to a stance of grief all his own. The speculation that the late-arriving mourning figure may be Hunt allows Shelley to introduce his own voice as one of compassionate judgment. In proclaiming "Let me not vex," he aligns himself with Hunt, who as someone who was first among Keats's champions is the truest, though latest, to join the procession of mourners.

Perhaps inspired by his own advocation of Keats's great advocate, Shelley opens the next stanza by declaring, "Our Adonais has drunk poison" (316)—his bold use of the possessive case having been secured through Hunt's implicit mediation. Whether "our" defines the rather limited company of truly sympathetic mourners (e.g. Hunt and Shelley), or whether it includes all true appreciators of poetry, it is clear that Shelley is at the center of this universalist vision, having finally made Keats his own. The reason for the temporary ambiguity in identifying Hunt becomes clear in retrospect: he is also a figure for Shelley's own belated, anti-elegiac mourning. As he intervenes to spare a fellow melancholic mourner from judgment for reasons of self-interest as much as generosity, the spectral Hunt not only legitimates Shelley's mourning, but typifies it.

Having recast his own early ambivalence about Keats's poetry as an anti-elegiac belatedness, Shelley suggests that those who come late to appreciation may come most fully to it. Much as Hunt arrives last (even after the late arrival of the "frail Form" who represents Shelley) but nevertheless remains first among Keats's appreciators, Shelley can proceed confidently with his lament because lateness may be a deceptive form of appreciation, the very sign of a yet-to-be-articulated grief. As Shelley proceeds to cast his own anti-elegiac suspicion of mourning in relief through the figure of Leigh Hunt as one "[i]n mockery of monumental stone," he also recalls the flowers that earlier mocked the corpse. This latter example of "mockery" cuts two ways: first, it is an attribution of internal affect, announcing "[t]he heavy heart heaving" that belies the quiet of stone; and secondly, rather like Wordsworth considering Peele Castle's "unfeeling armour," it is a moral example, demanding imitation of the stone. As the second connotation subsumes the first, the belated mourner's quieter and newer sorrow effectively contains the examples set by the procession of mourners. Since "monumental stone" connotes the epitaphic task of elegy and its commemorative conventions, Shelley implies that such an iconic cessation of affect does not so much restrain the pathos of loss as prolong it.

Of course the most likely precedent for Urania's own paradoxical heartlessness in Shelley's poem is Niobe, who as the very epitome of stone-hearted weeping seems also to provide the allusive referent of "monumental stone" in stanza 35. Indeed, throughout "Adonais" Niobe is the background for much of the poem's anti-elegiac typology. In construing Hunt as a Niobe figure, Shelley would have been influenced not only by the literary precedents of book 24 of the *Iliad* as well as Ovid's account of her transformation in the *Metamorphoses*, but also by a famous sculpture from the Uffizi Gallery at Florence (sometimes attributed to Skopas) of Niobe with her youngest daughter.[21] In a letter to Thomas Jefferson Hogg from April 20, 1820, dated almost exactly a year before the composition of "Adonais," Shelley had spoken of enduring a severe winter in Italy and of having "suffered in proportion." Yet he also appreciated some of the time spent in Florence, since he was able to "[dedicate] every spring day to the study of the gallery there; the famous Venus, the Minerva, the Apollino—and more than all, the Niobe and her children there." As he put it, "No production of sculpture, not even the Apollo, ever produced on me so strong an effect as this Niobe."[22]

In the final book of the *Iliad*, Niobe's story is a crucial reference in the scene where Priam ransoms the body of Hector from his son's killer, Achilles.[23] Ordered by the gods to relinquish Hector, after he has for twelve days dragged the dead Trojan's body around the tomb of Patroclos, Achilles calls for the body to be washed and anointed for burial and tells Priam he shall see his son's body at dawn; and then Achilles invites Priam to dine by invoking Niobe's extraordinary tale:

> Now you and I must remember our supper.
> For even Niobe, she of the lovely tresses, remembered
> to eat, whose twelve children were destroyed in her palace,
> six daughters, and six sons in the pride of their youth, whom Apollo
> killed with arrows from his silver bow, being angered with Niobe, and shaft-
>   showering Artemis killed the daughters
> . . . .
> Nine days long they lay in their blood, nor was there anyone
> to bury them, for the son of Kronos made stones out of
> the people; but on the tenth day the Uranian gods buried them.
> But she remembered to eat when she was worn out with weeping.

And now somewhere among the rocks, in the lonely mountains,
in Sipylos, where they say is the resting place of the goddesses
who are nymphs, and dance beside the waters of Acheloios,
there, stone still, she broods on the sorrows that the gods gave her. (24.601–17)[24]

Citing Niobe in order to encourage a pragmatic relation to loss is a rather astonishing piece of effrontery. Achilles's turn to food anticipates Hamlet's use of dining as trope for his objections to the speedily ebbing flow of grief: "Thrift, thrift, Horatio. The funeral baked meats / Did coldly furnish forth the marriage tables" (1.2.179–80). The crucial difference, however, is that whereas Achilles would emphasize the mutual humanity of Priam and himself in their bodily turn to self-remembrance, Hamlet disdains food precisely as a signifier of our too limited human dimension, crying "What is a man / If his chief good and market of his time / Be but to sleep and feed?—a beast, no more" (4.4. [9.23–25]).[25] Indeed Hamlet's disdain for food and for our beastly being is tied closely to his prior invocation of Niobe while criticizing his mother ("Like Niobe, all tears, why she, even she— / O God, a beast that wants discourse of reason / Would have mourned longer!" [1.2.149–51]). Indeed, the pair of oppositions in 1.2 and 4.4—"Niobe" to a "beast" wanting reason, and "a man" to a mere "beast"—may implicitly recall Achilles's speech, as Gertrude proves more Niobe-like in her turn to food than Hamlet's superficial meaning would suggest. It is not hard to imagine, if we see Achilles through Hamletic eyes, an implicit condemnation of the warrior's rhetorical use of Niobe. Since Achilles has been behaving in a beastly way, absurdly dragging the dead body of Hector around the tomb of his slain lover, his advice might be read as yet another example of self-interestedness.

Still, even apart from Achilles's rhetorical deployment of Niobe as self-serving anecdote, we may well wonder what the eating he celebrates signifies, since she is so soon to turn to stone. One might infer that she briefly ceases her sorrow, as Cytherea in "The Lament for Adonis," in order that she may later resume it; yet this is not Achilles's point. In his eyes, Niobe proves human when she fails her grief and cares for her own body, and by implication, it is only her inhumanity (the fact that she is "stone still") that permits her to extend her grief and brood upon the "sorrows that the gods gave her." Achilles seems to suggest that before she chose to prolong her grief and except herself from ordinary human sentiment, Niobe had, if only once, submitted wisely to her humanity, by accepting a place at the dinner table. Much as Urania's grief in "Adonais" fails as a model because it is heartless in its immortal premise, in Achilles's reference to Niobe and in Shelley's allusion to the literary typology of her story she illustrates the point past which extended mourning becomes potentially inhuman. As Achilles recalls a mourner who has to eat in order to endure and to remember, in Niobe herself he has imagined a tension between an imperfect, humanly unenduring form of mourning and a legendary, monumental example of grief.

With the Homeric story in the background, Shelley's allusion to Niobe in "Adonais" probably drew most directly upon the Niobe sculpture group at the Uffizi gallery. In his "Notes on Sculptures in Rome and Florence," notes that were originally intended as part of a major work on sculpture, Shelley admires the countenance of the central Niobe figure for signifying unadulterated grief— not terror, not anger, not "selfish shrinking from personal pain," not "panic at supernatural agency," Shelley argues, "only grief—deep grief."[26] Nancy Goslee has effectively shown how Shelley's responses to sculpture derive in part from the double influence of Johann J. Winckelmann and Augustus W. Schlegel, with Winckelmann's interpretations of classical sculpture tending to emphasize the relation between stasis and transcendent perfection, and Schlegel's tending to focus on the energy generated by contrary qualities and the subjective expressionism evident in the protohumanism of the Greeks. Though the terms of Shelley's admiration borrow from each sculptural critic, Goslee notes that Shelley's "emotional and moral involvement" with the sculptures, especially those in the Niobe group at the Uffizi, went beyond either, as Shelley perceived an energy in these sculptures "emanating toward the perceiver" and in his responses to them seemed unable to acknowledge "the difference between stone and living flesh."[27] Intent on describing the "consummate personification of loveliness" in Niobe's countenance, Shelley interprets her ideal beauty as deriving from a purely human etiology, which is to say, from the sculptor's act of imagining the anguished moment immediately prior to her last child's death. Blurring the distinction between the sculpture's mock humanity and the mock permanence of profound anguish, Shelley momentarily forgets the artistic medium and refers to the "pathetic beauty of the mere expression of her tender and serene despair, which is yet so profound and so incapable of being ever worn away," finally proclaiming it "beyond any effect of sculpture" (331).

Shelley's personifying interpretation of the sculpture may have relied upon his enthusiastic identification with the subject (one no doubt fed by the recent deaths of his own children and his anxiety about the child that Mary Shelley was carrying at the time), but it also involves a willful revision of the connotation of sculpture qua monument according to the classical norms of idealism and perfection. Turning us from the commemorative moment as more typically situated in the aftermath of loss, Shelley proposes that permanence in such a context will have become relatively meaningless, which is to say, too belated to be protective or ethically effective. He adds, with reference to the sculpted Niobe, "As soon as the arrow shall have pierced her last child, the fable that she was dissolved into a fountain of tears, will be but a feeble emblem of the sadness of despair, in which the years of her remaining life, we feel, must flow away" (331–32). In deriding Niobe's fabulous transformation into a fountain, Shelley denudes her of that retrospective function of perpetual mourning because such oddly staid sorrow seems merely an analogy to the poignance—or arrow-sharp precision—of her original loss.

Shelley's anticommemorative interpretation of the Skopaic sculpture seems to draw out metaphoric connotations of Niobe's monumental countenance that are explicitly rendered in the Ovidian account of her metamorphosis. There Niobe functions as an extension of a grief so extreme as to be beyond grief, and the gradual arresting of her movement connotes the end of grief's conventional modes. In Humphries's translation of Ovid, Niobe is "fixed and staring, / The picture of utter grief, and in the picture / No sign of life at all," and when the narrator refers briefly to her affective reaction ("and the vitals hardened / To rock, but still she weeps"), her grief is no longer expressive, but a peculiarly formal incongruity.[28] Here is the conclusion that Shelley, while viewing the Skopaic Niobe, wished to avoid. Ovid suggests that to be enduring, commemoration must be separate from the affective function of grief. Monumental stone, as an enduring instance of mourning, cancels both the cathartic function of grief and the ethical reciprocity on which grief would depend and to which (in remembrance of a reciprocity now forever denied) it would still refer. By the end of the Ovid story, Niobe's transformation into stone is almost perversely merciful, no longer part of her punishment (the wrath of the gods seeming pretty well exhausted by the time they have killed her fourteenth child); and Ted Hughes's looser translation of the tale nicely captures the note of mockery in Niobe's newly appointed commemorative function:

> And there, a monument to herself,
> Niobe still weeps.
> As the weather wears at her,
> Her stone shape weeps.[29]

Compare this with Humphries's more prosaic translation, "even to this day the marble / Trickles with tears" (139), which emphasizes the supplemental agency of the rain, but misses the subtly mocking tone of the Ovidian narrative in which the gods as the agency of the natural world interpret human limitation. Though Humphries clearly identifies the pathos implicit in the rain's doing for Niobe what she cannot continue to do for herself (namely, to cry eternally), Hughes's translation adds the insight that the weather is not merely supplementary, but antagonistic. Indeed, Hughes makes it seem as if Niobe also weeps because the "weather wears at her," the natural imitation of her grief no longer having anything to do with its original referents.[30]

Hughes's translation of Ovid is loosest and perhaps most modern when he calls Niobe a "monument to herself," thus making explicit the degree to which commemoration is always self-referential in its subjective affect. Perhaps cued by Shelley's own Ovidian allusion in the phrase "in mockery of monumental stone," Hughes captures the mock epitaphic dimension of Ovid's final line: *et lacrimas etiam nunc marmora manant* (6.312). Interpreting the poetic logic in Ovid whereby Niobe becomes the epitaph her weeping would intend, his interpretive translation emphasizes the interiority designated and contained by the stone. Whereas Ovid depicts the metamorphosis as taking place between the transportation of the weeping Niobe, who has in her heart already become like stone (*intra quoque viscera saxum est* [6.309]), and the description of the tears trickling from the marble, Hughes, by calling Niobe a "monument to herself," recalls her visceral hardening in the Latin text (6.309) and makes explicit the commemorative function of *marmora* as "marble" or "statue" (6.312). There is an ironic banishment of subjective agency at the heart of Ovid's commemoration of Niobe, Hughes suggests, and he forces us to negotiate the gap between the objective task of cultural commemoration and the subjective longing it simultaneously signifies and contains.

It is certainly worth noting that as Shelley's mourner leans over the deathbed he is similarly epitaphic in his quiet, given over implicitly to an Ovidian logic whereby grief is contained in a figure of mock (or mocked) endurance.[31] As a figure in "mockery of monumental stone," Hunt recalls not only the sculptural precedent of Niobe, but Shelley's greater suspicion that Niobe's symbolic transformation into a stone fountain is a "feeble emblem" of commemorative steadfastness. As Shelley sees all too clearly, there is a defeat inherent in mourning, since tears become over time self-reflective and less capable of referring to the other who has occasioned grief. The appeal of the Skopaic sculpture of

Niobe is that it represents a moment prior to the necessary detachment of retrospective commemoration and takes us seemingly inside an unsustainable fantasy of intimacy. Niobe is depicted as leaning protectively over her youngest daughter, her left arm with cloak in hand and in motion, the arm descending (too slowly, we already know) to protect her child from imminent and inevitable harm. Significantly, the child's own cloak has fallen, exposing the flesh of her back and buttocks, her flesh a site of vulnerability anticipating her fate since it is there that the arrows will enter the body. The sculpture embodies, in Shelley's own words, the premise of an impossible protection of the other, a wish for permanent reciprocity:

> There is embodied a sense of the inevitable and rapid destiny which is consummating around her as if it were already over. It seems as if despair and beauty had combined and produced nothing but the sublime loveliness of grief. As the motions of the form expressed the instinctive sense of the possibility of protecting the child, and the accustomed and affectionate assurance that she would find protection within her arms, so reason and imagination speak in the countenance the certainty that no mortal defence is of avail.[32]

Recall that in Ovid's tale it is by taunting Latona that Niobe earns her terrible grief, having foolishly declared the plenty of her own intimate relations and their relative permanence—"Suppose she takes much from me; there is more / She will have to leave me still" (Humphries trans., 135). Referring to her fourteen children as extensions of her satisfied ego, Niobe falsely perceives in relationship a reciprocity that amounts to possessing the other as property. Her moment of ethical insight, if it comes at all, arrives with thirteen of her children and her husband already dead, as she pleads for the gods to leave her youngest and tries to protect the child, in the words of the Humphries translation, "[w]ith body bending over, and wide robes spread / To make some kind of shelter" (139). Having begun as someone who sees her own children as substitutable, believing that the loss of one or even seven of the fourteen would be compensated for by the mathematical remainder, Niobe finally surrenders the premise of possessive reciprocity and identifies instead with the child's vulnerability. In Ovid's rendering substitutive economy is devastated, and Niobe's futile solicitation prior to the death of her last child is already an act of mourning, for "while she prayed / The littlest one was dying" (Humphries, 139). In the simultaneity of the wish and its failure, Shelley interprets the implicit ethics of mourning to be an absurdly imagined—and, as I have defined it in my introduction and first chapter, also wishful—protection of the dead. Niobe's grief signifies an imminent rather than retrospective defeat of relationship, as she tries belatedly and futilely to prolong her act of protection.

What this means for our reading of "Adonais" is that Shelley's use of Hunt as a figure of "monumental stone" involves a similar temporal inversion. According to the purely commemorative or retrospective function of protection, Hunt is a specter of protectiveness, like Niobe bending over her child, that arrives always too late. Yet his lateness also sets him apart by recalling an anterior time of remembrance (Hunt's historically situated appreciation of the living Keats). For it is Hunt both then and now who figuratively protects Keats from the critics trying, in Shelley's terms, to take his life. Such an elegiac desire only seems more ethically wishful to the extent that the poet has already admitted its futility.

The Defensiveness of Elegy

In his *Apology*, Sidney had declared, "If you have so earth-creeping a mind that it cannot lift itself up to look to the sky of Poetry, . . . when you die, [may] your memory die from the earth for want of an epitaph."[33] In Sidney's mind, the value of poetry is intricately tied to epitaphic function and its capacity to preserve the memory of the dead—a function that yields poetry a transcendent value tantamount to the rhetorically exaggerated claims Sidney makes for it. Though Shelley was capable of such visionary idealism, and his own "A Defence of Poetry" partakes of Sidney's overwhelming rhetorical confidence in poetry, in "Adonais" Shelley offers us a defense of the other through poetry that is more circumspect, anxious precisely in proportion to its skepticism about idealism and the enthusiasms of idealized remembrance. Having acknowledged protection as the guiding conceit of elegiac reciprocity, Shelley lets down the defenses built up by the elegiac tradition—namely, those defenses that would preserve the other in a fantasy of ethical continuity and mutuality. If Freud has helped us articulate the defenses of language as they deflect the unpleasurable phenomena of the real, in "Adonais" Shelley more closely explores a tension between this basic psychic defensiveness and a defensiveness on behalf of language and ethics.[34]

The effectiveness of elegiac protection is, by definition, retrospectively wishful, overemphasizing or exaggerating a prior condition of ethical reciprocity. Such is the case with the elegy's fondness for the pathetic fallacy, where the personifying turn to the natural world functions both as a screen for the mourner's projective, compensatory imagination and as the terrain of an impossible, indeed mythic agency standing in for or in advance of remembrance itself: "Cry me waly upon him, you glades of the woods, and waly, sweet Dorian water; you rivers, weep I pray you for the lovely and delightful Bion. Lament you now, good orchards; gentle groves, make you your moan; be your breathing clusters, ye flowers, disheveled for grief" (Moschus, "The Lament for Bion," 1–5). Milton and Shelley place themselves directly in the line of such hyperbolic reciprocity between poetic remembrance and the natural world, and just such a fantasy of reciprocity lies behind so many of the elegy's mournful personifications of the natural world. By imagining the responsiveness of nature, the poet allegorically recalls the hypothetical responsiveness of his society to the now absent other. But by also displacing this wish for social reciprocity onto the natural world, he recognizes failures in relationship that everywhere disprove reciprocity.[35]

So, when Milton accuses the model of reciprocity offered by the natural world ("Where were ye Nymphs when the remorseless deep / Clos'd o'er the head of your lov'd *Lycidas*?" [50–51]), his antipastoral, self-reflexive gesture confesses the artifice of all pastoral elegy and at the same time supposes that the reciprocity for which it stands may itself be an exaggeration. It is partly for this reason that the initial accusation of the nymphs (through the convention of elegiac blaming) represents Milton's own responsibilities as attached to an order other than the self. The nymphs are the very form of an exaggerated and impossible reciprocity that Milton would avow rather than disavow. Occupying the hypothetical realm of causation so crucial to moral consciousness, they temporarily hold the place of responsibility as if waiting until the poet could answer for himself; and the way the poet finally answers for himself is through the poem's culminating fantasy of an interpersonal relationship sustained as pure reciprocity, through an elegiac apotheosis that symbolizes the other's value in order to ensure the form of reciprocity. Through idealization a mourner compensates for a crisis that has interrupted reciprocity. By belatedly protecting one who is already beyond protection, a mourner recuperates reciprocity as an act of self-protection, expecting that the apotheosized one "shalt be good / To all that wander in that perilous flood" (184–85).

Just as Milton had anti-elegiacally lamented the failed protection of the nymphs and their mythic realm in "Lycidas," Shelley's lament for Keats reads elegiac grief even more radically to be about a crisis in protection. Ethical reciprocity has been violated by the premature death of Keats, and in his defense

Shelley must compensate not only for this, but for the violences of Keats's detractors, for whom Shelley himself was an earlier, if lesser, prototype. Thus when he defends Keats's protector Hunt, promising not to "vex" this loyal mourner, Shelley figuratively holds in suspension his own critical impulse and anxiously imagines the disdain with which sincerest mourning may be met. Even so, he self-consciously suggests that mourning is a mockery—that is, an imitation—of itself, already contained by the models or precedents of grief. In the end, the rhetorical momentum of the poem's defensiveness is on the side of commemorative idealization, culminating in the overt apotheosis of the final lines where the idealization works in the service of a restored reciprocity. But the poem's anti-elegiac interrogation of its own commemorative task creates a dialectic between melancholia and idealization in which the melancholic identification of mourning, like that state in which Niobe leans over her last child, becomes a vulnerable receptivity to the other.

From the mourner who "leans sadly" over the dead Adonais, we proceed quickly toward the melancholic accusation of idealization itself. Ultimately, Shelley reads the other's idealized state as a mere compensating projection, and he confesses demystifyingly, "*We* decay / Like corpses in a charnel" (348–49). It is through such melancholic emphasis that a mourner approximates the other's vulnerability to death retrospectively. In making this admission coincide with the poem's moment of elegiac apotheosization, Shelley suggests that the fantasy of reciprocity only veils the melancholic risk that comes from contemplating and perhaps identifying oneself with the dead—a risk that is not so much a dialectical opposition to idealization as a corollary to it. The imaginative succession whereby Keats becomes a "portion of loveliness" and part of the "one Spirit" demands suppression of his human alterity. As the idealized form "[s]weeps through the dull dense world, compelling there, / All new successions to the forms they wear" (382–83), Adonais, as transcendent principle, would call for the end of mourning ("Mourn not for Adonais" [362]), but only by looking away from the other's original vulnerability and alterity.

It is usually conceded that Shelley's visionary idealism conquers the poem's melancholy, but it seems to me that the poem's apparent restoration of reciprocity has ethical costs. For Shelley reads idealization itself as complicitous with a death wish: if the other has become perfect and perfectly content after death, if he is also a spiritual guide in the carnal world, then should he not lead beyond the world? *What Adonais is, why fear we to become?* Not quite able to answer his own query, at least not in the visionary terms the poem has established, the poet rediscovers the alterity of the other as a function of his fear, in his resistance to the implicit beckoning of the idealized other. Having previously displaced the elegiac apostrophe into an address of audience and into a procession of mourners, some of whom address Adonais (see, for example, Urania's lament in stanzas 26 through 29), Shelley now inverts the order of apostrophe to arrive at a more fearful version of address: "'Tis Adonais calls! oh, hasten thither, / No more let Life divide what Death can join together" (476–77). Immediately before this, he testifies to Adonais's unpleasurable hold on him—"what still is dear / Attracts to crush, repels to make thee wither" (473–74)—anticipating Tennyson's ambivalent imaginings of the continued proximity of Hallam in *In Memoriam*. According to a melancholic compulsion, the other here threatens the security of apostrophic address because the subject is no longer able to dictate the terms of idealization.

In the grips of mortal fearfulness, Shelley sets out in the poem's final stanza for an encounter with Adonais that is at best ambivalently motivated:

> The breath whose might I have invoked in song
> Descends on me; my spirit's bark is driven,
> Far from the shore, far from the trembling throng
> Whose sails were never to the tempest given;
> The massy earth and sphered skies are riven!
> I am borne darkly, fearfully, afar:
> Whilst burning through the inmost veil of Heaven,
> The soul of Adonais, like a star,
> Beacons from the abode where the Eternal are. (487–95)

With Lycidas's apotheosized protection in the literary historical background, Shelley weighs the principle of protection that should govern an elegiac apotheosis—the guarantee that the idealized other in his "large recompense . . . shalt be good / To all that wander in that perilous flood" (184–85). In Milton's eyes, it is only proper that Lycidas pay back the reverence that has belatedly protected him from harm by in turn protecting other travelers in their peril, especially those who have given their "incessant care" to his remembrance—namely, the true shepherds, or poets, of the world. So too Shelley, having positioned himself as a figurative wanderer at sea, in a bark like the one in which Lycidas drowns, would inherit the legacy of elegiac protection as his economic compensation, a reward for having protected the significance of the dead in the surviving world.[36]

It is in fact his anti-elegiac mourning that has created this expectation by distinguishing Shelley from the routine mourners whose "sails were never to the tempest given." If the others have failed to make the journey—whereby one risks a melancholic identification and responds to the other's call by placing oneself in peril—they are therefore not in need of protection. My point is that Shelley's melancholic journey has been premised on an ironic revision of elegiac reciprocity: when Shelley sees himself paid back by "[t]he breath whose might I have invoked in song," he submits to a rule greater than his own desire, beyond even the anticipations of his original invocation. The muse that now "descends" on him will lead Shelley "far from the shore," recalling the Spirit that compelled cooperation by "[t]orturing th'unwilling dross that checks its flight / To its own likeness, as each mass may bear" (384–85).

In this final stanza Shelley wanders further into fear and a subjective state denoting his alienation from the visionary principle that is supposed to be guiding him. Figured as a regression in the midst of an otherwise compensatory vision of idealization, Shelley's desire appears finally to have been surrendered to an identification that literally endangers him. This spirited guidance is ironic at best, since the elegist's peril increases as his journey comes more and more under the sign (or "star") of the apotheosized other, and if we insist on reading the other even now as a projection of the mourner's desire, we would have to say that the final stanza realizes the death wish as a motivating principle for melancholia. As the poet is transported by obedience to a relation beyond his intention ("my spirit's bark is driven"), Shelley makes a fearful, unpleasurable apprehension of the other the very ground of difference. If we ask what precisely it is that Shelley fears, we can answer only—Adonais himself. That Adonais fails to oversee the scene as a protector of a fearful Shelley, as the more generously figured Lycidas had promised to do at the end of his poem, is very much to the point. If Adonais himself is the source of Shelley's fear, the ending of the poem partakes of the ambiguity of Mark's strangely elegiac resolution to his Gospel, where in the final scene the disciples arrive at an empty tomb and report their finding to no one—"for they were afraid." Clearly, in Mark the trajectory of redemption as an economic return on faith is only *apparently* disrupted by such an ending, since the severely ironic logic supposes that the audience will distinguish itself from the disciples' lesser example and understand the true meaning of the empty tomb. But can we really understand the fear at the end of Shelley's "Adonais" as similarly redemptive, or does it rather obviate the assertion of idealization that accompanies it?

Even if we are supposed to travel the idealistic journey at the end of Mark's Gospel, the story still inscribes its fearful possibility—that we may remain rooted instead in the literality of our fear, in bodies that are unredeemed by the economy of salvation, perhaps too much occupied by the mournful remembrance of the crucified Jesus to imagine his apotheosized state. So too Shelley inscribes the potential of melancholic identification as a rejection within idealism. It is in danger or vulnerability that Shelley becomes like Keats, with the result that the redemptive logic of elegiac consolation seems subverted by the force of his ethical imagination. So moved is he by the loss of Keats that Shelley half imagines a nightmarish return of reciprocity, one that would be premised on melancholia instead of the healthy norms of a substitutive mourning. Placing himself on the threshold of danger in order to suggest the impossibility of a mutually beneficial relation to the dead, Shelley refuses to complete this vulnerable state of mourning. Here, in poetic terms, is an earlier version of that question Freud supposes the ego always faces when confronted with the loss of a beloved other: "the question whether it shall share this fate."[37] In Freud's view, our "narcissistic satisfactions" ought to bring us back from the threshold of self-destruction. But as Shelley pauses there at the nexus between melancholic identification and commemorative idealization, as the elegiac hypothesis of protection seems also in danger of collapsing, the other's alterity has been dramatically and fearfully inscribed on poetic conscience. Since the idea of a mutually beneficial protection continues to have its appeal and might even function as that which legitimates any elegy as a work of mourning, the fantasy of reciprocity remains most stable when an elegist is able to declare his elegy an effective protection of the dead. Until this moment occurs—if it ever really occurs—all elegy will incline toward anti-elegy.

CHAPTER FIVE

Wishful Reciprocity in Thomas Hardy's *Poems of 1912–13*

It is the often delusive, always wishful quality of elegy as a recuperative hypothesis of reciprocity—whether the elegist writes that reciprocity anew or, as is often the case with nostalgically inflected revisionings, for the first time—that constitutes much of its emotional, surprisingly ethical persuasiveness. Time and again in the life of the elegy, even when it is burdened by the melancholic signification of self-accusation or failed responsibility, mourning moves toward its end as toward a former or presumed vision of reciprocity. In contrast and complement to the elegy, the anti-elegy exposes the mythic structures of consolation and the cultural determinations by which grief is made to serve cultural ends, but even as it resists the ordinary progression of grief, it traces therein a hypothesis of elegiac action. For if an elegiac ethics of reciprocity grudgingly gives place to alterity, it ultimately demands some qualification of alterity in the service of ethical aim, care, and action.[1]

If in the preceding chapter I have suggested how anti-elegy begins to undertake a critique of the speculative hypotheses of reciprocity, in this chapter I consider the way Thomas Hardy's anti-elegiac poems simultaneously enlist and dishearten the psychological and ethical appeals of reciprocity. Hardy is not entirely skeptical of the wishful reaction to loss, and his *Poems of 1912–13* move subtly and dialectically between the wish for reciprocity and an accusation of self in which ethical responsibilities are exposed through the self's failings. Perhaps the easiest way to imagine the biographical plot of Hardy's elegies would be to imagine three subsequent states of ethical reciprocity—the first, corresponding to the early intimacy of his marriage, designating a primary reciprocity and an original model of relationship; the second, corresponding to the alienated period of the marriage, representing a failed reciprocity; and the third, occasioned by Emma's death, denoting an impossible reciprocity. Hardy would contrast the first phase, in which the address of the other is guided by the speaker's presumption of intimate personal relation as a ground for understanding, to a late phase in which he must account for her seeming indifference to him by way of an intermediate stage of relationship in which impersonalism (as a sign of genuine, irreconcilable differences between two people) had begun to characterize the marriage. But Hardy's uncompromising exposure of the play between personalism and impersonalism, between reciprocity and its failure, is more complex than this.[2]

For one thing, his use of the personal idiom enacts what is transparently a fantasy of reciprocity, the idiom of impersonalism seeming, even as it threatens to defeat the very possibility of relationship, to obtain an ethical function by criticizing the egoism of desire and the fallacious premise of reciprocity desire enacts. Perhaps more importantly, in the third state of impossible reciprocity Hardy arrives at a self-accusing interpretation of the second state of failed relationship, the interdependence between these two states occasioning the memory of an originally harmonious relationship. Since the harmonious past is always enacted as an interpretation of present reality and its more immediate precedents, it is imbued with the fantastical nature of all nostalgic longing, which seeks an origin that would simplify, by clarification or contrast, present reality. Eventually Hardy's elegies bring us to the sober, melancholic awareness that primary states of reciprocity in which a self's desire is equivalent to the intentions of the other do not exist anymore, and, by implication, never have. None of which prevents the fantasy of reciprocity, as it answers a historical failure of relationship, from exerting its appeal.

What all of this sets up within Hardy's anti-elegiac species of mourning is a rubric of secondary reciprocity. By secondary I refer to the compensatory aspect of the proposed reciprocity (which wishfully stands in for a reciprocity that can no longer be retrieved), as well as to the mourner's slightly diminished aspiration (which no longer reaches for idealizing mechanisms or grand consolatory structures translating the other into the realm of dignified abstractions). The call for a secondary reciprocity is part of mourning's grudging realism. It follows from an ethical desire to find again or for the first time an equality with the other from within the harder acknowledgment of an absolute inequivalence determining all relationship. The other seems either too great or too diminished to answer the mourner's need for reciprocity, yet from within mourning's surprising ethical attentiveness every sign of the other's fading significance questions the entire history of relationship preceding the moment in which vigilance became, practically speaking, unnecessary. This apprehension of responsibility is always partly confused with a blaming impulse in the poet, who might prefer to project responsibility for his wife's death elsewhere (even unto the dead wife herself), but eventually finds his way, as Hardy accuses himself in his elegies of having failed to observe the encroaching signs of his wife's death, to a more difficult self-accusation.

By accusing himself even in his innocence (whatever he has done to make Emma unhappy, he did not cause her death), Hardy reads mourning's impossible ethics through the concrete precedent of deteriorated relationship. The mournful memory of personal history increases the burden to recuperate the possibility of relationship, which will happen only if Hardy can recover a history of mutuality and create at the very least the impression of some equivalence in his relation to his wife. Even as Hardy imaginatively explores the hypothesis of secondary reciprocity, however, he persistently signifies Emma's ethical value through the prior alienation of their relationship, and these painful confrontations with his wife's incontrovertible alterity render all of his provisional arrangements with her memory wishful fantasies of reciprocity, always bordering on a denial of real ethical relationship. Although I treat many of the elegies in the *Poems of 1912–13* in what follows, my working rationale is itself slightly melancholic. Against several other readers of these poems I assume that Hardy's elegiac sequence does not make any significant advance toward resolution and that all of these poems exist under the spell of a fiercer anti-elegiac interrogation derived, as it were, through the other's reproach.[3]

Reciprocity, Redux

"Adonais" ends divided between the mourner's more conventional wish for a reciprocity that has been denied him and a melancholic identification with the other that trespasses all of the poem's compensatory structures. If the final fantasy of reciprocity is disturbed by the other to whom the mourner responds, we are not to conclude that the demand for reciprocity has finally been superseded. For insofar as mourning returns and is repeated—not traumatically, but as a cultural imperative to locate the dead—the requirement of reciprocity will also return and the mourner will continue to seek a reciprocity with the other even in the presently lamentable world. Shelley's melancholic motivation leads him at the end of "Adonais" into a dangerous isolation, but there is every reason to believe that the poem urges and implicitly constructs a community of mourning in which such peril would not be required, a communal horizon for mourning such as the one Esther Schor perceives to have been at least partly in place in the nineteenth century. Since the Enlightenment, Schor contends, appeals to the language of mourning have with ever greater frequency shifted the ethical emphasis from virtue to value, and it is in part the lapsing of this progress that accounts for our largely twentieth-century tendency to treat grief as an aberrant moment and focus on its individualistic symptoms, as if mourning were quintessentially about such isolation. By granting grief "greater extension and duration," we might learn (again) to give mourning a role in constituting communities, in providing a rationale for our historiographies, and even in offering mechanisms for moralizing contemporary social relations.[4] In effect, what Schor advocates is a more realistic account of the cooperative mechanisms of social economy in which the dead have been of tremendous use and value to the living.[5] What I take from Schor's account—which shares with mine the goal of revising the perception of mourning as a pathology, but differs in granting the psychoanalysts and utilitarians their assessment of the too stubborn mourner as pathological—is the persuasiveness of our cultural narratives of reciprocity between the dead and the living. Much as Michel de Certeau before her, Schor makes the case for a mournful language of reciprocity that, though it may in fact be imaginative, is much more than mere fantasy.

This move has its corollary in the field of ethics quite apart from the perspective of mourning and, more particularly, in the work of philosophers as diverse as Martin Buber, Stanley Cavell, and Paul Ricoeur, each of whom gives considerable attention to those structures of reciprocity that make ethical relationship and agency possible. Allowing Levinas's philosophical suspicion of reciprocity to function as a dialectical counterpart to the advocation of reciprocity in the three philosophers just named, let me elaborate here a theoretical account of *reciprocity* as a term in ethical discourse. Buber describes the existential relation as characterized by a paradoxical reciprocity that challenges the sphere of impersonal, objective knowledge. There is an ambiguity to reciprocity in Buber's account, since what Buber describes as the "bounded" relation of every object, functioning as an "it" in the sphere of objective knowledge, might almost be mistaken for a kind of reciprocity.[6] Yet though this restricted province of conceptual knowledge orients much of ordinary language usage, the personal, existential relation stands always, for Buber, in relation to a *Thou* exceeding the objectifying tendencies of language. Ultimately the articulation of the *I-Thou* relationship is, as Levinas assesses it, "dialogical in nature," requiring a "liaison of responsibility and dialogue" that is quite plainly "reciprocal."[7] Situated in the accomplished and reciprocal relation, the Thou inspires truthfulness, requires response, and as such institutes the person who must respond. Although Buber's Thou has a religious signification that yields to every encountered other its transcendent function, in the everyday world the full, existential, and ethical Thou can only be founded in the communal relation, since "[man] can become whole not in virtue of a relation to himself but only in virtue of a relation to another self."[8] Arriving at much the same point through a different critical genealogy, Cavell rejects a definition of reason as the sphere of autonomous agency and insists that the human person is defined from the outside, most particularly in relationship. Any assessment of the claim to reason or moral rightness requires an examination of that for which the agent takes responsibility and demands that she ask whether the position she has adopted can be called worthy from the larger purview of commitments responding to and serving communal ends.[9]

For Buber and Cavell alike, subjectivity is only meaningful in and through the larger context of relationship. For any self to become adequate to itself (Buber's emphasis) or for any claim made by a self to be deemed morally justifiable (Cavell's concern), either must be weighed in terms of a preestablished mutuality. Implicit in every form of mutuality is a simultaneous privileging and curtailing of the other (or Thou), who nevertheless renders to the self the very possibility of a meaningful, moral existence. In Buber, the reciprocal relationship affords the self an opportunity to live beyond the forms of alienated existence, which are the result of both knowledge as a mode of objectification and institutionally defined relationship, whereas in Cavell, who more emphatically dispels the mythic autonomy of the liberal, Western self, the recognitions of relationship codetermine the description of any thought or action, which according to the properties of knowledge can never quite be enacted in existential freedom. If Buber imagines an especially cooperative version of reciprocity, Cavell more frankly admits that the judgment from the perspective of reciprocity—that is, according to "the nature or quality of our relationship to one another" (268)—must also be restrictive.

Levinas, too, expresses an anxiety about the "formalism" of the I-Thou relationship, worrying that in Buber "the meeting, which is formal, can be reversed, read from left to right just as well as from right to left," and so restricts the very meaning of the other in his radical alterity. It is Levinas's suspicion, in other words, that the I-Thou relationship participates in the formal aspect of reciprocity characterizing the sphere of objective knowledge, if only because the I and Thou are necessarily subject-positions relative to a formal economy in which they take place.[10] In the seventh study of *Oneself as Another*, Ricoeur embraces precisely this reversibility, seeing it as one of the elements—along with nonsubstitutibility and similitude—that promote mutuality as a condition for moral knowledge. All ethics for Ricoeur depends upon the possibility of reciprocity, in the similitude between esteem for oneself and solicitude for others, in the very ability to think and act through the sympathetic principles of "you too" and "as myself." There is no ethics without equivalence: "The equivalence between the 'you too' and the 'as myself' rests on a trust that can be held to be an extension of the attestation by reason of which I can believe that I can (do something) and that I have worth."[11]

By moving from Buber (and Cavell) to Levinas to Ricoeur—or from reciprocity to the critique of inequivalence to a restatement of reciprocity—we glimpse the highly dialectical function of the other in several competing formulations of ethics. Ricoeur intuits the danger in a Levinasian account of ethics to be that it is—if we recall the split between ethics and morality that I suggested in my introduction—morally impossible. This is so, most particularly, because such an ethics aspires to the ruination of mutuality:

> E. Lévinas's entire philosophy rests on the initiative of the other in the intersubjective relation. In reality, this initiative establishes no relation at all, to the extent that the other represents absolute exteriority with respect to an ego defined by the condition of separation. The other, in this sense, absolves himself of any relation. This irrelation defines exteriority as such. (188–89)

The term *irrelation* is especially apt, since it glimpses the radically anti-economic dimension of Levinasian ethics in which difference opposes itself to relationship and summons the self to a responsibility so severe that it might erode the very self-esteem that makes ethical aiming and action possible. Under the burden of such alterity, Ricoeur fears, a self may come to "detest itself to the point of being unable to hear the injunction coming from the other" (189).

Ethics, in Ricoeur's view, must recuperate the resources of self-esteem and the capacity for benevolently regarding others; it must overtly emphasize a balance between the self and other and thus avert the potentially awful dissymmetry of the other's injunction because "a dissymmetry left uncompensated would break off the exchange of giving and receiving and would exclude any instruction by the face within the field of solicitude" (189). Ricoeur is quite clear that for ethics to be possible, the fact of otherness must involve a return for self, even if we are to understand what is given back to the self only as "a capacity for giving in return" (189), and so he speaks of a benevolent spontaneity through which the ethical agency of sympathy is construed. More particularly, by putting the other also in the position of the one receiving, Ricoeur restores the self's initiative in its capacity to respond. According to the self's talent for imaginative approximation, ethics becomes again a "suffering-with" quite opposite to the singular and potentially stultifying "assignment of responsibility by the voice of the other" (190).

According to Ricoeur, ethics becomes impossible when the phenomenological condition of selfhood deteriorates to a point where ethical action appears inhibited or prevented by either a deficiency or excess of reciprocity. Ethics is sociality in praxis. In a certain respect, Levinas and Ricoeur are not far apart here. For Levinas agrees that ethics coincides at some level with sociality, but more pointedly as the anterior construct or impossible form of sociality. When ethics translates merely into the realm of possibility and the set of intentional propositions that articulate and orient responsiveness, it pronounces the defeat of its own signification; it becomes morality or a system of answerable codes and obligations. For Levinas, ethics as reciprocity leads toward a defined set of answerable responsibilities that anticipate fulfillment, thus establishing a relation of equivalence between the responsive self and that to which it responds and, ironically, bringing to an end the very source of its provocation in the relation of inequality. For Ricoeur the problem of ethics is how to admit this inequality through which the other has been designated without proposing it as irremediable—in short, without being ruined by it. The task of ethical solicitude is a "search for equality in the midst of inequality," with ethics demanding to be returned always to the idiom of the possible (192).

Addressing the Other Who Beckons

I want to maintain that the elegy as it is emblematic of the social rhetoric of mourning proves a site for imperatives about reciprocity that we can read very much in the light of Ricoeur. In *The Interpretation of Dreams* (1900), Freud presents a number of dreams that recount the death of the other, all of which involve a basic temporal confusion. Most typically these dreams anticipate or imagine the other's death either as a symptom of a past and now repressed aggression or as a displaced wish, which Freud is sometimes able to discern as having been associated with an altogether different person's real death. According to this hermeneutic, dreaming the death of the other is only provisionally focused on the particular death about which one dreams. More significantly, such dreams would refer to the subject's complex and frustrated history of desire in the real world.

All the same, it is worth pausing over the anticipatory structure of death dreams, if only because anticipation or the associated idea of anxiety has played such an important role, especially since Wordsworth, in the imaginative life of the elegy. In a poem such as "Strange Fits of Passion Have I Known," which is itself a kind of death dream, as well as in the famous "spots of time" from *The Prelude*, Wordsworth inverts the temporality of loss and employs an imaginative anxiety preceding the other's death as a preliminary figure for the poet's retrospective grief. There is, at the very least, a formal resemblance on this point between Wordsworthian poetics and Freud's description of the dreaming psyche. Whereas Freud suggests that anxiety literally pre-vents loss in order to protect the self (since as she worries, the subject also prepares for the eventuality of loss), Wordsworth more surprisingly proposes that anxiety sustains or poetically elaborates the ethical relation: even though it is part of the fantasy protection of self, anxiety also glimpses a potential neglect of the other. After describing his eagerness to be with his lover and his journey in the dead of night to her cottage, the speaker of "Strange Fits" is overtaken by "fond and wayward thoughts" (25) that end the poem by predicting her death:

> "O mercy!" to myself I cried,
> "If Lucy should be dead!" (27–28)[12]

At the very least, Wordsworth plays upon the more callous reading that Lucy's death would result in the disappointment of his specifically erotic desires, but he has also rendered anxiety an ironic figure for the subject's protective fantasy and even suggested the desire for the other as the causative principle behind her death. Thus Wordsworthian anxiety is riven by a doubled temporality: even as it narratively precedes loss, it simultaneously signifies the poet's retrospective search for a cause. Anxiety after the fact may be precisely a figure of belated responsibility, evoked through accusation: *if only the subject had been on guard and anticipated loss, if only he had known,* he might have averted the psychic trauma occasioned by sudden loss. He might have altogether prevented—for this is the ultimate fantasy of mournful anxiety—the other's death.

In *The Interpretation of Dreams*, only one of the dreams about the death of the other in fact refers to a recent death. As such it bears all the signs, even though Freud does not quite see it this way, of a work of mourning. In this dream, a father has been standing vigil at the bedside of his sick son "for days and nights on end." When the son dies, the father goes into the next room to get some sleep, but before leaving he assigns an old man (possibly a servant) to "keep watch" over the child's body:

> After a few hours' sleep, the father had a dream that *his child was standing beside his bed, caught him by the arm and whispered to him reproachfully: "Father, don't you see I'm burning?"* He woke up, noticed a bright glare of light from the next room, hurried into it and found that the old watchman had dropped off to sleep and that the wrappings and one of the arms of his beloved child's dead body had been burned by a lighted candle that had fallen on them.[13]

The physical phenomenon that governs the dream seems obvious enough to Freud, for even while dreaming, the man is able to perceive the glare of light from the next room and conclude in his sleep that a candle has fallen over and a fire has started. What is more perplexing to Freud is why the man continues to dream once this information becomes available, since according to this delay during which the dream continues to translate reality into the imaginative, non-referential terms of dreaming, the father fails to awaken and prevent further damage to his son's body. Despite the fact that the unpleasurable details of the dream have not disguised the son's death, Freud concludes that the dream proves the strength of wish fulfillment, which is stronger even than the intrusive reality the dream is forced to register. The peculiar content of the father's wishing is this: in the dream the dead child has behaved "like a living one," and if the father were to respond immediately to reality and wake up, "he would, as it were, have shortened his child's life by that moment of time" (5:510). This is an elegant and sympathetic account of a father's prolonged attachment, but what Freud oddly underestimates, or perhaps chooses to ignore, is that the dream is already an act of mourning. As such, the dream's conversion of a real fire into an anxiety about the son's bodily demise offers a psychic repetition of the damage already done to the son. According to the terms set out by Freud's own economic model of mourning, the dream would thus denounce the father's incapable cathexis and lay the ground for severance and substitution.

There is more to it than this, however. For although Freud receives the story of the dream secondhand and so is deprived of the biographical details upon which a psychoanalytic reading would depend, several of the dream's details suggest that it has been shaped by a mourner's guilty perspective. Most striking is the father's unremitting vigilance until the time of the child's death, and then his designation of the old man as his substitute in order to extend by proxy his own vigilance on behalf of his previously living child into an act of vigilance on behalf of the dead. In allowing his protective imagination to relax so that another may stand in for his love, the father might well be said to have begun mourning's work (at least in the Freudian scheme) of relinquishing the dead. Inasmuch as he has come to regard his wakefulness as the signature of care, his sleep is already an act of decathexis. But if this is so, he still feels a great deal of uneasiness about this quite natural process.

Freud speculates that this uneasiness has a practical determinant: the dream so effectively interprets what is happening in reality because the father may have "felt some concern when he went to sleep as to whether the old man might not be incompetent to carry out his task" (5:510). It seems to me, however, that the question of the old man's competence has to be read as preeminently a symbolic one. To the extent that the dream supposes an anxiety about his competence, such an anxiety pertains to the father's own responsibility, since the old man as the father's stand-in already signifies a lapse in his attentiveness. Thus the child's voice in the dream ("Father, don't you see I'm burning?") figures what is already an ethical anxiety. How well has he kept guard over his son? Not well enough to prevent his death or even the second harm by fire that befalls the boy. In treating the boy as a living child, the dream finally puts the father's neglect in the place of causation and so enacts a perversely compensatory control over death: for the father has (at least in formal terms) less reason to regret that which he has caused.

The pathos of the boy's speech arises as a complaint within consciousness about the release being demanded by consciousness. In other words, the boy calls attention to his own burning as a symptom of the father's formal neglect, but also of the already initiated psychic work of relinquishing the child to death. Thus I would amend Freud's interpretation and insist that the dream has not treated the dead boy as "a living one," for it is hardly imaginable that a burning child would merely whisper *(und ihm vorwurfsvoll zuraunt)* that he is on fire. Rather, the boy's whispering has two functions: first, it suppresses the real shock of the other's death, which is repeated in a softened, fantasy form; but secondly, it traces the distance enacted by death as a measure of the boy's alterity. The whisper is the sign that this boy who speaks like a living one is already dead. As such, it predicts the demise of the other's voice. This may seem an odd way of putting it, since death has already occurred, but the otherworldly beckoning of the dead is a recognizable cultural fiction, enacted by so many of our literary ghosts, perhaps most famously King Hamlet himself, that the point hardly seems controversial. What the beckoning ghost signifies is an intermediate stage, a realm ambiguously denoted as hovering between the interpersonal claim of the other and the final death that is forgetting—an intermediate stage in which the other occupies in absentia a cultural space defined by his vestigial voice, what we might almost call the cultural afterlife of the dead. Such beckoning necessarily competes with idealization, which would preserve the other in the act of commemoration by resolving the other's value through an act of representation and thus arriving at a symbolic, cultural estimation of the other.

In the dream Freud recounts, the boy asserts that he is being burned and that his father permits it, yet his whisper quiets his complaint and predicts his deteriorating significance as an obligation upon the father's consciousness. When the dead child speaks as a living one, his accusation demands that the father be vigilant in death as he was in life, quite as if protecting a dead body were as important as tending to a live one.[14] All of our commonsense responses to melancholy, encouraged by our many utilitarian accounts of psychic health, depend upon an instinctive rejection of this analogy between protection of the dead body and care for the living person, and a conflation of these two realms contributes to the ethical absurdity of the Allende parable with which I began this book as also to the absurdist pathos of Niobe's too-late intervention on behalf of her daughter. Yet, as I have been suggesting, it is an ethical analogy persistently pursued by anti-elegiac mourning. The implicit principle is that our capacity to revere the living other as an unassimilable, yet irremissible precondition for both relationship and subjectivity depends upon the paradoxical capacity of our consciousness to be dedicated to the permanently absent other as to the primary and abiding signification of alterity.

Idealism would prefer to step in and resolve the analogy. In the elegiac tradition, it is the particular function of the apotheosis, drawing especially upon the Christian mythos of resurrection, to create a formal space for honoring the dead, but to do so only by allocating to the deceased a predetermined, idealistic state of being. Apotheosis relates to the dead other as on a substitute plain of living relationship, as the ethical anxiety occasioned by the death of the other is alleviated by a reassurance that he lives on as essentially the same being. Quite probably, the old man who in Freud's second dream attends to the body of the dead child is performing religious duties. In the dream's logic—which would make no theological distinction between accidental and intentional burning, since the accidents of dreams are masked intentions—the fire jeopardizes the boy's religiously defined symbolic status.[15] Which is to say that the old man who fails in his work has been employed symbolically in the service of idealization. Though the boy accuses the father's laxness and perhaps also the idealizing, substitutive resolution upon which his grief depends (for it is the father's duty to see the child through his ambiguously embodied status until the act of ritual idealization), his voice also signifies the ethical potential that coincides with the elegy's wish-fulfilling prolongation of the other's life.

When the boy implicitly accuses his father of negligence, it is not just because the old man who substitutes for the father is incompetent, but because he is precisely not competent as a substitute for the father's vigilance. In provoking the father's recognition of his own ethical negligence, the dream becomes what Cathy Caruth, interpreting Lacan's counterreading of Freud on this same dream, calls "the story of an impossible responsibility of consciousness in its own originating relation to others, and specifically to the deaths of others."[16] This apprehension of an impossible responsibility is not merely retrospective, but prospective, since the child's accusation reinstitutes and indeed redefines the father's protective agency. When the child, as Lacan observes, complains of the father's sleep, which is both the condition of his negligence and an analogy for it, the father awakens to renew his responsibilities, but yet again too late to defend his child. It is this second life of reciprocity—enacted as fantasy after the fact, as the wish for the second chance—that Hardy's elegiacs so eloquently express with very much the same pathos and ironic belatedness of the father's protection of his burning boy in Freud's story.

The "Dulled" Example of Responsiveness

Thomas Hardy's *Poems of 1912–13* are alternately a registry of an irredeemable death and an occasion for an imaginative ethical vigilance on behalf of the dead wife. As Hardy foregrounds the analogy between the ethics of remembrance and any ethical accounting of relationship among the living, he at the same time demystifies the sentimental aspect of reciprocity governing each. Like "Adonais," Hardy's elegies frequently deploy the trope of belatedness to signal the difference of his mourning, and so, for instance, in a poem offering more recuperative possibility than perhaps any other in the series, Hardy imagines that Emma speaks to him and wishes to return his belated love:

> Ay, there beside that queen of trees
> He sees me as I was, though sees
>   Too late to tell me so! (40–42)[17]

Throughout these poems, Hardy's belatedness takes form as a relentless insistence on the reality principle.[18] Similarly, in "Beeny Cliff," the only poem in the series to speculate on an afterlife that is not merely an act of haunting or a shadowing of the mourner's grief, Hardy sobers his quasi-religious speculations about Emma's immortality with the reminder that, even if Emma is enjoying herself "elsewhere," she will laugh at Beeny "nevermore" (14–15).

There are of course many elegies in the tradition that proffer a religious apparatus of consolation, even while simultaneously representing the poet's grief as momentarily inconsolable. In poems such as Ben Jonson's "On My First Son," John Donne's *The Second Anniversary*, or Anne Bradstreet's elegies for her grandchildren, or in the opening sections of Tennyson's *In Memoriam*, we encounter mourners on their way to consolation who are not quite there yet. Even recalcitrant grief is consoling when it is set against the formal apparatus of consolation, since such grief demands a better fate for the dead, implicitly sanctifying the dead or preparing them for otherworldly transformations. But though Hardy's occasional references are as idealistically determined as those of any elegist in the tradition, he suggests that the elegy's ideal sphere has no genuine relation to the real world of the elegist.

In the final poem in the series, Hardy invokes the conceit of eternity in service to an ironically secular perspective:

> —But two have wandered far
> From this grassy rise

Into urban roar
Where no picnics are,
And one—has shut her eyes
For evermore ("Where the Picnic Was," 25–30)

An almost too neatly rhyming remembrance of the "nevermore" from "Beeny Cliff" operates here. Recalling his severe version of the reality principle in the prior poem, Hardy makes Emma's eternal state of rest (how she will lie "evermore") an echo of such severity. Then too there are vestiges of pastoral protection in this final poem. Just as Milton had worried about all those who abandon pastoral idylls to "wander in that perilous flood" (185), in Hardy's poem the principle of departure signals catastrophic possibility. By repeating the scenario of Lycidas's own tragic departure as a more ordinary prospect of travel to be undertaken by others at the end of his poem, Milton would make the elegiac example seem not so distant from our lives; indeed, it is Lycidas who will guarantee that fact by watching over those subsequent travelers who must progress beyond pastoral innocence. In Hardy's poem departure is an absolute. Although throughout the elegiac series he imagines many retrievals of relationship, these efforts come always too late to alter anything. "All's past amend" (36), he says in "The Going"; and in "Your Last Drive," he pronounces Emma "past love, praise, indifference, blame" (30).

While Hardy's elegies relentlessly unveil the principle of exchange governing all more or less conventional recuperations of the dead and also deconstruct the idealizing and compensatory substitutions through which the other may be exchanged for an abstracted version of her ethical value, his grieving personas repeatedly yield nonetheless (if only momentarily) to fantasies of recuperation in which the responsiveness to the other would be based on a perfected mutuality. Even when these imaginings are not fully nostalgic, Hardy's acute sense of anti-elegiac belatedness and his guilty remembrance of his personal history with Emma interpret them as fragile fantasies. In Hardy's scenarios of reciprocity, the hypothesis of communication he envisions is eventually (or already) undone by the other's ambiguous status as a product of wishfulness. But rather than being produced merely for the sake of the poet's expressive will, these fantasies of responsiveness provide the other with a forum for her uncooperativeness. Time and again the mourner's guilty compensations are met with what is at best ironic gratitude and more often a deep ingratitude, and always it is a vision of reciprocity that begets Emma's challenging alterity. As the poet repeatedly runs in the face of his wife's accusations in order to encounter her one last time—much as the father of Freud's burning boy stays to hear his whispering son, even while the boy burns and even as he unpleasantly accuses the father of negligence—the idea of responsibility is glimpsed in the fantasy of attentiveness. Governed thus by an aspect of wishfulness, the poet acknowledges the culturally and psychologically insistent demand for reciprocity and searches at the same time for an appropriate social form for his ethical attentiveness.

Let me recall Ricoeur once more. Fearing that our potential for ethical attentiveness may be damaged by modes of signification that too harshly accuse the self as inadequate to its responsibilities, Ricoeur foresees a ruinous end to the traditionally constructed moral self if the Levinasian connotation were to be played out practically. While offering a fundamental insight into the demanding disposition of the other, the Levinasian system must ultimately find the self hateful. At a basic level, the difference between Ricoeur and Levinas can be articulated by distinguishing between a phenomenological plane of experience in which the self's activity is the measure of its moral worth and a mode of signification in which the self's necessary passivity is what requires it to be ethical in the first place. In practical terms, however, Ricoeur holds it against Levinas that he fails to imagine the means or actions by which the ethically assigned self is extended toward the other in order to act on behalf of the one who suffers. In placing too great an emphasis on the authoritative injunction from the other, Levinas dedicates the ethical subject to the other's mastery—to a scene of instruction, as it were, before which the self must submit without any proper capability. Ultimately, Ricoeur fears that Levinas trusts too much in this accusative mode of signifying ethical responsibility, as in the following representative passage from Levinas:

> Obsessed with responsibilities which did not arise in decisions taken by a subject "contemplating freely," consequently accused in its innocence, subjectivity in itself is being thrown back on oneself. This means concretely: accused of what the others do or suffer, or responsible for what they do or suffer. The uniqueness of the self is the very fact of bearing the fault of another. In responsibility for another subjectivity is only this unlimited passivity of an accusative which does not issue out of a declension it would have undergone starting with the nominative. . . . Everything is from the start in the accusative.[19]

According to the play that binds *accusation* to the grammatical accusative case, responsibility is assigned as an accusation—not for anything a subject has already done in the way of neglecting or harming another, but as a precondition of relationship according to which the subject answers to all the other may do and suffer. Whereas in the ordinary scheme of moral philosophy ethical decision making is always metaphorically an act of cognitive extension by which an already constituted self ventures toward the other, an ethics derived through accusation assumes that the subject's fault arises even in the fault of another, not as a contracted or even discernible reciprocity, not in balance and fairness, but as a preconditioned and implicating mode of relationship.

The very construct of reciprocity Ricoeur upholds against Levinas is perhaps more compensatory or wishful than it is corrective. An ethics of reciprocity would compensate for the "initial dissymmetry resulting from the primacy of the other in the situation of instruction" (190).[20] Reciprocity must be renewed especially in response to those moments of suffering through which the other reveals herself in an aspect of superiority that names the subject's own fragility— the very type of extreme situation that characterizes mourning. Though Ricoeur may well venture too far into the supposed psychology behind Levinas's conceits when he worries that the horizon of Levinas's accusative mode of signification is self-hatred, he describes well the potential devastation of melancholic mourning, in which an ethical consciousness such as Hamlet's may become debilitated. Melancholic mourners give validity to Ricoeur's concerns, positioning themselves always at the threshold of what Hardy conceives in "The Going" as a final *undoing*.

Hardy's mourning personas suggest that the only real measure of an ethics based in the other's alterity resides in the construct of relationship as that which may fail. To the degree that unfailing, reciprocated relationship competes with the unrelenting fact of alterity, little might remain to ethics in the confrontation with death as the final failure of relationship were it not for the mourner's ability to insist upon reciprocity despite the evidence of death. Reciprocity also assures the mourner that all his attentions to the other are to be renewed and relived in the other's attentiveness to himself.[21] By thus envisioning a highly cooperative other, reciprocity seems to become a rhetoric of consensus, which forbids the other any dissenting significance that does not already cooperate with the privileges of the mourner's desire.[22] Hardy would like to reach consensus with Emma's less-than-obliging memory, especially in his nostalgic renderings of the early portion of their relationship, but he is either too honest or too skeptical to be entirely persuaded by the fantasy he constructs for himself. The question throughout the elegies is whether the state of remembered reciprocity is invoked as an ethical model implicit even in failure, or whether it is figured as part of the past in order to signify that a former hope for an ethics of reciprocity has been eclipsed by a starker ethics of difference, wherein the measure of any other's authenticity resides in her capacity to oppose the self's pleasures.

Hardy sets himself up as a figure for conventional mourning and, with much the same intensity attached to Levinas's tropes of accusation, makes his own delusive wish for reciprocity stand for the larger historical pretensions of the tradition of elegy. For instance, in "The Going" he focuses on the temptations of nostalgia, immediately revisiting a fantasy of intimacy that Tennyson had constructed to counteract his mournful disappointment in section 22 of *In Memoriam*. Initially Tennyson recounts a history premised on mutuality:

> The path by which we twain did go,
>   Which led by tracts that pleased us well,
>   Through four sweet years arose and fell,
> From flower to flower, from snow to snow. . . . (22:1–4)[23]

Envisioning memory as perfect concord, Tennyson presents the wills of two friends harmoniously joined together in a country walk. Only as the path begins to slant and the pair "following Hope" descend more rapidly toward their goal does the "Shadow" of death intervene:

> Who broke our fair companionship,
>   And spread his mantle dark and cold,
>   And wrapt thee formless in the fold,
> And dulled the murmur on thy lip,
>
> And bore thee where I could not see
>   Nor follow, though I walk in haste,
>   And think, that somewhere in the waste
> The Shadow sits and waits for me. (22:13–20)

Oddly enough, Tennyson conflates the permanent separation brought about by death with the simpler conceit according to which the two become separated during their descent of the path. Yet the simpler event of separation seems less an analogy than a parallel to the final abandonment of death. In other words, Tennyson does not attribute to the former moment the weighted significance, say, of Wordsworth's famous "anxiety of hope" scene from *The Prelude*, in which the young Wordsworth's eager waiting for his father's arrival figures the subsequent and radical disappointment of death. In Tennyson, death interposes as though it were the euphemism (and not the other way around) for the fog into which the figure of Hallam has vanished, and the poet who "walks in haste" is again walking in present time, repeatedly revisiting the same path, each time perhaps with renewed hopes of finding Hallam there.

Tennyson's revisioning haste, which is quite basically the hope of seeing the other again, anticipates Hardy's revisionary turns against elegiac lament:

> Why did you give no hint that night
> That quickly after the morrow's dawn,
> And calmly, as if indifferent quite,
> You would close your term here, up and be gone
> > Where I could not follow
> > With wing of swallow
> To gain one glimpse of you ever anon! ("The Going," 1–7)

This is not merely a cathartic expression of anger or an ordinary example of what I have called elegiac blaming, which so often questions nature, providence, or God in an attempt to turn plaintive apostrophe into accusation. Hardy here finds fault with the beloved herself, as if her death occurred by intention and as if the objective phenomenon of his loss involved an ironically interdependent dimension of fault in both parties, Emma and the poet.[24]

Much depends on Hardy's subtle revision of Tennyson's lines "And bore thee where I could not see / Nor follow, though I walk in haste" (22:17–18). Whereas Tennyson interprets the already announced death as if only his limited seeing prevented the other's company (much as someone who has fallen behind a companion during a walk can no longer follow his lead), Hardy emphasizes the delusive quality of Tennyson's grief in order to interpret his own attachment to impossible scenarios. In his naïve confidence that he could again pursue and perhaps rejoin the beloved if only he could see his way clear, Tennyson nearly lapses into sentimentality. All that keeps his sentimental consolation at bay is the poet's subtler and self-conscious hint that a delusive persuasion must, by definition, inform the very life of grief. In other words, since the fact of death has intervened in the poem's remembrance of a real-life incident wherein the poet became separated from his friend on a path, Tennyson's intent to follow is both belated and slightly aberrant, his haste contributing to our sense that this entire episode is a species of self-delusion, a trick of memory the poet deliberately plays upon himself. When Hardy takes up the possibility of a similarly delusive attempt to follow the beloved, he inverts the order of *following/seeing*, and thus renders the hope of seeing the other (or "gain[ing] one glimpse" of her) less a restoration than a parting vision. According to Tennyson's syntactical arrangement, if he could see, he could also follow. Whereas death similarly prevents Hardy's following, he translates Tennyson's seemingly naïve wish to follow from a fantasy about recuperated reciprocity into the much less ambitious desire simply to have witnessed the other's departure. In one sense, the "glimpse" he imagines is his own, as he wishes to have anticipated his wife's going. But at the same time it is her cognitive glimpse of him that he longs for—to be once more recognized in the eyes of another.

According to the lesser ambition of Hardy's elegies for his wife, he imagines a renewal of relationship before the interruption of death, as if he could extend the past ever so slightly. This is anti-elegy by way of a reduction, with Hardy dissenting from the conventionally idealizing restorations of elegy precisely because in falsifying the past they also cancel it. By contrast, Hardy's lesser (but no more realistic) recuperation focuses minimally on past possibilities, on a time when wife and husband might really have recalled their mutual history of desire; and because this could have happened, he interprets the loss itself through the wishful hypothesis of communications that might also have occurred. As Hardy pursues his own wishfulness, he holds it up to close examination and interrogates a tendency in desire to suppress that which is other to its longings. Persistently in Hardy's elegies, the alterity of the dead is signified in opposition to the poet's projected intimacies, to a relationship he would construct anew as though true reciprocity were possible. Even Emma's death proves to be more willful departure than tragic disappearance, reinforcing her alterity as that which is by definition in opposition to the poet's own desires. At times, as in stanza 4 of "The Going," Hardy briefly revisits the past as if Emma's recollected proximity could sustain a fantasy of intimacy ("And, reining nigh me, / Would muse and eye me, / While Life unrolled us its very best" [26–28]), but immediately his remembrance is troubled by the fact that the mutuality he imagines was already, even at the distant time he remembers, a thing of the past. If Hardy cannot follow the other "in haste" as Tennyson does, this is because Tennyson's haste presumed a reciprocity only recently violated by death, whereas Hardy's pursuit of the other must acknowledge an already lapsed reciprocity. In his "haste" Tennyson appears confident that his desire cooperates with Hallam's, but for his part Hardy redirects the emphasis of haste and attributes it to the abandoning action of Emma, who closes her term and goes "quickly" (2) from Hardy, her death figured as a "swift fleeing" (40). In its anti-elegiac effect, Emma's rapid departure traces a subjectivity that does not want to be contained by Hardy's desire or to be made available to an elegiac myth of preserved intimacy.

In this respect, there is most likely some resonance between Hardy's real-life remembrances of Emma and the difficult mode of memory practiced in his elegies. Among the oddest details in the background of these poems is Hardy's own biographical experimentation with nostalgia in and around the time he wrote them. In the spring after Emma's death, having already written much of the elegiac series *Poems of 1912–13*, Hardy would revisit many of the natural sites associated with their real-life courtship that loom so large in his elegiac landscape. During much the same time, as David Gewanter has observed, Hardy carefully studied his wife's notebooks and made the self-interested decision to destroy a particular volume of what he called her "diabolical diaries." The volume, which had been titled "What I think of my Husband," most likely made for uncomfortable reading, putting Hardy into much the same position Emma had found herself in while reading *Jude the Obscure*. It is something of a literary historical irony that Emma's infamous campaign against her husband's novel, which had made its case for liberalizing divorce laws by drawing recognizably from details of their own unhappy marriage, had anticipated his own private decision to destroy some of her writings.

The writings Hardy did preserve, from a notebook entitled *Some Recollections*, offered him a glimpse of the sentimental and enthusiastic young woman he had married before she had become disenchanted with her husband and his literary life, and Gewanter concludes that these writings reinforced Hardy's own mournful and selective memory of the Emma he wished to remember in his elegies. Written in "conversation and collaboration" with Emma's personal notebooks, then, the elegies imagine the relationship as recoverable in large part because they focus on a time Hardy could wish to recover.[25] This all might suggest a biographical basis for Hardy's elegies as subjectively recuperative acts of mourning and selective fantasies of reciprocity. But to follow this line of thought is perhaps also to underestimate the extent to which the breaks in reciprocity inform almost every recognition of Emma in these poems, as well as the poetic patterning by which the other is inscribed consistently in opposition to lyrical voice and the manifest desires of the poet figure. We do not need to speculate on how much of a bad conscience Hardy might have developed over his decision to burn his wife's less-balanced, or simply less-flattering, diaries to observe that these poems often allude to Emma's voiceless (should we say muted?) complaint against her husband. Whether it is death or her husband's willful suppression of her voice that has rendered her silent, Emma's accusative stance survives the denial of its more overt expression.

To illustrate further Hardy's strangely poetical use of his own alienated marriage, I want to build on one of Gewanter's central and most persuasive points. Observing Hardy's conflicted reactions to a passage from *Some Recollections* in which Emma remembers that at their first meeting she thought Hardy "much older than he was" (to which Hardy had penciled defensively in the margins, "he being tired," later suppressing his notation) and also recalls that "[a]t first I was not greatly interested in him, for the church matters were paramount," Gewanter makes a strong case that Hardy's selective revisionings have been put in the service of largely idealized modes of memory.[26] It was quite possibly against the implicit charge that Emma had been "not greatly interested" in him that Hardy attempted to incorporate a revised version of this detail into his biography. In the original typescript for the biography, Hardy had in fact accurately recorded her words and then with what Gewanter calls a stroke of "some petulance perhaps" (195) crossed out Emma's "not" in order to make her "greatly interested in him" (*Some Recollections* 56). A later revision went a step further and declared, with ventriloquist virtuosity, "At first, though I was equally interested in him, the church matters were paramount"—only to have Hardy cross out his own use of "equally," perhaps realizing it was too wishful a word. Including a section from Emma's memoir in his ghost-written *Life and Work of Thomas Hardy*, the poet settled on "though I was interested in him," a clause that when attached to the qualification about the priority of church matters, appears to preserve the basic sense of her observation.[27] More than giving evidence of Hardy's troubled debt to Emma, his temporary insistence in the biography that they were "equally interested" emerges in the elegies as an experimental hypothesis referring not only to an early history of reciprocated interest, but to a more general mutuality of perspective in a mythical earlier time Hardy seeks now to renew. Inasmuch as the demise of love in Hardy's real-life marriage may have been a catalyst for his visions of reciprocated love, we have not traveled all that far from Gewanter's argument. What I want to stress about Hardy's alienated past, however, is its bearing on the poetry, where it is persistently figured as an aporia in his imaginative and retrospective relationship to Emma. In other words, the very distance between Hardy's reciprocal account of his former love for his wife and his awareness of the negative realization of that love over time indicates, even perhaps assigns a permanent place for, the other apart from the self and its desires.

Throughout these elegies, Emma is opposed to Hardy's vision (and re-visioning), to all his efforts to "gain one glimpse" of her, even in a past incarnation. What she does remind him of—as in the poem "After a Journey," where she appears to speak from her distant state—is the irrevocable *di-vision* that has marred their relationship in life as in death:

> Yes: I have re-entered your olden haunts at last;
>   Through the years, through the dead scenes I have tracked you;
> What have you now found to say of our past—
>   Scanned across the dark space wherein I have lacked you?
> Summer gave us sweets, but autumn wrought *division?*
>   Things were not lastly as firstly well
>   With us twain, you tell?
> But all's closed now, despite Time's derision. (9–16; emphasis added)

In short, their divisiveness is de-visioning, opposing itself to all the visual metaphors of retrieval through which the poet would track dead scenes and scan dark spaces. Throughout Hardy's elegies, vision competes with the conceit of listening.[28] With regard to this same passage, Gewanter offers a rather ingenious reading of an act of listening that would precede the second stanza, arguing that Hardy's "yes" resembles his own conversational writing style in letters and thus offers itself as a response, perhaps to words Emma has implicitly spoken in the space between stanzas 1 and 2.[29] We might well imagine the second stanza as a gentle retort to Emma's voice in *Some Recollections*—offered, as it were, from the midst of Hardy's scrupulous reading of his dead wife's words, a response akin perhaps to Hardy's accounting for Emma's observation that he looked older than he was when she first met him with the highly plausible explanation, offered in her voice, "he being tired." But Hardy's conversational form has another, grimmer precedent. For the Hardy who inquires "What have you now found to say of our past," sounds a lot like Hamlet melancholically taunting the skull of Yorick: "Where be your gibes *now*, your gambols, your songs, your flashes of merriment that were wont to set the table on a roar? Not one *now* to mock your own grinning?" (5.1.175–77, emphasis added). By echoing Hamlet's "now," in which the deictic declaration of the contemporary moment insults the uselessly absent dead, Hardy similarly draws attention to the irrevocable divide of time that will not permit a former and lively adversary (as Yorick to the court, so Emma is to Hardy) to speak as she was "wont." And as Hamlet ironically imagines sending Yorick as emissary to his lady to "tell her" (5.1.178) that she must someday arrive at death, Hardy also permits Emma's silenced being to send him a message: "Things were not firstly as lastly well / With us twain, you tell?" (14–15).

All of this has been a hard lesson to learn, for time itself would permit Hardy to forget the former lack of reciprocity and to remember more fondly. Hardy's elegies often work by subtle twists of expectation, and I would suggest that, according to the syntactical flow of the second stanza of "After a Journey," we want initially to read the last line, "But all's closed now, despite Time's derision" (16), as if derision referred to the mockery death makes of all human efforts to avoid it—whether one has in mind, as Hamlet does, the effort of the lawyer, the land-buyer, or Alexander himself to survive mortality through accumulated cultural capital, or perhaps, less ambitiously, the example of a woman such as Emma, who if she could still be heard from the beyond the grave might signify a fuller mode of reciprocal memory.[30] But according to Hardy's surprisingly anti-elegiac turn—and it is the "despite" clause that insists upon this contrastive meaning—the derision of time must refer not to death's final closure but to temporal endurance itself.

Surviving brings with it, if only through the subjective endurance of desire, a promise of renewal, teasing the poet with the possibility of relationship, which even if defeated by present circumstances would be compensated for in memory. Part of what the poet has to unlearn, then, are the compensatory mechanisms of mourning, which have historically misrepresented the real history of relationship. Hardy refers us to the conventional procedure of elegiac idealization, but suggests that what all such compensatory remembrance leaves out may be precisely what it must most remember. For to choose selectively one's memories of the other already implies a defensiveness that is itself part of the coping process: what is left out or repressed contributes to the illusive momentum of commemorative idealization in which the dead become so much larger than life that an ordinary mourner might no longer regret their absence from a world too small to contain them.

Though Hardy is less prone than most elegists (perhaps only because his memory will not permit him the luxury) to be naïvely idealistic about the dead, his nostalgic remembrances of the harmonious period in his marriage do sometimes incline toward elegiac idealization. More often, however, he avoids conventional solutions and represents Emma as dissenting from idealization, thus also from any reciprocal memory the poet might imagine for the couple. In their late domestic life, Emma took often to retiring while company visited or immediately thereafter, and in a poem such as "Without Ceremony" Hardy conflates this habit of withdrawing unannounced with the well-kept secret of her approaching death:

> It was your way, my dear,
> To vanish without a word
> When callers, friends, or kin
> Had left, and I hastened in
> To rejoin you, as I inferred. (1–5)

How much reprimand Hardy took from those real-life occasions of his wife's apparent moodiness we can only speculate, but what is striking in the poem is the pathetic claim that he never became accustomed to it, that each time, it would appear, he hastened to her only to find her already departed. The quick return is a sign of an original eagerness for reciprocity, as if he had wishfully "inferred" her desire as synonymous to his own. According to the odd syntax, the object of inference is in fact buried in anticipation of Hardy's interpretive act, so that the inference itself is a belated and impossible recollection of motive. Though it is clear that Hardy wrongly conjectured that he would return to find her, the grammatical ambiguity suggests that in rejoining her he had also inferred (again wrongly and thus adding to the pathos) a shared desire. Throughout *Poems of 1912–13*, Hardy admits to having often guessed his wife's intentions, and since his inferences are so frequently depicted as wrong, these poems make suspect all those remembrances in which he too-confidently represents the girl Emma once was, intuiting her voice in light of their former happiness.

Doing without Ceremony

Reading *Poems of 1912–13* in order, we arrive at "Without Ceremony" through "The Going," so that Emma's habit of vanishing "without a word" seems a rather deliberate revision of her failure in the earlier poem to "utter a wish for a word" (10). Hardy characterizes her—in death as in life, or in life as in death—through her aversion to address. Seen in this light, "Without Ceremony" reads as Hardy's attempt to exonerate himself before the charges of failed communication that arose from the melancholic insights of "The Going."

In its anti-elegiac attack on the sentiment of good feeling, "Without Ceremony" exposes what is elsewhere so well covered up by elegiac conventions—namely, the complexity and ambivalence of attachment.[31] At the same time, by investigating the formal closure a mourner achieves through his parting addresses to the other, the poem thoroughly demystifies the elegiac ceremony of departure.

Elegies, and Hardy's are no exception, are belated "good-byes," whether they embrace the logic of severance and its symbolic accoutrements or whether they anti-elegiacally interrogate the wishes behind the good-byes and denounce the psychological work of mourning as mere severance of feeling. If we read "The Going" through a slightly anachronistic perspective that includes the larger apparatus of Hardy's ethics of mourning and also remembers "Without Ceremony" (which was composed a few months later), much of the earlier poem's anti-elegiac persuasiveness obtains through Hardy's apparent attachment to a ceremony he no longer believes in. Less severe in its anti-elegiac fervor than "Without Ceremony," the earlier poem is the stronger one not so much for its ambivalence about the dead as for its ambivalence about its own demystifying inclinations. There is a strange pathos to "The Going" as Hardy mournfully accuses Emma of never bidding "good-bye" (8) and laments a lack of closure that might have occurred as a real-life reconciliation. Ordinarily, mourning as a praxis of psychological coping might offer the one who grieves the opportunity to reach a compromise with the past and its unpleasant persistence, but Hardy exposes the contrived hopefulness behind such a hypothetical accomplishment by treating mourning as an implicit, yet admittedly impossible, wish (since no such wish was ever uttered between Emma and him in real life) for the renewal of the couple's former love.

With regard to such impossible wishfulness, much of Hardy's ostensible anti-elegiac labor appears yet again to occur through his revision of Tennyson and the ceremonial forms of broken "companionship." In Tennyson the event of the break is largely the work of an allegorized death that wraps Hallam "formless in the fold" and, according to Tennyson's extremely pathetic figure of address, has "dulled the murmur of thy lip" (22:16). At all times, but especially in the strongly anti-elegiac middle sections 50–58, the reader of *In Memoriam* is under the impression that Tennyson's apostrophe draws its strength from having been predicated upon a former reciprocity.[32] According to an elegiac pathos that delusively preserves and extends relationship as if it might still be the thing it once was, Tennyson does not doubt that Hallam continues to speak to him; it is only that the poet has trouble hearing him. It takes Tennyson a rather long time to concede the fact that his relationship with the dead friend cannot be as it was when Hallam was living. Only after he succumbs in section 50 to a wish that Hallam should be near him in the many aspects of his desolation does the impossibility of such an intimacy impress itself upon him, and at this point he finally interrogates his own wishfulness by asking whether "we indeed desire the dead / Should still be near us at our side" (51:1–2). For the idealized dead who watch over us, positioned like Lycidas as guardian spirits, would watch over us "[w]ith larger other eyes than ours" and thus would see those things about us we would rather not have seen (51:15). This extended narrative unit of 50–58 is the closest Tennyson comes to attributing to the other an accusative function on the order of Hardy's technique of elegiac blaming, and it is also the moment in which Tennyson casts elegiac hope finally as mere wishfulness, first declaring himself but an "infant crying in the night: / An infant crying for the light," one who has "no language but a cry" (54:18–20), and then beginning the very next section by exposing the religious premise of elegiac consolation as a transparent wish ("The wish, that of the living whole / No life may fail beyond the grave" [55:1–2]), clung to by the poet only because it coincides with his desperation.

Whereas Tennyson arrives at his statement of departure in section 51 by having clung so obdurately to his faith in their relationship before finally admitting that he must relinquish the dead or be watched over by him in a most unpleasant manner, in "The Going" Hardy laments the absence of formal parting with Emma by alluding to and revising the "dulled" sound Tennyson hears on Hallam's "lip":

> Never to bid good-bye,
>   Or *lip* me the softest call,
> Or utter a wish for a word. . . . (8–10; emphasis added)

Behind Tennyson, Hardy hears the more remote echo of *Hamlet*, whose hero muses elegiacally over Yorick's skull and makes his absent "lips" a metonymy not only for absent voice but for intimacy itself. Hamlet first declares, "Here hung those lips that I have kissed I know not how oft," before considering Yorick's lost voice and asking, "Where be your gibes now?" (5.1.174–75). If Hardy finds himself in a Hamletic situation, wherein intimacy does not signify a contemporary or even recent condition of ethical interaction but a distant and, as it were, lost possibility, he simultaneously attributes to himself a vigilance (as extraordinary as Tennyson's or as Freud's dreaming father's), a state in which he would certainly have heard a "good-bye" and can confidently assert that no such communication has taken place. The irony is that Emma's failure to provide even a faint call, such as the one Hallam appears to utter, inspires Hardy's heightened attention. As Hardy listens for Emma to have uttered her "wish for a word," he approaches the question of her intentionality, speculating on a renewal she too might have wanted. In "Without Ceremony," Hardy figures his diminishing trust in reciprocity by representing Emma as having intentionally refused all ceremony of departure: "Your meaning seems to me / Just as it used to be: / 'Good-bye is not worth while!'" (13–15). Quoting Emma's past intentions and remembering her habit of leaving as an analogy for sudden death, the poet appears to gain an interpretive ability that corresponds to her control over the meaning of her death. Emma's "swift style" (12) of departure attributes to her an intention in dying and thus responsibility for the rupture that has defined their relationship. Interpreting her habit of disappearing, Hardy appears to achieve a paradoxical consolation whereby he is alienated from his own responsibility. Though at first impression we might be hard pressed to see the poem's presentation of Emma's stark opposition to the ceremony of good-byes as a species of wish fulfillment, it is just that—a radically negative form of wish fulfillment through which the poet intuits his wife's implicit intentions to be so greatly in opposition to his own that his inability to respond to her seems unavoidable, almost an ontological testament to the difference between them.

What a poetic persona wishes, however, is not necessarily what a poem means—in aesthetic or ethical terms. For even as Hardy embraces this negative fantasy (of denied reciprocation), he exposes the ethical lie behind our constructs of reciprocal responsibility—the premise that one is only responsible to the other to the degree that she makes her intentions known or expresses her desires. This sense of contractual reciprocity may be necessary for many forms of legal, social, and political dealings in the liberal society, but as such, reciprocity always involves a reduction of the ethical responsibility for the other that exists before and beyond the limits of knowledge. By the strict terms of contractual reciprocity, the other is also responsible for her fate, whether she endures alienated marriage or death. Reciprocity not only permits but encourages a distribution of blame, since any principle of exchange must also allow for the passing of blame.

Elegists are very good at sharing blame, even when they make their charges in the name of the other, but the apportioning of blame is often a convenience through which the mourner begins to work through grief and the specters of responsibility. If we recall the example of Bernard Williams's driver who accidentally hits and kills a child with his lorry, what is ethically striking about the scenario is that Williams attaches such importance to the lorry driver's sense of blame. Despite the almost immediate attempts of others to comfort the driver by moving from the "state of feeling" in which he claims the special onus of agent-regret, we would have "some doubt . . . about a driver who too blandly or readily moved" to the position advocated by his comforters.[33] The sharing of blame and consolation alike may have everything to do with mitigating the feeling of responsibility, but it is an especially cynical or desperate form of grief that would apportion the largest share of the blame to the victim herself, as if the lorry driver took special comfort in reminding himself that the child impulsively ran out into the road and so brought his misfortune upon himself. It is hard to escape this connotation of grief in "Without Ceremony," in which the other's own intentions seem an excuse for the subject's failure, and largely for this reason the poem lacks the ethical complexity of "The Going," in which every potential act of distributing blame seems driven by, but also answerable to, the poet's acute sense of uncancellable responsibility. What is most valuable in the lesser poem, "Without Ceremony," is the critique of the elegist's too-conventional efforts—pursued through the presumptions of elegiac address and the elegy's ceremonial forms of reciprocity—to be relieved of his responsibility for the other.

The Orphean Specter of Hardy's Mourning

What elegy also discerns—at least elegy as Hardy handles it—is the basic presumption that inheres in address, especially in its apostrophic function. So often the elegiac address to the other occurs as a demand rather than as a response, as a monologic vision imposed upon the ostensible situation of dialogue. Though the disappearance of the other is the most literal reason for such a phenomenon, insofar as any speech act is conceived as ordering the world it addresses, all language stands potentially, by the means of projective and aggressive acts of personification, to conform the element or object of alterity to a psychic system that accounts for subjectivity as a function of economy. For instance, in *The Future of an Illusion*, in a remarkable chapter that is itself an exercise in address, Freud recognizes the dangers of his own monologism and so invents an interlocutor who mistrusts Freud's argument, an interlocutor much like the many adversaries of Socrates in Plato whose inevitable fate—and indeed true function—is to be overcome. Freud's interlocutor objects to the thesis that the humanization of nature derives from humanity's helplessness and our need to put dreaded forces in relation to us, arguing instead that the motives of primitive humanity are superfluous since it is the very "nature" of primitive thought, apart from the psychological question, to project subjective existence outwards. Human speech is the sign of a psychic need for mastery over the environment, and much of the emergent anthropological theory about primitive culture seemed in Freud's time merely a myth-making version of this intuitive premise.

Closer to mourning's peculiar concerns, the hermeneutic of psychological mastery informs Freud's discussion of the trauma, with the unconscious repetitions of an unpleasurable event serving as an attempt to establish some power over an event that caught the self unprepared. This traumatic motive might even account for Hardy's many poetic repetitions of his loss, except that Hardy's striving for the upper hand remains at the rhetorical surface of his elegiac poetry. By treating Emma's death and her failed communication as if they were her choices, Hardy might seem to provide himself with an opportunity for interpretively mastering her departure. More generally, however, such elegiacally motivated behavior recalls an impulse at the center of our conventions of address, one dramatically illustrated by the personifying tendencies of apostrophe.

At some deep level, apostrophe traces the ethical premises of language itself. Whereas we may suspect with a philosopher such as Buber that any too-elaborately impersonalized or abstracted language loses its sense of urgency as a speech act, strictly personalizing language may veil a monologic, narrow view of the world in which the other is treated as an object to be read projectively. If apostrophe is a convention of address that as often takes for its audience the inanimate world, a loosely personified nature, or an abstract principle or event, it seems only appropriate to ask ourselves how (or how well) modes of address based in a personal context differ from those modes of address focused on the impersonal—for instance, when Milton first addresses a natural world personified under the religious conceit of paganism ("Where were ye nymphs?"), before proceeding to his more elaborate personifications of Christian justice in the figure of Saint Peter and of Lycidas as a deity who will benevolently protect those who wander at sea from this peril, which is the very sign of the natural world. According to its pastoral logic, the poem translates personal significances into an impersonal realm where they can be made meaningful, but it does so by treating the absent other through an abstracted mode of address.

Similarly, since Tennyson addresses with equal ease Christ (section 1), yew trees (section 2), sorrow (section 3), time (section 13), and the ship carrying Hallam's body (section 14) before turning more persistently to his elegiac conversations with the dead Hallam, the element of personal address in his apostrophe represents not a merely residual form of past habits of interpersonal communication, but an active personifying impulse that confronts the specter of impersonalism evoked by the other's absence in death. In other words, the dialectic between personalism and impersonalism cuts two ways: on the one hand, by speaking to the alienated, impersonalized other as though he were determined by intimacy, the elegist personifies alterity in order to master it; and on the other, the resistance of the impersonal world (or to use Freud's word, "nature") checks the subsuming and personalizing propensity of grief as a mode of subjective consciousness.

Since elegiac address is always in part constructed by its implication in compensatory patterns of thought, to be attentive even in a state of impossible reciprocity might be to correct death's insult by granting real authority to the apparently diminished other. The attentiveness of elegiac address, in which the speaker must build and at the same time inhabit the role of listener, would repair reciprocity, even while admitting that reciprocity necessarily lapses—has in fact already lapsed—in its encounter with alterity. Paradoxically, as Ricoeur himself might argue, it is the very function of the other to inspire the balancing of ethical relationship or, in elegiac terms, the compensatory fantasy of reciprocity. In elegy, this seems true even, or perhaps most significantly, when the other frustrates the speaker's attentions. When Emma is referred to in "The Going" as departing from her husband "calmly, as if indifferent quite" (3), she is defined as thwarting his intimate imaginings and as altogether alienating the personalist musings of lyrical voice in which the other might have been obtained, at least as an ideal, through the erstwhile earnestness of the poet's longings. The belatedness of the poet's own desires coincides with the poem's oddly posthumous voice, by which I mean simply that there is little possibility here that the poet's lyrical imaginings could aptly signify the reciprocity for which he longs.

The basic disjuncture between the present possibility of lyrical voice and the impossible, even indifferent past it represents is captured nicely in "Your Last Drive," as Hardy remembers a trip Emma took past the same graveyard she was to be buried in a week later. Hardy explores the occasion as a missed opportunity for his attentiveness and elects to represent Emma, rather like Freud's accusatorily burning boy, as having full knowledge of her fate. Lamenting his

failure to have accompanied Emma on this ordinary trip, Hardy accuses himself of being absent from a scene that might have yielded knowledge of Emma's
intentions and helped him anticipate her death. Yet this extraordinary and revisionary attentiveness is as futile as it may be self-serving, since Hardy appears
likely to have used the time to accuse her of having surpassed his judgment
("You are past love, praise, indifference, blame" [30]) and having abandoned
him to her own imperceptibility, her symbolic impersonality. The charge of
"indifference" functions oddly in line 30, since it might as easily refer to his set
of conflicting psychological responses to her as to the state of her obvious
indifference. His own potential indifference—a figure for the therapeutic
goal of psychic detachment of which he is already skeptical—hardly seems
relevant in light of Emma's monumental indifference to him. Though Hardy
imitates the angry attitude of many mourners, he simultaneously caricatures
the self-importance of such a stance. The beloved has severed the very premise
of reciprocity upon which the mourner's outrage depends, and has done so
long before the poet had occasion to explore his own lingering and ambivalent
attachment. Indifference in "Your Last Drive" is at best an ironic site for
reciprocity.

In the very next poem in the series, "The Walk," Hardy recounts a walk he
took alone during Emma's illness, permitting his solitude on this occasion to
characterize a more general willingness to neglect her memory even while she
was alive: "I did not mind, / Not thinking of you as left behind" (7–8). The
mournful occasion of this remembrance is developed further in a second stanza
where Hardy takes another walk after her death and considers the "difference"
between his two moments of museful strolling, as this second occasion demands
from the poet remembrance of an event not included in the walk of the first
stanza. Hardy's mournfully guilty conscience is objectified in the second stanza
by "the look of a room on returning thence" (16), the emptiness of the room
seeming a cruel fulfillment of the poet's abandoning thoughts. But of course
the note of retrospective guilt has already been sounded in the phrase "Not
thinking of you as left behind." According to the retrospective reading, "as left
behind" is not simply a narrative descriptor but rather the implicit object of the
poet's phrasing of his nonthought—or, in paraphrase: *I was not yet thinking of
you as someone I had abandoned.* He has not thought of what it feels like from
Emma's perspective to be left behind, nor of the moment in which she will be
permanently abandoned to death. And this failure of foresight has resulted in
her unwitnessed departure.

There is an unmistakable allusion here to Orpheus's infamous example of unsuccessful mourning. As the archetypal elegist, Orpheus sings so persuasively as to win from the gods the second chance of desire for which any mourner might futilely hope, but, when, in his eagerness for the other, he looks back to view Eurydice, Orpheus defeats his own desire by violating the one condition placed upon him. At the very moment in which reciprocity would be restored, Orpheus's backward glance ironically abandons Eurydice to Hades. There is no small irony in the fact that this backward glance is only to be expected from a man who has won such an opportunity for retrieval by obdurately holding to what he should already have abandoned.

In this sense, Orpheus's gesture is a figure for mourning itself, and it almost appears as though the permission the gods have given Orpheus to enact a singular exception against the rule of death had been intended to convey the impossibility of his wishfulness, as if his posthumous glimpse of Eurydice were all that he had the right to hope for. As such, the glimpse itself stands for the mourner's absent witness to the moment of death, and since the moment Orpheus actually catches sight of her is also the moment of Eurydice's second death, his story figures mourning itself as implicated in the demise of the other. In part, the story well anticipates Freud's assessment of every mourner's characteristic reluctance to surrender a formerly pleasurable attachment, and might almost be read as an admonition to submit to the reality principle. Yet the Orpheus story troubles as much as it anticipates the Freudian definition of successful mourning, teasing us with the possibilities of a success (what if he had not looked back and had regained her?) that is entirely opposed to Freud's advocation of the realistic work of mourning. In its pure unrealistic pathos, the Orpheus myth accuses the mourner of his own attentiveness, which has been both excessive and inadequate to the task of recuperation he has pursued.

As Melissa F. Zeiger has established, the Orpheus story is part of the allusive texture of Hardy's elegies, perhaps most evidently in an elegy Hardy began at the time of *Poems of 1912–13* but finished years later. In "The Shadow on the Stone" (1916), the poet is wandering by the Druid stone when he is suddenly convinced that an unnamed woman (presumably Emma) is standing behind him.[34] As if he has learned Orpheus's lesson only too well or perhaps recalled his own history of disappointed wishfulness, he refuses to turn and risk a final loss, keeping his head, as he says, "unturned lest [his] dream should fade" (24). Reading the elegiac premise of recuperation in the Orpheus story, Hardy's poem suggests that the story's melancholic end and its mournful hopefulness are one. Orpheus's too eager desire is really just a figure for the necessary defeat of desire in the face of death: all mourners turn too early in their search for the other because their wishful visions are substitutes for presence or mere extensions of their own necessarily appropriative desires. In Ovid's rendering of the story, it is of great significance that, during the moment when Orpheus turns his loving eyes (*flexit amans oculos* [10:57]) and Eurydice fades, he tries to confirm his vision by grasping for her (*bracchiaque intendens prendique et prendere certans* [10:58]), but the other remains in mourning only an impossible hypothesis.[35] Whether the mourner wishes symbolically to have witnessed the other's death or merely to glimpse and hold the other once more, his subjective mode of vision is, by definition, neglectful of the mystery, elusiveness, and alterity of the dead one he has loved.

Very much attuned to this Ovidian premise, the Hardy persona of "The Shadow on the Stone" elects not to defeat the other's value by visionary grasping, deciding that he will "not unvision / A shape which, somehow, there may be" (19–20). The self-accusing line "I did not mind, / Not thinking of you as left behind" (7–8) from "The Walk" is clearly alluded to here when Hardy declares, "I thought her behind my back" (9). If the Orphean allusion is more overt in the later poem, it also prepares us for the final paradoxical and wishful assertion that the woman remains a figure of desire only insofar as she is not turned to or grasped. In a sense, Hardy answers Orpheus's dilemma—his desire divided between erotic urgency and elegiac remembrance—by letting the symbolic ascent from Hades continue unabated. It may well be, Hardy suggests, that there is nothing to the elegist's belief in retrieval ("I would not turn my head to discover / That there was nothing in my belief" [15–16]), but the hopefulness is all. The fact of the other's nothingness is the very thing Ovid's Orpheus confirms when he tries to embrace the already ghostly Eurydice and "seizes nothing but the unhappy yielding air" (*nil nisi cedentes infelix arripit auras* [10:59]). According to the Latin, *aura* ("air") carries with it the humanizing connotation of "breath," as Eurydice seems here to exhale her last breath once more. But it is also possible that Ovid's irony is even more severe, since *aura*, which is also the "breath of fortune," could signify a fortune that had remained at Orpheus's back before he turned with such unhappy or unfortunate results (both connotations are part of the Latin *infelix*) to possess it. If Ovid emphasizes the violence of Orpheus's act with the verb *arripere*, which means not just "to grasp" but "to drag into court" or "to seize violently," Hardy refuses to render as harsh a verdict against the foolishness of desire. Since Hardy's Orphean figure never turns or grasps the beloved he awaits, the poem permits the abiding pathos of incomplete desire or unaccomplished grief, allowing his mourner to retain at least the hint of the other's immemorial value, be she Eurydice or Emma.

Along similar lines, Hardy frequently associates the valuation of Emma with the natural impossibility of appearing. So when Emma makes the poet of "The Going" leave his house and "think for a breath it is you I see" (16), Hardy's eventual choice of *breath* over the word *instant* from an earlier draft of the poem may have been inspired by the play on *air* in Ovid's telling of the story.[36] Reading in the other direction, from "breath" to "air," Hardy creates an ambiguity that allows Emma, like Eurydice, to be withheld in and by the impersonality of air. This is also much the sense of "The Voice," in which Hardy's desire projects itself onto an infelicitous natural scene:

> Or is it only the breeze, in its listlessness
> Travelling across the wet mead to me here,
> You being ever dissolved to wan wistlessness,
> Heard no more again far or near? (9–12)

According to the Ovidian resonance, the mourner delusively believes he has heard Emma, but thinks better of his fancy, deciding her hypothetical breath must be just a "breeze." Whereas Ovid's Eurydice dissipates at the ascendant moment of Orpheus's visionary desire, Hardy more soberly imagines her dissolution into air ("being ever dissolved to wan wistlessness") as having already occurred in the absolute past. Emma's utter unobtainability is very much in keeping with the impersonal function of nature as an opposition to human desires. The implication is that personal grief can never be a measure of the absent other, and the impersonal, natural phenomena of the world will prove this so. Accordingly, "The Shadow on the Stone" oddly revisions the renunciation of grief and makes it appear that the poet has done the right thing in keeping Emma behind him. Through his anti-Orphean gesture of refusing to turn, he ironically preserves her, but he does so only by surrendering the eagerness of his desire and yielding to an impersonalism in which the poet seems symbolically to have no thought of what he has left behind. Whereas Ovid's Orpheus is extremely aware of his loss, becoming so self-conscious of his desire that he defeats it, the Hardy persona seems oblivious to what he is about to lose.

Perhaps most perverse of all Hardy's rationalizations of human loss is "The Convergence of the Twain," written in commemoration of the victims of the

Titanic in 1912, the year of Emma's death and of many of Hardy's finest elegies to her. Historical catastrophe and personal loss intersect outrageously in the central conceit of this poem in which the meeting of the Titanic with the fateful iceberg is compared to an awful marriage. As the Titanic meets her "sinister mate" (19) the poem recalls the "intimate welding of their later history" (27) as though the disaster signified less a potential for error informing all human technologies than the basic folly of culture as an endeavor to defeat nature. Though there is some ironic play on personal modes of attachment in calling the ship's encounter with the iceberg an "intimate welding," all other vestiges of personally connoted elegiac voice have been suppressed in this caricature of an epithalamium. According to the poem's resurgent sense of nature, signified by the iceberg, which grows in "shadowy silent distance" (24) while awaiting the ship, personal attachments should yield to their impersonal fate as though to a moral lesson. The poet's desire seems slightly less reconciled to stoical yieldings in "The Shadow on the Stone," where his plaintive rebellion against impersonalism is vestigial, signified by his pathetic inability to act on his own behalf. Since even in this very cool later elegy of 1917, written several years after Emma's death, the poet's absorption in the impersonal world of nature has not well protected him against loss, longing returns once more, albeit less explicitly, as a fantasy of personal reciprocation.

By subtle contrast, a poem such as "The Spell of the Rose" concedes from the start that the play of personal feeling will inform the objective lessons of fate. In this poem, Emma's having planted rose bushes before her death means that the poet has to trace her significance amidst a natural world that proves her absence. By deftly muting the pathetic fallacy, Hardy dismantles the mythic structure whereby nature so often serves, in poems such as "Adonais," the fantasy of reciprocity. Typically in a pathetic fallacy nature mirrors the poet's grief and objectifies his wishful vigilance on behalf of the dead, but here Hardy enfolds such a transparently poetical device within the closer range of personal history by recalling his intentions to build Emma a hall and "[p]lant roses love shall feed upon" (6). Of course the roses were never planted, and the memory of unplanted roses makes the poem rather straightforwardly an allegory for love as (un)enacted passion or deteriorated affection. The rose bush is the very sign of a failed reciprocity. Yet the poem, as one of only two poems in the series written largely from the posthumous perspective of Emma, has not altogether surrendered the hope for reciprocity. Even as she recalls an incident that proves their inability to reenact their early love for each other in the later portion of their marriage, this hypothetical Emma is someone who cares enough about reciprocity to note its absence.

Along these lines, Emma defeats their alienated history when she sympathetically understands his failure as theirs ("And misconceits raised horrid shows, / And agonies came thereof" [20–21]), finding in their history of mutual misunderstanding an explanation for subsequent miseries. Ultimately, the poem fantasizes, Emma would have liked to "mend these miseries" (22), and Hardy even imagines her act of gardening as having been performed for his belatedly appreciative eyes, as if she had planted the rose bush to be a sign of the poet's returning—and somewhat revisionary—wish for reciprocity. According to this poem's allegorical artifice and its double bracketing of the poet's own voice, Emma attributes to Hardy from within the voice he attributes to her a wish for restored relationship. Her act of mending offers itself as a corrective hypothesis in tension with the persistently melancholic posture of Hardy's grief, pronounced so starkly at the end of "The Going" (where the poet concedes that "[a]ll's past amend" [36]). Here, in the "The Spell of the Rose," Emma's wish would even repair the divisiveness of their past—"'This,' said I, / 'May end divisions dire and wry, / And long-drawn days of blight'" (26–28).

If "The Spell of the Rose" further elaborates Hardy's strategy of making Emma's imagined intentions stand for his own surprise after her death (as if she had meant by leaving him to have this very effect), less typically for these elegies it also gives her a benevolent intention. When she designates her death as accidental rather than intentional, suggesting that she has been "called from earth—yea, called / Before my rose-bush grew" (29–30), Emma alludes to a transcendent, perhaps provident intention other than the merely sinister negation of desire so often attributed to her in Hardy's elegies. In this way, Emma's unrealized desire seems less conspicuously opposed to the poet's own:

> And would that now I knew
> What feels he of the tree I planted,
>   And whether, after I was called
>   To be a ghost, he, as of old,
>   Gave me his heart anew! (31–35)

According to these deceptively simple lines, Hardy discovers his own hopefulness by attributing it to Emma, and he makes the poem's fantasy imagining of the other stand as a difficult act of self-interpretation. Part of the pathos comes from what we must already presume—when Emma inquires as to whether her husband has surrendered himself to hope and given her "his heart anew," she acknowledges his wishfulness as already in place and gives it a value apart from anything it might practically achieve. As yet one more ironic figure of reciprocity, this moment nevertheless strikes a different note, Hardy's wish for reciprocation serving as a sign of the ethical relationship he has not yet forsaken, even though he has already failed it.

There is even sympathy for such sturdy impossibility in Emma's gentling vision of a nostalgic Hardy who "as of old" would give his heart "anew." In the simplified chronology of the three states of reciprocity I outlined at the top of this chapter (the reciprocity of their early love, the failed reciprocity of their later years of marriage, and the wishful restoration of reciprocity after her death), it was the older and not the latest state of relationship that signified affection, but one cannot literally give *anew as of old*, since newness, as Kierkegaard reminds us, is a condition that must exhaust itself in the present of experience, unable even to suggest meaningful repetition.[37] In "The Going," Hardy hints at this impossibility when he asks Emma why they did not seek "[t]hat time's renewal." Still, even if such renewal were once possible, it is no longer. Playing with the conventional temporal scheme of the elegy in which the invocation of nature cooperates with the hypothesis of renewal and a season of resurrection, Hardy says,

> We might have said,
> "In this bright spring weather
> We'll visit together
> Those places that once we visited." (32–35)

As it both reflects and melancholically suspends the elegiac consolation of springtime renewal, "The Going" locates a missed possibility within the history of relationship. Hardy is either incapable of embracing, or more simply unwilling to embrace, a redemption that depends entirely on retrospection. By contrast, the speaker of "The Spell of the Rose" hopes to renew hopefulness by inverting the temporality of redemption and foregoing a "renewal" that is *revisionist* in the most falsifying sense of the word, instead figuring Emma's desire as prospectively open-ended, much as it was when she and the poet first met. In her ignorance of Hardy's mind and of the future, Emma is positioned on the verge of a new state of knowledge in which she would be able to discern whether Hardy's heart is to be given anew. The pathetic force of her attention is ethically poignant, especially if we go so far as to argue that Hardy himself does not fully know whether his own heart has been given anew.

A Remembrance beyond Reproach

As the elegy cooperates with a cultural propensity for repairing identity's esteem and the damage done to the symbolic system, two principles inform all elegiac action—the hypotheses of retrieval and protection. Though surely Hardy understands these actions to be mere caricatures of the morally deliberated acts of which he was once capable, in the "The Spell of the Rose" he depicts an Emma who seems conciliatory and unreproachful, who permits him his symbolically recuperative action of tending to her rosebush. Still, the poem's real concern resides in the hypothesis of seeing the other properly. An Emma who would "end divisions dire and wry" (27) reflects the limits of Hardy's own capacity to conquer the divisions at the heart of relationship:

> Perhaps now blooms that queen of trees
>   I set but saw not grow,
>   And he, beside its glow—
> Eyes couched of the mis-vision that blurred me—
>   Ay, there beside that queen of trees
>   He sees me as I was, though sees
>   Too late to tell me so! (36–42)

These last lines extend the fantasy of reciprocity that runs throughout *Poems of 1912–13* to a point where the poet's elegiac vulnerability seems completely reversed. If Hardy has previously sought in "The Going" an Orphean "glimpse" of Emma that would figure his own recuperated identity in the recognition of her eyes, Emma's longing is now made dependent on his recognition.

There is hardly a more pathetic touch in the whole of Hardy's canon than this Orphean play upon second vision. As Emma longs to be seen as she truly was, she reminds us of all those absent others who are threatened, according to poetic convention, by what Alexander Pope calls in the "Elegy to the Memory of an Unfortunate Lady" the poet's "closing eyes" (79). Whereas Pope anxiously refers us to the conventional anxiety of elegiac representation—that even if the poet could sustain a lifetime of grief as a sign of reciprocity, the grief which has become tantamount to the poet's remembrance must die with the poet[38]—the original for such anxious remembering is of

course Orpheus's extraordinary poetic agency, which only defeats itself by becoming too urgent:

> They were near the margin, near the upper land,
> When he, afraid that she might falter, eager to see her,
> Looked back in love, and she was gone, in a moment.
> Was it he, or she, reaching out arms and trying
> To hold or to be held, and clasping nothing
> But empty air?[39]

There is a confusion here between vision and the act of reaching, as well as
about who is doing which. If we proceed from the perspective of Orpheus's
gaze, then his vision is the matter of most import; but as soon as we picture
Eurydice reaching for him in order to be held, the question of what she apprehends through her seeing must be included in the scene's denotation of responsibility. When Hardy speaks for Emma in "The Spell of the Rose," he
also speaks for the muted voice of Eurydice in Ovid's story, who might similarly have remarked upon Orpheus's eyes as "couched of the mis-vision that
blurred me" (39). Of course Hardy's "mis-vision" refers not to the other's
second demise, but to the poet's past mistaken views of who or what Emma
was. Yet the unmistakable Ovidian resonance necessarily refers us (as a conflation of retrieval with revision) to the poet's late revisionary efforts to see
the other, which include a presumptuous attempt to characterize Emma in
her own voice.

   In all of this, there is also an aspect of implicit reproach, a connotation of the
original Ovidian text made explicit in Rolfe Humphries's translation:

> Dying the second time,
> She had no reproach to bring against her husband,
> What was there to complain of? One thing, only:
> He loved her.
> [*iamque iterum moriens non est de coniuge quicquam*
> *questa suo (quid enim nisi se quereretur amatam?*)] (Humphries, 236; 10:60–61)

In the Latin there is a deliberate continuity between Eurydice's hypothetical
complaint (*questa*) and the narrator's interpretive interrogation of what she
could possibly have had to complain of (*quereretur*), as if Ovid needed to reiterate the point by implying that only the most ungrateful and querulous of
women would speak against Orpheus's tremendous act of faithfulness (indeed,

Ovid's mythic quarrel with women in general becomes overt later on when he describes what happens to Orpheus at the hands of the Thracian women). In substituting "reproach" for the more obvious "complaint," however, Humphries invokes a connotation that derives from the scene on the whole. To reproach is quite literally to "bring near again," but also, in its original connotation, to cast up a thing as though to bring it against a person. As a form of moral accusation, reproach is stronger than complaint for the simple reason that it already implies a legitimacy to its objection, that there is in fact something to be brought forward or near in order to make this charge. It could be argued, then, that Humphries slightly distorts Ovid by construing the connotation of a hypothetically legitimate objection from Eurydice's perspective, a possibility the Ovidian narrative clearly rejects in the end. But I would argue that what Humphries brings to the surface is the sense we have that Ovid's rhetorical overemphasis, in which he overtly declares that there would be no legitimacy to an objection offered from the perspective of Eurydice, is more a suppression of her dissenting perspective than an innocent profession of Orpheus's reproachless effort.

What Humphries's translation also brings to the surface is the narratological connotation according to which Eurydice, on the verge of surfacing in the upper world, is the very thing being brought near. In narrative terms alone, Eurydice is a sign of reproach; she is something being brought near as if her true function were to be brought against someone. Once she disappears, her "double death" stuns Orpheus, and we might read this as an allegory for grief and the futililty of the mourner's attempted retrieval. But according to the mythic story line, wherein the fictive status attributed to Eurydice is slightly more than a symbolic placeholder for the absent dead, she has become significant, even after her death, as an other with whom memory must still reckon. Her being brought near allows the reader to arrive (almost) at the meaning of this other as someone with a separate, even contrary, set of intentions, and Orpheus's successfully completed act of retrieval requires him finally to concede her right to object, even if it is to protest the retrieval itself (in this sense, a feminist reading of the Orpheus legend, such as Zeiger's, is much less in tension with the story than it might seem to the casual reader). Even in worrying about Eurydice's opinion, whether she meant blame or praise, Ovid credits Eurydice with making a moral claim upon Orpheus.[40] Since he has maintained desire in his grief (being unable to separate the two), Orpheus is almost able to grasp her again, but it is quite as if his turning toward her forces him for the first time to account for Eurydice's tremendous otherness and to apprehend a woman whose alterity includes also all the strange alterity of death. As desire turns to grief, Eurydice becomes obscure in the poet's vision, her voice muted to his ears. Even in these most simple facts of mourning, acknowledged by Orpheus for the first time, there is already a reproach from the other—who might be forgotten by the mourner, who is already less than she once was, who is accusing the one who would remember her of a responsibility for this diminution.

As Hardy plays, then, upon an Orphean topos in "The Spell of the Rose," Emma is not only "blurred" in the form of her ghostly reappearance, but obfuscated as the corollary to the poet's subjective, and indeed projective, properties of both visual perception and ethical imagination. As she speculates on what Hardy now sees and imagines that "he sees me as I was" (41), Emma seemingly possesses a self-understanding (what she truly "was") that the poet has been trying to approximate. Her idea of herself is that which absolutely cannot be revealed in the present tense of vision. Most of what prevents a more perceptive vision is not the poet's desire or even ability, but the fact that it is "too late." The emphasis is somewhat different in "Your Last Drive," where Hardy contemplates a look he might have gleaned from Emma's face as though it were a reprimand of the ethical distance to which he has become accustomed. In her state of irretrievable alterity, Emma will not know how many times Hardy visits this familiar haunt and she "shall not care" (22).

In Ovid's story, the almost-retrieved Eurydice, as she chooses not to accuse her lover of his inability, makes a final show of solidarity with him who sought so extraordinarily to retrieve her. Her faint good-bye ("He could hardly hear her calling / *Farewell!* when she was gone" [Humphries, 236]) guarantees that even in her absence she will seem to have cared for all of Orpheus's efforts. There is still a possibility, however, especially if we read the story from the outside, unenchanted by its affect, that the mourner has sought less the other herself than her approval of his desire and grief. When Hardy takes up Ovid's archetypal story in "Your Last Drive" as his own, Emma's silence finally forbids even the posing of this question: "Should you censure me I shall take no heed, / And even your praises no more shall need" (23–24). According to Hardy's anti-elegiac demystification of Ovidian mourning, there is a loss greater even than the self-recognition one obtains through having been reproached for one's failings, and that is the loss that comes from having moved beyond reproach.

It is tempting to dismiss the pathos "Your Last Drive" derives from Emma's unwitnessed loyalty by observing as Jahan Ramazani says more generally of the *Poems of 1912–13* that "in death [Emma's] objectionable self can be effaced" (57), since a dead woman is obviously less contentious than an alienated and bitter wife. There is a truly Ovidian insight in Ramazani's point, since the Orpheus story is in part about the silencing of a potentially querulous woman. Yet, as I have suggested, the specter of reproach looms large in Ovid and even larger in Hardy's elegies. This question of reproach is voiced perhaps most explicitly here in "Your Last Drive," when Hardy anti-elegiacally places Emma "past love, praise, indifference, blame" (30)—which is to say, past the reach of her own accusations. What we have finally to confront in Hardy's elegies is the extent to which reproach, while proceeding from the surprising difference of the other, also preserves the possibility of her response and the last vestige of relationship as that for which he can in some way be reciprocally responsible. Even though Hardy defends against Emma's allegation by proclaiming himself immune to the needs of reciprocation ("Dear ghost, in the past did you ever find / The thought 'What profit,' move me much?" [27–28]), we already know this sobering statement is only a half-truth.[41]

It is the lapsed premise of reciprocity, according to which Emma gave "no hint" of going, that creates the awkward position of the poet in the second stanza of "The Going," a stanza that so well characterizes the larger dilemma of Hardy's mourning:

> Never to bid good-bye,
> Or lip me the softest call,
> Or utter a wish for a word, while I
> Saw morning harden upon the wall,
> Unmoved, unknowing
> That your great going
> Had place that moment, and altered all. (8–14)

Hardy is denied both the moment Orpheus obtains through persistence (the soft call of "Farewell" as Eurydice disappears for a second time) and the reassurance that comes with it—that Emma like Eurydice would have uttered some wish for a word if only she had had the chance. In the absence of such a sign from Emma, Hardy is emotionally desolate, literally "[u]nmoved" by what has occurred, unable to respond to his loss. Through his elegiac series, Hardy contrives for himself several such versions of fantastically Orphean opportunity, nowhere more explicitly than in "The Haunter," where Emma addresses a hypothetical third party who might assure Hardy that she also longed for a restoration of reciprocity:

> What a good haunter I am, O tell him!
>   Quickly make him know
> If he but sigh since my loss befell him
>   Straight to his side I go. (25–28)

Articulated as an emanation of a mourner's wish-fulfilling fantasy, solicitous even to the point of erasing her otherness, Emma speaks as though trying to make amends for having been unresponsive in her difference from the poet's desire. Though she claims as the idealized "faithful one" to be "doing / All that love can do" (29–30)—seeming to render the protection that the apotheosized offer to those who still care for them—there is an obvious limit to what her love can do. In the poem's opening, she has drawn attention to Hardy's inability to recognize her, to his ignorance of the fact that the very reciprocity he seeks is being impossibly fulfilled:

> He does not think that I haunt here nightly:
>   How shall I let him know
> That whither his fancy sets him wandering
>   I, too, alertly go?—(1–4)

Reciprocity is fulfilled precisely in the moment when the other can no longer be witnessed. What this means is that Hardy must commit himself to an elegiac witness that can never have the full evidence of reciprocity it seeks, though Emma's lingering is the hint of a possibility that was with him more fully than he knew. What Hardy glimpses in the past state of failed reciprocity—in those words he now speaks to his wife, even though, as she says, "When I could answer he did not say them" (9)—are his own too limited expectations of the other.[42]

Whereas other elegists perfect their own examples of mourning by imagining an ethical failure in the distant future, one most often beyond their control, Hardy turns more soberly throughout this series of elegies to the present time (or recent past) in which the other's remembrance is threatened less by the prospect of the mourner's death than by a survivor's closed eyes or unturned head. Through this technique, the reproach of mourning parallels the ethical resistance to representation and commemoration, since each turns on a "misvision" marking the radical division between the self and the other. But Hardy's elegies also suggest how fully, if also uncooperatively, the other approaches the mourner through this question of reproach. As Hardy's desire begins to exceed what he can reasonably expect—"Now that he goes and wants me with him," as Emma says, "More than he used to do" ("The Haunter," 13–14)—he first apprehends the value of her alterity. In this way, the ethical desire for an impossible reciprocity opposes itself to commemorative logic, for in the present tense of his inordinate desire, Hardy is vigilant on behalf of a value he has previously disregarded. His protection, like that of Freud's father dreamily guarding his burning son, may be futile as an act of literal preservation, but it suggests, first of all, that mourning opposes the literal demise of the other by proffering itself as a demand beyond that which seems reasonable; and secondly, that, as mourning also poses itself as a wish for the other's approach, it is always within range of her reproach. Since according to Hardy we are ethically vigilant on behalf of another who must find fault with our efforts, in mourning we venture finally toward an Orphean otherworld of meaning as toward the highly ethical claims exerted by the other in her persistently meaningful state of impossibility.

CHAPTER SIX

The Bad Conscience of American Holocaust Elegy

The Example of Randall Jarrell

Randall Jarrell had begun to observe the fate of Europe's Jews in his poetry as early as 1940, but by the time he wrote "A Camp in the Prussian Forest" (1946) he had gained, along with the rest of America, fuller knowledge of the Nazi genocide.[1] In 1945 Jarrell had taken explicit account of the death camps in his review of a book of poems about Jews by A. M. Klein, and in an essay on W. H. Auden in that same year, which built on a 1941 essay also highly critical of his once-revered precursor, Jarrell held Auden accountable for his schematic interpretations of politics and his tendency to find trivial fault with the social absurdities of the contemporary world at a time when the Jews were dying under a great cultural lie of anonymity, suffering the unique atrocities of World War II.[2] As Auden had moved increasingly toward a language of abstraction, he had sought to make himself more accessible and to oppose the obscurity of the modernists, but the result of his experiment had been to mystify many of the social forces of which he had previously been so critical and to settle for a rhetoric of bureaucratic depersonalization. For Jarrell as critic and poet, the quality of Auden's aesthetic failure was so closely related to as to be almost interchangeable with his morally defective vision. The coming together of these two fields of judgment is evident in the 1940 poem "The Refugees," which much like Auden's own "Refugee Blues" (1938) had been written to address the European refugee crisis resulting from the increasingly oppressive policies of the Nazi regime in Germany.[3] Jarrell focuses the entire cognitive mechanism of his poem upon a question of anonymity, asking his audience to "read" in the faces of refugees remote in place, if not yet in time, a fate to which all involved—the refugees and those here learning of their plight—were consenting.

By adhering to the limited perspective of the refugees who seemingly cooperate with their own disappearance, Jarrell treats the question of their fateful anonymity as if it were incontestable. There is a persuasiveness to such a view of history, in which we seem automata of our prior beliefs and presumptions, participating in currents of history that are at the same time beyond our immediate ken. In the poem's movement from the refugees' initial speculation as to what they possessed that they were "willing to trade for this" to a final speculation in which they wonder what it was they possessed, if anything at all, that they (written as a *we* of internal discourse) were "unwilling to trade for this," the poem hangs finally on the ambiguity of the unwilling "we" (6.24). Since the *we* might also be read as the interruptive voice of Jarrell's reading audience, the American public's own unwillingness to have traded present pleasures for attitudes translating into practical actions on behalf of the refugees is here indicted. The dire and fatalistic symbiosis between the minds of the refugees and the audience the poem provides for them confronts us, as it were, with the inevitability of history. For Jarrell, it is largely a matter of moral discernment whether or not one consents to a view of history in which the plight of refugees must be interpreted fatalistically. To consent to this worldview entails quite literally an aesthetic failure: if we do consent, we will have altogether missed the poem's crucially ironic and moral turn, which demands, if only at the level of a proper aesthetic attentiveness, that we separate ourselves from the modes of political thoughtlessness that have so far described the refugees' lives.

The moral difficulty entailed in reading a poem such as "The Refugees" recapitulates a central hermeneutic conflict between the personal and public elegy, even as it also approaches a characteristic paradox of the cultural reception of Jarrell, who has been remembered more for his critical voice and judgment and the difficulty of much of his poetry than as an advocate of a public poetry to be written in more colloquial, less esoterically modernist idioms.[4] Although Jarrell had pronounced the waning of the modernist epoch and accused poetry under the mantle of Eliot and Pound of having inclined toward obscurity and become irresponsible to its audience, he had himself been accused in early reviews of a penchant for obscurity, intellectualism, or unearned profundity. This was much the verdict, for example, of a review of *Losses* in the pages of *Poetry*, where W. S. Graham took Jarrell to task for the "self-consciously modern" surface of poems that, through the use of devices such as ellipses and liberal dashes and an immersion in incidental detail, were aimed at representing an "honest, thorny reality" even as Jarrell's poetic voice lagged behind the attempt, as if from a different, vaguely archaic era.[5] Deploring the combination of an overly crafted casualness and a fondness for phrasings that were "old-fashioned and laboriously clichéd," Graham insisted that the insights reached by Jarrell's speakers were often banal and that Jarrell (rather like Jarrell's Auden) littered much of the poetry with abstractions and "big verities" meant to bring us to the edge of insight (303, 304). The result, quite contrary to the intention, was a "deafening organ-peal of the pseudo-profound" (305).

Though Graham's judgment is harsh, it is not altogether inaccurate, touching Jarrell where he is most vulnerable as a poet. For Jarrell has a habit (which Graham traces to Hardy) of insisting rhetorically and dramatically upon his poem's moments of moral insight. Such a habit of reaching for the profound has to be understood, I think, in light of Jarrell's attempt to find a more public idiom for poetry, and it casts the pseudoprofundity to be found sometimes even in Jarrell's best poems in a new light—as having arisen from the imposed obligations of public poetry, as also from the necessary extravagance of collective voice. It is also the corollary, I want to argue, to Jarrell's use of the figure of the bad conscience, which we might understand as an attempt to emphasize the difference between personal and public, collective, or historical understanding. According to Jarrell's figurative logic, not only does the profundity of historical suffering seems too large for personal apprehension, but the personal becomes the sign of a discomfiture in public meanings, an unsettling of received historical knowledge.

To speak directly in the collective voice, even provisionally, puts lyric under tremendous strain. Theodor Adorno's famous defense of the social meaning of lyric proceeds, in fact, from this very assumption. For Adorno, the world most fully articulated by lyric is seemingly quite private, and it is as the perfection of a type of speech, belonging especially to its bourgeois ethos, that the lyric poem must be reckoned an important measure of prevailing ideology.[6] Whether or not one holds such a view of lyric (and in chapter 3 I have offered my own reasons for rethinking this model), for a poet writing directly in the shadow of the modernists, the effort to contradict the modernist descent into subjectivity and myth seemed to require an extraordinary exertion of voice and vision. As Jarrell saw only too well, in Auden's attempt to return poetry more directly to the world of social meaning, he had become, even in the early poetry of which Jarrell largely approved, mired in folkish politics, often teetering on the edge of fascistic sympathy. Thereafter, Auden's tremendous disdain for the bourgeois world—which in Adorno's terms is the very foundation of contemporary lyrical voice—caused him to veer more desperately into generalized descriptions and to employ heavy-handed devices delineated by Jarrell in his 1941 essay, from capitalized personified abstractions to esoteric phrases such as the "Bureaucratization of Perspective by Incongruity" (344), in order to reveal a world that had delivered itself over to the absented hands of anonymous social forces. The social critique informing these devices was at best quasi-Marxist, with Auden making Marx over in his own image through a series of abstractions substituted for Marxist materialist causes that had themselves been substitutes for idealist conceptions of human agency.

As Jarrell saw the matter, Auden's "degeneration into abstraction" had been an almost inevitable consequence of his critical vision and his concerted effort to become "increasingly abstract, public, and prosaic" (347). Though the language of the early poetry held the seeds of such abstract flowering, it had not been allowed to succumb to rhetoric. By the late 1930s and early 1940s, however, Auden was trying to keep pace with a world in which he had begun to glimpse the gathering persuasiveness of the bureaucratic idiom. His poetic language becoming more and more a rhetoric, Auden eventually found solace in a "quasi-scientific method," a technique of naming mechanisms through which the world might be explicated (347).[7] It was quite evident to Jarrell that Auden's experiment, which he'd ventured with the aim of making himself a more overtly public poet, had been conducted at the expense of his poetry.

In a parenthetical remark anticipating Adorno's observations about the lyric more than a decade and a half later, Jarrell closes his earlier 1941 essay on Auden by observing that such a poetic method might have been better suited to a "didactic or expository poetry than to lyric poetry," before speculating on how poetry might best accommodate the requirements of political vision: "Our political or humanitarian interests may make us wish to make our poetry accessible to large groups; it is better to try to make the groups accessible to the poetry, to translate the interests into political or humanitarian activity. The best of causes ruins as quickly as the worst. . . ." (348–49). It would be too easy to account for Jarrell's implicit distrust of popular taste as the habit of cultural privilege and the product of an aesthetic dedicated to the refined ears (as also the political ideology) of the socially elite. To do so is to underestimate the truly humanitarian and political voice Jarrell sought to achieve in much of his poetry. Like Adorno after him, Jarrell valued the difficulties of high cultural aesthetics for their implicit moral claim: only through the cognitive trials of a more difficult reading could poetry espouse genuine critique or dissent. To bring poetry to the masses—say, in the cultural moment of 1938–44 or immediately after the war—might have obligated the poet to serve the cultural tastes and prejudices of his moment, to toe the political line on isolationism or the more severely anti-immigrant and antisemitic stances of the American public. But if Jarrell's socially inflected poetry pushes especially hard on matters of social conformity, it reflects a historical moment of conformity in order to implicate both speaker and listener in the very social phenomenon to which they might wish to object. At the same time, this mimetic impulse works in the service of an ironic vision that demands from the reader a dissent from the laxity characterizing so much of the public's sentiment and social analysis.

The rhetorical leanings of Jarrell's early poetry, if they are better concealed than those of Auden's wartime poetry, are never entirely assimilated to the fictive possibilities of the world espoused in any single poem.[8] Still, I want to argue that this is only as it should be for a poetry that asks the hard question of what idioms remain to poetry in which it might speak of the ethical responsibility for contemporary historical atrocities. Obliged by the memory of atrocity even as he also recognizes the futility of ordinary elegiac commemoration, Jarrell foregrounds the bad conscience both as a sign of an ideological false consciousness in the American public and as a manifestation of responsibilities either unmet or only mournfully, belatedly, ineffectively answered for.

The Rhetoric of Grief

At least some of the rhetorical flourishes W. S. Graham and others had begun to criticize in Jarrell's poetry should be read, I am arguing, in light of his struggle to write a poetry of greater public relevance. An illustrative case is provided by Jarrell's biographer William H. Pritchard, who recounts an incident in which Jarrell refused an editing suggestion from Allen Tate. A significant patron of Jarrell's early work, Tate had brought Jarrell to the attention of Edmund Wilson at the *New Republic*, but when he later recommended through Wilson that the poem "90 North" (1941), which was soon to be published in the pages of that magazine, could be improved if the fifth stanza were dropped, Jarrell absolutely refused to take his mentor's advice.[9] "90 North" charts the retrospective judgment of an Arctic explorer who having "reached [his] North" finds it to be existentially meaningless. Only in retrospect does he come to understand that he has been flung from darkness to darkness; the narratives of achievement he has lived by, in which pain is supposed to be translated into wisdom, are merely ineffective lies about pain. As the persona speaks from his bed, his exploratory consciousness intersects with the world of childish dreams, giving rise finally to the elaborate conceit of the fifth stanza and those lines that Tate wanted excised:

> And it is meaningless. In the child's bed
> After the night's voyage, in that warm world
> Where people work and suffer for the end
> That crowns the pain—in that Cloud-Cuckoo-Land
>
> I reached my North and it had meaning. (17–21)

The source of Tate's objection is not hard to imagine. As the stanza brings us back proddingly to a perspective innocent of what the explorer will have learned, the point seems to be precisely that we can never get back to such a world. We are soon confused as to whether the "Cloud-Cuckoo-Land" is a world of dreams prior to reality or a designation for the end toward which one strives, but in either case, the bed of rest is no longer separate from the world of suffering and disillusionment—the world as it really is. That the adult bed recalls in the persona's consciousness his former child's bed seems a rather obvious, sentimental, and inflated conceit. As the speaker's self-indulgent musings become indistinguishable from Jarrell's own morally serious tone, we are reminded in a way that can only be called platitudinous of a world "[w]here people work and suffer." Finally delivered from the heavily handled dream world into the sixth stanza's reporting of the explorer's impermanent triumph, the poem improves drastically, as if by a modulation of voice: "I reached my North and it had meaning." The lines Tate would have excised and that Jarrell refused to surrender suffer from extreme rhetorical artifice. That Jarrell defended them as central to the poem's meaning does not mean that they are successful lines of poetry; it does suggest, however, that such moments of rhetorical inflation were not mere aberrations of poetic voice but rather deliberate attempts to jolt the poetic line, as Graham himself had suggested, toward a greater confrontation with a hard reality.

The ending of "The Refugees" is also given over to rhetorical assertion bordering on trite moralization:

> What else are their lives but a journey to the vacant
>   Satisfaction of death? And the mask
>   They wear tonight through their waste
> Is death's rehearsal. Is it really extravagant
>   To read in their faces: What is there that we possessed
>   That we were unwilling to trade for this? (19–24)

For the fragility of the *we* in the final line—"What is there that we possessed / That we were unwilling to trade for this?"—depends entirely upon a colloquial slippage according to which it is hard for us to pronounce *we*, even as part of the language of free indirect discourse, apart from the pronominal connotations of self-reference; that is, without having recourse to a thought of ourselves. It is this accident of speech that characterizes our hypothetical opposition to the refugees' fate and to the uncompassionate politics that have determined their lives. In other words, the rhetorical excess of the poem is performing the work of conscience, as if Jarrell feared his readers would not otherwise meet their responsibilities. This is an all-too-familiar strategy of progressive-minded sentimental narratives. One thinks of Stowe's narrator in *Uncle Tom's Cabin*, intervening to make sure that her reader is with her and, more importantly, with her heroine on the night Eliza takes her child in arm and flees from slavery:

> If it were *your* Harry, mother, or your Willie, that were going to be torn from you by a brutal trader, to-morrow morning,—if you had seen the man, and heard that the papers were signed and delivered, and you had only from twelve o'clock till morning to make good your escape,—how fast could *you* walk? How many miles could you make in those few brief hours, with the darling at your bosom,—the little sleepy head on your shoulder,—the small, soft arms trustingly holding on to your neck?[10]

The close relation between the politics of sentimentality and moments of rhetorical excess is a conspicuous (though not necessarily determinative) one in literary history, and if there is a single, readily identifiable aesthetic weakness of Jarrell's poetry, most of his critics would suggest it is his sentimentality. For the most part, Jarrell employs the rhetorical excess of sentimentality by simultaneously alluding to a history in which it has functioned as an often too easy substitute for conscience. The self-accusation occasioned by reading the closing "we" of "The Refugees" as the audience's collective responsibility is, strictly speaking, a bad reading. Having inserted herself into the story and become responsible by an accident of spoken language, the reader must also confront the full force of an interpretive presumption ("Is it really extravagant / To read in their faces: What is there that we possessed / That we were unwilling to trade for this?" [22–24]) according to which we are as presumptuous when we claim to understand the final thoughts of the refugees as we are when we read the story of our own failure in what has happened to them.

Clearly, part of Jarrell's point is that responsibility itself is a presumption. In order to become imaginatively responsible, even if only accidentally, the intervening reader has to overstep a constitutive boundary of aesthetic mimesis, much as she would have been required to transgress the parameters of nationalistic identity to have truly met the refugees in their political abjection. But it is also Jarrell's point that the reader has not yet performed this work of conscience, and it is for this reason, I want to suggest, that Jarrell writes responsibility as an accident of speech. Uncertain that the reader will arrive at the moment of true conscience or perhaps wishing to remind her that the very fate of the refugees names her conscience as a yet ineffective extravagance, Jarrell pronounces a gap between the conclusions of conscience and a responsibility that persists whether we arrive there imaginatively or not. If more conventionally sentimental authors often seem mere rhetoricians, it is in part because they remain too naïvely confident in the good conscience of their readers. When Stowe assumes that a reader (who has been typed implicitly as a liberal, white Northerner and mother) can put herself in Eliza's place, she also assures us that to do so will mean that sympathy has become tantamount to political solidarity.[11] To sympathize truly with Eliza is not only to walk in her shoes, but to wish that no one else will have to; it is to align oneself with the progressive, abolitionist cause and to lend oneself finally to the liberatory politics of good feeling. By contrast, in Jarrell's poem, not only does conscience arrive by accident, it occurs in remission, in the moment of failure.

"The Refugees" concludes on a note of bad conscience entirely worthy of Levinas's denotation of an "anxiety of responsibility" that befalls "individuals

who live on after the violent death of the victims": "A kind of scruple about surviving dangers which threaten the other. As if everyone, though with clean hands
and in presumed or certain innocence, had to answer for the starvation and murders!"[12] To maintain a good conscience while others suffer injustice depends
upon the presumption of an innocence amounting to indifference. To assert
one's innocence in relation to the suffering of the other is to exonerate oneself
before her fate, and even if this were a fairly accurate description of the matter
in political or social terms, it would amount to an ethical failure—the wish not
to have been responsible. Just as Levinas imagines an ethical subject who answers
for starvation and murders that are not directly of her own doing, Jarrell's poem
ends with a question preventing any return to the good conscience of innocence.
Whatever else the reader might have traded, she has been (as a sign of all of us)
unwilling to trade it. Once we have crossed this border of knowledge—knowing
what will happen to the refugees, being able to read (however speculatively) their
secret thoughts, and discerning the absence still of political intervention—we
cannot answer in either good faith or good conscience that there was nothing we
possessed that would have helped avert the fate of the refugees.

With regard to rhetorical excess as a substitute for conscience, then, we can
observe that the simple extravagance of Jarrell's poem resides in the possibility
of a collective responsibility, one that has gone unheeded, indeed undefined.
Then too, there is extravagance in the poem's collective voice, which finds the
ground for its *we* only by having contemplated the fate of those who remained
outside the purview of the reader's privilege at the very moment when they
could least afford to be there. Any collective idiom is a language of political
permission, within which we can locate ourselves only as a consequence of the
benefits we derive through our cultural affiliations. For this very reason, collective identity may require that others be sacrificed in order that the privileges of
identity can be discerned and maintained. Just so, Jarrell imagines his audience's unwillingness to be hard fought—a battle not only for an illusory innocence but for the exemptions from harm that coincide with the privileges of
nationalist identity. The failure of the collective imagination at the end of
"The Refugees" does not so much signal the need for a better and more inclu-
sive version of collective identity as argue, instead, that to be meaningful at all
collectivity must define itself on the hard edges of bad conscience, searching
always for what it has already neglected.

Jarrell ends "The Refugees" by implicitly encouraging an act of public mourning that would be tantamount to ethical vigilance. There is an ambiguity in

such vigilance, which is characterized by anti-elegiac belatedness and inefficaciousness, and yet is also pronounced as a resistance within the resigned fatalism that characterizes so much of our grief. With the phrase "satisfaction of death," Jarrell caricatures the history of elegiac resolution as an eminently sacrificial mode in which the survivor's peace of mind is secured by commonsensically surrendering the other to a fate he or she has already met. Revising the anti-elegiac figure of belatedness in which responsibility arrives as a protection of the other that is already too late, alluding also to mourning's regular praxis of learning to accept the other's death, Jarrell travesties the good sentiments of successful mourning by representing the acceptance of death as having arrived prematurely—that is, before the other has died. If the collective reader has moved to the threshold of responsibility at the very moment in which the refugees are about to perish, this belatedness of conscience occurs at a time when it would be obscene to resign ourselves to the refugees' deaths. Yet, according to Jarrell, that is precisely what his audience is in the midst of doing, as they read a poem about a group of refugees perishing because the major world democracies refused to liberalize their immigration standards and failed to make a concerted effort toward providing political asylum for Europe's mostly Jewish refugees. What makes the last stanza of the poem perhaps hardest to read, if one pays attention to its elegiac ambivalences, is that Jarrell insists on inhabiting the moment before mourning becomes finally necessary, in which we, by imagining "what else" the lives of the refugees might refer to besides their death, might still exempt them from the necessity—or "satisfaction"—of death and preserve them instead among the living.

Mourning as the Occasion of History: "A Camp in the Prussian Forest"

From a reading of "The Refugees," one might imagine that Jarrell's critique is directed primarily at the laxity of collective conscience, which absorbs the urgency of a direct personal responsibility into the political doctrines and practices of nations. Certainly it is along such lines that, in his second major essay on Auden from 1945, Jarrell would argue for the ethical irrelevance of Auden's easy language of the abstract and anonymous, in which the reader who was a de facto witness to the era of Hitlerism could glimpse little of her own world of recent remembrance. The villains of Auden's world were in his own words "bores and scoundrels," and Jarrell demands to know of his reader: "Were *these* your enemies, reader?" before insisting, "They were not mine" (457). As he had turned to a collective idiom, Auden seemed altogether to have abrogated the terms of personal responsibility, and Jarrell's suspicion of abstractly collectivist politics seems to owe something to the many American affirmations of the liberal tradition, by authors such as Dorothy Thompson and Walter Lippman, that came to prominence during the war.[13]

In both his essays on Auden, Jarrell accuses Auden of a penchant for increasingly simplistic and satiric assessments of bureaucratic modern culture, but in the second essay Jarrell concludes by focusing on the specter of the war's atrocities, accusing Auden of saving "his own soul" by way of such platitudes, while losing the "whole world" (456). Auden writes too glibly of the modern malaise "within the months that held the mass-executions in the German camps, the fire-raids, Warsaw and Dresden and Manila; within the months that were preparing the bombs for Hiroshima and Nagasaki; within the last twelve months of the Second World War." Finally, after diagnosing its bureaucratic, sometimes Marxist and sometimes Freudian natural laws, Auden "submits to the universe without a question," but it is a universe only of psychological affect, a universe that is "his own shadow on the wall beside his bed" (456). It is a world without public seriousness and without individual agency. Much of Jarrell's impassioned interrogation of Auden's ethically empty phraseology might prepare us to find Jarrell's own poetry, when it is explicitly devoted to the memory of such catastrophic events, infused with personal grief and the recuperative energies of moral indignation.

When we turn to Jarrell's overt Holocaust elegy, "A Camp in the Prussian Forest," we find that any such expectation is only ambiguously met. The poem opens by attempting to approximate the voice of an American soldier participating in the liberation of the camps:

> I walk beside the prisoners to the road.
> Load on puffed load,
> Their corpses, stacked like sodden wood,
> Lie barred or galled with blood
>
> By the charred warehouse. No one comes today
> In the old way
> To knock the fillings from their teeth;
> The dark, coned, common wreath

Is plaited for their grave—a kind of grief.
The living leaf
Clings to the planted profitable
Pine if it is able;

The boughs sigh, mile on green, calm, breathing mile,
From this dead file
The planners ruled for them. . . . One year
They sent a million here:

Here men were drunk like water, burnt like wood.
The fat of good
And evil, the breast's star of hope
Were rendered into soap. (1–20)

Though Jarrell provided a note to this poem explaining that the speaker was supposed to be an American soldier, we quickly discern the inadequacy of the conceit. Pritchard has called Jarrell's descriptive note "wishful thinking," since nothing in the poem "identifies it as emanating from an American soldier" (163). The speaker's description of the camps and of his feeling about them, his full awareness of the Jews and their fate, and his general savvy about the Prussian forest—all of these seem implausible, if not altogether impossible knowledge for a soldier who has been immersed in combat with the Germans until the moment in which he participates in the liberation of the camps. If we seek a historical ground for Jarrell's voice, it would appear that he attributes to the ordinary soldier an overarching political perspective akin perhaps to that of General Dwight D. Eisenhower, who upon first entering camps at Ohrdruf and Buchenwald claimed to have witnessed scenes eroding his very powers of description.[14] Uttering words now so well etched into American memory (as they are literally etched in relief on a wall outside the United States Holocaust Memorial Museum and also spoken in a voice-over accompanying the documentary footage one views while riding the industrial steel elevator up to the museum's main exhibit), Eisenhower provided us with a virtual trope of access to the Holocaust: "I saw there scenes that beggar description." What he has witnessed, he claims, affronts the ordinary historical imagination in its most basic capacity to assemble, recount, and place evidence in a rational narrative. As Eisenhower was to recall in his postwar memoir, he forced himself to examine every gruesome detail and then began to oversee the documentation of the evidence, believing it should be "placed before the American and British publics in a fashion that would leave no room for cynical doubt" (409). Already, long before the Holocaust had been placed at the center of contentious debates about the limits of representation, we hear Eisenhower advocating, as it were, a new historical idiom, demanding that the evidence be recorded without understanding—that the audience witness, in effect, without knowledge.

Yet if Jarrell's soldier is an ordinary American standing in for a personage such as Eisenhower, he is also a stand-in for the audience that Eisenhower constructs as witnesses to these events. In his official military capacity, Eisenhower spoke for the political will of the American people, and much of the footage he oversaw soon made it into the studio newsreels regularly played at movie houses across America. Indeed, as Jeffrey Shandler has noted, it was largely at Eisenhower's behest that some theater owners agreed to show these horrific images to ordinary American audiences accustomed to coming to the theater for entertainment and at best superficial coverage of world news.[15] Though World War II had facilitated the transformation of the newsreel from what Shandler calls a relatively "frivolous news source" into an "important source of war-related information and propaganda . . . closely monitored by the newly created Office of War Information" (10), this material was shocking even for wartime propaganda. The prominent film critic and author James Agee argued in the *Nation*, soon after the newsreels began to be shown, that audiences viewed such footage under the extended auspices of the wartime propagandistic enterprise. Clearly part of the purpose of showing these images was to educate audiences about the American triumph over German barbarity.[16] What comes across, for instance, in the Universal newsreel entitled "Nazi Murder Mills!" or the Paramount newsreel entitled "History's Most Shocking Record!" is the exclamatory rhetoric of a narrator who demands from the audience a vicarious encounter with this horror, quite as if these images were a corrective to fascism and hateful ideologies of all varieties; and Agee's point is ratified by much of the journalistic coverage of the screenings.[17]

The images from the 1945 newsreels, the wave of reporting that facilitated the presentation of atrocities, and Eisenhower's public exhortation that ordinary Americans view the footage of the camps—all are part of the background and morally charged occasion of witness in Jarrell's poem.[18] There is more involved here, however, than Jarrell's anachronistic inclusion of information readily available to his audience a year subsequent to but not necessarily during the liberation of the camps. For as Jarrell's speaker bears a knowledge greater

than what is possible according to his historical location in time as a soldier directly involved in the events, a discrepancy emerges between the rhetorical demands of the poem and its described occasion. I would like to suggest that this
discrepancy traces a deeper conflict between the public and personal voices of
poetry, a problem with which Jarrell had been much concerned throughout the
1940s. In order for poetry to have a persuasive public dimension and to intervene in the political conscience of its readers, Jarrell maintained, it needed
somehow to shed the modernist, Eliotic requirement of an impersonal mediat-
ing vision, as well as the vaguely collective, but altogether too abstract and
anonymous idiom of a poet such as Auden. Yet in much of Jarrell's historically
oriented and ostensibly public poetry, he introduces the personal idiom only
to describe at the same time a world in which it will not take hold. So, for example, in the much anthologized (and largely overestimated) Jarrell poem
"The Death of the Ball Turret Gunner" (1945), the conflict between the personal point of view and public responsibility amounts to an overly contrived
poetic tour de force:

> From my mother's sleep I fell into the State,
> And I hunched in its belly till my wet fur froze.
> Six miles from earth, loosed from its dream of life,
> I woke to black flak and the nightmare fighters.
> When I died they washed me out of the turret with a hose.[19]

According to the structuring conceit of this short poem, the impossible posthumous testimony of the gunner as a casualty of the war effort is ironically denoted through the pathetic hypothesis of his quasi-infantile speech. Not only
does the womb imagery connote the speaker's youth and unrealized potential,
but it sets up the personal idiom as though it depended upon an unsustainable
or unrealistic posture of innocence. Much as in Freudian family romance an innocent attachment to the mother cannot endure, the personal idiom here falls
out of a domestic plot, which might have progressed toward self-possession, toward a dangerous mode of public responsibility. Before the gunner even knows
who he is, he is a member of the "State," transplanted from the womb of the
mother into the "belly" of his plane, waking to find himself no longer in a dream
but in a historically significant nightmare. Much of the poem's popularity undoubtedly develops from its rather free-floating pathos, which can be as well
harmonized with a patriotic celebration as it can with a pacifist critique of the
American war effort. If there is any troubling dissonance in the poem, it would

have to be the final detail of the dead body recalling for us how he was "washed . . . out of the turret with a hose" (5). Even here, however, Jarrell's prosopopeia works by a rather obvious pathos in which the impossibly speaking dead airman seems the only one to have taken account of his death. As such his anonymity seems less a comment on depersonalizing codes of military honor than an exemplification of the fate of the personal idiom in the midst of extreme circumstances. Perhaps most interestingly, then, Jarrell suggests that one falls into public roles as into modes of impersonality, and the final pathos of the poem is that the speaker does not protest his own anonymity, but rather describes his fate as a matter of routine and necessity.

For all his criticism of Auden's abstract, bureaucratized rendering of history, Jarrell's poetic attempts to locate a personal responsibility standing in the full light of history often present historical events as if they were governed by an externally motivated progression over which his poetic personas can exercise little if any control. "A Camp in the Prussian Forest" begins with the soldier who in walking "beside the prisoners to the road" (1) has been put in position to walk beside history at one of its most enormous moments. But the question soon arises as to whether there is any way for his consciousness to catch up with history, to take in and remember the cultural significance of the scene he has glimpsed and also to sustain his own identity as historically significant. To the extent that the speaker's response is made to seem beside the point, the personal idiom fails in its effort to appropriate the event of witness as an occasion pertaining to a self's intentions and capabilities. With the divided sensibility of a bad conscience, which always dedicates a self to remembrances greater than its intentionality, Jarrell's speaker's identity dissolves almost immediately into the occasion of witness, his observations marked as being complicitous with all they observe. When the soldier's eye imposes a figurative order on the scene of corpses, imagining them "stacked like sodden wood" (3), he has unwittingly participated in those "language rules" according to which Nazis referred to their dead victims as *Figuren* (dolls) or employed other depersonalizing euphemisms in order to prevent recognition of their victims' humanity.[20] The use of internal rhymes contributes to the effect, as the speaker's consciousness discerns a symmetry between corpses that lie "barred" with blood and the complexion of the "charred warehouse" (4, 5). A truly menacing connotation of such rhyming symmetry follows when Jarrell contrasts the contemporary moment of "today" with a past Nazi routine designated as "the old way": "No one comes today / In the old way / To knock the fillings from their teeth" (5–7). Having approximated the rhythm of the ballad stanza, with its shortened second and fourth lines, while altering the more common *abab* rhyme scheme, Jarrell here treats the shortened second line as a kind of internal rhyme both hastening the observation and making it casual in its hastiness. According to this trick of rhythm, the reader becomes aware only after the fact that atrocity has just been referenced in the singsong voice of folk ballad.[21] There is undoubtedly some parodic intention at work here since Jarrell means to evoke the terrifying casualness with which such horrors were routinely performed and perhaps also some of the folk sentiments that masked Nazi criminality. Given his own strenuous objection to the folkish habits of the early Auden's voice, it seems implausible that Jarrell's own quasi-folkloric rendering of atrocity could be anything less than ironic, even if such an irony would most likely have been lost on a soldier who had been fighting a war and not reading Auden.

As the soldierly conceit comes to seem too narrowly contrived, the rhetorical burden placed upon the witnessing voice pushes beyond the immediate personal idiom of the soldier to trespass upon a perspective that is in fact much closer to Jarrell's own ideal citizen's conscience. If this implicitly divided consciousness is, as Graham had worried, imperfectly marked in Jarrell's poem, it is largely Jarrell's distrust of the way objective or collective views tend toward impersonal abstraction that obliges him to this imperfectly fictional, but also fictionally imperfect, voice. An odd thing happens in the transition from the second to the third stanza, where the speaker's eye turns ostensibly from the historically significant scene of stacked corpses (lines 2–5) to the funeral wreath that is to mark their common grave (lines 8–9). In the first place, when the wreath is called "a kind of grief" (9), the poem has shifted into a deliberately elegiac register, returning us to a familiar, well-worn convention of literary mourning—the decking of the funeral bier. Coming abruptly as it does, the effect can only be called contrived. When the stilted transition from witness to mourning is next followed by free-ranging reflections on the surviving natural world, the poem shifts registers once again, this time into what we might call a pastoral meditation (lines 10–20).

In all of this there is an awkward alteration between the living and the dead, which may take its cue from the Paramount newsreel footage of Nazi atrocities, in which the camera symbolically panned from shots of the living to the horrible piles of dead bodies. Having opened his poem (lines 1–7) by moving quickly from the surviving prisoners to the grotesquely imaged bodies, Jarrell moves next from the dead wreath back out to the living world of the forest. The alterations are rather sharp, except for the fact that they have been harmonized by Jarrell's use of approximate rhyme to connect lines 7 and 8 with lines 9 and 10 ("teeth / wreath," followed by "grief / leaf"). This approximate rhyme scheme makes the elegiac convention of the wreath occupy an oddly chiasmic center, and we move from gruesome Nazi souvenirs of the victims (remembered only for the gold of their teeth) to the formal object of commemoration, and from the commemorative object as a metonymy for grief to the world of nature now horribly rendered a souvenir of history.

Mock-pastoral Sensibility and the Holocaust Elegy

Of course, Jarrell's funeral wreath is already by convention a grudging acknowledgment of the opposition between life and death, its freshly cut flowers or branches remembering their own fullness of life and so signifying the recently abbreviated life of the one being mourned, even as their temporary beauty—the very fact that they have been cut in order to appear beautiful—also recapitulates the death of the other. The wreath employed as a solitary figure of elegy, symbolically severed from its natural setting, carries with it the artifice of the pastoral apparatus, in which the poet discovers a world that was once plentiful and might have remained meaningful if death had not disillusioned the premise of natural beauty.

In this sense, the pastoral background of the elegy seems always on the verge of becoming obsolete, without ever quite getting there. The perceptions of pastoral are already inflated and unlikely in Milton's "Lycidas," and in Shelley's "Adonais" they are tilting toward irrelevance, with Wordsworth's apparent faith in the natural world, which comes to a crisis at least as early as "Elegiac Stanzas" (1805), seeming perhaps both a historical center and turning point for pastoral persuasiveness. After Wordsworth, elegists from Walt Whitman to Thomas Hardy to moderns such as William Butler Yeats, T. S. Eliot, and Wallace Stevens continue to invoke pastoral scenes, almost perhaps as a poetic reflex, but with perceptibly diminished expectations about the consolations they will offer. Holocaust poets, writing in a variety of languages, are no exception. To name only two of the more famous examples, both Paul Celan's "Deathfugue" and Czeslaw Milosz's "Song on Porcelain" employ highly pastoral scenarios in order to measure the impact of the Holocaust. In each case, the pastoral scene stands for a European tradition of poetry that had fostered the relationship between the land and the people only to be suddenly, perhaps permanently, interrupted by violence; and one of the central questions the reader of these poems must ask is whether the implicit memory of violence is somehow endemic to the naturally imagined world or whether it has intruded upon a genuinely or relatively innocent national past. Even more so after it has been charged with implausibility, pastoral is a hypothesis of continuity, whether national, natural, or poetic, that quite possibly cannot survive the things done in its name or in its places.

By convention, then, a wreath is a sign of the natural continuity of the life cycle, but as Jarrell overemphasizes the claim of continuity through the use of approximate rhyme, he draws attention to an impossible abridgment of atrocity and the natural world. What I would like to suggest is that the insufficiency of the speaker's witnessing finds a parallel in an insufficiency of elegiac convention, which is also to say (framing it from the other direction) that an inadequate gesture of mourning points to an inadequacy in personal remembrance. Also implicit at this moment is the elegiac precedent whereby the natural world approximates the function of an otherwise absent witness. It is such a function of substitute witness that Milton's nymphs, as spirits of the pastoral world, are supposed to signify. Even as they fail in their protection of Lycidas, it is hypothesized that they could have done and seen more. So too the deep complicity of Shelley's natural world is predicated upon a sympathy for Adonais that can only have turned to betrayal because nature was there in the first place, even perhaps functioning as the cause of his demise. If much Romantic New Historical criticism has forced us to see how often a rhetoric of the natural world veils the material reality of history, it has not often enough been insisted upon that this pastoral device, in which there is a turning to nature as to an impersonal principle greater than the poet's subjective understanding, is also a rhetorical marker for a history the poet or subject could not otherwise remember.[22]

In the 1930s there was some understanding that the pastoralizing techniques of Romantic poetry were confused significations of the collective and revolutionary impulse, although Edmund Wilson's verdict that Romanticism was "the indulgence of the imagination and the emotions for their own sake—what artists and poets tended to do when the purposes of the Revolution seem frustrated"—was not in the least an atypical estimation of where such language led.[23] A familiar of Wilson and the strain of American Marxist thought he represented, Jarrell was similarly inclined to be suspicious of the Romanticist cult of the natural world as a veiled code for nationalist sentimentalizings. With Kenneth Burke's *Attitudes toward History* (1937) providing the analytic framework for the 1941 revaluation of Auden, Jarrell's criticisms of the early Auden focused in part on his astonishing use of a *we* and *they* language that connoted a "Lawrence-Hitler-*Golden Bough* folk-mysticism" (334).[24] Arguing against the prevalent view of Auden as urbane poet, Jarrell pointed to the "surprisingly *rural* character of most of Auden's early poems," observing his use of what I would call pastoralizing oppositions between capitalist idioms rendered bankrupt by the era of the Great Depression ("They are aridly commercial, financial, distributive"; "They are bourgeois-respectable or perverted") and the folkish idioms through which the renewal of society was to be produced ("We represent real production, the soil"; "We are folk-simple, or else consciously Bohemian so as to break up Their system and morale"). In other words, as Jarrell put it, in Auden "They represent the sterile city, We the fertile country" (330).

With this suspicion in the background, the movement into the pastoral scene of lines 10–20, as well into those subsequent connotations of "A Camp in the Prussian Forest" that remain internal to its pastoral scene (lines 21–36), advances Jarrell's own deep revisioning of pastoral idyll. Much as Shelley had anti-elegiacally interrogated the claim of reciprocity through which the deceased were customarily made to inhabit the meaning of the natural world ("He is a portion of the loveliness / Which once he made more lovely" [379–80]), Jarrell here supposes that the natural world incorporates the violence it has beheld and quite literally upheld, as if the forest itself remembered the atrocities committed there:

> The boughs sigh, mile on green, calm, breathing mile,
> From this dead file
> The planners ruled for them. . . . One year
> They sent a million here. . . . (13–16)

At first, the sigh of the boughs—literally, the wind through the trees—seems a familiar use of the pathetic fallacy, with nature made, as it is in Shelley, to cooperate with the poet's grief for the remembered dead. This sympathetic figure cannot be sustained, however, and the calmness of the forest starts to seem both a betrayal of the dead and a complicity in their death.

Such a mock-pastoral logic has a trajectory that finds its fulfillment among a now vast canon of aesthetic responses to the Holocaust in several of our more memorable, if also sensational, tropes for Holocaust memory. One such example occurs in the poem "During the Eichmann Trial," where Denise Levertov constructs the memory of the Holocaust upon a pastoral eruption of

Eichmann's and indeed our collective bad conscience. During his trial, Eichmann had at one point testified to witnessing a mass grave in Lwow and seeing
there the earth moving as if it were alive, with blood seeping—or in his words,
shooting—from the ground. Hannah Arendt would cite the same passage in
Eichmann in Jerusalem: A Report on the Banality of Evil (1963) as a blatant
example of Eichmann's bad faith and self-pity, but in Levertov's independent
account, the earth's momentary rejection of mass death seems a kind of moral
indigestion.[25] Quoting Eichmann from the trial as he recalls visiting a mass
grave where "A spring of blood / gushed from the earth," Levertov declares this
episode a "Miracle / unsung" because the earth, as a substitute for human conscience, "cannot swallow / so much at once."[26] In short, the natural world has
offered a sign of resistance to the inhumanity of the Nazis, but this sign is
"unrecognized" since it is Eichmann who witnesses it without apprehending its
true portent. As the earth's belated rejection of death comments ironically on
what the rest of us have been too willing to stomach, Levertov offers a scene
of pastoral grotesque in which the humanized landscape becomes a figure for
disgust.

Similarly invoking the pastoral apparatus in his famous film *Shoah* (1985),
Claude Lanzmann preserves the hypothesis of pastoral innocence in order to
reveal the fundamental dishonesty upon which it is constructed. Once one begins to consider Shoah through the lens of pastoral, so many of the shots in
which the camera pans over the contemporary landscape, displaying what
Jarrell had called "mile on green, calm, breathing mile," seem directed toward
a distinctly antipastoral end. For instance, in the opening sequence Lanzmann
presents us with an image of survivor Simon Srebnik rowing up the Narew
River, singing a Polish folk tune he had been made to sing as a young boy for
the pleasure of the Nazis, but with all those who were nearby also able to hear.
After briefly narrating Srebnik's history, including how he bizarrely survived a
bullet to the head during one of the Nazi "work details," Lanzmann intermin-
gles Srebnik's song with the testimony of villagers, who recall his beautiful
singing voice and admit to reliving for an instant what happened in this place.
The film then shifts to a lush field of grass in which Srebnik is made to stand
and testify: "It's hard to recognize, but it was here. They burned people here.
A lot of people were burned here. Yes, this is the place. No one ever left here
again" (5).[27] Without Srebnik's surviving words, without Lanzmann's own
probing of the land and its people, memory would not exist in this perfectly pastoral scene. There can be little doubt that Lanzmann wants the empty beauty

of the countryside to function as an ironic *J'accuse*, the land as a metonymy for the people's forgetfulness.

As *Shoah* concentrates so much angry attention on the bystanding peasants, they are revealed through Lanzmann's constant probing as well as his selective sampling of their words to be complicitous to the highest degree with what they once witnessed, indeed, to what they saw as if it were a fantasy projection of their own antisemitism. Their collective indifference to the Jews' sufferings seems, according to the film's rhetorical construction and their own unwittingly self-condemning words, a wishful upholding of the atrocities they did not themselves commit, but easily might have. In a sequence where he first elicits from the peasant Czelaw Borowi an admission that to work his fields he had to cross the train tracks in plain sight of Treblinka and its everyday atrocities, Lanzmann next interrogates a group of villagers who admit to the same routine:

> *But they could work a field a hundred yards from the camp?*
>
> They could. So occasionally he could steal a glance if the Ukrainians weren't looking.
>
> *He worked with his eyes lowered?*
>
> Yes.
>
> He worked by the barbed wire and heard awful screams.
>
> *His field was there?*
>
> Yes, right up close. It wasn't forbidden to work there.
>
> *So he worked, he farmed there?*
>
> Yes. Where the camp is now was partly his field. It was off limits, but they heard everything.
>
> *It didn't bother him to work so near those screams?*
>
> At first it was unbearable. Then you got used to it.
>
> *You get used to anything?*
>
> Yes. (26)

In pursuing what the villager has had to accept in order to work the fields, Lanzmann savages an entire history of pastoral innocence in which the simple folk who work the soil are supposed to be better than the modern civilization they have not fully entered. His questions demand memory from the villagers, and they stand also in place of conscience, implying a responsibility for others that would surpass the narrow purview of self-interest. What Lanzmann eventually exposes in the peasants is an utter lack of bad conscience, a lack that has become tantamount to the premise of pastoral itself. No longer can the Polish country-side be figured as if its natural beauty exonerated those who partake of it from

the corruptions of civilization, for *Shoah* persistently exposes pastoral innocence as a dangerous peasant ignorance through which a deep tradition of
antisemitism (with its active myths, such as the idea of the Jews as Christ-killers)
has been preserved.

Still, it is important to note that Lanzmann's demystification of pastoral
innocence depends upon his own exilic perspective, which is to say upon a
mock-pastoral mechanism of projecting onto the land the moral (or in this case,
mostly immoral) qualities he wants to see there. The hypothesis of bad conscience comes upon the scene extrinsically, as Lanzmann asks questions of conscience that appear never to have been asked by the peasants themselves. Even
the ambiguity of what it means to be "bothered" by atrocity is to the point here.
For although Lanzmann undoubtedly wants his audience to hear this as a speculation pertaining to the bad conscience, the peasant—who may feel the sting
of the question, if not of remorse, or who may be altogether innocent of the
filmmaker's standard of moral conscience—can respond to a literal meaning of
Lanzmann's question. The screams are a noise, a disturbance of his tranquillity,
an objective unpleasure. So at first they bother him; then later he gets used to
even this extraordinary unpleasantness. Clearly in whatever way we understand
this ambiguity to have been elicited, it is Lanzmann who has shaped it and made
us come to expect it.

According to the rhetoric of *Shoah*, to be bothered by the screams means
only that the bad conscience must arise through a pun, as a figurative specter
presiding over the literal fact of being psychologically upset by the proximity to
another's pain. The spectral connotation has been prepared for by Lanzmann
when he asks whether the man lowered his eyes, an unmistakable gesture of
shame that is probably also an allusion to the archetypal scene of the murderous bad conscience—specifically, to Cain's fallen face. According to the story of
Genesis 4, in which Cain's face falls because God has rejected his offering,
Cain's shame precedes his murderous action and as a gesture of failed responsibility almost holds the place of an intention.[28] Similarly, in *Shoah*, Lanzmann's
godlike questions figure the consciousness of responsibility through the figure
of the averted eye, as if such shame might have preceded the historical moment
of indifference and the recollective act of responsibility alike. Of course, Cain is
also the archetypal farmer, a "tiller of the ground" (KJV 4:2), so Lanzmann's
peasants are hardly original in conjoining a murderous ideology with the hypothesis of pastoral good conscience. According to the extrinsic demands of
responsibility, in which the questions put by God or Lanzmann would parallel

the ethical obligation the other should have imposed upon Cain or a Polish peasant during the Holocaust, pastoral seems an intention to maintain innocence against the hard fact of a murder for which one is responsible, whether as perpetrator or complicitous witness.

I have traced these two seemingly anachronistic examples of pastoral bad conscience because they trace a horizon predicted by Jarrell's "A Camp in the Prussian Forest," and also because the difference between Levertov and Lanzmann represents a tension explored by Jarrell's antipastoral, anti-elegiac work of mourning. In Levertov's imaginative appropriation of Eichmann's testimony, the bad conscience speaks in the outrage of the land, which sides mythically (in the sense of a universalist, transcendent standard) with truth against the murderer's and Western culture's conveniently poor memory of atrocity. In Lanzmann, however, the bad conscience is articulated in the narrator's taking exception to the land, which has its own mythic capacity (in the sense that it designates ideological complicity) for naturalizing all phenomena that occur on its soil. Jarrell's poem portrays this latter tendency most startlingly in the fifth stanza:

> Here men were drunk like water, burnt like wood.
> The fat of good
> And evil, the breast's star of hope
> Were rendered into soap. (17–20)

The naturalized euphemisms for atrocity—drinking water, burning wood—render the agents of historical atrocities oddly anonymous, as if what they did plays a habitual, integral part in the pastoral scheme of the Prussian forest. There is protest and even outrage implicit in the voice of the speaker who records these facts, but as is the case with Lanzmann's relation to the villagers, the moral distinctions, the capacity to name the "fat of good / And evil," remains external to the scene and to the naturalizing idiom. In other words, according to Jarrell's deeply negative use of irony, the forest has an endless capacity— much as Lanzmann's villager might first have looked down and then accepted what should be "unbearable"—to assimilate its perpetrators and provide the victims with only a horrid asylum in the soil. Certainly, it is part of Jarrell's point to invert the familiar strategies of projection that ordinarily preside over pastoral perception, offering us instead a strangely literal, historical, and violent pastoral world to be projected back onto a civilized perspective. By this inversion, the pastoral world is suddenly more historical than ideal (rather like

Marlow's proceeding into the heart of the jungle's darkness, this is what the soldier has not known about history), as it is also a world more dependent upon real and terrible exclusions than any hypothetical harmony or inclusivity.

I think we badly misunderstand Jarrell if we do not see how the fourth and fifth stanzas of "A Camp in the Prussian Forest" suggest just such a pastoralization of atrocity, even as they also present us with the poem's most ostensibly historical voice. As Jarrell's speaker turns to statistical measures ("One year / They sent a million here" 15–16) and sensationalistic rhetoric ("Here men were drunk like water, burnt like wood," their fat "rendered into soap" 17, 20), he might well be speaking the voice-over for the Paramount or Universal newsreels of 1945 or approximating the idioms of the prosecutors at Nuremberg.[29] Though the poetic voice lacks the moderated, objective perspective we associate with an empirically reasoned construction of history, it displays that rather strange combination of detachment and moral judgment characteristic of the American media's reporting on domestic and political violence in the late twentieth century. And whatever criticisms we may want to offer of the frequent sensationalism and the overt nationalist ideology informing the techniques of popular news reporting, this more than anything else is the voice of history as presented in the immediate moment, the words of mass media already constructing an American cultural memory of events such as the Nazi genocide. One of the most generalizing observations we might make about the sensationalism of American print, film, and television journalism is that it makes a spectacle of the bad conscience, thus deflecting any more challenging claim that might be made upon the audience. One might even argue that the American mediated relation to violence supposes or fosters pastoral in the Empsonian connotation of that word, since the corruption and violence of the contemporary world are invoked in order to construct and reify the innocent simplicity of an audience ostensibly removed from the sensational event being reported.

The occasion of pastoral harmony in the fourth and fifth stanzas in Jarrell's poem might recall the dangerous folk nationalisms of the Germans and the Poles, in which the land is celebrated as a trope for their own belonging and the impossible belonging of scapegoated Jews, but there is at least an oblique allusion in this poem to American innocence as a trope for Holocaust reception: when Jarrell's speaker's language progresses into the universalizing idiom of the final stanzas, we are not permitted to abandon such history to folk provincialisms, but rather forced to claim it as property of us all. Still, when Jarrell's speaker does finally come to plant his commemorative sign in the soil, there is every reason to wonder what such a gesture of mourning for the victims of atrocity can signify in a pastoral context that coincides with the hateful ideology of those who perpetrated these crimes:

> I paint the star I sawed from yellow pine—
> And plant the sign
> In soil that does not yet refuse
> Its usual Jews
>
> Their first asylum. But the white, dwarfed star—
> This dead white star—
> Hides nothing, pays for nothing; smoke
> Fouls it, a yellow joke,
>
> The needles of the wreath are chalked with ash,
> A filmy trash
> Litters the black woods with the death
> Of men; and one last breath
>
> Curls from the monstrous chimney. . . . I laugh aloud
> Again and again;
> The star laughs from its rotting shroud
> Of flesh. O star of men! (21–36)

Implicit here in stanzas 6 through 9, though also suppressed, is a possibility Levertov would choose more than a decade later—namely, that the land itself might stand for moral outrage, in mythic rejection of the crimes of men.

Indeed, the idea that the land might literally refuse the victims of atrocity provides the opportunity for Jarrell's syntactical play on the enjambment that bridges stanzas 6 and 7. As the reader pauses mistakenly but almost naturally at line 24, expecting "[i]ts usual Jews" to complete the sentence as a direct object, what she would imagine is a pastorally complete scene. The speaker's planted sign would be received naturally, much as the Jewish victims of atrocity were also received into the land. The planting of the sign might suggest a continuity with the prior act of burial, supporting the oft-emphasized point of pastoral elegy that death is part of a natural cycle. Of course we know already that these are the most unnatural of deaths, and that such visions of pastoral harmony are artificially and ironically conceived. Still, in bringing an ironic charge against pastoral entirely consistent with the prior charge of stanzas 4 and 5, Jarrell makes the act of burial (originally performed by the perpetrators or their forced laborers) complicitous with murder. The natural burial of elegiac convention is perversely rendered, as if the one who hastens to complete the past were (as Hamlet had always suspected) in a hurry for a reason. All of this, including the possibility that the past is complete, becomes merely a spectral connotation as one continues the sentence across the enjambment and discerns Jarrell's almost callous syntactical play—as "its usual Jews" slides into the position of indirect object and "[t]heir first asylum" becomes the direct object—on what exactly it is that has been refused.

Jarrell's syntactical play brings with it the fully anachronistic connotation according to which history is no longer simply the completed past. For if this first spectral meaning of refusal has to do with the connotation I have just outlined—that the land might refuse to let the victims be buried—it is also governed by the memory of the international refusal to grant Jewish refugees asylum, the explicit subject of Jarrell's "The Refugees." Here once more is the specter of bad conscience, the implication being that an audience hearing of these events after the fact might nevertheless bear some responsibility for their original unfolding; but this recognition is suppressed in order for the poem to progress toward its most sinister connotation. In what might almost be termed an intertextual pun, Jarrell finally names the "welcomer" country that had hovered as the hypothesis of refuge in his 1940 poem "The Refugees" (line 9): here in the pastoral world the Jews received their first and only "asylum," to be buried in the soil of the Prussian forest. There is a rhetorical extravagance to this pun, as Jarrell makes a bitter joke at the expense of the victims. Although the joke alludes to a shame that should redound to those who have substituted murder for real asylum, it operates entirely from outside the victims' perspective and so positions the speaker as one who feels helplessly complicitous with the history he encounters. Perhaps more importantly, Jarrell's joke about "asylum" signals the inappropriateness of the speaker's mournful voice. It is in fact a strange combination of helplessness and inappropriateness that characterizes his final lament.

The Cessation of the Personal Idiom

As mourning heightens the rhetorical inflections of his poetic voice, Jarrell's penchant for adopting overstated rhetorical postures in his poetry should perhaps be understood not only as an attempt to override the influence of the impersonalist, modernist idiom of many of his contemporaries, but as an explicitly ethical project. The sign of disproportion in his poetry marks the limits of the personal idiom of lyric, as that which might measure itself as a consequence of intentionality. But neither can Jarrell simply turn to public voice, for Auden had already taught him how easily such a voice could descend into dangerous collectivist platitudes. Suspended somewhere between the formal requirements of public elegy and the ostensibly private emphasis of personal elegy, Jarrell's poetic voice is positioned in such a way as to render suspect all the ordinary confidences of identity conceived through either personal or more public idioms, since these are really always two sides of the same coin. The bad conscience is, then, his figure for an ethics residing in just such a culturally ambiguous space between individual remembrance and collective structures of responsibility, and Jarrell's interrogation of the limited remembrance of personal voice would force us to encounter our historical responsibility for others in the remembrance of what we have failed to do for them, but also as an impossibly sustained grief that is horribly incapable of mending the history to which it attends.

Though it invokes a number of elegiac conventions, employs a pastoral apparatus, and even attributes a superhistorical knowledge to its speaker, "A Camp in the Prussian Forest" can plausibly be read as the speech of a single soldier through the first six stanzas. After that it cannot. For the last three stanzas are pitched at a level of rhetorical extravagance that finally and absolutely violates the premise of the personal idiom. In particular, there are three rhetorical excesses at the end of this poem that altogether disregard its previous construction of personal voice: the introduction of high elegiac language, the aspect of impossible contemporaneity (or, the anachronistic perspective on history), and the ridiculous elaboration of personal grief. All three are in fact deeply interrelated. So, with regard to the first, when Jarrell suddenly introduces the speculative moment of elegiac apotheosis ("the white, dwarfed star— / This dead white star" [25–26]), he begins by skeptically diminishing an elegiac trick of valuation whereby the other's idealized state often provides consolation for her absence. There is an ambiguity at work in this moment, since if we are reading from within the speaker's contemporary perspective, the star to which he specifically refers, which also remembers the star of David now rendered a sign of Nazi persecution, is the one he has carved from pine to commemorate the graves of the dead Jews. Yet the high elegiac language demands that we imagine the star for a moment as if it stood for the transvalued others—or millions of others—now fixed in the firmament. The poem recoils from this transcendent solution, not as Shelley's "Adonais" does by coming under its sphere and being attracted ambivalently to its otherworldly connotations, but rather by treating the otherworldly hypothesis as mere figure for an awful history. Reversing the sacralizing trajectory of ordinary elegy, the "dwarfed star" is not a resolution opening toward the future, but an epitaph that is itself a horrid souvenir of the past.

My point is this: according to the poem's anti-elegiac rejection of consolation, it is quite as though the suddenly introduced apotheosis arrives too early, much as the "first" (25) and only asylum provided for the Jews, which was in fact their death, also arrived too early. And so begins a series of anachronistically conceived and disorienting images in the final three stanzas. A once transcendent star is instantly marred by the smoke as by a secularizing "yellow joke" (28), and our modes of valuation are obliged to refer to a harsh reality before which language is found lacking. Since the smoke is quickly associated with the ash that "[l]itters the black woods with the death / Of men" (31–32), we are positioned suddenly between the speaker's contemporary moment, in which atrocities have already become part of the strangely pastoral past, and an anachronistically surviving specter of history (the "one last breath" that "[c]urls from the monstrous chimney" [32–33]). In anti-elegiac terms, we might argue that it is the prospect of completing the past that forces this anachronistic eruption of atrocity into the present moment, as the woods seem again to be littered with death. So too, it is an implicit reversion from the ordinarily projected future of elegiac grief, the moment of transcendence and resolution in which history becomes merely the past, that promotes an anachronistic extravagance at the end of Jarrell's poem.

Perhaps the oddest of the three excesses presiding over this ending is the harmony of laughter with which the poem ends. By this rather overt inversion of reverent elegiac tears into sardonic or despairing laughter, Jarrell concludes on a final anti-elegiac note that has less to do with a critique of mourning's conventions than with the basic suspicion that any sincerely expressed grief has become extravagant. In chapter 4 I discussed a number of the anti-elegiac tendencies that promote a dialectical interrogation from within the elegiac tradition, but one might also venture a reading of resistant mourning through the more severely demystifying gesture of a laughter supplanting grief. For instance, there is that odd passage at the end of book 20 in The Odyssey where Athena casts a spell over the suitors that results in a violent fit of laughter, and, as they laugh without knowing the source of their hilarity, we are offered a glimpse of the brutal death that awaits them all.[30] Perhaps the spell of laughter functions to prevent Homer's reader from developing an inappropriate pathos for the suitors (a pathos that might cause us to resist Odysseus's extremely violent act of self-restoration); or perhaps, if we look for a rationale more internal to the narrative, the fit of laughter descends upon the suitors in order to prevent them from mourning or fearing for themselves—from becoming, in other words, vigilant in the cause of their own defense. At any rate, the distance of the laughter from all subjective motive is part of the point. The Homeric laughter keeps the suitors slightly alienated from a knowledge of their motives and their fates, which is to say it positions them as antithetical to the very restoration of identity Odysseus is about to achieve.

For more modern examples, we might think of Virginia's Woolf's confession in her posthumously published memoir "A Sketch of the Past" that as a young child she had laughed after visiting her mother's deathbed. Woolf offered several versions of such a scene elsewhere in her writings, and in each case it was the extravagantly performed grief of her father Leslie Stephen (or some fictional counterpart) that inspired her laughter or stood in stark contrast to it. With Leslie Stephen symbolizing the high sentimentality of Victorian mourning, the young Virginia becomes a prototype for modern anticonsolatory grief. Yet as such this is also an entirely involuntary model for protesting grief, the laughter motivated (rather like laughing in church) by its inappropriateness as a response to a solemn occasion.[31] Implicitly the laughter becomes a symptom of Woolf's inability to occupy her own grief for her mother. Not yet capable of understanding the depth of her loss and not able to perceive how the father's too-public grief could have anything to do with a sincere and private grief, Woolf laughs as a sign of the disproportion between grief and its effects.

As a final example, in which anti-elegiac laughter is provided with a more fully sardonic tone approaching Jarrell's own, we might think of Darl's insane laughter at the end of *As I Lay Dying* (1930). Throughout the novel, Darl has been the one who understands the absurdity of the family's sense of duty to the mother's body, the only one who understands how the quest to get Addie buried in Jefferson, despite the storm and flood and the series of misfortunes opposing their journey, has resulted in an absolutely irreverent treatment of her corpse, what Cora at one point calls an "outrage" to the mother's dead body. Darl's anti-elegiac opposition culminates in his attempt to set fire to a barn where the family has stopped for the night and in which his mother's body lies rotting and attracting vultures. After Jewel heroically rescues the obnoxious casket, the family quietly prepares to betray Darl; and at the novel's end, as Darl is seized by his family, handed to the authorities to be put in a straightjacket, and loaded on a cart to be taken to an insane asylum, his almost demonic laughter substitutes for grief. It is not just that he is unable to grieve for what has befallen him. It is also that grief has over the course of the novel been rendered its farcical opposite. What form could Darl's grief for himself or his hypothetical grief for the mother take in a world where the forms of mourning have been turned so severely, albeit accidentally, into a mockery of the dead?

I think we have to understand the laughter at the end of "A Camp in the Prussian Forest" as similarly signifying the final inappropriateness of grief itself to the historical discovery of incomparable atrocity and mass death. In a passage from his memoir in which he recalls watching the newsreels of 1945, Alfred Kazin rounds out his description of the almost indistinguishable "sticks" of corpses and of living dead by recalling the audience's markedly uncomfortable reaction to what they saw: "Then the sticks would come back on the screen, hanging on the wire, looking at us. It was unbearable. People coughed in embarrassment, and in embarrassment many laughed."[32] So uncomfortable is Kazin himself with the people's response that he has to interpose a motive of embarrassment between the images on the screen and the objective response in the theater—in which he hears coughing and laughter, but conspicuously no weeping. No doubt in remembering the coughing and laughter, Kazin wants to emphasize that there cannot be an appropriate response to the images projected on the screen. Yet it would be quite a different point to conclude that the most inappropriate of responses, laughter, has now become all that remains to pity or sincerest grief.

Though Jarrell's poem does not quite come to this conclusion, it does ask us to consider whether elegiac pity remains a valid response to atrocity or whether we can only laugh despairingly at the remains of our humanity put so publicly on display. Jarrell, like Kazin, may have attended a screening of the Paramount or Universal newsreels of 1945 in which members of the audience laughed uncomfortably before the spectacle of such incredible suffering. Whether or not his poem has been cued by some such real-life inappropriate response, the laughter of his speaker arises as a direct response to the historical facts of atrocity—indeed, precisely at the moment in which the crematoria chimneys anachronistically exhale their final breath. Not only this, but the speaker's laughter is soon joined by the laughter of the star on the rotting shroud, as the perspective of the victim is conjoined with a moment of mock apotheosis in order to ridicule the pity with which we might ordinarily respond to such severe suffering.

All told, the poem's ending signifies an impossible, even ridiculous attempt to find a proportion between what any person might feel upon hearing such news and the historical depth of the victims' sufferings. What the laughter itself finally signifies, I would contend, is the free-floating bad conscience, which cannot be made to seem merely the function of a soldier's individually conscientious grief. Much like Darl's insane laughter, which articulates a prophetic disdain for the moral and mourning frameworks operative in *As I Lay Dying*, Jarrell's laughter surpasses the soldier's ordinary capacity for judgment of himself or others. It is a remnant of public voice, perhaps a sardonic reflection on the exclusions of folkish sentiment that stood for collectivity in its most dangerous form, and perhaps also a remembrance of the inappropriate laughter of audiences of the 1945 newsreels; but most importantly, it signifies the gap between collective and individual idioms. According to its conventions, elegiac mourning would reconcile traditional, collective frameworks for bereavement to the particular occasion of the contemporary mourner's grief, but Jarrell proceeds by rendering the contrivance of those frameworks transparent and by exposing the final inability of personal voice to find therein its sympathetic measure. If there must always remain an uncomfortable gap between personal grief and public significance, if there is little we can do to reclaim the ordinary idioms of emotion in the face of such enormous and catastrophic historical events, the effect of the laughter is both to surpass and disintegrate the possibility of relatively ordinary expressions of personal grief premised upon simply discernible responsibilities for the other. In confronting the history of atrocity, the speaker is overwhelmed by the sheer excess of an event for which he would still find some means of expressing his responsibility, and it is in this sense that the poem is propelled at the end toward a fantastic, vaguely public scenario.

There is in "A Camp in the Prussian Forest" finally an impulse to side with the rhetorical contrivance of public meaning because the personal idiom must still be found accountable, even though it has lacked the means of responsibility. For this reason, Jarrell imposes the star's public significance (as a sign of propaganda, ethnic pride, and epitaphic commemoration) upon grief, rather than projecting any personal response onto the star. We may well take issue with the aesthetic merits of Jarrell's having turned at poem's end to extreme poetic rhetoric, but the rhetorical extravagance of high elegiac form, the anachronistic invocations of history, and the spell of inappropriate laughter all emphasize a necessary disproportion between convention and grief, between the public and the personal, and between responsibility and its results.

This is precisely what the rhetorical bombast of the final line—concluding with the heavy-handed lament "O Star of men!"—must signify to the reader who expects to be moved by witnessing atrocity. Whereas the ordinary expression of grief might bring at least a provisional end to our historical responsibility by recuperating our social good conscience—that is, by restoring the proportion between our sympathy for others and our historical sense of ourselves as beings who would demonstrate a better form of responsibility for others were they in our hands—Jarrell's deeply ironic and deliberately contrived use of apotheosis refuses to arrive at such a satisfactory end. Finding its analogy and expression in the inappropriate, sardonic, and involuntary laughter of the mourner, the star is also a souvenir of the American audience's unpleasurable response to the history of atrocity and, quite possibly, an emanation of our bad conscience in relation to that history. The epitaphic star, which is a memory both of Nazi persecution and Jewish identity, becomes finally the mock-transcendent star of humanity, an elegiac identification toward which we must be drawn if we are to come to any terms with the grief we feel over historical events. In explicating the bad conscience of mourning, Jarrell suggests, we must consider the facticity of unjust death that—as a matter of social or political circumstances, as a matter, for example, of highly restrictive American immigration policy and the absence of aggressive diplomatic policy with regard to the European refugee crisis—might have been, at least in part, prevented. Such overtly historical connotations insist upon mourning's misgivings as a form of conscience, even as they also emphasize that the expressions of grief are never adequate to the responsibilities they signify.

CHAPTER SEVEN

The Holocaust She Walks In

Sylvia Plath and the Demise of Lyrical Selfhood

The rhetorical excess of Randall Jarrell's "A Camp in the Prussian Forest" is jarring because it signifies a grief that disrupts the poet's conceit for mourning, never allowing the reader to characterize the persona who responds to loss or the particular quality of his grief. According to the ambiguity that presides over the ending of Jarrell's anticommemorative Holocaust elegy, once the narrator's despairing laughter finds its objective correlative in the laughter of a star, which had historically mocked personal dignity but now functions as a universalizing designation for the fallen dignity of all human beings, the historical plight of the Jews has infected the transcendent, cathartic possibilities of poetic expression. In short, we have been transported into a world forever bereft of elegiac pity. Indeed, it may be the relative absence of such elegiac pity—or, for that matter, of self-pity—that has spared Jarrell's most famous Holocaust poem, despite the imaginative contrivances and rhetorical extravagances through which he brings the bystander into a more intimate relation with an already neglected history, the severe criticisms directed at a poet such as Sylvia Plath.

In the tradition of elegy, the affect of literary mourning most often depends upon a poem's rhetorical distribution of pity—which is to say, the ethical ratio a poem establishes between pity for the dead and pity for the poem's mourner, as well as the historical ratio it supposes between this central mourner and the rest of a grieving world populated, sometimes universally, sometimes quite thinly, by all those other natural or human figures who also survive the dead. Especially when the latter ratio seems to involve a claim of one-to-one correspondence—as it does, for example, in Milton's "Lycidas"—we may suspect the poem's objective world of having become merely an emanation of personal affect, with the result that the historical component of loss seems muted:

> But O the heavy change, now thou art gone,
> Now thou art gone, and never must return!
> Thee Shepherd, thee the Woods, and desert Caves,
> With wild Thyme and the gadding Vine o'ergrown,
> And all their echoes mourn. (37–41)

Not only do we not believe that grief was ever as general as this, we are not supposed to believe it. For if poetry were required to imagine history as obedient to the sterner logic of mimetic representation—which is to say, as responsible for recording the world as it really was—there could be no gap between what happened and what might also have happened. And it is partly because of this gap between the sense of factual necessity presiding over our conception of a historical event and an imaginative understanding developed through a hypothesis of subjective agency internal to the event that we can say it might have been possible for history to occur otherwise, thus creating space for critical dissent, imaginative revision, or ethical correction.

Likewise, to the extent that a poem's rhetorical affect seems concentrated on the ratio between the narrator's personal grief and the poem's objective or historically oriented expressions of grief—this is true whether we suppose that there is a one-to-one correspondence between the former and latter such as one finds in the pathetic fallacy or an alienated relation in which the grieving poet seems set apart from her peers and the conventions that orient their responsiveness—we may be inclined to perceive the poem's ethical ratio as having been subsumed by the subjective poetics of expressiveness. It has to be acknowledged, however, that the attempt to restore a greater sense of historical proportion to a poem's ideological evasions or wishful revisionings (in other words, to adjust its historical ratio) will not necessarily amend the ethical ratio governing elegiac pity, if only because of the basic disjuncture between history and morality so effectively articulated by Nietzsche when he argues that morality is most fundamentally a lie told against its own genealogy. Most often the morally obligated subject, who believes she can discern the premises of social utility presiding over any particular instance of guilt or bad conscience, involves herself in a lie told against those historical relations of power governing any moral system as also against those social premises to which she is already subservient.[1] From this perspective, the problem with pity is not that it is an artificial or an excessive construct of moral sentiment, but rather that it is a perfectly apt expression of the logic of morality, which in itself is an ideological perception in excess of its historical genealogy.

Insofar as Levinas offers a revaluation of the Nietzschean bad conscience, his greatest debt to Nietzsche would be traced in his reclamation of the inequivalence that institutes moral consciousness.[2] Indeed, if not for Levinas's own reluctance to embrace the representational claims of historiographical method, one might speak of the responsibility for the other as being both linguistically and historically signified by a relation of inequivalence or disproportion. For the historical situatedness of the ethical relation—in which the moral subject can never answer fully enough to the plight of the other, a situation most poignantly demonstrated by the Holocaust—characterizes and contributes to responsibility's surpassing of obligation. Like Nietzsche, Levinas writes history against our limited modes of historical understanding and finally transumes history itself into the ethical relation of responsibility. By giving responsibility the very structure of a disproportion, Levinas especially attunes us to a sense in which the subject is never for itself without being also for others. Though this is not a version of sociality that simply refers us to collective consciousness as a corrective to a too private notion of ethics (since the collective consciousness is structured according to largely the same prescriptive limitations and economics as personal identity), Levinas nevertheless provides a collective or political connotation for all memory of the self—a horizon according to which one stands in responsibility in the full light of history, even if one perceives it partially or not at all.

Building then on the strangely ethical connotations of disproportion and attending to those particular questions of disproportion that inhere in elegiac voice and also trouble Plath's controversial use of Holocaust language, I propose in this final chapter to read the ironic sociality of Plath's rhetorical *I* as a measure of the cultural impact and memory of the Holocaust. In few poets has the rubric of what I have been calling the personal idiom of poetry been as consistently interrogated for its failure to abide by more appropriate public modes of memory. Most of the criticisms of Plath's Holocaust poetry focus on her apparent disregard for a sense of historical or ethical proportion in her imaginative uses of Holocaust victims and their sufferings. However we finally judge the outrageousness of Plath's Holocaust figures, I want at least to propose that much of their trespass inheres in the rhetorical performance of the poems. To read the poetry or the excesses of her language strictly as symptomatic of the tragic excess of her life is problematic not so much because it belittles her conscious and crafted manipulation of language (we do not need here to rehearse all the poststructuralist questions that trouble the field of an author's intentions), but because it permits us to underestimate how the Holocaust functions as history in her poems or, in more ethical terms, as a figure for the difficulty our society has in commemorating victims of atrocity.

Some of Plath's strategies are those of the modern anti-elegy. For a variety of reasons, including the Freudian revolution in conceiving of the psyche's motives for attachments and, more spectacularly, the historical scale of mass death in World Wars I and II, the modern elegy has turned with ever greater urgency to considering the intersection between the mournful valuation of the dead and the so-called aggressive instincts or emotional ambivalences of those who grieve for them. In poems such as "Mary's Song" and "Daddy," Plath employs psychological terms that are reminiscent of both Nietzsche and Freud as she interrogates the mystifications of mourning and returns them seemingly to the aggrieved sentiments of a mourner's personality. Even as she does this, however, Plath foregrounds many of the very tensions that preside over the Nietzschean hermeneutic with its fluctuating mythic valences, demanding that her reader face the signifying power of history as an excess to ordinary rationality and responsibility, quite as though she perceived in us already a turning away from the meaning of atrocity, a wish not to come face to face with it.

Whatever metaphoric license Plath might appear to take with Holocaust history, if we are to insist that an ethical response to the Holocaust is possible then the fault in this straying from history cannot be laid too simply on metaphor itself. For already there is a historical willfulness that accompanies her use of metaphor. Like Jarrell before her, Plath's experiments in historical sensibility seem a mixed success; but also like Jarrell before her, she would have us understand the bad conscience as central to any ethical meaning we can take away from Holocaust history. By bringing the burden of the bad conscience to bear upon the personal idiom, she runs the risk of making the Holocaust stand as a figure for interiority. Still, even if such a complaint were to be admitted as at least partly true, what interiority has meant within the lyrical tradition of mourning will have been largely revisioned by Plath's elegiacs, forced to a new reckoning with a history it would prefer to forget.

Reviewing *Ariel* Once More

The Holocaust poems of *Ariel* have often been taken as proof of the ahistorical and thus ethically inappropriate nature of a personal, emotional, and imaginative response to the Nazi genocide.[3] While applauding Plath for being one of a few contemporary writers to "counter the general inclination to forget the death camps" and also offering some appreciation of the poems themselves, George Steiner suggested in a 1965 essay that a poet who so translates her private grievances into the idiom of a great historical horror commits a "subtle larceny" threatening the very legitimacy of the poems themselves (301); and in a 1969 essay he realized his early doubts in a fuller condemnation of Plath's imaginative trespass.[4] When in 1973 Irving Howe dissented against Plath's ascendant literary critical reputation, he invoked the Holocaust as a moral barometer for his suspicions about the merits of Plath's poetry. For Howe, as for Steiner, drawing attention to Plath's troubling representation of the Holocaust functioned as shorthand for questioning her accomplishment as a poet, but the note of moral condemnation had become more strident in Howe, as he suggested there was something "monstrous, utterly disproportionate" about poems in which one's emotions about one's father are "deliberately compared with the historical fate of the European Jews."[5] Emphasizing the rather obvious historical point about a disproportion between her life and that of the victims of atrocity, Howe makes this disproportion a signifier of Plath's intention and thus, implicitly, of the poetry itself. This is also much the line held later (in 1980) by Alvin H. Rosenfeld, when he remarks upon the "rhetorical appetite for atrocity" evident in Plath's poetry and insists that the terms of her comparisons are simply "not apposite," the gap between personal horrors and those brought about by the Nazis too severe to be repaired by the pathetic patchings of a non-Jewish American woman's imagination.[6] Among the esteemed company of Steiner, Howe, and Rosenfeld, Plath's metaphors are interpreted as if they were strict analogies—all of these criticisms proceeding from an anxiety that Plath found her individual sufferings not only similar, but somehow proportional to the fate of Holocaust victims.

There is an escape clause, however, for if the "comparison [was] made spontaneously" (166), Howe suggests, then the case may well be less monstrous than sad. Undoubtedly, in adding this slight qualification, Howe has in mind a perception of Plath that had begun to emerge through A. Alvarez's premise, in *The Savage God: A Study of Suicide* (1970), that Plath's suicide had itself been an elaborate performance, a cry for help.[7] She could not really have meant to die, if anything she was attempting to exorcise the theme of death in her life; like her persona Lady Lazarus she fully expected another "[c]omeback in broad day." Making passing reference to her Holocaust language, Alvarez claimed that Plath had developed the "queer conception" that to be an adult was to be a survivor, "an imaginary Jew from the concentration camps of the mind" (20), but in this respect she was finally, in his eyes, a representative witness to modern death.[8] What I find most interesting is that the two points seem interdependent. It is quite as if the real intention of self-destruction would make Plath's use of the Holocaust merely a screen for her personal pain and thus either an unconsciously expressed pathology or a deliberately sensationalistic intention (thus anticipating the two options Howe's severe judgment permitted these poems). Alvarez's influential study insisted that Plath's obsession with suicide, like her interest in the Holocaust, was the poetic reflex of a talented and troubled mind, which is to say, a symptom of a personal malady that quickly became representative of the pain and suffering of others. I think it safe to say that there is not another literary figure of late-twentieth-century America who has been as consistently interpreted through her biography or for whom the equation between the voice of the lyrical poem and the poet who speaks in the poem has been made quite as strongly.[9]

The perhaps misguided effort of Alvarez and a number of Plath's feminist readers to defend her poetry as if the cultural and gender politics pervading Plath's tragic life could legitimate such an imaginative exchange of sufferings only made the suspicions of those who were critical of her appropriations all the more germane. For both the defenses and criticisms of Plath's Holocaust language depended on the broad cultural impulse to associate these poems with the confessional school of poetry made famous by Robert Lowell and—closer to home for Plath—by the recent success of Anne Sexton's *All My Pretty Ones*.[10] Again, it was Steiner who had implicitly framed the terms of this debate by relating Plath's poems to those of Lowell and the confessional school, while hesitantly admiring the honesty with which she treated the "nervous-physiological makeup" of women. In his earlier review, Steiner suggests that it is Plath's "rhetoric of sincerity" that makes her poems so difficult to evaluate.[11] Conceding the rhetorical authority Plath gained by introducing into her poetry directly a woman's difficult apprehension of her own body, Steiner assumed, as so many critics have since, that the poetry's claim to the Holocaust proceeded along these very lines. The rhetoric of Plath's sincerity had to do with her manipulation of a radically personal idiom, and if at times the rhetoric ventured where it should not, what was not to be doubted was that she had done it all with "desperate integrity" (302).[12]

Though Steiner recognized the limits of an overly biographical hermeneutic, he also believed that Plath's poems put themselves inevitably in the way of such a reading. Having turned her desperate integrity toward the Holocaust and pushed her poems to a threshold where poetry might "give to reality the greater permanence of the imagined," Plath "could not return from them" (302). When James E. Young turned to these poems in 1988, offering what is perhaps the most sustained sympathetic reading of Plath's imaginative appropriations of Holocaust history, he expanded Steiner's speculation into full argument. Steiner had all but said that Plath's poems were too strident, too sincere. In them she had perhaps risked too much of her real self, and as a consequence she could not reclaim herself from the poems she had become.[13] Young also read the poems as confessional utterances, beginning from the premise that in them Plath was figuring herself as a Holocaust Jew, but then proceeded by way of a paradox to extend Steiner's hint of what it might mean for Plath not to return from her poems into a reading of what it should mean for us that Plath was unable to return more specifically from the figures of atrocity with which she had identified herself.[14]

By reversing the burden of appropriation, Young suggests that, rather than the other way around, it is the Holocaust that finally appropriates the poet. As he takes seriously an observation made by Alvarez elsewhere—that of the half-dozen suicides or near-suicides he had known personally, each had "prepared his act with a fierce immersion in the literature of the camps"—Young offers a revaluation of Plath ultimately based upon this loss of self to an imagined history.[15] There are two basic strands of argument in Young's reading of Plath, the first being that the Holocaust has become an archetype entering the public imagination and therefore inclining toward universalizing connotations; and the second, that there is a measure of authenticity in Plath's use of these figures that cannot be reduced to a bad faith use of an experience not properly her own. Taking issue with Rosenfeld's attempt to distinguish between a historical and a biographical order of pain, Young argues that insofar as history converts into cultural memory it will be hard for any reader to separate biographically determined pain from historically determined pain—which is to say, her private history from what is more properly public history. Since we are beings immersed in culture, Young takes it for granted that our figures are necessarily our reality. What this means is that for the poet who comes to the event through cultural memory, the realities of the inner life can be generated by knowledge of the Holocaust.[16]

While granting the Holocaust the status of a broadly circulating signifier, Young suggests at the same time that it is a signifier in excess of its significations, one that extraordinarily destroys ordinary usage. Legitimated in a sense by her self-destruction, it is quite as though Plath's pain has become a paradoxical measure of history. What I am implying is that despite an admirable effort to hear the figures of the Holocaust taking their toll on the sensibility of a poet frequently accused of taking too much license with this history, Young nevertheless upholds the notion that Plath's poems are inescapably confessional. Having constructed herself in language as a site of vulnerability, Plath offers the strange—but perhaps not atypical—case of a poet traumatized by her own literary imagination. Like those who had preceded him, Young concentrates on the specter of Plath's life and death, either looming omnipresently above or intruding directly upon the fictive world she creates in her poems. Yet he also intimates that the real meaning of these poems might reside in their implosion of the personal idiom. If the line between personal and public modes of memory is hard to maintain historically, it may be almost impossible to draw imaginatively. By means of this logic, Young places us within range of an effect that I want to attribute to the strange rhetoric of the poems themselves, rather than to Plath's intrusive life—namely, the effect whereby the personal idiom yields to the extrinsic event of history as to the very possibility of collective meanings.

Indeed one might almost argue—according to a chronology of these poems in which "Daddy" (composed October 12, 1962) and "Lady Lazarus" (October 23–29, 1962) are succeeded by "Getting There" (November 6, 1962) and "Mary's Song" (November 19, 1962)—that Plath's confessional appropriation of the Holocaust subsides over time. "Daddy," as the first of her overt Holocaust poems, is the poem that continues to provide the most fodder for the objections I have outlined above, with "Lady Lazarus," the next chronologically, running a close second. The two poems composed in November seem more properly designated as Holocaust poems in the sense that each offers a sustained imaginative encounter with the Holocaust as history, rather than an appropriation of its most terrific images as a mode of self-interpretation. Such a view of "Getting There" has been advanced recently by Susan Gubar, who argues that readers have underestimated Plath's self-critical and sophisticated deployment of the trope of prosopopeia, which registers Plath's doubt about being able to speak from within the historical parameters of another's voice and thus admits the real distance between herself and the atrocities of which she writes.[17] Although I doubt that such a direct figurative sensitivity is as readily discernible in the earlier "Daddy," my subsequent reading of "Mary's Song" does emphasize Plath's growing unease with her own use of the personal idiom.

In my view, then, the chronological hypothesis I have just outlined—according to which Plath became, in a little more than a month's time, a more sensitive reader of the Holocaust—seems a bit too easy and schematic, but it is not altogether misleading. What it helps us do is unsettle an interpretive imperative to read Plath's Holocaust imagery as veiled confessional language, for if we were to emphasize the latter two poems in discussing Plath's poetry on the Holocaust, we would have to observe that the difficulty of the subject matter is reflected in its resistance to the imaginative appropriation with which Plath has so often been charged. In focusing on "Mary's Song" and "Daddy," I choose the two poems where a crisis in the personal idiom seems to me most evident, and if I do not read them according to the chronological order of composition, this is because I want to see how reading in the other direction—from the more overt historical sensitivity of "Mary's Song" to the seemingly confessional utterance of "Daddy"—might help us discern Plath's subtle engagement with Holocaust history.

Sacrifice, History, and the Personal Idiom: "Mary's Song"

In beginning, then, with "Mary's Song," we confront a poem that falls among the controversial grouping of poems that Ted Hughes included in *Ariel* in lieu of other slightly more biographical poems Plath had slated for her volume. Moreover, "Mary's Song" appeared only in the 1966 American edition of *Ariel* (appearing in Britain five years later in the volume *Winter Trees*). Reviewers of the British edition, such as George Steiner and M. L. Rosenthal, lacked this poem in formulating the early picture of Plath's exploitation of the Holocaust that has remained very much with readers ever since. Though the poem is not less sensational in treating outrages of atrocity as poetic spectacle—as it arrives in the final lines at a reading of the Holocaust as a mock-Eucharistic moment and even perhaps the very epitome of Christian culture—its sensationalism is clearly concentrated on the Holocaust as historical event. More specifically, I would contend that in this poem we observe a pronounced yielding of the personal idiom to history as an extrinsic force.

Immediately the poem's deep pursuit of a memory of victims is vexed by having to run in and at the same time against the grain of a cultural logic of sacrifice, which has its basis in a Christian hermeneutic so forgetful of its origins as to ignore the violences it once perpetrated and continues yet to uphold. It is the difficult fate of the personal idiom to be troubled and moved by forces beyond the persona's immediate capabilities of memory, as we approach the Holocaust through a consciousness remote from the events it evokes:

> The Sunday lamb cracks in its fat.
> The fat
> Sacrifices its opacity. . . .
>
> A window, holy gold.
> The fire makes it precious,
> The same fire
>
> Melting the tallow heretics,
> Ousting the Jews.
> Their thick palls float
>
> Over the cicatrix of Poland, burnt-out
> Germany.
> They do not die. (1–12)[18]

As the poem opens, a Christian woman symbolically named Mary by the poem's title cooks her Sunday lamb, innocent of both its religious and historical connotations. The metaphoric connotation of "sacrifice" in the third line is strictly visual: we are supposed to picture a lamb in the oven, the fat losing its white opacity as it cooks. With the ellipsis ending the first stanza, however, Plath denotes an imaginative trespassing of the poem's narrative frame, as the persona is liberated from her immediate or contemporary context to pursue what seems to be either personal hallucination or, perhaps more ambitiously, a quasi-visionary transportation. Indeed, the contrived visual transition causes the entire scene to shift to the inside of a church, but not (I am assuming) as a function of the woman's piety. Even before it makes reference to the Holocaust, then, "Mary's Song" has begun to overreach the imaginatively associative mind of its narrating persona, as if history were capable of producing its own ironic and corrective remembrances of events that might otherwise be diminished or neglected.

There is a startling disproportion between the characterized personal voice and the poem's imaginative reach. As Plath traces the muted sacrificial logic of Christian Sundays, the specter of a Jewish past begins to preside over the phenomena of historical memory and only thus to refer us to the more recent history of the Holocaust. The "fire" of the second stanza, coming from the implicit votive candles that illuminate the church's windows, immediately evokes a ghastly historical memory when it is presumed to be the "same fire" used to burn heretics, all of whom might be figurative, unrepentant Jews. Or perhaps Plath wants to draw upon the memory of antisemitic pogroms, so often the by-product of Christian holy days and the Easter season with its liturgical recapitulations of Jesus as sacrificial lamb and its somewhat schizophrenic celebration of a theologically necessary sacrifice that is nevertheless blamed on the Jews as instigators of Christ's misery.

What seems inescapable in Plath's poem are the traces of severe violence hidden in the by now banal connotations of Christian Sundays and liturgical recollections of the paschal sacrifice. Plath's insistence that the fires of Mary's Sunday oven or the votive candles of a contemporary church are the "same fires" that burned heretics and ousted Jews is rhetoric of the strongest kind, imposing memory where it has been absent. Since Christian memory remains willfully innocent of its own center, the poem conflates Christ the sacrificial lamb with all Jews who have been historical victims of the implicit or overt menace of Christian righteousness, a conflation likely to outrage both Jews and Christians alike. Although one might read the participles of the second stanza as simply serial ("Melting the tallow heretics, / Ousting the Jews" [7–8]), I would suggest that the force of the juxtaposition is oddly appositional. The heretics and Jews are in effect the same: they are significant here as the sacrificial objects of Christian liturgy, reenacting, however unconsciously, those deep ambivalences about violence imperfectly contained by the story of Christ's redemptive crucifixion. Indeed, a rather gruesome allusion seals this conflation of the Lamb of God and those heretics and Jews burned in his name: for the term "tallow heretic" remembers not only the burning flesh and fat of the heretics burned by the Inquisition (so many of whom were charged as being unconverted Jews), but also recalls the rumors that Nazis were harvesting the fat of their Jewish victims for industrial and commercial purposes. Plath's densely figured substantive refers in the first place to altar candles made of tallow and then proceeds by metaphoric extension to include the memory of all the atrocities upon which holy candles have thrown their light, and this personifying movement from objects to persons imagines the candles grotesquely as if they were the literal by-product of the Holocaust.[19]

If this figurative turning of candles themselves into the Jews they should remember seems far-fetched, we have to see that all the fetching belongs to Plath's poem, which has been carried forward entirely by a series of imagistic associations beginning with the dripping fat of a Sunday lamb. The subsequent reference to the "thick palls" alludes to the mystery of Christian transubstantiation, recalling sardonically, in an image employed by Randall Jarrell as well as by a number of Jewish Holocaust poets, the exterminated Jews who exist only in the sooty smoke of the chimneys of Birkenau.[20] Again the metaphoric aptness of the image begins at a visual level, as "pall" describes the illusory concreteness and thickness of smoke in the sky. But surely, in a poem that puns so openly and associatively on Christian space and mind, we are supposed also to hear these "thick palls" as referring to the many palls of Roman Catholic liturgy—whether to altar cloths, the vestments donned by popes and bishops, or perhaps (with special elegiac aptness) the cloth spread over the hearse at a funeral. Through these vestments and adornments of Catholic or perhaps Anglican tradition (Plath was irregularly attending Anglican services during the final two years of her life), the poet signifies the hateful history that so often accompanied Christian holiness, from burning heretics as Jews or Jews as heretics to the infamous pogroms of Eastern Europe, forcing us to see in these events the precedent and precipitating conditions of the Holocaust.

With the beginning of the fourth stanza, the poem assumes a mythic topography expressing the inadequacy of Western culture's derivatively Christian narratives for redeeming loss.[21] Plath ironically contends—as a funereal pall of smoke made literally of Jews lingers in the Polish and German sky and travesties resurrection—that this history will not die. As she speaks next of the "cicatrix of Poland," it is possible that Plath refers to a sutured wound in the Polish map, which would then stand for the excised Jewish population of Poland, but this more precise meaning of the metaphor is overridden by the connotations of what I want to call the *lazy genitive*, which is to say, a genitive of predication. According to this not quite grammatical usage of the genitive, which recalls both the inflated liturgical language of Psalm 96 with its imperative to "worship the Lord in the beauty of holiness" and American advertising or Hollywood colloquialisms such as "a beauty of a car," "a gem of a movie," or "a peach of a girl," Plath refers to Poland itself as a cicatrix.[22] Floating imprecisely between a claim of metonymic proportion and descriptive attribution, rendering illustrative metaphors as if they were substantive truths, the lazy genitive is mostly a shorthand technique. Indeed, the relation between the high (biblical) and low (advertising) modes of the lazy genitive is continuous, as in each case a language of stunned appreciation degenerates into easy attributions of supposedly incomparable worth.

Such a confusion of rhetorical levels seems an especially apt locution for Plath, who veers so often between a self-important, almost mythic rhetoric and casual observations spoken in the rhythms of everyday speech (as, for example, when she descends masterfully in "Tulips" from the devastating significance of an unwanted gift of hospital flowers—"I didn't want any flowers, I only wanted / To lie with my hands turned up and be utterly empty"—to a perfectly appropriate and petty rejection of their beauty—"The tulips are too red in the first place, they hurt me" [36–37, 43]).[23] The lazy genitive is symptomatic of a speech that cannot do justice to what it appreciates or, in this case, to what it laments. Thus though the phrase "cicatrix of Poland" approximates a grievance standing for history, it is not quite enough that the cicatrix should refer to what Poland has lost. As historical scar, it must signify Poland itself as a wounded topos, a place in history forever abandoned by redemptive or healing mythologies. Through this bathetic designation of a hurtfulness and lack belonging to its history, Plath refuses to permit Poland to inhabit a nationalist identity vestigially rooted in Christendom and forces it to play host to a negatively allegorical meaning as it signifies violences suppressed by nationalist memory.

Having thus exposed the wounds of nationalist mythology, Plath ventures further into mythic language in the final three stanzas of "Mary's Song," only now she employs a rather free-floating sense of myth as that which is entirely extrinsic to personal memory as also to collective memory:

Gray birds obsess my heart,
Mouth-ash, ash of eye.
They settle. On the high

Precipice

That emptied one man into space

The ovens glowed like heavens, incandescent.

It is a heart,

This holocaust I walk in,

O golden child the world will kill and eat. (13–21)

The ordinary woman is suddenly obsessed by extraordinary meanings that will not be imaginatively appropriated, but settle, rather, on her consciousness.

If one were to apply the method of René Girard here, one could perhaps conclude that Plath has discerned the function of all sacred myth as a veil for historical violence.[24] In "Mary's Song," however, mythic meaning does not remain continuous with ideology so much as it marks a rhetorical excess irreconcilable to either personal or cultural memory. As Plath's mythic apparatus specifically recalls the victim as one who is cast outside collective memory and the nexus between history and culture, the persona here moves in or into history only by getting caught up in a mythic narrative greater than her understanding. The moment is not unlike Plath's association of history and corpses in "Letter in November":

This is my property.

Two times a day

I pace it, sniffing

The barbarous holly with its viridian

Scallops, pure iron,

And the wall of old corpses.

I love them.

I love them like history. (16–23)

There is perhaps in this passage an Eliotic fondness for those overly naturalized corpses that remember both fertility rites and sacrificial praxis as though they referred to better times ("That corpse you planted last year in your garden," Eliot's speaker had asked, "Has it begun to sprout?" [71–72]).[25] But rather than accept the conflation of nature's indifferently regenerative pattern and the history of human violence upon which Eliot's allusion to the myth of the recuperative natural world depends, Plath insists upon reading the ordinary pastoral usage of the vegetable world as if the holly were "barbarous" for lending itself to such meaning. As opposed to the famous mock fertility rite of *The Wasteland*, Plath's "wall of old corpses" seems a strangely literal and si-multaneously unaccommodated memory, or at least it seems so until a few stanzas later she completes the reference by alluding to the "mouths of Ther-mopylae" (35), to that famous battle of 480 B.C. in which the Greeks turned the Persians back from Europe, with the corpses of the fallen Greeks symbol-izing this last wall of defense against colonization.[26] What Plath has done is invert Eliot's rhetorical move. Unlike Eliot's Stetson, who desperately per-forms fertility rites with dead bodies as if the dead might still be of sacrificial use in history, Plath's speaker insists on excavating the corpses of Greek sol-diers even in her English garden, quite as if all the evidence of acculturated nature could finally reveal the very intention of mythic (and pastoral) mean-ing to be the dead bodies of Greek soldiers or, in "Mary's Song," of quasi-Jewish martyrs.

It is every bit Plath's irony—and not just my own—that takes exception to a sacrificial logic that would redeem Jewish victims to the progress of culture. That Plath loves vaguely remembered corpses much as she loves history seems in her "Letter in November" both slightly glib and ironically quaint (the scene is, after all, an English garden). Still, at times the reader may be almost grateful for Plath's ironic qualifications of her own mythic rhetoric, since they provide respite from her otherwise relentless accumulation of allusion and metaphor and her dense poetic topography. What generates the impression of glibness in so many of Plath's poems is not only a frequently bathetic descent into the personal idiom, but an ironic defensiveness that characterizes the per-sonal idiom as though it served to deflect the history to which it might suc-cumb. If "Mary's Song" lacks the same mixture of rhetorical levels one hears in a poem such as "Letter in November" and in her previous Holocaust poems "Daddy" and "Lady Lazarus," this is largely because the poem's personal idiom poorly withstands the mythic force of history. Thus, as the sixth stanza mounts toward archetypal Christian space, Plath's previous conflations of the lamb and Christ and of Jews and Christ turn suddenly toward the poem's most historic and simultaneously horrific reference—namely, the ovens of the cre-matoria. With this move, not only must the Nazi atrocities be included in Christian memory; they occupy its most sacred claims and its transcendent myths. Much as Paul Celan's famous "Deathfugue" had troubled the future of transcendence by remembering Jews who "shovel a grave in the air," Plath here joins the space of transcendent meaning to the historical memory of the crematoria.[27] Suddenly degraded and incorporated into the memory of a

violence that history would otherwise have abandoned, in these final two stanzas the transcendent meaning of Christian sacrifice reverts to its etiology in
pure violence.

Much as I admire James E. Young's revaluation of Plath's Holocaust language, I do not see how the final lines of "Mary's Song" can be read, as he
reads them, as if Plath were addressing herself and "making herself the sacrifice here" (123); and I say this in light of the critique of sacrifice with which I
have so far credited Plath, and also because this is a poem that has worked
quite hard to establish its fictive setting and persona. Even if the poem's feminine persona might speak in part for Plath herself, the child of the final line
would have to be an emanation, according to the poem's ruling conceit, of a
maternal anxiety for her own children. Whether the poem's title names a pro-
tagonist outright or conflates her ironically with the Virgin Mary, it is clear
that the final line is uttered as a lament for a child who is soon to be sacrificed
or who already has been sacrificed. Accordingly, Plath uses the lowercase
word *holocaust* at a time in which it was used with some frequency to refer to
the Nazi genocide, but had not yet become common parlance for those events.
The pun is perhaps richer and less manipulative at the time she uses it than it
would be even two years after her death when *Ariel* was first published and had
begun to be reviewed.[28] Having used the word *holocaust* in previous poems
with an eye toward investigating its sacrificial connotations,[29] Plath here renders a Mary who reluctantly or defiantly yields her son to the sacrificial logic
of the world, her apostrophic address to an already dead child signifying a contrafactual elegiac wish, a wishfulness that is futile precisely to the extent that
she walks already within the memory of the Holocaust of recent history. The
ambiguity of the phrase "holocaust she walks in" derives from the fact that this
is nothing less than history extrinsically imposed against desire, much as we
might imagine a Virgin Mary who meets the requirements of Christian history not as the bearer of God and of God's mythic intentions, but as a woman
alienated by the cultural violence that takes her son's life. By de-Christianiz-
ing Mary and characterizing her as a contemporary mother lamenting a son
who is also an archetypal Jewish victim, Plath has not historicized emotion so
much as drawn attention to a history pronounced mythically as beyond the
mother's desire.

The poem's elegiac pathos resides within history as an ethical wish that history could be written otherwise; and the final line seems a desperate interjec-
tion following upon the grim acknowledgment of the history of sacrificed Jews

who haunt the Christian redemptive scheme, almost as if Plath would have been better served to employ Dickinsonian dashes in her final stanza:

> It is a heart -
> This holocaust I walk in -
> O golden child the world will kill and eat.

The nexus between a potentially receptive heart and a history of atrocity turning to redemptive sacrifice is supposed to be troubling. The apostrophic exclamation of the final line disrupts grammatical sense, and my hypothetical dashes would highlight the disruption to reveal an appositional relation between "heart" and "holocaust" that is already inadequate. In what structures of meaning, "Mary's Song" asks us, might the persona's consciousness or her poem itself take refuge once either has been besieged by history?

There is finally a tension between the mythic excesses of Plath's language and the woman's semiconscious incorporation of this history. A too innocent mother comes to recognize the world's violence, and as she witnesses to the enduring claim exacted upon Christian culture by the Jewish victims of the Nazis, she universalizes the violence done to them by finding an analogy to their sacrifice (but not their sufferings) in the crucifixion of Christ, who is figured as both a historical Jew and any contemporary child. By the poem's demystifying logic, however, the analogy has to be ironic: it is simply too convenient, too historically reductive. To put the suffering of the Jewish victims back into this Christian narrative scheme of sacrifice functions as a desperate strategy for coping with an unpleasure whose largeness signifies the expansive insignificance of unnarrated history. Surely, as coping this seems mere travesty. Having foregrounded the smallness of the woman's experience at the opening of the poem—with the ellipsis at the end of the first stanza marking a challenge to identity, rather than an affirmation of it—"Mary's Song" eventually opens toward historical connotations far beyond her immediate grasp, never able to effect a containment that would stand for the resolution of grief or historical injustice.

Though the containment of history may be the goal and perhaps also the necessary condition from which an *I* speaks to affirm its place in cultural identity, such a resolution has become impossible. Indeed, I am inclined to read the final line ("O golden child the world will kill and eat" [21]) as a lament for a former mythic innocence enacted throughout Christian sacred history and lived, albeit as a violent lie, until the contemporary cultural moment in which the apocalyptic scale of the Nazis' genocidal violence revealed the many violences upon which the Christian mythos of Europe had been founded. It is only by walking within range of the historical truths of a Holocaust greater than those violences traced but also contained by biblical holocausts and Sunday lambs that the mother figure comes to apostrophize the child with elegiac pity. As she laments, "O golden child the world will kill and eat," we imagine a child abandoned by its own as also by others' mythic resources, and thus left exposed to the real atrocity of history. The questions as to whether writing the poems of *Ariel* was an imaginative task from which Plath could not return and whether the Holocaust figures she had used played a determinative role in preventing that return are by definition biographically speculative and undecidable. But in "Mary's Song" we can at least say that there is no returning from history to a personal idiom, unless it is to suggest the incommensurability between a bourgeois woman's story and a Holocaust she can walk in only imaginatively. History has been imposed extrinsically as that from which there is no refuge. Once we recognize this unpleasurable plot, we begin to see how the poem enacts the very mistake (or mistaking) of personal voice that presides over so many of our literary critical readings of Plath.

"Daddy" and the Moral Difficulty of Making Nazis Familiar

In "Mary's Song," a singular consciousness—be it strictly Mary's or some amalgamation of Plath and her fictive persona—is challenged by a violent history without ever becoming an object of the violence to which it witnesses. The poem's fictive posture elaborates a historical specter of bystanding, and one might argue that Holocaust history is preserved in its separateness from and incommensurability with ordinary suffering by the very fact that we are never presented with a personal history of the lyrical persona through which we might discern analogous sufferings.

In "Daddy" this is infamously not the case. The self-reflexive tendency of this poem has led many critics to emphasize Plath's troubling imaginative transpositions as if they stood for the interchangeability of her metaphoric terms, so that, according to Jacqueline Rose, Plath's most severe critics commit themselves to a "repudiation of metaphor itself—that is, of the necessary difference or distance between its two terms" (206).[30] In order to work toward a better understanding of this most controversial of Plath's poems, I want to explicate in as efficient a manner as possible the theoretical suppositions informing

Rose's insightful and influential reading of "Daddy." Although it is astute on many particulars of the poem, Rose's reading does not do enough to redress the critique that the Holocaust functions as mere metaphoric fodder for the poet's personal pain or to suggest, in more general terms, how personal grief measures itself against the claims made by a history of atrocity.

Much depends here on the status we give Plath's Holocaust figures—whether their aspect of unpleasure seems an emanation of the personal idiom or that which is inappropriately translated into the pleasurable capability of a self, or whether the unpleasure functions as a violation or transgression of the self's ordinary capabilities. From Rose's point of view, the metaphoric reach of the psyche is what constitutes its basic capability in history, this range of imaginative positionality functioning as the very material of reality. Thus Rose attributes to metaphor and the associated mechanism of psychic fantasy the therapeutic capacity to restore to the personal idiom a viability and freedom from within history and, in her reading of "Daddy," she implicitly valorizes the Nietzschean confession of an aggressive instinct in the animal man (or in this case, woman), while also upholding the viewpoint that sociality is constituted through the self's capacity to credit itself with a construct of power according to which it is viable in the world. A psyche's most basic responsibility to itself and to the history to which it responds would be to deflect those abiding states of unpleasure that tend to mark it as other than for itself. In other words—to adopt a Nietzschean phrasing—in order to be in history the psyche may require the defeat of the bad conscience.

In her approach to Plath, Rose proceeds by way of a significant "detour," first providing her reader with an overview of a number of papers presented at the 1985 Hamburg Congress of the International Association of Psychoanalysis, which was convened in Germany for the first time since 1932. The German hosts had made an odd stipulation, forbidding any direct reference to Nazi history in the proceedings unless it was deemed unavoidable—as, for instance, in the case histories of patients who were children of Holocaust survivors or Nazis. According to Rose, perhaps as a necessary consequence of this suppression, there was what almost amounted to a consensus fascination at the conference with patients whose cases testified to the burden of second-generation memory. From within the therapeutic situation, the children of survivors and the children of Nazis found that they shared a paradoxically similar plight: "Over and over again these patients found themselves in fantasy occupying either side of the victim/aggressor divide" (209).

What the Hamburg Congress would seem to prove is that if we fail to speak directly to the facts of Holocaust history, we (or at least many among us) may continue to inhabit the subject-positions of victim or aggressor without the beneficial mediation of metaphor and fantasy through which such fixated definitions of self might be exorcised. By this line of thought, fantasy has, as it were, two sides: it facilitates a retrospective coping with violence and the subject-positions imaginatively occupied in relation to acts of violence, and it promotes the creative play of a psyche that is at least partly determined by the self's naturally or animally inclined instincts toward aggression. Not surprisingly, it is this question of fantasy—or, more particularly, of how the psyche is constituted in fantasy through the very terms of its metaphors—that draws Rose's attention in "Daddy." In a certain sense, Rose answers critics of Plath's Holocaust language by refusing to answer them directly. They have missed the point and power of these poems, which were never meant to be read as history, but as reflections on the mechanisms of fantasy through which each of us works out a relation to history. Moreover, Rose suggests, when Plath reads the metaphoric properties of a psyche already determined by patriarchal cultural meanings, the internal disposition of aggression, and the aggressive demonstrations of the self's own vitality, she is a perceptive reader of the very nexus upon which fascistic culture is unconsciously constructed.

It has to be said in qualification of Rose's position that she is advancing neither a historical nor, for that matter, a moral argument so much as she is putting forth a reading based in a therapeutic rationale. Indeed, it might be more accurate to say that according to Rose's psychoanalytic hermeneutic, moral or historical meaning has been referred to the constitutive moment of the psyche, which is congenitally defined by two basic subject-positions that in themselves trace a sociality defined by conflict. In Freud, the outward signs of a social struggle for power have been so radically internalized that one comes to speak of the self as divided between masochistic and sadistic tendencies, with an aspect of aggressivity functioning as a predisposition for each psychic attitude. In this view, passivity is always an introversion of an original aggressive impulse, veiling a potentiality in the subject for enacting the fantasy terms of its own internal drama at the expense of others. The real danger, as psychoanalysis imagines it, is that a self will excise the memory of its constitutively aggressive impulses and conduct itself as if it were innocent of these most basic, albeit often unconscious, intentions.[31]

From the psychoanalytic perspective, the most dangerous memory is necessarily one that cannot be remembered. As Rose puts it, summarizing one of the papers presented at the 1985 Hamburg Congress, psychoanalysis requires a return to the troubling event, a return that is made "in order to *restore* the function of metaphor." What the patient has been troubled by is a "literalness of language which makes memory impossible," a position from which she can have "no real knowledge that the Holocaust even took place" (213). In Rose's view, Plath's most severe critics align themselves, in the name of history, with an impossibly literal conception of testimonial speech that would prevent the subject from achieving the distance from the past by virtue of which one also achieves historical perspective. This perspectival distance is in fact the same distance from which metaphor speaks in its imaginative graftings of disparate realms of experience. As metaphor takes hold of that which is remote from the subject's experience, it refuses to allow an event to remain literal and therefore unintelligible. For Rose, the implicit ethical value of metaphor is that it refuses to ascribe an absolute alterity to experience, in part because such an alterity, whatever it has meant in history, will necessarily be experienced as a violence against the self. It is for this reason that metaphor is "the recognition and suspension of aggression" (213).

When Freud theorized the unconscious as a realm given over to a private and collective history of intentions impinging upon and determining consciousness without ever becoming fully present to it, he discerned responsibility as a cultural narrative written onto an ego, which would otherwise be driven more pragmatically by the perception of its own needs and instincts. The two realms of motivation, conscious and unconscious, are finally as hard for Freud to separate as those actions dedicated to a private sphere of satisfaction are from actions taken in the service of collective ideologies. The specter of aggression Freud discerns in every cultural activity is evidence of this view. By much the same logic, reason is necessarily subject to a fictive or provisional dimension, so that the task of working through the past by way of symptoms in the present must always also allow for the possibility that reason will lapse into what also (secretly) motivates it. Such a hemeneutic is Nietzschean in its distrust of the manifest content of rationality and is also tied to a tradition of philosophical skepticism, which testifies to much the same point—that is, to reason's vulnerability, its capacity to be wounded by the lapsing premises of transcendence, idealism, or self-possessive agency.

In terms of the larger distinction I have made throughout this book, the imbrication of rational and irrational motives and of voluntary and involuntary action suggests that morality cannot mean only what it has understood itself to mean; and so, too, history produced as a narrative interweaving of causes, acts, and agents must be revised to account for the provisional dimension of its narratives. This is in fact the ethical meaning Rose would like to attribute to "fantasy" in the poetry of Sylvia Plath. According to her psychoanalytic hermeneutic, the perception of reason or history through the lens of fantasy is, at least potentially, an emancipating experience for the subject, but the significance of such an emancipation also pertains to history. Since fantasy acknowledges the basic metaphoricity of the self, which is to say, the multiplicity of subject-positions that inhabit and construct any particular self, one can play upon the "fantasies underpinning metaphor" (214)—and this is what Rose says happens in "Daddy"—in such a way that one need not become preoccupied by history to the point where one is only a symptom of one's own history or of larger collective histories that befall individuals in time.

Specifically, when one brings fantasy to bear on the Holocaust, it offers to liberate the one who remembers such history from an unpleasurable preoccupation that could only inhibit the self in its present and future capacity to assume pragmatic positions of political responsibility in the world. In fantasy, one negotiates extrinsic realities by way of the self's intrinsic and multiple preoccupations, and this lack of fixity in identity teaches the self that it might at any moment also be its own other. Rose is by no means anomalous in her set of ethical concerns, for any psychoanalytically informed treatment of Holocaust history (the examples of Saul Friedländer and Dominick LaCapra come immediately to mind) focuses in large part on how such a history is going to make sense in the present (or make nonsense of it).

To all of this, the skeptical historian would do well to object that fantasy often proceeds as if history itself could be renegotiated or as if the parties of a particular history (as, say, the group of agents who made up the Nazi party) might have been negotiated toward another course of action—in this case, toward a less horrific implementation of their ideology. The problem, simply put, is that the revisionistic tendencies of fantasy incline toward a radical underestimation of unpleasurable historical realities. A fair reading of the fantastic mechanisms of the *Ariel* poems must negotiate, then, between Plath's construction of a fantasy of reason and her potentially trivializing representation of fantasy atrocities. Among those readers who find that these poems, though conceived and expressed in great rage, have clearly articulated the constrictive social reality of the 1950s woman awakening to the implication of her life in patriarchal structures, the poems of *Ariel* articulate a reasonable, if still fantastic and distant, horizon of expectations for women's political and cultural reality. For those readers who reject the fantastic urgency of Plath's voice, perhaps the greatest cause for concern is her willingness to map the experience of one group's political frustration onto another entirely different group's historical experience of suffering.[32] Though it is by no means an easy matter to decide what Plath thought she was doing by invoking the Holocaust in these poems, it is abundantly clear from a letter she wrote her mother on October 21, 1962, (only nine days after she had completed "Daddy") that she understood the ethical texture of these poems to be intimated in their willingness to address unpleasurable realities:

> Don't talk to me about the world needing cheerful stuff! What the person out of Belsen—physical or psychological—wants is nobody saying the birdies still go tweet-tweet, but the full knowledge that somebody else has been there and knows the *worst*, just what it is like. It is much more help for me, for example, to know that people are divorced and go through hell, than to hear about happy marriages.[33]

Certainly a tossed-off comment in a letter to one's mother should not be made to stand as an aesthetic credo, but in the span of only three sentences Plath here manages to provide fodder enough for the most generous and most grudging of readings. On the one hand, with her turn against the easy conventions of optimistic reading Plath insists that much of what we call heartening literature becomes merely platitudinous in the face of atrocity. Offering her own take on Adorno's famous dictum, Plath might be paraphrased as saying: *It is insulting to write poems about birds that still sing once you get out of Belsen.* Much of the 1950s and early 1960s scholarly literature on the Nazi genocide and its survivors, at least some of which Plath would have been familiar with, consisted of psychoanalytically framed studies by authors such as Eli Cohen and Bruno Bettelheim that addressed the symptoms of a horrible history as having become manifest as a pathology in the survivor.[34] To her credit, Plath intuits the limits of such discourse, arguing that the therapeutic demand for survivors to become like the rest of us and to focus on "cheerful stuff" discredits their historically transformative experience of suffering; and so she imagines, instead, how we—or at least she—could go to them.

But there soon follows the other hand, what we might call a sleight of hand whereby Plath makes at least two dangerously reductive conflations and a positively trivializing comparison of Belsen to a bad marriage. When she refers to the "person out of Belsen—physical or psychological," she may refer sympathetically to the Belsen that endures in a survivor's mind, long past the actual moment of liberation from the camps. But there is already an irreality in her phrasing, which consequently blurs the distinction between a physical and psychological Belsen, as if one could suffer a psychological Belsen without ever having encountered a Nazi. There may be an ethical bravery in Plath's willingness to hear the worst of what another has suffered and to go imaginatively to meet him there, but as soon as one claims to know "just what it is like," the other's experience has been reduced to the scale and map of one's own experience of suffering.

Though there are many who would disagree with me, I do not find it likely that Plath's statement about the moral imagination's capacity to equate experiences, even when one is speaking about Belsen, is meant to find its answering term or analogue in the very next sentence. More likely, she has been trying to speak down to her mother, illustrating her grander moral philosophical claim by way of an anecdote from her own life. Rose's emphasis on fantasy as the imaginative manipulation of subject-positions is again germane, but such a facility with history has the potential to become merely facile. With her too-easy slide into the familiar example, Plath takes back as much as she had yielded to the alterity of Belsen's historical victims.

Grief's Impossible Redemptions

So much of the debate over imaginative uses of the Holocaust has centered on the potentially falsifying legacy of attempts to universalize the Holocaust as a case of injustice, making it only one, albeit a serious one, in a series of atrocities that characterize the destructive bent of the modern world. My entry into this ongoing debate has been to suggest that we might begin to refocus it through the question of proportion that ethics itself is founded upon. Indeed, if we define ethics by way of a disproportion—whether as a gap between the complexities of motive and the self reflected in the process of unitary moral deliberation (Bernard Williams) or as the constitutive difference between the other who resists conceptualization and the subject who responds to the call of responsibility through acts of cognitive reduction (Emmanuel Levinas)—much of the currency of analogy, which is so charged an issue in discussions of Plath's poetry, might be read not as simplifying statements of equivalence, but as comparative idioms immersed in the inequivalence of ethical relationship as conditioned by an irrevocable and disastrous history.

With respect to the task of reading Plath's poetry, this would demand first of all that we do a better job of wrestling with the function of mythic voice in her poetry. Her feminist advocates, the poet-husband who helped canonize her, and the critics who lament her appropriation of the Holocaust all share a tendency to read Plath as though the mythic register of her voice and her use of the personal idiom were easily conflated and as though they represented by and large, as Amy Hungerford has recently suggested, experiments in auto-biographical personification.[35] Yet there is every reason to believe, from the poetry as also from her journal entries and much of her personal correspondence, that Plath was attuned to the sense in which her poetry might reflect larger problems of ideology and cultural memory. The mythic register of her poetic voice is supremely representative on this front. There is no mistaking, for example, the immediately mythic pitch with which "Daddy" opens, as Plath presents a speaker who emerges from the realm of children's fairy tales to find that she can no longer remain in the "black shoe / In which I have lived like a foot / For thirty years" (2–4), and we have absolutely no question that "Daddy" is, at least in part, an allegorical rendering of a modern woman's besieged identity. From within this mythic version of aggrieved voice, Plath defines in stanzas 2 and 3 the poem's first and grounding elegiac loss, namely, the loss of the father:

Daddy, I have had to kill you.
You died before I had time—
Marble-heavy, a bag full of God,
Ghastly statue with one gray toe
Big as a Frisco seal

And a head in the freakish Atlantic
Where it pours bean green over blue
In the waters off beautiful Nauset.
I used to pray to recover you.
Ach, du. (6–15)

In these stanzas, Plath directly invokes elegiac conventions and alludes to the possibility of elegiac resolution. Her readings in psychoanalysis, to which she makes pat allusion by speaking of the girl's Elektra complex in a conversation recorded for the BBC, have caused her to render the work of mourning as implicated in the more ordinary work of psychic separation that is so crucial within the plot of the family romance.[36]

This also means her murderous conceit need not be seen as proportional to the family history she has endured. According to the poem's rhetorical, quasi-mythic exaggerations, the father must be murdered in fantasy as in grief precisely because he is, as Freud would suggest, the necessarily patriarchal father of language and culture. Since his premature death prevents the young woman from assailing the symbolic reign of the father in real life and therefore from articulating a separated identity for herself, her mourning is shadowed by a fantasy of independence. All of this is obliquely brought to a head through the commemorative dead weight of the "[g]hastly statue" (9), most likely a funereal statue at the father's graveside, that has marked the father's identity as a task for the young girl's further remembrance and interfered with her effort to define herself apart from the culturally signified memory of the father. The statue becomes quite literally a grotesque, its sealish appearance connoting the grotesque's defamiliarizing configuration of animal and human form, but also, in somewhat more comical terms, the living memory of the father with whom the speaker has been enraptured. As a reflection on the hypothesis of a completed work of mourning, the speaker's attempts at resolution, as quickly becomes apparent, have been unsuccessful. She has sustained the memory of the other to the detriment of self.

It is in the throes of such an incomplete mourning that Plath's speaker confesses with almost superstitious wishfulness, "I used to pray to recover you" (14). This is nothing less than an elegiac fantasy of recovery, much like Milton reproving the nymphs absent from the scene of Lycidas's death in order to elaborate a belated fantasy of protection enfolded in the simple, seemingly far less ambitious wish to recover Lycidas's corpse from the sea, as if consolation might depend upon the proximate body. In the modern elegiac idiom, in Tennyson or Hardy, the fantasy of recovery means that a dead Hallam or Emma may take on intensely unpleasurable connotations with the seeming aim of opposing both a history of conventional elegiac resolutions and a contemporary cultural praxis of forgetting. So too, when Plath's speaker turns to the fantasy of recovery, she has been living with her commemorative task as with the dead weight of funereal statues and God, with what Nietzsche might call the heft of a bad conscience obliged to a contract it can never fulfill.[37]

Stanza 4 picks up, then, with an ambivalent realization of the fantasy of recovery expressed in stanza 3, as Plath transposes the recovered history of the Nazi past onto the simpler personal fantasy of recovering the dead body of the deceased: "In the German tongue, in the Polish town / Scraped flat by the roller / Of wars, wars, wars" (16–18). The thought here is an oblique fulfillment of the speaker's stated wish to recover the father, as if she were saying, *I used to pray to recover you—how silly!—in the German tongue and in a Polish town laid low by incessant German warfare.* Far from supposing, however, that what follows in the poem involves the simple transfiguration of the tyrannical father of personal history into a Nazi, with the two terms made to stand as roughly equivalent, I want to argue that Plath has represented the task of commemoration as a work of unpleasurable recovery, one that now takes on a larger collective and historical connotation. It is precisely to this end that the oppressive acts of the speaker's biographical father are never named, indeed may even be nonexistent. Rather, the father's oppressiveness derives from what he stands for in memory, as an emblem of what the speaker's identity necessarily owes to inherited meanings and the cultural reign of the father.

As she imagines finding her father "[i]n the German tongue," Plath begins to unfold a genealogical fantasy according to which the cost of Germanic ancestry is to have to locate oneself forever inside the recent German past. All of the language referring to the father's mythically connoted history remains firmly speculative: "So I never could tell where you / Put your foot, your root" (22–23); and thus too the daughter's own imaginative acts of identifying herself as Jewish remain couched in the conditional. Father and child are alike implicated in a history in which neither has directly participated. And if the metaphorically adopted subject-positions of this poem eventually prove troublesome, we have always to keep in mind that Plath creates the poem as a mock genealogy, even perhaps as an experiment in what her own bad conscience about the Holocaust can recover of its own implicit guilt.[38]

My claim is that Plath thus explores the ethical meaning of a subject whose rhetoric of identification is profoundly an acknowledgment of her implication in history. In "Daddy," as in "Mary's Song," the original motive for the speculative encounter with the Holocaust is a mourner's bad conscience, a version of elegiac blaming that finds in its own pain a mode of reference aimed at the father as at larger collective meanings built upon the social history of pain. In turning to the ordinary fantasy of recovering the dead, she finds that the dead bring with them the history of their time, but it is also possible that this is why she beckons to the father in the first place—precisely because the unpleasure that signifies her identity as an obligation to an absent other will be suddenly enlarged into a trope by way of which she stands in history. As Plath told her mother, she wanted to write poetry that could be read as historically meaningful by "the person out of Belsen": the Holocaust victims are not mere figures for herself, but the irremissible audience for a poetry of suffering.

In this respect, the unpleasurable force of the bad conscience as a proportion to history—and, specifically, Holocaust history—is given a connotation much like that attributed to it by Jean Améry. In the essay "Resentments," Améry alludes to Nietzsche's critique of the resentfulness of the victim and argues for the moral reliability of the victim's perspective precisely because it coincides with a history—of atrocity, torture, and victimization at the hands of the Nazis—that cannot be imaginatively reversed except at the expense of truth. Confessing his own antitherapeutic ineloquence and referring ironically to the possibility that he is himself a ready example of "concentration camp syndrome," Améry objects to the forms of collective memory he witnesses in Germany in the early half of the 1960s.[39] What the Germans of that moment lack is precisely a bad conscience about their national history. Although Améry's argument relies on anecdotal proofs,[40] when these proofs are read in the context of Germany's rapid restoration on the international scene they suggest that Germany and much of the rest of the world are eager to treat National Socialism as a mere aberration in Germany's glorious history. Still, unless Germany wants "to live entirely without history," Améry argues—and he doubts that the world's "most history-conscious national community" would be willing to do so—those twelve years must assume a prominent place in the memory of collective, national identity (76). What Améry constructs therefore is a mode of ethical vigilance in which one stands in relation to the past as to an enduring influence and a living effect. From our place in history, the Holocaust makes Germany and the good conscience forever incompatible. Though this configuration might well be extended to a broader rubric of responsibility, including those who were responsible for this history without participating in it, there must, according to Améry, be some historical literalism to such an emphasis. Otherwise ethics becomes merely a utopian hypothesis, even in its negative formulations—at best, an abstract standard for constructs of agency or, at worst, a wishful connotation of personal responsibility without social context or precedent.

When Plath renders identity under the hypothesis of genealogy, as if bloodlines literally ascribed a legacy of guilt, she yields personal identity to collective meanings, finding in stanzas 5 through 7 that not even the German language can remain untainted by history:

> I never could talk to you.
> The tongue stuck in my jaw.
>
> It stuck in a barb wire snare.
> Ich, ich, ich, ich,
> I could hardly speak.
> I thought every German was you.
> And the language obscene
>
> An engine, an engine
> Chuffing me off like a Jew.
> A Jew to Dachau, Auschwitz, Belsen.
> I began to talk like a Jew.
> I think I may well be a Jew. (24–35)

Alluding to that permanent separation in time upon which all elegiac apostrophe depends, Plath here recalls Hardy's fantasy terms of incommunication, which in themselves are manifestations of a bad conscience about the dissolution of the poet's love for his wife. For the speaker of "Daddy," however, the beginnings of guilt are to be found ironically in ever having loved the father. Rather than hearing the poem's mounting fantasy of aggression as an implicitly mimetic response to a father and daughter's personal history, the poem offers a more overtly elegiac explanation: the father is oppressive because he is dead; he is the sign of obligations and cultural constructions of identity that the daughter inherits without any choice in the matter.

It is in this respect that the father also calls forth the bad conscience, his German past suddenly grafted onto a German national past that reached its most horrific stages only after Plath's father had died in the fall of 1940. The anachronistic transposition of the Nazi genocide, which entered its systemic exterminating phase in the fall of 1941, onto the stand-in father's biography is hardly accidental. The dead father of "Daddy" signifies the past by occupying the very space of history, of all those things from which the speaker's identity might be derived and for which it might be responsible. For this reason, the persecuting connotations of Plath's ancestry are distributed between the father and her no-longer-native tongue. We know that Plath made consistent efforts to learn the German language and as consistently failed in her studies. In

The Bell Jar (1971) Plath downloads some of her frustration with German onto her autobiographical heroine, who confesses while studying German that "the very sight of those dense, black, barbed-wire letters made my mind shut like a clam."[41] If the speaker of "Daddy" is similarly alienated from her heritage, she imaginatively encounters the historical referent behind the "barbed wire letters" by getting her tongue caught on the "barb wire snare" of Nazi concentration camps. It is as though Plath had sought an image through which she could literalize the imaginative trajectory of her voice, as if to enter into the German language were to enter into the history of atrocity once spoken in German.[42] One might well picture the German who speaks in his native tongue in that time shortly (but how shortly?) after the Nazi reign, hesitating each time he is about to speak, trying to find uncontaminated German words. Such a conscientious or guilty relation to language is what Plath intuits only too well, her speaker's voice marred by bad conscience. The voice that is called forth is a function of the duress imposed by German history; it is only through the stuttering *I* of her half-Germanic identity that she can speak at all of that history.

It is clear that Plath gives to the German language the power to impose its history upon the one who enters into it. As one tries to make sense of those lines ending stanza 6 and beginning stanza 7, the interruptive punctuation oddly increases the negative power the German tongue exercises on the speaker:

> I thought every German was you.
> And the language obscene
>
> An engine, an engine
> Chuffing me off like a Jew. (29–32)

The period at the end of line 29 prevents "the language obscene" from arriving as a direct object of the speaker's thoughts. Of course that meaning is at least partly fulfilled, since, as any reader of Dickinson surely knows, we continue to abide by and search out grammatical rhythms even after they have been frustrated. In reading these lines aloud, we are likely to treat the period as a comma and read the fragment as if it were a larger direct-object clause oddly enhanced by a dependent participle of simultaneity. Yet by disassociating the participle from its proper grammatical function, Plath gives it the force of an active verb and yields the nominal phrase "the language obscene" the activating force of an agent or grammatical subject. Accordingly, we cannot account for the obscenity of the language as though it were the speaker's fantasy sense of persecution, but must call the German language objectively obscene, its every utterance containing the memory of deported Jews and threatening to carry the speaker off as one more victim. In this sense, Young is quite right to attribute an appropriating power to the figure itself, as though it acted on the poet—except of course that the extraordinary power he attributes to the figure is already a figured moment in Plath's poem. It is only as an *I* possessed, as it were, by a terrible past it cannot articulate that Plath's speaker eventually utters a personal history in which her imagined subject-positions begin to approximate and to appropriate metaphorically the terrain of the Holocaust.

In the second half of "Daddy" there can be little doubt that Plath employs a language of vicarious victimization. As the speaker's imaginative recovery of the father brings with it the specters of a past for which she has not imagined herself responsible, the plot of the first half of the poem has involved the speaker involuntarily in the German past. But in the second half she works through those specters of the past, seemingly, by enfolding them into her own personal history and exorcising their power over her. The persecuting force of history causes her to adopt the subject-position of the victim and to speak, but only in metaphoric terms, as a virtual Holocaust victim. In other words, as the poem begins to speak from within the perspective of the victim, it moves into what is at least ostensibly a confessional idiom. Under this sway, Plath offers a string of metaphoric descriptions of the father ("your Luftwaffe, your gobbledygoo," "your Aryan eye, bright blue," and a "man in black with a Meinkampf look" [42, 45, 65]) that seem to trivialize the very history by which the speaker has been quite literally preoccupied. Rose's reading of "Daddy" seems most persuasive once the unspeakable history of the German past begins to be caricatured, say, as an oppressive father who stands looking slightly satanic at a blackboard (51–54). In all of this, there is just a note of the slapstick desperation of Charlie Chaplin's famous caricature of Hitler in *The Dictator*, as Plath's speaker in turn chants, "And your neat mustache / And your Aryan eye, bright blue. / Panzer-man, panzer-man, O You—" (42–45).

In my judgment, we must also hear the poem's most infamous lines, which are dangerously banal if taken at face value, as part of the poem's deliberately trivializing performance of the past: "Every woman adores a Fascist, / The boot in the face, the brute / Brute heart of a brute like you" (48–50). Pronouncing the utter complicity of the victim of fascism in her oppression, these words declare such an interpretation to have been produced as fantasy by our cultural idioms of power. In other words, this is mock profundity, the "gobbledygoo" of the Nietzschean hypothesis that the reverences of guilt are veiled confessions of a mass cultural submission to those who are powerful, willful, and violent. So too is the poem's performance of a marriage in which the speaker marries, not a husband, but an image of the father as an oppressive specter of history: "I made a model of you, / A man in black with a Meinkampf look / And a love of the rack and the screw. / And I said I do, I do" (64–67). Indeed, these lines almost read as though Nietzsche were demystifying the motives of obligation in fairy-tale form.

Plath, I am suggesting, begins by figuring history as an unpleasure in which a personal mourning for a dead father is opened surprisingly toward a larger unpleasurable aspect of collective memory, but she moves in the second half of the poem to convert the resistances of unpleasure—the very phenomenality that makes them unpleasurable (according to Freud)—into psychic emanations or fantasies of the one who is too beholden to history. Once the poem begins to enact the necessary forgetting of all therapeutic narrative, it does so only at the expense of the history to which it has witnessed. In Rose's view, unpleasure as a subjection to the past is ahistorical because it cannot be acted upon, because a subject loses her agentive relation to the present. Yet it is only because she has been gripped by mourning's unpleasure that Plath's speaker, or the psychoanalytic subject, has been thrown back upon history in the first place. Since the historical past is by definition that from which a psychoanalytic subject would be released, psychoanalysis—or for that matter, any largely therapeutic or redemptive narrative—must finally argue for a trivialization of the past. With the ending of "Daddy," Plath glimpses the Nietzschean terms underneath her quasi-Freudian language for those modes of forgetfulness beneficial to the self.

Contrary to Rose's reading of "Daddy," then, I am contending that the poem's represented therapeutic phase is what contributes to its seemingly ahistorical trajectory. Spoken from the perspective of a victim-subjectivity vicariously inherited through the German legacy of atrocity and ranging far enough to include the speaker's imaginative understanding of what her memory owes to the dead father, the poem becomes a performance against unpleasure, indulging a fantasy of vengeance in which aggressivity would deliver the victim from the hold of history. As it moves into a mythic register that only vaguely remembers history, the poem proffers a rhetorical transcendence obviously not available to Holocaust victims. This is a mythic mode distinct from that which we observed in "Mary's Song," where the mythic connotations elaborated a history too large to be apprehended through the ordinary personal idiom. Though the sacrificial note upon which myth is constructed is also sounded in "Daddy," Plath's mock-mythic language is produced in this earlier poem not as a fantastic survival of history, but in opposition to the burdens imposed by recovered history. According to the poem's deliberately farcical gesturing toward elegiac resolution ("If I've killed one man, I've killed two—" [71]), no distinction is made between the metaphorical psychic killing of the husband through divorce and the completed act of mourning as burying a father in memory (a symbolic second killing); nor is any distinction made between the murderous memory of Nazi genocide and the fantastically imagined revenge of its victims.

Though the poem ostensibly sides with the victims of history in its claim to avenge them by striking blows against a father's oppressive memory, we are within our rights to proclaim that such a resolution has nothing to do finally with their history. Indeed, when Plath adds yet another level of conceit to the ending and calls the dead father a vampire, she rather crudely encapsulates the father's survival in memory with the associated sufferings of history he elicited in the idea of a vampiric living death. Certainly, the ritual killing of a vampire seems a poor figure for avenging Jewish victims of Nazi murder, not least of all when one considers that according to the antisemitic lore of the blood libel the Jew was virtually charged with vampirism. When the villagers take their vengeful satisfaction upon the already dead body of the vampire, who is himself a figurative hybrid of both perpetrators and victims, they dispel the responsibility of history into the mythic resolution of a contrived, but also displaced, scenario of mourning. And this sounds perhaps the oddest note in this poem's elegiacally unsatisfying ending, for the speaker appears at the last minute to have exempted herself from participation in the vengeful fantasy. As the villagers kill the vampire knowing it was the father, the speaker whispers, "Daddy, daddy, you bastard, I'm through" (80), almost as if she were dying with the murder of the father's memory. Though it might well appear a social demand for resolution has been enacted, such a resolution altogether fails to overcome the daughter's vexed attachment to the father. Unable to contain the history of atrocity that coincides with the unpleasures of personal memory, as she is unable finally to suppress her mourner's bad conscience, Plath's persona remains, in her uneasy attachment to the father's memory, a symptom of a larger cultural responsibility for the Holocaust.

What I have tried to stress in my reading of both Jarrell and Plath is that each poet exposes the radical insufficiency of the personal idiom to the commemorative task that besets the modern poet and her audience. By turning to the bad conscience as a figure for the disproportion between personal capability and the responsibility that arises through history, each poet signifies a responsibility distinct from intentionality and the ordinary moral capabilities of the self, as she or he also insists that each of us is called nevertheless into relation to the events that constitute the Holocaust. If, for Levinas, ethics is defined against intentionality, as a paradoxical impossibility really existing within history, then responsibility is greater even than the moment of its historical expression and any intention that might offer itself in the foreground of a particular action. By definition, there is a noncoincidence that always characterizes responsibility, a refusal of the other to enter into the time and history of the self's intentions, which means that ethics always signifies prior to the cultural definitions of morality and what is pragmatically conceived as possible. By such an emphasis, the suffering of the other cannot be beyond the pale of the self; it can never be irrelevant.

Throughout this book, I have read mourning as both a figure for and expression of an impossible responsibility wherein one refuses to yield the other to the more comfortable freedoms of identity. At the same time, I have contended that responsibility, even in the most everyday of situations, proceeds toward the extraordinary circumstance, confronting the other's death and opposing it to the very life of subjectivity itself. In such a view, responsibility can never finally be fulfilled or satisfied. Responsibility is always in part a relation to loss. Indeed, ethics arises through its own failure and impossibility: one cannot ultimately prevent the death of the other, but one remains nonetheless responsible for her. This is the uncomfortable, indeed unpleasurable fact of ethics, and it is an insight persistently put forward by the elegiac tradition, especially in the modern era, in melancholic or anti-elegiac strains of literary grief. When modern psychology speaks of a necessary realism wherein the subject confesses a deep ambivalence informing all attachment, this very notion might be read as if it were based in a cruder elegiac logic. Since the other can never be what I would like her to be—which is to say, ideal or fully reciprocating or permanently responsive—and because the other is necessarily one who dies, all attachment is governed by a realism that yields the other to her death before it has occurred. What the poems of Jarrell and Plath conclude from the historical example of the Holocaust is that the yielding of others to death, even by those who did not directly participate in the event of persecution or atrocity, is far too easily achieved in both its original and subsequent historical moments. Such a history must, rather, exercise an extraordinary demand on individual conscience as on our personal idioms for grief, so much so that it may be the specter of unpleasure and the unsettling promptings of the bad conscience that would hereafter denote us as historical and potentially responsible beings.

Notes

Introduction

1. See Ruth Behar, *The Vulnerable Observer: Anthropology That Breaks Your Heart* (Boston, MA: Beacon Press, 1996), 1. The Isabel Allende story, "And of Clay We Are Created," is included in the collection *The Stories of Eva Luna*, trans. Margaret Sayers Peden (New York: Atheneum, 1991), 319–33.

2. Allende's story is in fact narrated by the reporter's lover, who imagines her lover's pangs of sympathy more consistently than the sufferings of the girl Azucena. As the narrator watches her lover on television and receives his desperate dispatches about the girl, she realizes he is succumbing to his own past and confronting fears he has long kept at bay. As this strange identification overcomes him, the narrator declares at one point, "He *was* Azucena" (328). A short while later, the dying girl observes him crying and tells the reporter not to cry for her, to which he replies extraordinarily that he has not been crying for her, but for himself: "I'm crying for myself. I hurt all over" (329).

3. See Sophocles, *Loeb Classical Library: Antigone; The Women of Trachis; Philoctetes; Oedipus at Colonus,* ed. and trans. Hugh Lloyd-Jones (Cambridge: Harvard University Press, 1994).

4. Jacques Derrida, *Writing and Difference,* trans. A. Bass (London: Routledge, 1978), 111.

5. See Bernard Williams, *Ethics and the Limits of Philosophy* (Cambridge: Harvard University Press, 1985) (hereafter referred to as *ELP*), 71–92.

6. For his part, even though Levinas entirely omits prescriptive terms from his discussion of ethics (declaring the Good a transcendent signification derived through the relation to the other), when he insists that the relationship to the other provides the anterior significance of all language and sociality, he would implicitly prescribe the necessary conditions of thought for all of us who propose thinking more concretely about a way the world ought to be or the way we ought to be in the world. Simon Critchley explores one way of reading this assignation of responsibility when he speaks of the language of "indication" in Levinas. See Critchley, *The Ethics of Deconstruction: Derrida and Levinas* (Cambridge, MA: Blackwell, 1992), 169–82.

7. See Geoffrey Galt Harpham, *Getting It Right: Language, Literature, and Ethics* (Chicago: University of Chicago Press, 1992), 23. From Harpham's point of view, the slippage between these two modes seems a constitutive element rather than a theoretical weakness of ethics, a difficulty that leads him to inquire, playfully, when it is that a fact is like a value and then to answer his own question, "When it is ethical." It should be noted that Levinas is introduced into Harpham's discussion as an example of a descriptive discourse all about "the priority and autonomy of the prescriptive" (23).

8. Both Williams and Ricoeur admit that the distinction cannot be made simply by tracing each concept to a truer or root origin, since the Latin and Greek etymological and genealogical origins of morality and ethics do not encourage such a distinction. Ricoeur announces his decision to adopt the distinction in order to separate the realm of practical morality from the phenomenological and idealistic terrain of ethical aims. See Paul Ricoeur, *Oneself as Another*, trans. Kathleen Blamey (Chicago: University of Chicago Press, [1990] 1992), 169–71. Whereas Williams also admits that the two terms mean roughly the same thing (disposition or custom) and that moral philosophy has used them interchangeably, he finds a subtle difference at the level of connotation, inasmuch as the Latin *mores* gives greater emphasis to a "sense of social expectation," whereas the Greek *ethos* concentrates more on "individual character." Williams explores the nuances of ethical decision making and the dispositions of the agent left out of the most basic accounts of obligation offered by moral philosophy. By creating a narrower and systemic view of ethical behavior, moral philosophy delineates boundaries between what is moral and what is not, but if we were able to get past such presuppositions, Williams proposes, we would have to widen the playing field of ethics, including a far wider range of considerations— as opposed to, say, behaviors—that would also count as ethical. See Williams, *ELP*, 4–11.

9. The Levinasian suspicion is that imagination, as a cognitive act ordered by the rules governing all our knowledge, always reduces alterity to a play of the *same*, that which is already signified by language and thought. As Jill Robbins rightly suggests, Levinas's writings have been significantly and repeatedly shaped by his encounters with literature, not only with regard to a vast though often subtle web of allusion running throughout the Levinasian canon, but also through an ongoing dialogue with contemporaries such as Bataille, Blanchot, and Derrida. See Robbins, *Altered Reading: Levinas and Literature* (Chicago: University of Chicago Press, 1999), 39–40, 53–54, 75–82. Also relevant here is Robert Eaglestone's reading of Levinas's highly dialectical engagement in "Reality and Its Shadow" (1948) with Heideggerian aesthetics. See Eaglestone, *Ethical Criticism: Reading after Levinas* (Edinburgh: Edinburgh University Press, 1997), esp. 98–128.

10. See J. Hillis Miller, *The Ethics of Reading* (New York: Columbia University Press, 1987).

11. See John Searle, *The Construction of Social Reality* (New York: Free Press, 1995), esp. 127–47.

12. Jahan Ramazani, *Poetry of Mourning: The Modern Elegy from Hardy to Heaney* (Chicago: University of Chicago Press, 1994).

13. See Freud, "Formulations Regarding the Two Principles in Mental Functioning," in *The Standard Edition of the Complete Psychological Works of Sigmund Freud*, ed. and trans. James Strachey (London: Hogarth Press, 1953–74), 12:224.

14. See Julia Kristeva, *Black Sun: Depression and Melancholia*, trans. Leon S. Roudiez (New York: Columbia University Press, 1989).

15. Harold Bloom, *The Anxiety of Influence* (New York: Oxford University Press, 1973), 9.

CHAPTER 1. Toward an Ethics of Mourning

1. For Bernard Williams, the fundamental "mistake of morality is to try to make everything into obligations," a mode of thinking that often leads practically to an impasse in decision making, since once a subject recognizes herself to be under an obligation, that

obligation cannot be canceled without blame and may only be outweighed by another recognized moral obligation. See Williams, *Ethics and the Limits of Philosophy* (Cambridge: Harvard University Press, 1985) (hereafter referred to as *ELP*), 180. In a Kantian world the compelling reason to act morally could only be that "moral universality was a requirement of practical reason itself" (190), and this unremitting nature of obligation fails as a realistic description of what it would mean to make an ethical decision.

2. See Emmanuel Levinas, *Otherwise Than Being or Beyond Essence*, trans. Alphonso Lingis (Pittsburgh, PA: Duquesne University Press, [1974] 1998), 29.

3. This is roughly the Aristotelian point of view, as set out in *The Eudemian Ethics*. See Aristotle, *Loeb Classical Library: The Athenian Constitution; The Eudemian Ethics; On Virtues and Vices*, trans. H. Rackham (1935; repr., Cambridge: Harvard University Press, 1996), esp. 234–56.

4. See Bernard Williams, "Utilitarianism and Moral Self-Indulgence," in *Moral Luck: Philosophical Papers, 1973–1980* (New York: Cambridge University Press, 1981), 40–53.

5. For a discussion of the tensions in Levinas's metaphoric strategies and the question of whether he can ever get beyond metaphor, see John Llewelyn, *Emmanuel Levinas: The Genealogy of Ethics* (New York: Routledge, 1995), 162–79.

6. When obligation takes the form of an answerable question (have I voluntarily done what I ought to have done?), it is limited to a predetermined judgment. According to Williams, the particular failure of the voluntary model is that first person deliberations may take the self's relation to a conceptual obligation as the essential content. See Williams, *ELP*, 93–119.

7. For a discussion of Levinas's work in relation to the conventional tension in moral philosophical discourse between universal principle and the individuating circumstance of responsibility, see Fabio Ciaramelli, "Levinas's Ethical Discourse between Individuation and Universality," in *Re-Reading Levinas*, ed. Robert Bernasconi and Simon Critchley (Bloomington: Indiana University Press, 1991), 83–105.

8. See Paul Ricoeur, *Freud and Philosophy: An Essay on Interpretation*, trans. Denis Savage (New Haven: Yale University Press, 1970).

9. Freud, "Mourning and Melancholia," in *The Standard Edition of the Complete Psychological Works of Sigmund Freud*, ed. and trans. James Strachey (London: Hogarth Press, 1953–74) (hereafter referred to as *SE*), 14:239–58.

10. Much relies on the meaning we give to the acceptance of death, whether we understand acceptance to denote a mature confrontation and working-through of the event of death in the subject's life, or whether we believe, for example, that acceptance proceeds by an ideological evasion that displaces the reality of death toward some other meaning. Much of Herbert Marcuse's canon, of which *Eros and Civilization* remains perhaps the most enduring work, is dedicated to the optimistic premise that humankind might in fact be liberated from the mythic reification of death and the deathly ideologies that follow from such an uncritical acceptance of death. Ironically, as Jonathan Dollimore emphasizes, it may be the death drive itself (as perhaps also the sexual perversions) that testifies as though by "unconscious protest" against our cultural narratives of death and names both their inadequacy and destructiveness. See Dollimore, *Death, Desire, and Loss in Western Culture* (New York: Routledge, 1998), 220–27.

11. Even as Freud continues from here and suggests that the "economic means by which mourning carries out its task" resist his understanding, he has presumed an economic model of utility in which the ego struggles with its pains and pleasures in a manner

very much patterned after Aristotle's description of temperate morality or Jeremy Bentham's view of utilitarian reason in *An Introduction to the Principles of Morals and Legislation* (London: W. Pickering, 1823). Since reason must give itself to the dictates of pleasure and elicit the principle of utility in order to work toward the good as a measure of proportionate advantage to the whole of society, Bentham contends that pain is the enemy of our reasonable agency, a demon always to be exorcised for the utilitarian good.

12. See Geoffrey Galt Harpham, *Getting It Right: Language, Literature, and Ethics* (Chicago: University of Chicago Press, 1992), 113–16. In its most literal application, as Martha Nussbaum has argued, utilitarianism must disown not just aberrant states of sympathy, but the very possibility that sympathy could inform ethical decision making. See Nussbaum, *Poetic Justice: The Literary Imagination and Public Life* (Boston, MA: Beacon Press, 1995).

13. Sympathy for the dead might provide an exceptional case or it might simply be proof of the charge utilitarianism makes more generally against sympathy. Yet from the utilitarian standpoint of what it is best for the mourner to do and how it is best for him to live in a world that now lacks the other, an aberrant sympathy for the dead jeopardizes the mourner's capacity to gain pleasure from existence and might even lead him to make decisions contradicting the rules of utilitarianism and thus the good of society.

14. Freud, "Mourning and Melancholia," in *SE* 14:255. Each of us constitutes our world of meaning under the influence, if not the unmediated sway, of a primary narcissism, and so any mourner's aberrant sympathy, his staying too long on the thought of the lost other, recalls the same motive for attachment we find, albeit in exaggerated form, in the melancholic. Though Freud argues for anaclitic (or object-based) attachment as a necessary cultural progress beyond the narcissistic motives for attachment, the self characteristically reverts to its cruder or earlier form of relationship because egoistic satisfaction continues to drive its attachment to objects and its very modes of identification. Attempting to locate an origin for this basic mechanism of language and human thought, Jacques Lacan gives the name "mirror stage" to that early developmental period of childhood wherein the child acquires language as the resource of meaning and identity. According to Lacanian theory, from the earliest phase of our identity we respond to the real world as if it were a mirror, as if each object were an *imago*, or a specular image of one's identity, so that a self depends on or refers to the other "in the full sense that analysis gives to the term [identification]: namely, the transformation that takes place in the subject when he assumes an image" (Lacan, "The Mirror Stage," in *Écrits: A Selection*, trans. Alan Sheridan [New York: Norton, 1977], 2). Facilitating identification with the other, language at the same time universalizes the ego and makes it truly into a subject, quite frequently and practically amending the I in its self-conception. But the talent at the base of identity—an ability to see in others the projections and possibilities of self—is never unseated.

15. Elisabeth Kübler-Ross, *On Death and Dying* (New York: Macmillan, 1969), 4.

16. Ovid, *Metamorphoses*, trans. Rolfe Humphries (Bloomington: Indiana University Press, 1955), 135.

17. See Jacques Derrida, *The Gift of Death*, trans. David Wills (Chicago: University of Chicago Press, 1995); Derrida, *Mémoires for Paul de Man*, trans. Cecile Lindsay et al. (New York: Columbia University Press, 1986).

18. For the controversy over Paul de Man's wartime writings, see *Responses: On Paul de Man's Wartime Journalism*, ed. Werner Hamacher, Neil Hertz, and Thomas Keenan

(Lincoln: University of Nebraska Press, 1989); Alan B. Spitzer, *Historical Truth and Lies about the Past: Reflections on Dewey, Dreyfus, de Man, and Reagan* (Chapel Hill: University of North Carolina Press, 1996).

19. Emmanuel Levinas, "Dying For . . . ," in *Entre Nous: On Thinking-of-the-Other*, trans. Michael B. Smith and Barbara Harshav (New York: Columbia University Press, [1991] 1998), 216.

20. Earlier in his career, in *Totality and Infinity* (1961), Levinas had strongly associated death and the other's irreplaceability: "Death, source of all myths, is present only in the Other, and only in him does it summon me urgently to my final essence, to my responsibility." *Totality and Infinity*, trans. Alphonos Lingis (Pittsburgh, PA: Duquesne University Press, [1961] 1969), 179. In a 1982 interview, Levinas argues that since the death of the other demonstrates an alterity that will not reduce to self-knowledge, as it demands that the subject venture beyond self-concern, "the death of the other has priority over yours, and over your life." "The Philosopher and Death," in *Alterity and Transcendence*, trans. Michael B. Smith (New York: Columbia University Press, [1995] 1999), 164.

21. Jill Robbins, *Altered Reading: Levinas and Literature* (Chicago: University of Chicago Press, 1999).

22. Levinas, *Totality and Infinity*, 199.

23. Levinas, "The Proximity of the Other," in *Alterity and Transcendence*, 103–4.

24. Several critics of Levinas, perhaps most famously among them Paul Ricoeur, have worried that the subjective resources that make ethical agency possible and inform any particular ethical praxis on behalf of the other are drained by Levinas's failure to provide an ethical horizon upon which the self might position itself formidably. See especially Ricoeur, *Oneself As Another*, trans. Kathleen Blamey (Chicago: University of Chicago Press, [1990] 1992), 188–89, 335–41.

25. Williams, "Moral Luck," in *Moral Luck*, 20–39.

26. For a fuller discussion of moral luck and its origins as a classical mode of thought, see Martha Nussbaum, *The Fragility of Goodness: Luck and Ethics in Greek Tragedy and Philosophy* (New York: Cambridge University Press, 1986), esp. 1–21.

27. Using the case of an artist he names Gauguin, Williams explains, for example, that although an agent may adhere to a consistent and rational life project at odds with normative reality and coming at considerable costs to others, he will be unable to determine whether his project has been justified until it fails or succeeds. See Williams, "Moral Luck," 22–27.

28. Emmanuel Levinas, *Difficult Freedom: Essays on Judaism*, trans. Seán Hand (Baltimore: Johns Hopkins University Press, 1990), 215.

29. Williams's formulation at this point is undoubtedly influenced by Michel Foucault's elaborate inversion of the question of responsibility in *Madness and Civilization*, where he suggests that only through texts by authors such as Nietzsche and Antonin Artaud that conjoin art and previously occluded forms of madness do we arrive at a moment in which a work of art demands that we become responsible before it. When Williams metaphorically accuses morality of "insanity," he alludes to Foucault's famous revaluation of insanity and his demystifying account of the institutions and protocols by which certain experiences are in the Classical Age deemed unreasonable because unspeakable (or perhaps vice versa). Like Foucault, Williams suggests our adherence to morality can become a kind of blindness more "insane" than what it discounts. See

Foucault, *Madness and Civilization: A History of Insanity in the Age of Reason*, trans. Richard Howard (New York: Random House, 1965).

30. However ambivalently Foucault portrays his debt to Freud, I am inclined to agree with Derrida when he argues that psychoanalysis is not only that of which Foucault speaks but at least in part also that from which he speaks. In the essay "'To Do Justice to Freud': The History of Madness in the Age of Psychoanalysis," Derrida shows how Foucault ambiguously characterizes Freud as a kind of threshold signifier or doorkeeper, one who both ushers in a new era and acts as the guardian of an epoch that comes to a close with him. Against positivist psychology, Freud represents a progress insofar as he attempted to listen and speak to unreason. However, at the center of Foucault's book, Derrida locates a chiasmus whereby the Freud who had been initially aligned with Nietzsche in service of the liberation of madness and unreason is eventually perceived as someone who aligns himself more consistently with the institutions of medicine and the mystification of the doctor as an "alienating figure." See Derrida, *Resistances of Psychoanalysis*, trans. Peggy Kamuf et. al. (Stanford, CA: Stanford University Press, 1998), esp. 70–84.

31. See Peter Sacks, *The English Elegy: Studies in the Genre from Spenser to Yeats* (Baltimore: Johns Hopkins University Press, 1985), esp. 1–8, 64–89, 106–17.

CHAPTER 2. Mourning and Substitution in *Hamlet*

1. See Peter M. Sacks, "Where Words Prevail Not: Grief, Revenge, and Language in Kyd and Shakespeare," *English Literary History* 49 (1982): 576–601; *The English Elegy: Studies in the Genre from Spenser to Yeats* (Baltimore: Johns Hopkins University Press, 1985), esp. 82–89.

2. The history of the critical interpretation of *Hamlet* has been largely blind to the fundamental absurdity of this dilemma as a nonchoice. The critical obsessions with Hamlet's delay, ranging from Bradley's focus on Hamlet's characteristic melancholy to the psychoanalytic solution of the Freud-Jones hypothesis to more structural solutions such as William Empson's, all appear to take for granted that Hamlet should choose between loyalty to Claudius and murderous defiance.

3. William James, *Varieties of Religious Experience: A Study in Human Nature* (New York: Mentor Edition, [1902] 1958), 121.

4. Ernest Becker, *The Denial of Death* (New York: Free Press, 1973), 21.

5. Elisabeth Kübler-Ross, *On Death and Dying* (New York: Macmillan, 1969) and Philippe Ariès, *Western Attitudes toward Death: From the Middle Ages to the Present*, trans. Patricia M. Ranum (Baltimore: Johns Hopkins University Press, 1974). See also Ariès, *The Hour of Our Death*, trans. Helen Weaver (New York: Vintage, 1982). Other prominent studies in the field of thanatology include Jessica Mitford, *The American Way of Death* (New York: Simon & Schuster, 1963); Geoffrey Gorer, *Death, Grief, and Mourning* (Garden City, NY: Doubleday, 1965); and Robert Jay Lifton, *The Broken Connection: On Death and the Continuity of Life* (New York: Basic Books, 1979). For a concise reading of what I would call the self-legitimating trope of thanatology—namely, the assertion of a cultural "denial of death"—and Ariès's elaboration of this idea, see Jonathan Dollimore, *Death, Desire, and Loss in Western Culture* (New York: Routledge, 1998), 119–23.

6. See, for example, David Dempsey, *The Way We Die: An Investigation of Death and Dying in America Today* (New York: Macmillan, 1975), esp. 17, as well as Becker, *The*

Denial of Death, Kübler-Ross, *On Death and Dying*, and Ariès, *Western Attitudes Toward Death*. Dollimore identifies a similar tendency in Baudrillard's critique of Enlightenment rationality (*Death, Desire, and Loss in Western Culture*, 123–27), which emphasizes the pathologization of death, or exclusion of the dead, at the center of the Enlightenment narratives of reason, the consequence of which is, not so ironically, a "culture of death." Baudrillard, *Symbolic Exchange and Death*, trans. Iain Hamilton Grant, intro. Mike Gain (London: Sage Publications, [1976] 1993), 127.

7. See Herbert Marcuse, "The Ideology of Death," in *The Meaning of Death*, ed. H. Feifel (New York: McGraw-Hill, 1959), 64–76, esp. 71; also on Marcuse, see Dollimore, *Death, Desire, and Loss in Western Culture*, esp. 220–27.

8. Ernest Jones strongly advocates reading *Hamlet* as though the very action to which Hamlet objects (Claudius's murder of the father) were a buried desire of the hero's psyche. See Jones, *Hamlet and Oedipus* (Garden City, NY: Doubleday, 1954). Though no psychoanalytic critic, T. S. Eliot arrives at an oddly parallel insight when he concludes that the play altogether lacks an "objective correlative" for Hamlet's disgust with his mother and that, since Gertrude is too insignificant to be worthy of such contempt, the play seems mostly an emanation of its hero's pathology almost as if the pathology were the author's own. ("Hamlet," in *Selected Essays* [New York: Harcourt, 1932], 123). For an essay that efficiently brings the Eliotic and psychoanalytic critique together by suggesting that the figure of the feminine is at the center of Hamlet's pathology, see Jacqueline Rose, "Hamlet—the Mona Lisa of Literature," *Critical Quarterly* 28 (Autumn 1986): 35–49.

9. All references to *Hamlet* and to other plays by Shakespeare are to *The Norton Shakespeare*, ed. Stephen Greenblatt et al. (New York: W. W. Norton, 1997).

10. Cf. Alexander Welsh's explanation of the relative sparsity of critical attention paid to grief and mourning in *Hamlet*. See Welsh, *Hamlet in His Modern Guises* (Princeton: Princeton University Press, 2001), esp. 26–27.

11. Focusing on the many instances of incomplete mourning in *Hamlet*, Lacan directs his attention to the status of ritual in mourning and suggests that what most commonly characterizes mourning in Hamlet is that in each case "the rites have been cut short and performed in secret" ("Desire and the Interpretation of Desire in *Hamlet*," in *Literature and Psychoanalysis: The Question of Reading, Otherwise*, ed. Shoshana Felman. [Baltimore: Johns Hopkins University Press, 1982], 40). Arriving independently at a similar interpretation of maimed rites in the play, Lawrence Danson argues, "The murder of old Hamlet and his reappearance in ghostly form introduce a fatal anomaly that destroys ritual observance and makes the demand for a new ritual that can accommodate it." See *Tragic Alphabet: Shakespeare's Drama of Language* (New Haven: Yale University Press, 1974), 26–27. Cp. also Francis Ferguson, *The Idea of a Theater* (Princeton: Princeton University Press, 1949); Linda Woodbridge and Edward Berry, *True Rites and Maimed Rites: Ritual and Anti-Ritual in Shakespeare and His Age* (Urbana: University of Illinois Press, 1992).

12. See Freud, "Mourning and Melancholia," in *The Standard Edition of the Complete Psychological Works of Sigmund Freud*, ed. and trans. James Strachey et al., 24 vols. (London: Hogarth Press, 1953–74) (hereafter referred to as *SE*), 14:248.

13. Mourning, Freud says, begins as "the reaction to the loss of a loved person," but in melancholia the importance of the person or object recedes from consciousness as dissatisfaction becomes more general, focused less on the particular case of loss and

evolving more from individual pathology or personal lack. In mourning "it is the world which has become poor and empty; in melancholia it is the ego itself" (*SE*, 14:246).

14. Cf. Henry Staten, who traces the intersection of Hamlet's mourning and his erotic loathing, remarking especially upon those moments, such as 2.3.303–8, where Hamlet's obsessiveness about death seems to entail a rejection of organic being. Staten reads Hamlet as symptomatic of a Western cultural propensity for an idealist, transcendental flight from the erotic drives because they necessarily partake of the corruptible body. The purity of mourning Hamlet desires also proves his desire for an exemption from organicity, for a life greater than life forces. Staten, *Eros in Mourning: Homer to Lacan* (Baltimore: Johns Hopkins University Press, 1995), esp. 102–3.

15. The line that Freud in fact cites in his footnote reads, "Use every man after his desert, and who should scape whipping?" (2.2.508–9).

16. Cp. Philip Fisher's recognition that the self-critical tendencies of Hamlet's delay are tied to social complaint and that his strangely passionate nature resists a bogusly progressive society. See Fisher, "Thinking about Killing: Hamlet and the Paths among the Passions," *Raritan* 11, no. 1 (1991): 43–77, 61.

17. See Julia Kristeva, *Black Sun: Depression and Melancholia*, trans. Leon S. Roudiez (New York: Columbia University Press, 1989).

18. With regard to the social meaning in Hamlet's negative praxis, Terry Eagleton speaks of Hamlet's "reluctance or inability to enter the symbolic order" and describes Shakespeare's most famous hero as a transitional figure located between traditional and bourgeois models of subjectivity, who as a result functions as a "negative critique of . . . both these regimes." Eagleton says,

> Hamlet's reluctance or inability to enter the symbolic order, and his revulsion from the sexuality which reproduces it, are in one sense regressive states of being. . . . But this psychological regression is also, paradoxically, a kind of social progressiveness. Hamlet is a radically transitional figure, strung out between a traditional social order to which he is marginal, and a future epoch of achieved bourgeois individualism which will surpass it. But because of this we can glimpse in him a negative critique of the forms of subjectivity typical of *both* these regimes (*William Shakespeare* [New York: Basil Blackwell, 1986], 74)

Though Eagleton reads Hamlet's resistance to his society as a symbolic refusal to participate in either of the two ideological regimes available to him, he fails to credit Hamlet with any significant ethical dissent from the social patterns of injustice to which he is a witness.

19. Kristeva, *Black Sun*, esp. 40–42. In Kristeva's view, the antisymbolic force of melancholia is also the fount of creativity, which is so often produced as a crisis in inherited meanings. Just such a creative dimension of character is apparent in Hamlet, who flits in the mousetrap scene, for instance, between poetic accomplishment of the highest ethical import and a state closer to dementia, reflecting both the spontaneity of mania and quite likely his own prior capacity for joy. The traces of a former *jouissance* figure Hamlet's ethical obligation as more intimately connected with the disrupting force of unpleasure.

20. See Fisher, "Thinking about Killing," 45. Fisher's emotional schematism—studying the movement from mourning to anger, or from the delay that signifies mourning to action—would complement Peter Sacks's reading of *Hamlet*, in contrast to *Titus*

Andronicus, as a play that shows the movement from action to language or anger to grief. See Sacks, *The English Elegy,* esp. 74–82.

21. John Milton, *Complete Poems and Major Prose,* ed. Merritt Y. Hughes (New York: Macmillan, 1957).

22. As one who adheres practically to the dictates of his desires against unnatural idealisms, Claudius anticipates the sexual ethics of psychoanalysis. He associates reason with an acceptance of nature and believes that because Hamlet will not accept the unchangeable logic of experience, his protest is both a "fault to heaven" and "a fault to nature." Much *Hamlet* criticism assumes or infers that Claudius's advice to Hamlet is basically sound: our trust in such language would only be disrupted because the plot ultimately reveals Claudius as a hypocrite disguising his self-interest and criminality in the better form of reason and fairness. I cite G. Wilson Knight as an early, influential example of this position: "[Hamlet's] hope of recovery to the normal state of healthy mental life depended largely on his ability to forget his father, to forgive his mother. Claudius advised him well" (Knight, *The Wheel of Fire: Interpretations of Shakespearian Tragedy with Three New Essays,* 4th ed. [London: Methuen, 1949], 19). For a version of what might be termed the "that one may smile and smile and be a villain" interpretation, or the argument that it is primarily Claudius's hypocrisy that draws his advice into question, see Virgil K. Whitaker, *The Mirror Up to Nature* (San Marino: Huntington Library, 1965).

23. Cf. Danson, *Tragic Alphabet,* who argues that, whereas Hamlet's characteristic mode of speech is fierce punning, Claudius's patterns of speech are largely oxymoronic, as if he were subsumed by rhetorical contradiction.

24. The word *prophetic* is commonly used in Shakespeare to denote the act of predicting the future. Note for example "in her prophetic fury sewed the work" (*Othello,* 3.4.70) or "[Say] why / Upon this blasted heath you stop our way / With such prophetic greeting" (*Macbeth,* 1.3.74–76). This interpretation is further supported by associating *prophetic* with the role of the biblical prophets, who do not so much predict the future as denounce a present course of action or past deed in light of the future consequences to Israel. Indeed the polemic of biblical prophets often centers on an act of substitution whereby Israel has displaced or forgotten God for the sake of worldly objects and affections. Just as the prophet relies for validation upon God's action, so here the ghost's revelation has confirmed Hamlet's prophetic enterprise as one denouncing the evidence of substitution.

25. For an interesting discussion of the range of symbolic and antisymbolic meaning suggested by Hamlet's attire, see James L. Calderwood, *Shakespeare and the Denial of Death* (Amherst: University of Massachusetts Press, 1987), 77–86.

26. For a fuller reading of the problem of patrilinear identity in *Hamlet,* see Theodore Lidz, *Hamlet's Enemy: Madness and Myth in* Hamlet (New York: Basic Books, 1975), esp. 50–54.

27. For an extreme case for Hamlet's distrust of the ghost as indicative of Elizabethan culture's pious overthrowing of revenge, see Eleanor Prosser, *Hamlet and Revenge,* 2nd ed. (Stanford, CA: Stanford University Press, 1971). Robert Ornstein (*The Moral Vision of Jacobean Tragedy* [Madison: University of Wisconsin Press, 1960]) and Helen Gardner (*The Business of Criticism* [Oxford: Oxford University Press, 1959]) argue the reverse hypothesis that the ghost is a reliable indicator of an acceptable code. For more recent accounts of Shakespeare's complex relation to the Elizabethan revenge tragedy, see Peter Mercer, *Hamlet and the Acting of Revenge* (Iowa City: University of

Iowa Press, 1987) and Robert N. Watson, *The Rest is Silence: Death as Annihilation in the English Renaissance* (Berkeley: University of California Press, 1994), esp. 55–102.

28. Cp. Alexander Welsh's argument that the mourning situation is one of the basic scenarios of the revenge tragedy and that revenge is hardly an alternative to mourning, but an apt expression of grief in Elizabethan culture (38–53). See also Gordon Braden, *Renaissance Tragedy and the Senecan Tradition: Anger's Privilege* (New Haven: Yale University Press, 1985).

29. Adam Smith says,

> It is miserable, we think, to be deprived of the light of the sun; to be shut out from life and conversation; to be laid in the cold grave, a prey to corruption and the reptiles of the earth; to be no more thought of in this world, but to be obliterated, in a little time, from the affections, and almost from the memory, of their dearest friends and relations. Surely, we imagine, we can never feel too much for those who have suffered so dreadful a calamity. The tribute of our fellow feeling seems doubly due to them now, when they are in danger of being forgot by every body; and by the vain honours which we pay to their memory, we endeavour, for our own misery, artificially to keep alive our melancholy remembrance of their misfortune. . . . And from thence arises one of the most important principles in human nature, the dread of death, the great poison to the happiness, but the great restraint upon the injustice of mankind, which, while it afflicts and mortifies the individual, guards and protects the society" (*The Theory of Moral Sentiments*, ed. D. D. Raphael and A. L. Macfie [Oxford, UK: Clarendon Press, 1976], 12–13).

30. For a reading of how the ghost's oddly anachronistic status bodes the return of unrecognized political meanings, see Derrida, *Specters of Marx: The State of the Debt, the Work of Mourning, and the New International*, trans. Peggy Kamuf, intro. Bernd Magnus and Stephen Cullenberg (New York: Routledge, 1994).

31. The function of the sepulcher or sarcophagus, which is etymologically a flesh eater or that which digests body, is inverted, so that it now spits up and casts the body out into the world. The metaphor of consumption is part of the ritual center of funerals as well as marriages, so Hamlet's conflation of the two is not merely accidental. For a discussion of the metaphoric significance of eating or feasting as a denial of death, see Calderwood, *Shakespeare and the Denial of Death*, 17–29. Then too the eruption of the corpse challenges the symbolic apparatus that typically suppresses the evidence of death to preserve meaning. For a mode of interpretation that similarly draws out the potential for corpses to subvert symbolic structure, see Kristeva's reading of Holbein's "Dead Christ" in *Black Sun*, 107–38.

32. Roland Mushat Frye notes that incestuous liaisons such as Gertrude's and Claudius's were termed "adultery" in Tudor sermons and theological tracts, a cultural taboo that may have increased the audience's identification with Hamlet and cast both Claudius and Gertrude as villainous. See Frye, *The Renaissance Hamlet: Issues and Responses in 1600* (Princeton: Princeton University Press, 1984), 76–82.

33. In a conversation with the First Player, Hamlet intimates his authorship: "You could for a need study a speech of some dozen or sixteen lines which I would set down and insert in't, could ye not?" (2.2.517–19).

34. See William Kerrigan, *Hamlet's Perfection* (Baltimore: Johns Hopkins University Press, 1994), 34–62.

35. Cp. Welsh, *Hamlet in His Modern Guises*, esp. 60–70. Welsh argues that the murder of Polonius liberates Hamlet from an obsession with the death of his father and proposes that, given the strictures of the revenge code presiding over Hamlet's society, "the killing of Polonius may be justified under the circumstances" (69).

36. René Girard, *A Theater of Envy: William Shakespeare* (New York: Oxford University Press, 1991), 276.

37. Cf. Michael Neill, *Issues of Death: Mortality and Identity in English Renaissance Tragedy* (Oxford, UK: Clarendon, 1997), 217–61.

38. See Ted Hughes, *Tales from Ovid* (New York: Farrar, Straus, Giroux, 1997), 206.

39. She may even be the referent when Hamlet speaks of the ghost as "preaching to stone" (3.4.117).

CHAPTER 3. Lyrical Economy and the Question of Alterity

1. See Aristotle, *Loeb Classical Library* 20: *The Athenian Constitution, The Eudemian Ethics, and On Virtues and Vices*, trans. H. Rackham (Cambridge: Harvard University Press, 1952), 259.

2. See Bernard Williams, "Moral Luck," in *Moral Luck: Philosophical Papers, 1973–1980* (New York: Cambridge University Press, 1981), 20–39; Martha Nussbaum, *The Fragility of Goodness: Luck and Ethics in Greek Tragedy and Philosophy* (New York: Cambridge University Press, 1986).

3. For a discussion of ethical virtues as formulations that enact an idea of self and are motivated by "ethical egoism," see Bernard Williams, "Utilitarianism and Moral Self-Indulgence," in *Moral Luck*, 40–53; Williams, *Ethics and the Limits of Philosophy* (Cambridge: Harvard University Press, 1985), esp. 4–15.

4. For Williams's suspicion of obligatory conceptualizations, see *Ethics and the Limits of Philosophy*, esp. 182–96. For a pointed summation of the Levinasian objection to the Kantian universal law, see Jean-François Lyotard, "Levinas's Logic," trans. I. McLeod, *Face to Face with Levinas*, ed. Richard A. Cohen (Albany: State University of New York Press, 1986).

5. See Emmanuel Levinas, *Otherwise Than Being or Beyond Essence*, trans. Alphonso Lingis (Pittsburgh, PA: Duquesne University Press, [1974] 1998), 121–29, esp. 126.

6. For a critique of Levinas's own implication in metaphysics and of the way in which he may simplify the ontological method for the sake of contrast, see Jacques Derrida's groundbreaking essay, "Violence and Metaphysics," in *Writing and Difference*, trans. Alan Bass (Chicago: University of Chicago Press, 1978).

7. A related line of thought is glimpsed in critics, such as Barbara Hardy, who would attach the power of lyric voice to feeling and argue for the affective intensity of lyric as its peculiar virtue. Barbara Hardy, *The Advantage of Lyric: Essays on Feeling in Poetry* (London: Athlone Press, University of London, 1977).

8. See Alan Liu, *Wordsworth: The Sense of History* (Stanford, CA: Stanford University Press, 1989) and Marc Shell, *The Economy of Literature* (Baltimore: Johns Hopkins University Press, 1978).

9. Theodor Adorno, "On Lyric Poetry and Society," in *Notes to Literature*, vol. 1, ed. Rolf Tiedemann, trans. Shierry Weber Nicholsen (New York: Columbia University Press, [1974] 1991), 37–54, 43.

10. Jonathan Culler, "Changes in the Study of the Lyric," in *Lyric Poetry: Beyond New Criticism*, ed. Chaviva Hosek and Patricia Parker (Ithaca, NY: Cornell University Press, 1985), 38–54.

11. *OED*; s.v., "economy," 1a, 2a, 3.

12. For a discussion of the status of the foreigner in ancient Greek culture, see Julia Kristeva, *Strangers to Ourselves*, trans. Leon S. Roudiez (New York: Columbia University Press, 1991), esp. 41–64; see also John Boardman, *The Greeks Overseas*, 2nd. ed. (New York: Thames & Hudson, 1980).

13. Max Horkheimer and Theodor W. Adorno, *Dialectic of Enlightenment: Philosophical Fragments*, ed. Gunzelin Schmid Noerr and trans. Edmund Jephcott (Stanford, CA: Stanford University Press, [1944, 1947] 2002), 35–62.

14. Homer, *The Odyssey*, trans. and ed. Albert Cook, 2nd ed. (New York: W. W. Norton, 1993).

15. Observing the political and gendered reversal of which I speak here, Ralph Hexter says, "That the simile crosses not only enemy lines but gender lines as well is also significant, but is itself in no way unusual for Homer." Hexter, *A Guide to the Odyssey: A Commentary on the English Translation of Robert Fitzgerald* (New York: Random House, 1993), 119. For a fuller discussion of the method and meaning of Homer's gendered reversals, see Helene Foley, "'Reverse Similes' and Sex Roles in The Odyssey," *Arethusa* 11 (1978): 7–26; Sheila Murnaghan, *Disguise and Recognition in the Odyssey* (Princeton: Princeton University Press, 1987); John J. Winkler, *The Constraints of Desire* (New York: Routledge, 1990), 129–61.

16. Cf. Homer, *Loeb Classical Library: The Odyssey I, Books 1–12*, 2nd ed., English trans., A. T. Murray, revised George E. Dimock (Cambridge: Harvard University Press, 1995). The Loeb offers "clear-toned lyre" in order to capture the emphasis of the participial form of *ligus*, which here qualifies *lyre* and denotes a clear or shrill, indeed even a piercing or clamorous, sound. By letting *piercing* stand unattached to the quality of the sound per se, I mean to emphasize the extent to which Alcinoos has intuited the lyre's shrill sound as having pierced Odysseus with grief.

17. See Northrop Frye, *Anatomy of Criticism* (Princeton: Princeton University Press, 1957); Barbara Herrnstein Smith, *Poetic Closure: A Study of How Poems End* (Chicago: University of Chicago Press, 1968).

18. Ricoeur's discussion of the various aspects of Freudian economy remains the best account. See Paul Ricoeur, *Freud and Philosophy: An Essay on Interpretation*, trans. Denis Savage (New Haven: Yale University Press, 1970), 115–58, 230–80.

19. So efficiently does Sacks read the elegy's "enforced accommodation between the mourning self on the one hand and the very words of grief and fictions of consolation on the other," we might almost forget that his entire hermeneutical method depends upon a transposition of the economics of mourning onto the economy of the lyric. See Sacks, *The English Elegy: Studies in the Genre from Spenser to Yeats* (Baltimore: Johns Hopkins University Press, 1985), 2.

20. For Levinas's most direct discussion of the way in which economic relation presides over the other in a social totality, see "The Ego and Totality," in *Collected Philosophical Papers*, trans. Alphonso Lingis (Boston, MA: Kluwer Academic Publishers, [1987] 1993), 37–39.

21. Spenser, "Astrophel" and "The Doleful Lay of Clorinda," in *The Yale Edition of the Shorter Poems of Edmund Spenser*, ed. William A. Oram et al. (New Haven: Yale University Press, 1989).

22. For a version of this line of argument in relation to Hardy, see Jahan Ramazani, *Poetry of Mourning: The Modern Elegy from Hardy to Heaney* (Chicago: University of Chicago Press, 1994), 33–68.

23. W. David Shaw has suggested that paradox might be the elegy's characteristic mode. See Shaw, *Elegy and Paradox: Testing the Conventions* (Baltimore: Johns Hopkins University Press, 1994), 59–66, 147–79.

24. John Donne, "Holy Sonnet 17," in *The Divine Poems*, 2nd ed., ed. Helen Gardner (Oxford, UK: Clarendon Press, 1978), 14–15.

25. Kenneth Burke, *Counter-statement*, 2nd ed. (Berkeley: University of California Press, [1953] 1968).

26. In contending that his wife has been unfairly seized from him, Donne disguises an underlying premise whereby the poet conceives of his wife as his own property. To the extent that Donne sets up this work of mourning as a struggle over the wife as property and employs the ancient classical conceit of militaristic seizure of property (which included the seizure of wives and daughters), he recalls, for example, the specifically patriarchal grief of the Trojan father Chryses who petitions the Achaians at the opening of *The Iliad* for the return of the daughter Chryseis that Agamemnon has seized from him. See Homer, *The Iliad*, trans. Richmond Lattimore (Chicago: University of Chicago Press, 1951), 1.8–21.

27. The word *in* appears in some modern editions as *on*, following Edmund Gosse's misreading in his publication of this sonnet for the first time (Gosse, *Jacobean Poets* [London: J. Murray, 1894]). The error was first corrected by Roger E. Bennett (*The Complete Poems of John Donne* [Chicago: Packard, 1942]). For an explanation of this textual history that bears out the narrative I have been suggesting, see Gardner, *The Divine Poems*, 79.

28. Arnold Stein, *The House of Death: Messages from the English Renaissance* (Baltimore: Johns Hopkins University Press, 1986), 140.

29. *Ben Jonson*, ed. C. H. Herford et al., 11 vols. (Oxford, UK: Clarendon Press, 1925–63), vol. 8.

30. Jonson, "On My First Daughter," *Ben Jonson*, vol. 8.

31. *The Norton Shakespeare*, ed. Stephen Greenblatt et al. (New York: W. W. Norton, 1997).

32. For arguments about the propensity for renunciation in Dickinson's poetry see, for example, Richard Wilbur, "Sumptuous Destitution," in *Emily Dickinson: A Collection of Critical Essays*, ed. Judith Farr (Upper Saddle River, NJ: Prentice-Hall, 1996), 53–61; Jane Donahue Eberwein, *Dickinson, Strategies of Limitation* (Amherst: University of Massachusetts Press, 1985).

33. This is a quality observed and legitimized by Richard Chase, who argues that the paradoxical "abundance" of Dickinson as a poet turns on the spare quality of her verse and on limitations and various "exclusions of substance and means" in her life. See Chase, *Emily Dickinson* (New York: William Sloane Associates, 1951), 119.

34. This and all subsequent references to Dickinson's poetry are to *The Poems of Emily Dickinson*, ed. R. W. Franklin (Cambridge, MA: Belknap Press, 1998).

35. For an argument about Dickinson's opposition to traditional metaphysical teleology that nevertheless emerges in her own teleological version of poetics, see Shira Wolosky, *Emily Dickinson: A Voice of War* (New Haven: Yale University Press, 1984).

36. Sharon Cameron, *Lyric Time: Dickinson and the Limits of Genre* (Baltimore: Johns Hopkins University Press, 1979), esp. 136–57.

37. For the biographical background of Dickinson's restrictively gendered familial home and extended personal history, see Cynthia Griffin Wolff, *Emily Dickinson* (New York: Knopf, 1986), 163–78.

38. For an exploration of Dickinson's deeply adversarial perception of the relationship between human capability and nature, see Joanna Feit Diehl, *Dickinson and the Romantic Imagination* (Princeton: Princeton University Press, 1981).

39. For an insightful reading of how the rhetoric of secrecy enacts the presumption of privilege, see Frank Kermode, *The Genesis of Secrecy: On the Interpretation of Narrative* (Cambridge: Harvard University Press, 1979).

40. See Horkheimer and Adorno, *Dialectic of Enlightenment*, esp. 43–49.

41. Homer, *The Odyssey*, trans. Robert Fitzgerald (New York: Random House, [1963] 1990).

42. Hexter, *A Guide to The Odyssey*, 283–84.

43. Ibid., 282–85.

44. Honoré de Balzac, *Colonel Chabert*, trans. Carol Cosman (New York: New Directions, 1997).

45. The elliptical syntax of Poem 199 permits at least two grammatical possibilities here in this final stanza. According to the first, the infinitive of line 11 ("To wonder") would be an extension of the turning heads in line 10 and the "itself" of line 12 would be a futuristic, temporally alienated member of the family who wonders about the words to come out of his or her own mouth. In the second reading (which I prefer), the infinitive of line 11 does not continue line 10, but functions in apposition to the infinitive of line 9 ("To think"), so that "myself" of line 11 is a subjective rather than objective pronoun rooted in the present moment of speculation and the "itself" of line 12 becomes the object of its present tense wondering, the self as a future object that will respond unpredictably at that later time.

46. For this sense of the alterity of the future, see Emmanuel Levinas, *Time and the Other*, trans. Richard A. Cohen (Pittsburgh, PA: Duquesne University Press, [1947] 1987).

47. Sacks is surely right (at least from the Freudian viewpoint) to perceive in the artifice of poetry only a more efficient and capable use of the symbolizing work of language. See Sacks, *The English Elegy*, esp. 1–18.

48. See Freud, "Beyond the Pleasure Principle," in *SE*, 18:7–64, esp. 14–17.

49. See Hegel, *Phenomenology of Spirit*, trans. A. V. Miller with analysis and foreword by J. N. Findlay (New York: Oxford University Press, 1977), esp. 256–78.

50. For a helpful interpretation of the different referential levels of "reality" in Freud, see Ricoeur, *Freud and Philosophy*, esp. 261–80, 324–38.

51. Oddly, Freud presumes a coincidence between the thought of the real and its material reality, even as he also supposes that the real world provides the resistance to the psyche's tendency to construct a world it would have preferred. See Freud, "Formulations on the Two Principles of Mental Functioning," in *SE*, 12:218–26, 219.

52. There is only as yet an intimation of that greater disruption of the trauma, which Freud theorizes in *Beyond the Pleasure Principle* (1921) as a psychic function working against the ego's characteristic insistence on its own pleasure. See Freud, *SE*, 18:12–23.

53. See Althusser, "Freud and Lacan," in *Lenin and Philosophy and Other Essays*, trans. Ben Brewster (New York: Monthly Review Press, 1971), 195–219.

54. A similar point is made by Ricoeur when he names the unconscious as the structure and persistent register of disappointment. See Ricoeur, *Freud and Philosophy*, 261–76.

55. What traumatic dreams unfold is a reality that will not conform to the pleasures of self. See Freud, *SE*, 18:12–17.

CHAPTER 4. The Ethical Rhetoric of Anti-Elegy

1. The connotations of "anti-elegy" are implicit throughout *Yeats and the Poetry of Death: Elegy, Self-Elegy, and the Sublime* (New Haven: Yale University Press, 1990), where Jahan Ramazani explores Yeats's introduction of ambivalence and aggression into the elegiac tradition. In an article on Hardy's anti-elegiac poetry, with a special concentration on the epochal elegies for the Victorian era, Ramazani alludes to Romantic and Victorian forebears (specifically, Shelley and Tennyson) who had begun "subverting the restorative work of elegy," but Hardy is viewed as "more critical than they of the recuperative claims of the genre" (133). See Ramazani, "Hardy's Elegies for an Era: 'By the Century's Deathbed,'" *Victorian Poetry* 29, no. 2 (1991): 131–43. In *Poetry of Mourning: The Modern Elegy from Hardy to Heaney* (Chicago: University of Chicago Press, 1994), Ramazani uses the term "anti-elegy" frequently and there acknowledges that Celeste M. Schenck's perception of an anticonsolatory tendency in the "ceremonial poem" and in certain modern poems she calls "anti-elegies" anticipates his own emphasis on nontranscendence and nonconsolation. See Schenck, "When the Moderns Write Elegy: Crane, Kinsella, Nemerov," *Classical and Modern Literature: A Quarterly* 6 (1986): 97–108. Daniel Albright, on the other hand, uses the term in a way that is closer to Ramazani's category of "self-elegy" in his *Yeats and the Poetry of Death*, as the elegist and the elegized sink into mutual oblivion. See Albright, *Lyricality in English Literature* (Lincoln: University of Nebraska Press, 1985), esp. 201–7.

2. In supposing the modern anti-elegiac turn against elegy to be subject to the fragility of the concept "modern," I have also in mind Paul de Man's trenchant critique of the historicist perception that the lyric becomes decreasingly referential as it becomes modern and his crucial point that the lyric's range of and resistance to referentiality are far greater than contemporary estimations (which treat such problems as if they were unique to the lyric's late twentieth-century cultural context) often allow. De Man, "Lyric and Modernity," in *Blindness and Insight: Essays in the Rhetoric of Contemporary Criticism*, 2nd ed., trans. Wlad Godzich (Minneapolis: University of Minnesota Press, [1971] 1983), 166–86. Both Peter Sacks and Ramazani acknowledge the traditional role of what Sacks calls "elegiac questioning" (*The English Elegy: Studies in the Genre from Spenser to Yeats* [Baltimore: Johns Hopkins University Press, 1985]), but perceive a greater anti-elegiac emphasis to such questioning since Thomas Hardy. Sacks's history-of-the-genre approach forbids him from theorizing too radical a break in Hardy, whose use of elegiac features such as repetition, antiphony, apostrophe, interrogation, procession and eclogic division keeps him within the elegiac fold, in the company of the elegists from Virgil and Ovid to Swinburne and Tennyson, he himself recalls. So too Ramazani similarly supposes the inescapability of elegiac tradition when he suggests that modern anti-elegiac protest only strengthens the genre, becoming indeed an efficient means of psychic catharsis as other cultural means of consolation lapse or prove bankrupt. *Poetry of Mourning*, esp. 10–23.

3. Samuel Johnson, "John Milton," in *Lives of the English Poets*, 3 vols., ed. George Birbeck Hill (Oxford: Clarendon Press, 1905), 1:163.

4. By bringing under suspicion the mythic responsibilities of the pastoral world, Milton not only makes Christianity the modern principle of his poem, but extends the force of pastoral by converting it into a figure for his own potential responsibilities. A strategy of contrived retrieval would ironically distinguish Milton from his forebears as well as his contemporaries. Milton's pastoral elegy, with its obvious recuperation of Spenser and a recently bygone era, contrasts sharply with the other elegies in *Iusta Edouardo King*, which, as Ruth Wallerstein points out, tend to emphasize the contemporary preference for either a fusion of Christian piety and epigram or a more worldly account of rationality interacting with wit. Beaumont employs allegory in the cultivation of Christian virtue whereas Brown employs pastoral that emphasizes wit, and the others such as Cleveland and More reveal the influence of Donne and an individualist Christian ethos that rejects the "pagan sympathy of nature" and the neo-Platonism so vital to pastoral elegy. If Milton seems archaic by comparison, refusing to oppose pagan naturalistic feeling to religion, his willingness to use conventions that many of his contemporaries considered outmoded shows him, perhaps paradoxically, to be more confident in the distinctiveness of his modern Christian sensibility. See Wallerstein, *Studies in Seventeenth-Century Poetic* (Madison: University of Wisconsin Press, [1950] 1965), esp. 96–114.

5. John Milton, *Complete Poems and Major Prose*, ed. Merritt Y. Hughes (New York: Macmillan, 1957).

6. See Stanley Fish, "Lycidas: A Poem Finally Anonymous," *Glyph* 8 (1981): 1–18. Extending Fish's reading, I would suggest that Milton's personal crisis, be it vocational or mournful, would find relief in the art of the impersonal by effectively veiling the personal relation to King. Among two fairly recent readings of the poem, Elizabeth Hanson shades us toward the more autobiographical view of Milton's return to pastoral when she suggests that the poem originates "not merely in loss, but in the past failure of the poet's voice to produce a final, abiding consolation," and J. Martin Evans reads the poem as steeped in a vocational crisis. See Elizabeth Hanson, "To Smite Once and Yet Once More: The Transaction of Milton's Lycidas," *Milton Studies* 25 (Pittsburgh, PA: University of Pittsburgh Press, 1989): 69–88, esp. 73, and J. Martin Evans, *The Miltonic Moment* (Lexington: University Press of Kentucky, 1998).

7. Bion, "The Lament for Adonis," in *Loeb Classical Library: The Greek Bucolic Poets*, ed. J. M. Edmonds (Cambridge: Harvard University Press, [1928] 1977), 96–98.

8. Cp. Peter Sacks's argument to the effect that, even though modern elegists take aim against familiar expressions of grief and the elegy's central conventions, "[i]t would be absurd to suggest that these refusals . . . cancel out the survival of the genre" (*The English Elegy*, 306). Sacks argues further that those elegists whose work is most successful will be "those least afraid to repeat the traditional procedures of the genre" (326). Cp. also W. David Shaw, *Elegy and Paradox: Testing the Conventions* (Baltimore: Johns Hopkins University Press, 1994), who speaks of the modern elegy's habit of "qualifying its own momentum" and argues that "instead of being interpreted as mere restraints, as meanings half said or imitated, these breaking points dramatize the way a tactical stumble or ellipsis may turn the breakdown of language, a potential awkwardness or stammer, into a moment of breakthrough instead" (9). What Sacks and Shaw help us see is that the questioning of elegiac convention has always been the imaginary resource for any persuasive extension of our inherited and partially exhausted paradigms of grief.

9. See Martin Buber, *I and Thou*, trans. Ronald Gregor Smith (Charles Scribner's Sons, [1923] 1958), 58.

10. See Harold Bloom, *The Anxiety of Influence* (New York: Oxford University Press, 1973).

11. Samuel Johnson, "Pope," in *Lives of the English Poets*, 3.101.

12. Alexander Pope, *Poetical Works*, ed. Herbert Davis (New York: Oxford University Press, 1966).

13. Emmanuel Levinas, "Martin Buber and the Theory of Knowledge," in *Proper Names*, trans. Michael B. Smith (Stanford, CA: Stanford University Press, 1996), 24.

14. Arguing for the failure of redemption at the end of *King Lear*, Stanley Cavell (*Must We Mean What We Say?: A Book of Essays* [New York: Cambridge University Press, (1969) 1976]) sees the Lear of the final scene, much as I do, as one who is engaged in a "new tactic to win the old game" (296). One substantial difference between Cavell's moral philosophical reading and my own is that Cavell interprets the hero's many failures of recognition as failures in Lear's conception of intimacy, whereas I read intimacy itself—especially the fantasy of intimacy proposed in this final scene—as an extension of the terms of social reciprocity elsewhere in evidence in the play.

15. See, for example, Ramazani's comments on Hardy's self-critical awareness of having profited as a poet from the personal loss he suffered when his wife died. *Poetry of Mourning*, esp. 66–68.

16. I quote here from Earl Wasserman's revised version of his reading of "Adonais" in *Shelley: A Critical Reading* (Baltimore: Johns Hopkins University Press, 1971), esp. 502. See also *The Subtler Language: Critical Readings of Neoclassic and Romantic Poems* (Baltimore: Johns Hopkins University Press, 1959).

17. In much the same vein, Lawrence Lipking observes of Collins's tambeau for Thomson that "Collins seems to anticipate a time when poetry itself shall prove mortal." Lipking, *The Life of the Poet: Beginning and Ending Poetic Careers* (Chicago: University of Chicago Press, 1981), 148. Moschus, "The Lament for Bion," *Loeb Classical Library: The Greek Bucolic Poets*, 9–10.

18. Shelley, "Adonais," in *Shelley's Poetry and Prose*, ed. Donald H. Reiman and Sharon B. Powers (New York: W. W. Norton, 1977), 390. All references to "Adonais" are to this edition.

19. Ross Grieg Woodman, *The Apocalyptic Vision in the Poetry of Shelley* (Toronto: University of Toronto Press, 1964), 169.

20. Byron, *Manfred*, in *Byron*, ed. Jerome J. McGann (New York: Oxford University Press, 1986).

21. Pliny had in a famous note said of the Niobids in Florence, of which the statue of Niobe with her youngest daughter is the center, that no one was sure whether they were sculpted by Praxiteles or Skopas, which, according to R. R. R. Smith, "means of course that it was probably neither" (*Hellenistic Sculpture: A Handbook* [London: Thames & Hudson, 1991], 108). According to Andrew F. Stewart the group traces a debt to Skopas and can be accounted as part of the Skopaic school, but "on both stylistic and chronological grounds attribution to Skopas himself must be ruled out" (*Skopas of Paros* [Park Ridge, NJ: Noyes Press, 1977], 119).

22. *The Letters of Percy Bysshe Shelley*, vol. 2, ed. Frederick L. Jones (Oxford, UK: Clarendon Press, 1964), 186.

23. In the "Defence of Poetry," Shelley calls Homer one of the three sons of light, along with Dante and Milton, and indeed it seems that it is an elegiac Homer Shelley especially loves. Months before writing "Adonais," Shelley wrote to John Gisborne congratulating him on having finished the Iliad: "You must have been astonished at the perpetually increasing magnificence of the last 7 books.—Homer then truly begins to be himself—The battle at the Scamander, the funeral of Patroclus, & the high & solemn close of the whole bloody tale in tenderness & inexpiable sorrow, are wrought in a manner incomparable with any thing of the same kind" (*The Letters of Percy Bysshe Shelley* 2: 250).

24. Homer, *The Iliad*, trans. Richmond Lattimore (Chicago: University of Chicago Press, 1951).

25. For a discussion of the signifying opposition of food and death in Shakespearean tragedy, see James L. Calderwood, *Shakespeare and the Denial of Death* (Amherst: University of Massachusetts Press, 1987), 30–32.

26. See Shelley, "Notes on Sculptures in Rome and Florence," in *The Complete Works of Percy Bysshe Shelley*, vol. 4, ed. Roger Ingpen and Walter E. Peck (New York: Gordian Press, 1965), 331.

27. Nancy Goslee, *Uriel's Eye: Miltonic Stationing and Statuary in Blake, Keats, and Shelley* (University, AL: University of Alabama Press, 1985), 143, 141.

28. Ovid, *Metamorphoses*, trans. Rolfe Humphries (Bloomington: Indiana University Press, 1955), 139.

29. Ted Hughes, *Tales from Ovid* (New York: Farrar, Straus, Giroux, 1997), 208.

30. Translating *mano* loosely as "to wear," Hughes introduces Niobe's all-too-human exhaustion, as if he finds it most pathetic that she can never reach the limit of her grief, the point at which the inconsolability that would preserve the other becomes physically impossible and becomes one last loss, repeating the insult of an original loss.

31. Sacks, reading the metamorphoses in the Pan-Syrinx and Apollo-Daphne stories, sees in Ovid instances of what Freud would come to call the *successful* work of mourning: "Ovid presents a condensed version of this process, a metamorphosis in which the lost object seems to enter or become inscribed in the substitute, in this case the found sign or art" (*The English Elegy*, 6). Still, in the specific stories Sacks reads, substitution emphasizes the mourner's symbolic replacement of a lost or elusive other, and when Apollo dons the laurel Daphne has become or Pan plays the pipes that were Syrinx, we recognize that these substitutions for the other are also containments of otherness. The Niobe story, however, should trouble our confidence in these efficient containments of otherness by offering us a counterparable of contained subjectivity. In the substitution of stone for Niobe, our psychic substitutions, whether they are chosen or chosen for us, are exposed to mockery, since substitution is itself a mockery of both desire and relationship. Though mourning may yet signify the desire for relationship, it is also that which is immediately contained in the Niobe story.

32. Shelley, "Notes on Sculpture in Rome and Florence," 331.

33. Sir Philip Sidney, *Miscellaneous Prose*, ed. Katherine Duncan-Jones and Jan van Dorsten (Oxford, UK: Clarendon Press, 1973), 121.

34. Before Freud ever articulated the substitutive economy implicit in the work of mourning, elegies began to distrust the nature of their work because the substitutions seemed inadequate as a means of sustaining the other's value. See "Mourning and

Melancholia," but also *Beyond the Pleasure Principle*, in *The Standard Edition of the Complete Psychological Works of Sigmund Freud*, trans. James Strachey. 24 vols. (London: Hogarth Press, 1953–74) (hereafter referred to as *SE*).

35. As William Empson has noted with regard to the artifice of such pastoral logic, the allegorized natural world always reverts from its idealization by recalling the real for which it is a substitution and a compensation. See Empson, *Some Versions of Pastoral* (London: Chatto & Windus, 1935), esp. 3–23, 119–45.

36. As Ed Duffy has reminded me, the bark should also allude to the "little boat" of poetry, making the significant subtext the beginning of Dante's *Paradiso*, canto 2. Though I take the "perfidious bark" of "Lycidas" to be the more immediate elegiac precedent, it should be clear from much of my argument here that the Dante allusion would only enhance the degree to which the elegiac protection of Keats has also become about the protection of poetry itself. As Shelley tries to square his poetic calling with his ethical responsibility to the dead, the resulting implication is that all of poetry is herein implicated and in jeopardy.

37. Freud, "Mourning and Melancholia," in *SE*, 14:255. With regard to Shelley's "Adonais," though Keats is immortally protected at the end of the poem, the surviving elegist remains fearfully called by Adonais's radical alterity to the verge of self-negation, to a point where idealization seems merely a screening or denial of the real meaning of the death of another. Sacks clearly acknowledges this risk when he asserts that the "double death" is what must be avoided or at least postponed by the elegy as a work of mourning (*The English Elegy*, 148).

CHAPTER 5. Wishful Reciprocity in Thomas Hardy's *Poems of 1912–13*

1. Defining itself in the face of an impossible relation, the elegy most often seeks, as Peter Sacks has so fully demonstrated, an economic compensation for loss and for the crisis in the other's value posed by his or her absence. See Sacks, *The English Elegy: Studies in the Genre from Spenser to Yeats* (Baltimore: Johns Hopkins University Press, 1985), esp. 4–18.

2. For the move toward impersonalism in Hardy's elegies, see Jahan Ramazani, *Poetry of Mourning: The Modern Elegy from Hardy to Heaney* (Chicago: University of Chicago Press, 1994), esp. 46.

3. For the arguments toward resolution, see Sacks, *The English Elegy*, 237–44; Melanie Sexton, "Phantoms of His Own Figuring: The Movement toward Recovery in Hardy's *Poems of 1912–13*," *Victorian Poetry* 29, no. 3 (1991): 209–26; and Ramazani, *Poetry of Mourning*, 54–61.

4. Esther Schor, *Bearing the Dead: The British Culture of Mourning from the Enlightenment to Victoria* (Princeton: Princeton University Press, 1994), 4. According to Schor, the overt ethical rhetoric in which mourning intersects with constructs of value emerged in the Enlightenment and continued prominently in the Victorian era before lapsing in the twentieth century. Her thesis bears a relation, as do a number of prominent elegy studies, to the work of Philippe Ariès and Ernest Becker. Ariès charts the Enlightenment secularization of death and Becker remarks upon the even more conspicuous twentieth century cultural tendency to "disappear" our dead. See Schor, esp. 19–27, 230–40; see also Ariès, *The Hour of Our Death*, trans. Helen Weaver (New York: Vintage, 1982) and Becker, *The Denial of Death* (New York: Free Press, 1973).

5. Much to this end, Schor makes great use of Adam Smith's economy of sympathy, which begins by focusing on the privileged place a culture gives to its dead as the basis from which to build its constructs of sympathy. See Schor, *Bearing the Dead*, esp. 19–40.

6. Martin Buber, *I and Thou*, trans. Ronald Gregor Smith (New York: Charles Scribner's Sons, 1958), 4. As Buber insists, "where there is a thing there is another thing. Every *It* is bounded by others; *It* exists only through being bounded by others. But when *Thou* is spoken, there is no thing. *Thou* has no bounds" (4).

7. Emmanuel Levinas, "Martin Buber and the Theory of Knowledge," in *Proper Names*, trans. Michael B. Smith (Stanford, CA: Stanford University Press, 1996), 17–35, 26.

8. Martin Buber, *Between Man and Man*, trans. Ronald Gregor Smith (New York: Macmillan, 1948), 168.

9. See Stanley Cavell, *The Claim of Reason: Wittgenstein, Skepticism, Morality, and Tragedy* (New York: Oxford University Press, 1979), esp. 264–73. Qualifying the universalism so often associated with moral philosophy, according to which morality appears to depend upon "its competence to assess *every* action" (269), Cavell suggests that a claim of morality (versus a claim of knowledge) depends upon being able to establish a position such that others can decide whether they are living in the "same moral universe" (268), and that part of the enterprise of defining a position of responsibility necessarily involves defining precisely what positions one takes responsibility for. For Cavell, it is the field of cooperation—of what I have called reciprocity—that legitimizes any claim of morality.

10. Levinas, "Martin Buber and the Theory of Knowledge," 32.

11. Paul Ricoeur, *Oneself as Another*, trans. Kathleen Blamey (Chicago: University of Chicago Press, 1992), 193.

12. William Wordsworth, "Strange Fits of Passion Have I Known," in *The Poetical Works of William Wordsworth*, ed. E. De Selincourt, 2nd ed. (Oxford, UK: Clarendon Press, 1952).

13. Freud, *The Interpretation of Dreams*, in *The Standard Edition of the Complete Psychological Works of Sigmund Freud*, ed. and trans. James Strachey et al., 24 vols. (London: Hogarth Press, 1953–74) (hereafter referred to as *SE*), 5:509.

14. From the child's phrase "Father, don't you see I'm burning?" Freud cleverly deduces that when the boy was still alive he might have said the very words "I'm burning" while sick with fever. Echoing this much of the real child's speech, the dream would then have transposed his words onto the highly emotional context of grief, adding the interrogative form. This reading is perhaps less remarkable as an example of Freud's exhaustive method of accounting for the psychic origins of all the details of a given dream than it is for the analogy it glimpses between the father's guilty protection of the dead child and the vigil he has kept over the sick child.

15. It is of some interest here that when Jacques Lacan interprets Freud's reading of the dream and when Cathy Caruth gathers both of their readings under the rubric of trauma theory, Lacan and Caruth alike retain the force of prophetic announcement that belongs more to the father's dream than to Freud's interpretation of it. Lacan argues that it is through the dream that the father confronts the reality of death and so allows the father's awakening to the preternatural datum of the really burning dead child to be an extraordinary figure for his psychic awakening, an awakening stirred by the noise of the other's voice: "Is there not more reality in this message than in the noise by which the

father also identifies the strange reality of what is happening in the room next door?" See Lacan, "Tuché and Automaton," in *The Four Fundamental Concepts of Psycho-analysis*, ed. Jacques-Alain Miller, trans. Alan Sheridan (New York: W. W. Norton, 1978), 58. Caruth (*Unclaimed Experience: Trauma, Narrative, and History* [Baltimore: Johns Hopkins University Press, 1996]) emphasizes that this necessary awakening figures the father's survival as an "*ethical* relation to the real" (102). With echoes perhaps of Terrence Des Pres and Robert Jay Lifton, Caruth reads the dream as the inscription of the real in a survivor's testimony, so that trauma always carries with it the responsibility to the other's suffering that has been inadequately witnessed.

16. Caruth, *Unclaimed Experience*, 104.

17. Hardy, "The Spell of the Rose," *Poems of 1912–13*, in *The Variorum Edition of the Complete Poems of Thomas Hardy*, ed. James Gibson (London: Macmillan, 1979). All further references to Hardy's poems are to this edition.

18. Sacks ascribes the peculiar insistence of these elegies to the strange intersection they forge between the reality principle's characteristic repetitiveness (in which the mourner repeatedly reminds himself of the fact of death he would prefer not to acknowledge) and the traumatic compulsion to repeat (in which the mourner has been caught unprepared for loss and so finds himself returning over and again to the occasion "trying retrospectively to create the defenses that he had so utterly lacked" (*The English Elegy*, 239).

19. Levinas, *Otherwise than Being or Beyond Essence*, trans. Alphonso Lingis (Pittsburgh, PA: Duquesne University Press, [1974] 1998), 112.

20. For Ricoeur's articulation of the economic give and take of sympathy, see *Oneself as Another*, 191.

21. What I am calling the fantasy of reciprocity here bears a strong relation to what Ramazani sees as the obvious self-interest and self-deception and conflicted ambivalences of Hardy's *Poems of 1912–13*. See Ramazani, *Poetry of Mourning*, 57–67.

22. One might refer here to Foucault's suggestion that the languages of liberal consensus are emanations and reifications of the cultural mechanisms of power, and that even as desire is produced in tension with the evident principle of power in a culture, it is necessarily a symptom of—and as such in complicity with—the institutions upon which it is oppositionally based. See especially Foucault's elaboration of the "repressive hypothesis" in *The History of Sexuality*, vol. 1: *An Introduction*, trans. Robert Hurley (New York: Random House, [1976] 1990), 17–35.

23. Tennyson, "In Memoriam A.H.H.," in *The Poems of Tennyson*, ed. Christopher Ricks, 3 vols., 2nd ed. (Berkeley: University of California Press, 1987), vol. 2. All further references to Tennyson are to this edition.

24. Ramazani remarks upon this figurative pattern whereby Hardy "represents his wife not as a passive victim of circumstance but as an active agent" (*Poetry of Mourning*, 50), but though he recognizes Hardy's tendency to modulate his blaming with self-blame, for Ramazani these accusations are at best de-idealizations of the emotions of mourning: "Never in the canonical tradition of elegy had a poet vented such anger at the dead person for betraying him. . . . [S]he leads him on, abandons him, and even in this way sickens him" (51). This seemingly objective disdain for the other is modified, however, by Hardy's tendency not only to connote the traumatic surprise of Emma's death as if it were the product of an intention, but to read his own figuratively presented intention as a sign of the wife's alterity. Ramazani's reading tends to take Hardy's

descriptions as if they were largely self-justifying characterizations of the wife as a troublesome other, but there is always a highly fictive and figurative aspect to Hardy's characterizations of Emma such that her qualities sometimes stand for the fact of her alterity. For instance, the very attribution of haste to Emma in the opening lines of "The Going" indicates that, rather like Eve fleeing the projective desire of Adam in *Paradise Lost*, Emma's dying is a willed departure, but one that connotes the very possibility of her independence and difference.

25. See David Gewanter, "'Undervoicings of Loss' in Hardy's Elegies to His Wife," *Victorian Poetry* 29, no. 3 (1991): 193–207. Arguing that Hardy's engagement with Emma's voice is everywhere implicit in these elegies and perceiving Emma's beckonings and implicit voice as if they constructed these elegies as "conversation" poems, Gewanter is persuaded that Hardy portrays an independent, willful, and somewhat admirable woman, such as Emma was in real life before her resentments about Hardy's success kicked in and the couple became increasingly estranged.

26. See Emma Hardy, *Some Recollections by Emma Hardy*, ed. Evelyn Hardy and Robert Gittings (New York: Oxford University Press, 1961). The reserve Emma attributes to herself in the early courtship may be read as signifying nothing more than the gap between the events that dictate our desires and the degree to which our desires remain a mystery to ourselves. That there is at least some truth in Emma's reservations may be suggested by her reaction to *Jude the Obscure* and Emma's tendency to read Sue Brideshead as a figure for herself. In that infamous novel of 1895 Hardy presents his heroine (who seems a composite figure of Hardy's erotic frustrations with Emma and Florence Henniker) as a woman who neither knows her own desires well, nor has the strength of her non-conformist convictions. For an account of the biographical influences on Hardy's highly controversial novel, which many readers (including Emma) received as a declaration against marriage, see Michael Millgate, *Thomas Hardy: A Biography* (New York: Oxford University Press, 1985), 335–378.

27. My discussion here follows closely David Gewanter's assessment of the "Some Recollections" manuscript, Dorset County Museum, which shows Hardy's attempts to amend Emma's words. The editors of Emma's memoir followed Hardy's erasure and reported Emma as having written, "At first, though I was greatly interested in him. . . ." Emma Hardy, *Some Recollections*, ed. Evelyn Hardy and Robert Gittings (New York: Oxford University Press, 1961), 56. For Hardy's own solution, see Thomas Hardy and Florence Hardy, *The Life and Work of Thomas Hardy*, ed. Michael Millgate (London: Macmillan, 1984), 73.

28. Critiques of vision as an act of imperialistic or possessive gaze are manifold in contemporary theory. In vision, the self apprehends the other as though the self were capable of gathering, assimilating, or possessing the other's alterity. See Jill Robbins, *Altered Reading: Levinas and Literature* (Chicago: University of Chicago Press, 1999), 23; see also Emmanuel Levinas, *Difficult Freedom: Essays on Judaism*, trans. Seán Hand (Baltimore: Johns Hopkins University Press, [1963] 1990), 8.

29. Gewanter, "Undervoicings of Loss," 197.

30. According to Hardy's intratextual self-allusion—if we read the elegies as a series—this is also a reference to the wishful hypothesis from "The Going" of seeking "time's renewal." If the "time" of the earlier poem is a past state of being and an imagined permanence, the derisive time of the later poem connotes the verbal flow of temporality as an antithesis to conclusive or final conditions.

31. The question "Why, then, latterly did we not speak[?]" ("The Going," 29) would be severely answered in the later poem's suggestion that not only did Emma fail to ask Hardy to speak with her (the rough logic of the first poem), but she did not wish to in the first place. It is just such an uncomfortable insight into the ambivalence informing all attachment that Ramazani sees surfacing in the symptoms of modern elegiac grief and indeed bestowing elegies such as Hardy's (for Hardy is at the front of this modernizing curve) with many of their most forceful descriptions of grief. See Ramazani, *Poetry of Mourning*, esp. 4–6, 29–30, 49–61.

32. Sacks reads Tennyson's achievement of consolation as almost grudgingly achieved through "the slow, accretive structure of the poem," arguing that the poet's reluctant deployment of elegiac typology, though it may have been required by Tennyson's skepticism, also robs his mourning of "energetic, processional drive" so crucial to the elegy (168, 202). It is possible, Sacks worries, that "too much ground has been ceded" to the "counterpressure" of melancholy. See Sacks, *The English Elegy*, 166–203, 202.

33. Williams, "Moral Luck," in *Moral Luck: Philosophical Papers, 1973–1980* (New York: Cambridge University Press, 1981), 28.

34. See Melissa F. Zeiger, *Beyond Consolation: Death, Sexuality, and the Changing Shapes of Elegy* (Ithaca, NY: Cornell University Press, 1997), esp. 43–61. Overall, Zeiger builds from Sacks's deployment of the Freudian work of mourning for reading the elegy's substitutive work in order to suggest that there is a particular sacrificial quality to the gendered patternings of the traditionally *male* elegy, which has often deemed women less worthy as objects for poetic commemoration and, when it does treat them at all, has employed a gendered typology derived from the legacy of the Orpheus and Eurydice story. Explicitly tracing the gendered politics of elegy to the poetics of Orphean mourning, Zeiger suggests that the woman's replacement by poetic voice and vocation is hardly a coincidental, or merely sequential, result of Orpheus's tremendous grief. As Orpheus's song is predicated upon his loss of Eurydice, the contrapuntal theme to this sacrificial idealization is the poet's fear of women, eventually objectified by the actions of the Thracian women. Though the story questions the masculinity of mourning , it also "invents" homosexuality as a play between "heterosexual and homosexual motifs, as well as between misogyny and homophobia" (13). Much of Zeiger's specific reading of Hardy is anticipated by Ramazani, who similarly emphasizes the implicit aggression in Hardy's mourning through which he enacts his desire for control over Emma and her freedom (see e.g., Ramazani, *Poetry of Mourning*, 57, 61).

35. All references to the Latin are from *Loeb Classical Library: Metamorphoses*, trans. Frank Justus Miller, 2 vols., 3rd ed. (Cambridge: Harvard University Press, 1977).

36. In the MS text (the bound-up volume of manuscripts in the Dorset County Museum), line 16 of the poem reads "And think for an instant it's you I see," before Hardy revises the line to read "And think for a breath it is you I see." What the revision loses in temporal precision it more than makes up for in figurative force. In keeping with the likely Ovidian allusion, the "breath" also emphasizes the duration of the vision as if it depended upon the poet's own visceral being. It is almost as if the breath inspires a vision of the other, while at the same time signifying the contrary pull of life on the poet—his exhalation functioning also as a release of the other. For an explanation of Hardy's manuscript variants, see James Gibson's introduction to *The Variorum Edition of the Complete Poems of Thomas Hardy*, ed. James Gibson (London: Macmillan, 1979), esp. xix-xxxii, 338.

37. For Kierkegaard, complete immersion in the "new," which the pure aestheticism of a figure such as his Seducer in *Either / Or* partly represents, is tantamount to meaningless existence. Yet since Kierkegaard as firmly renounces recollection as a merely stultifying response to the existential demand for meaning, he proposes repetition as a "recollecting forward" that approximates the continuousness of life itself. See *Fear and Trembling / Repetition*, ed. and trans. Howard V. Hong and Edna H. Hong (Princeton: Princeton University Press, 1983), 132–33.

38. For a concise statement of the way in which the poet's self-regard operates as a constitutive ambiguity of the elegiac text, see Eric Smith, *By Mourning Tongues: Studies in English Elegy* (Totowa, NJ: Rowan & Littlefield, 1977), 9–13.

39. Ovid, *Metamorphoses*, trans. Rolfe Humphries (Bloomington: Indiana University Press, 1955), 236.

40. This relates to Cavell's basic point that the claim of reason must be qualified and interpreted by the claims others exercise upon us in our understanding of reason. See *The Claim of Reason: Wittgenstein, Skepticism, Morality, and Tragedy* (New York: Oxford University Press, 1979), esp. 247–73, 329–93.

41. Cf. Ramazani's reading of this same confession of a profit motive in grief. Hardy, Ramazani argues, "represses the dangerous knowledge that he is reaping poetic 'profit' from her loss: she has always known that his work was useless. Having denied that he is making gain of her death, he can move once more from mystification to knowledge: he admits she is beyond his multifarious poetic responses to her" (*Poetry of Mourning*, 54).

42. In elegies from earlier in his career, such as "He Never Expected Much" and "The Darkling Thrush," Hardy attacks his own expectations to cultivate a detached and impersonal stance, so it is all the more striking that these later elegies involve moments such as this in which the poet inverts his more defensive stance. Sacks rather openly admires "the unsheltered nature of these poems, their openness to loss" (*The English Elegy*, 235). Ramazani decides that Hardy's apparent vulnerability consistently "gives rise to his invulnerable detachment" (*Poetry of Mourning*, 34) and that the quality of achieved indifference in these later elegies seems largely an extension of Hardy's earlier defensive stance against expectation and vulnerability. See also Ramazani, "Hardy's Elegies for an Era: 'By the Century's Deathbed,'" *Victorian Poetry* 29, no. 2 (1991): 131–43.

CHAPTER 6. The Bad Conscience of American Holocaust Elegy

1. "A Camp in the Prussian Forest" first appeared in *Nation* 162 (June 22, 1946): 756; it was also included in Randall Jarrell's *Losses* (New York: Harcourt, Brace, 1948). All future references to Jarrell's poems are to Randall Jarrell, *The Complete Poems* (New York: Farrar, Straus, & Giroux, 1969).

2. See Jarrell, "These Are Not Psalms," *Commentary* 1 (Nov. 1945): 88–90; "Changes of Attitude and Rhetoric in Auden's Poetry," *Southern Review* 7 (Autumn 1941): 326–49; "Freud to Paul: The Stages of Auden's Ideology," *Partisan Review* 12 (Fall 1945): 437–57.

3. "The Refugees" first appeared in *Partisan Review* 7 (Jan.-Feb. 1940): 20–21; the poem was reprinted in the *New York Times Book Review*, Nov. 1, 1942, 8. It was included in Randall Jarrell, *Blood for a Stranger* (New York: Harcourt, Brace, 1942).

4. Not insignificantly, it was during the second half of the decade of the 1940s that Jarrell, after initially having disdained the poetry of Robert Frost, began to come round to the "popular" American poet, distinguishing in a 1947 review essay between the pub-

lic Frost and Frost as "he really is," a poet who was not yet understood for the subtlety and severity of his vision. Though, in this review of Frost, Jarrell places a greater mimetic burden on the writing of poetry—a burden far greater than any that had been taken up by the modernists—he did not mean that poetry should cease to demand much of its readers. See Jarrell, "To the Laodiceans," in *No Other Book: Selected Essays*, ed. and intro. Brad Leithauser (New York: Harper Collins, 1999), 19–41, 20.

5. See W. S. Graham, "Jarrell's 'Losses': A Controversy," *Poetry* 72 (1948): 302–7, 303.

6. Adorno, "On Lyric Poetry and Society," in *Notes to Literature*, vol. 1, trans. Shierry Weber Nicholsen (New York: Columbia University Press, [1974] 1991).

7. The link between a quasi-scientific use of abstraction and the desire for accessibility is by no means obvious, but seems to depend upon a peculiar relation between abstraction and collectivity, as if to speak in generalizing terms were to render a logical transparency to social forces and thus a greater degree of accessibility to a reader who was relatively uninitiated in the study of her own society. In general, this problem of initiation looms large in Auden's poetry, and his penchant for technical, abstract language may seem at times to be only a more elaborate version of his habit of writing poetry for an inner circle. For a discussion of the way in which the Mortmere circle Auden formed with friends at Cambridge University (including Edward Upward and Christopher Isherwood) fostered a habit of writing for a privileged audience that survives even in his ostensibly public poetry, see Frederick Buell, *W. H. Auden as a Social Poet* (Ithaca, NY: Cornell University Press, 1973), 22–27, 33–76.

8. Jarrell could never quite abide the politics or aesthetics of friends and mentors such as Allen Tate and Robert Penn Warren, who were in the midst of establishing the orthodoxy of New Criticism with its ruling principle that a poem ought to be a purely self-expressive icon of its own language. Perceiving the implication of Tate and Warren and their company in reactionary Southern agrarian politics as well as in Eliot's aesthetic obscurity, Jarrell insisted on going his own direction as poet and critic. See William H. Pritchard, *Randall Jarrell: A Literary Life* (New York: Farrar, Straus, Giroux, 1990), 64–87.

9. For an account of this incident and the negative repercussions it had for the friendship of Allen Tate and Jarrell (since Tate had decided that Jarrell was ungrateful), see Pritchard, 66–81.

10. Harriet Beecher Stowe, *Uncle Tom's Cabin*, ed. Elizabeth Ammons (New York: W. W. Norton, 1994), 43–44.

11. Jane Tompkins, *Sensational Designs: The Cultural Work of American Fiction, 1750–1860* (New York: Oxford University Press, 1985).

12. Emmanuel Levinas, "Uniqueness," in *Entre Nous: On Thinking-of-the-Other*, trans. Michael B. Smith and Barbara Harshav (New York: Columbia University Press, [1991] 1998), 189–96, 192.

13. Walter Lippman, *An Inquiry into the Principles of the Good Society* (Boston, MA: Little, Brown, 1937) and Lippman, *U.S. Foreign Policy: Shield of the Republic* (Boston, MA: Little, Brown, 1943); Dorothy Thompson, *Refugees: Anarchy or Organization?* (New York: Random House, 1938).

14. See Eisenhower's recollections in his memoir of what he saw and why he made immediate efforts to document these scenes of atrocity. Dwight D. Eisenhower, *Crusade in Europe* (New York: Doubleday, 1948), 408–9.

15. See Jeffrey Shandler, *While America Watches: Televising the Holocaust* (New York: Oxford University Press, 1999), 6.

16. James Agee's remarks must be understood in the context of his larger argument for a policy that did not punish the German nation too severely for its war crimes, since Agee felt that this had been the Allies' mistake in World War I. See Agee, "Films," *Nation* 160, no. 2 (1945): 342; "Films," *Nation* 160, no. 20 (1945): 579. As Shandler also observes, the images presented in the newsreels consistently "reflect an agenda to depict Nazi atrocities at their most thorough, extensive, and graphic"—which is to say they are images "entirely appropriate to the demands of wartime propaganda" (170).

17. There is certainly, as Shandler argues, an element of naïveté in presuming that photographic images speak for themselves, as if their meaning were not also "a product of the sensibilities of the modern age" (*While America Watches*, 9). Invoking Susan Sontag's oft cited account of first encountering photographs of the camps, Shandler recalls, for instance, her claim that her life could almost be divided into the time before and the time after she saw these photographs, but also reminds us that in the same essay Sontag insisted that photographs cannot create a moral position; they might only reinforce or help build one. See Shandler, 8–9; Susan Sontag, *On Photography* (New York: Doubleday, 1973), 19–20.

18. See, for just a few examples, "Nazi Prison Cruelty Film to Be Shown Tomorrow," *New York Times*, Apr. 25, 1945, 3; "Nazi Atrocity Films Real Shockers but U.S. Audiences Take It; Some Cuts," *Variety*, May 9, 1945, 6, 18; "Horror Pictures," *Motion Picture Herald* 159, no. 5 (1945): 8.

19. "The Death of the Ball Turret Gunner" first appeared in *Partisan Review* 12 (Winter 1945): 60; it was twice reprinted in anthologies in 1945, but was never included in Jarrell's books until *The Complete Poems* (1969). It was not anthologized again until after the Vietnam War, but from 1973 to 1980 it was reprinted fourteen times.

20. For an excellent study of the conceptual characteristics of the Nazis' self-styled "language rules" (*Sprachregelungen*), see Berel Lang, *Act and Idea in the Nazi Genocide* (Chicago: University of Chicago Press, 1990), 81–102.

21. That Jarrell was in fact experimenting with the rhythms of the folk ballad is apparent from his poem "Oh, My Name It is Sam Hall" (1946), which employs ballad stanzas to observe three American prisoners accompanied by a military policeman at a training base in Arizona and concludes with MPs starting to sing the old Irish folksong the poem is named after. The exploration of folk mythology is also apparent in a poem such as "The Märchen" (1946).

22. Thus, for example, according to Milton's pastoral logic the natural world that corroborates the poet's grief is conspicuously better than the historical world for which it is partly analogous, since if the poem's angry and digressive diatribe against the clergy in lines 103–31 teaches us anything it is that the pastoral machinery has been adopted in order to sustain an elegiac wishfulness and to indict the implicit ethical failure of those who survive Lycidas and remember him poorly. Of course as Milton elaborates his pathetic fallacy and imagines a pastoral scene forever tainted by his sudden loss ("As killing as the Canker to the Rose. . . . Such, Lycidas, thy loss to Shepherd's ear," 45–49), the demise of pastoral vision connotes Lycidas's death as if it were the consequence of a prior failure in the poem's pastoral, mythic apparatus ("Where were ye Nymphs when the remorseless deep / Clos'd o'er the head of your lov'd *Lycidas?*" 50–51). Still, it is less significant here that Milton has used the pastoral apparatus to refer allegorically to the historical occasion of his elegy—that is, to Edward King's death at sea—than it is that history has been introduced, much as it is through Saint Peter's excessive and digressive

diatribe against the clergy, as an accusation against or violation of the pastoral machinery. The flaw in the compensatory logic of the poem's pastoral system gives persuasive, if not yet fully anti-elegiac, force to Milton's grief.

23. The critique of pastoral was voiced most famously by William Empson in *Some Versions of Pastoral* (London: Chatto & Windus, 1935), and Edmund Wilson's suspicion of Romanticism resembles Empson's in associating the Romantic cult of the land with pastoral ideology. For a fuller discussion of the long history intertwining pastoral with its diverse and often tacit ideologies, see Annabel Patterson, *Pastoral and Ideology: Virgil to Valéry* (Berkeley: University of California Press, 1987). For a discussion of Wilson's rather vexed relation to Romanticism, see "Wilson's Romanticism," in Wilson, *Centennial Reflections*, ed. Lewis M. Dabney (Princeton: Princeton University Press, 1997). The contemporary skepticism of pastoral as a device to elude or circumvent history was honed further by the Romantic New Historicist critics, perhaps most famously by Alan Liu, who at one point punningly refers to the "vegetable 'tropics'" of the Wordsworthian eye, tracing the "need for imagery" to the strongly, even perhaps necessarily revisionist propensities of aesthetic perception. See Liu, *Wordsworth: The Sense of History* (Stanford: Stanford University Press, 1989), 315.

24. Jarrell's suspicion of Romanticism also informed his critique of modernism and his attempt to define his own poetic praxis as a break with the school of Eliot and modernism, which he interpreted in a 1940 essay, "A Note on Poetry," as "essentially, an extension of romanticism" or "what romantic poetry wishes or finds it necessary to become" (*No Other Book*, 85). Yet Auden was by no means a unitary signifier of Romantic habits, and in "The End of the Line" (1942) Jarrell cited Auden as the "most novel and successful reaction against modernist romanticism." We ought to make a distinction, then, between Jarrell's critique of the literary tradition of Romanticism as it extends into modernism, which is characterized by an experiment in subjectivity and cognitive difficulty that seems to Jarrell to have exhausted itself, and his critique of the implicit folkish politics of Auden, which cannot be innocent of the emergent fascistic tendency in the European politics of his time.

25. I use the term "moral indigestion" here as an implicit revaluation of Nietzsche's famous suggestion in section 3.16 of *On the Genealogy of Morals* that the "strong and well-constituted man digests his experiences (his deeds and misdeeds included) as he digests his meals, even when he has to swallow some tough morsels. If he cannot get over an experience and have done with it, this kind of indigestion is as much physiological as is the other—and often in fact merely a consequence of the other" (*On the Genealogy of Morals*, in Friedrich Nietzsche, *On the Genealogy of Morals*, trans. Walter Kaufmann and R. J. Hollingdale, and *Ecce Homo*, trans. and ed. Walter Kaufmann [1967; repr., New York: Random House, 1989], 129. For the account of Eichmann's witness of what Denise Levertov figures as the indigestive earth, see Hannah Arendt, *Eichmann in Jerusalem: A Report on the Banality of Evil* (New York: Penguin, [1963] 1964), 89.

26. Denise Levertov, *Poems, 1960–1967* (New York: New Directions, 1983).

27. Lanzmann, *Shoah: An Oral History of the Holocaust (The Complete Text of the Film)*, preface Simone de Beauvoir (New York: Pantheon Books, 1985).

28. Jill Robbins reads this scene as central to Levinas's articulation of the subject who faces responsibility. See Robbins, *Altered Reading: Levinas and Literature* (Chicago: University of Chicago Press, 1999), 63–72.

29. For a discussion of the American prosecutors' occasional use of sensationalist evidence and their tendency to treat the Nazis' crimes against humanity as atavistic in nature, see Lawrence Douglas, "The Shrunken Head of Buchenwald: Icons of Atrocity at Nuremberg," *Representations* 63 (Summer 1998): 39–64.

30. I am grateful to Amelia Zurcher for her suggestion that this odd conjunction of "quenchless laughter" and violent death at the end of *The Odyssey* (trans. and ed. Albert Cook, 2nd ed. [1967; repr., New York: W. W. Norton, 1993], 20.345–58) might well be an antecedent for such modern examples of anti-elegiac laughter as we observe in Virginia Woolf or William Faulkner, as also here in Randall Jarrell.

31. See *The Diary of Virginia Woolf* 2: 300–301, and also *A Writer's Diary.*, ed. Leonard Woolf (London: Hogarth Press, 1959), 224. In one example, laughter substitutes for the seeming intention of tears and might be imagined as childish nervousness about the appropriate response. In a second, she again recalls the inappropriate laughter: "Remember turning aside at mother's bed, when she was dead, and Stella took us in, to laugh, secretly, at the nurse crying. She's pretending, I said, aged 13, and was afraid I was not feeling enough." Taking his cue from Woolf's sense that in writing *To the Lighthouse* she had "explained" the emotion for her mother and so "laid it to rest," Mark Spilka argues that such incidents are characteristic of Woolf's flawed mode of grief, that Woolf expresses the "need to grieve, and through Lily Briscoe (to whom she gives no psychic history) she tried to meet it bravely enough for most human purposes, in her own belated way—the way of therapeutic elegy—with all the main chords muted." See Spilka, *Virginia Woolf's Quarrel with Grieving* (Lincoln: University of Nebraska Press, 1980), 81.

32. Alfred Kazin, *Starting Out in the Thirties* (Boston, MA: Little, Brown, 1965), 166.

CHAPTER 7. The Holocaust She Walks In

1. With regard to the two ratios of pity I have suggested, a Nietzschean reading would suggest that pity cooperates with and reifies moral institutions of bad conscience, which in turn veil the respective parties' implication in social relations of power, but also that our moral sensibility advances a mythical alignment of the mourner with a system containing her own interests and the interests of the one who is lamented. See section 3.14 of *On the Genealogy of Morals* in Friedrich Nietzsche, *On the Genealogy of Morals*, trans. Walter Kaufmann and R. J. Hollingdale, and *Ecce Homo*, trans. and ed. Walter Kaufmann (New York: Random House, 1989), 121–25.

2. Nietzsche describes the "bad conscience" as evolving from the weaker party's guilty feeling of indebtedness. See *On the Genealogy of Morals*, 2.14–2.20, 81–91. Levinas uses the phrase with frequency in his later writings, offering a revaluation according to which the bad conscience traces ethics as a dissent in advance from intentionality and from the ordinary properties of moral knowledge. For Levinas's most concise discussion of the bad conscience, see the essays "Nonintentional Consciousness" and "From the One to the Other: Transcendence and Time," in *Entre Nous: On Thinking-of-the-Other*, trans. Michael B. Smith and Barbara Harshav (New York: Columbia University Press, 1998), esp. 127–32 and 140–44.

3. M. L. Rosenthal, "Poets of the Dangerous Way," *Spectator*, March 19, 1965, 367; Stephen Spender, "Warnings from the Grave," *New Republic*, June 18, 1966, 23, 25–26.

4. George Steiner's 1965 essay "Dying Is an Art" was the first to bring a heightened sensitivity about the Holocaust to bear directly on an aesthetic judgment of Plath's

achievement. Made uneasy by the peculiar connotations of Plath's Holocaust conscious-ness, Steiner speculated as to whether in fact only someone not directly involved in these events could "focus on them rationally and imaginatively." Steiner, "Dying Is an Art," reprinted in *Language and Silence: Essays on Language, Literature, and the Inhuman* (New York: Atheneum, 1967), 295–302, 301. Later, in a 1969 essay on "Daddy" written for the *Cambridge Review*, Steiner wondered, "Do any of us have license to locate our personal disasters, raw as they may be, in Auschwitz?"—his questioning of the poetry seeming to presume, even more than before, a single answer. Steiner, "In Extremis," *Cambridge Review* 90, no. 2187 (1969): 247–49, 248.

5. Irving Howe, "The Plath Celebration: A Partial Dissent," *The Critical Point: On Literature and Culture* (New York: Horizon Press, 1973), 158–69, 166.

6. See Alvin H. Rosenfeld, *A Double Dying: Reflections on Holocaust Literature* (Bloom-ington: Indiana University Press, 1980), 176, 178. Rosenfeld—who following Lawrence Langer (*The Holocaust and Literary Imagination* [New Haven: Yale University Press, 1975]) and alongside Sidra Ezrahi (*By Words Alone: The Holocaust in Literature* [Chicago: University of Chicago Press, 1980]) helped define the parameters for critical study of Holocaust literature—takes Plath as the central example of a tendency among certain contemporary poets to employ the ghettoes and camps as a "public reference not for the pain of history but for private pain" (174–75). Also in 1980 Edward Alexander ("Stealing the Holocaust," *Midstream* 26 [Nov. 1980]: 47–51) coined his phrase "stealing the Holo-caust," referring to the cultural tendency to use the Holocaust as a comparative ground in order to express the gravity of issues and experiences other than the Holocaust that one really wished to address.

7. A. Alvarez, *The Savage God: A Study of Suicide* (New York: Random House, 1972), 3–41, 38.

8. When Alvarez speaks further on of Plath and other authors as symptomatic of the "awareness of a ubiquitous, arbitrary death . . . central to our experience of the twenti-eth century" (243), he briefly cites and seems significantly influenced by psychoanalytic critic Robert Jay Lifton (*Death in Life: The Survivor of Hiroshima* [New York: Random House, 1968]). Lifton employed psychoanalytic interpretation to elucidate the inevitable changes in the modern, socially determined psyche once all humankind had become wit-ness, near or far, to instances of mass death permanently altering the scale of death and suffering in the mind of the twentieth-century citizen. Survivors of Hiroshima or con-centration camps were, in this sense, representatively global citizens.

9. Alvarez himself, though he emphasizes the coincidence of Plath's final burst of cre-ativity and her descent into pathological depression, finds it unfortunate that her death was so quickly employed as a mythic explanation for her art—"the poet as a sacrificial vic-tim" (*The Savage God*, 434). Recent studies of Plath sharing my suspicion that the em-phasis given to Plath as a representative confessional poet functions as a distorting influ-ence on the ways in which she has been read include Christina Britzolakis, *Sylvia Plath and the Theatre of Mourning* (Oxford: Clarendon Press, 1999); Lynda K. Bundtzen, *The Other Ariel* (Amherst: University of Massachusetts Press, 2001); and Amy Hungerford, *The Holocaust of Texts: Genocide, Literature, and Personification* (Chicago: University of Chicago Press, 2003).

10. Plath and Sexton had studied together under Lowell, and Sexton's poem "My Friend, My Friend" (which contains the line, "I think it would be better to be a Jew") has often been read as an antecedent to "Daddy." See Heather Cam, " 'Daddy': Sylvia Plath's

Debt to Anne Sexton," in *Sexton: Selected Criticism*, ed. Diana Hume George (Urbana: University of Illinois Press, 1988), 223–26; Jacqueline Rose, *The Haunting of Sylvia Plath* (Cambridge: Harvard University Press, 1991), esp. 217–20.

11. Steiner, "Dying Is an Art," 299, 296. The perception of Plath as a confessional poet was largely determined by the way in which her posthumous collection was presented to the public. In selecting and arranging the British and American editions of *Ariel* (which differed only in the inclusion of three extra poems in the American edition, but each of which departed significantly from the collection Plath had planned to publish as *Ariel and Other Poems*), Ted Hughes ended the collection with poems that had been written close to the time of her death and thus seemed to make the death obsession of the collection the ultimate confessional utterance. When Plath's former teacher Robert Lowell was asked to write a foreword to the collection, he predictably focused on the courage of these poems in speaking from and for real life. In 1967 M. L. Rosenthal, who had reviewed the British edition of *Ariel* in 1965, would cite poems by Lowell and Plath ("Lady Lazarus" was the example from Plath) as representative examples of confessional poetry. Rosenthal, *The New Poets: American and British Poetry Since World War II* (New York: Oxford University Press, 1967); see also Rosenthal, "Sylvia Plath and Confessional Poetry," in *The Art of Sylvia Plath: A Symposium*, ed. Charles Newman (Bloomington: Indiana University Press, 1970), 69–76.

12. This line of reading Plath, as Steiner foresaw, was immediately overdetermined by her death by suicide, which seemed to rest—to borrow the words of Irving Feldman— "like a seal on these confessional poems, affirming the authenticity of their gestures by their eruption into life itself and drawing its own meaning from them." Feldman, "The Religion of One," *Book Week*, June 19, 1966, 3.

13. This claim is easily associated with what critics, approaching the poetry from a variety of angles, call the Plath "myth." Janet Malcolm borrows the term (with skeptical reserve) from Olwyn Hughes, who refers cynically to the cultural mythology by which Plath had become a martyred everywoman and Ted Hughes the villain of her tragic history (*The Silent Woman: Sylvia Plath and Ted Hughes* [New York: Random House, 1994], esp. 24–31). It is worth noting that Hughes played his own part in crafting the myth of his dead wife since his arrangement of the poems was guided by his reading of Plath as a poet who in the final months of her life finally found her true voice by becoming, in a sense, a martyr to her poetry. As Lynda K. Bundtzen argues, Hughes's view emerges implicitly in Judith Kroll's 1976 book on Plath, the only such book (before the controversial biography by Anne Stevenson) to have been endorsed by Hughes as executor of the Plath estate. Kroll, *Chapters in a Mythology: The Poetry of Sylvia Plath* (New York: Harper & Row, 1976), 42; Bundtzen, 29–32.

14. James E. Young, *Writing and Rewriting the Holocaust: Narrative and the Consequences of Interpretation* (Bloomington: Indiana University Press, 1988), 118.

15. A. Alvarez, "Literature of the Holocaust," *Commentary* (Nov. 1964): 64.

16. Young argues that the "massive suffering of the Jews becomes appropriate as a trope for the poet's pain precisely because it was also an agent of it" (126). This is a rather ingenious reformulation of Alvarez's estimation of Plath's sincerity—that she had not meant to kill herself, but her poetry was nevertheless representative of all modern victims. For Young, it is quite the other way around: it is the personal pain that signifies the authenticity of Plath's use of the Holocaust, rather than any representational claim made by the poetry itself.

17. "[N]o poet," Susan Gubar maintains, "has been more scathingly critical of the figure of prosopopoeia than Sylvia Plath" (Gubar, "Prosopopoeia and Holocaust Poetry in English: Sylvia Plath and Her Contemporaries," *Yale Journal of Criticism* 14, no. 1 [2001]: 191–215, 203). On Plath's "Getting There," a poem that does indeed employ prosopopoeia, Gubar is quite persuasive, but I think she may overextend the figure in perceiving it to be explicitly at work in Plath's other Holocaust poems.

18. All references to Plath's poetry are to the 1981 authoritative edition: Sylvia Plath, *The Collected Poems*, ed. Ted Hughes (New York: Harper & Row, 1981).

19. Plath here treats what has come to be known as the "soap rumor"—the idea that the Nazis harvested the fat of their Jewish victims and rendered it into soap (and sometimes candles)—as an apparently established fact, and indeed this historically unreliable charge against the Nazis has had a long life in popular lore, among certain segments of the survivor community, and also in American literature, including an early appearance in Randall Jarrell's "A Camp in the Prussian Forest" (1946). No evidence has ever been produced to prove this particular atrocity story (the United States Holocaust Memorial Museum even ran tests in the 1990s on German-produced wartime bars of soap). Raul Hilberg, perhaps the most prominent of Holocaust historians in America, has suggested that this particular atrocity story (against many that proved to be true) is indeed mere rumor. See Hilberg, *The Destruction of the European Jews*, revised and definitive ed., 3 vols. (New York: Holmes & Meier, [1961] 1985), esp. 520–21, 737–38.

20. See Jarrell, "A Camp in the Prussian Forest." For examples from Jewish poets employing the same image, we might turn to Jacob Glatstein's poems "Smoke" and "Cloud-Jew," the first of which opens with the lines: "Through crematorium chimneys / a Jew curls toward the God of his fathers"; or we might think of Paul Celan's poem "Tabernacle Window," based on one of Chagall's ironically sacralizing representations of atrocity, in which the poet refers to "the Hovering Ones, the / Humans-and-Jews, / the Cloud Crowd [*das Volk-vom-Gewölk*]" (5–7). Glatstein, *Selected Poems of Yankev Glatshteyn*, ed. and trans. Richard J. Fein (Jewish Publication Society, 1987), repr. in *Art from the Ashes: A Holocaust Anthology*, ed. Lawrence L. Langer (New York: Oxford University Press, 1995) and Celan, *Selected Poems and Prose of Paul Celan*, trans. John Felstiner (New York: W. W. Norton, 2001), 196–99.

21. Cp. Christina Britzolakis, who argues that Plath's complex engagement with an array of modern and modernist poetic precursors from Baudelaire and Lawrence to Eliot and Yeats centers especially on the woman's body as the site of a poetic and cultural mastering of nature. Drawing this literary historical narrative into an at least parallel relation to an Enlightenment narrative that progresses beyond barbarity and nature, Britzolakis observes Plath's resistance to myths of regenerative violence and Enlightenment rationality (as the site of Western imperialistic violence) partly through the figure of the *mater dolorosa*, of which the persona of "Mary's Song" is one characteristic example. See Britzolakis, *Sylvia Plath and the Theatre of Mourning*, esp. 177–78.

22. As Ted Hughes observed in his notes to the 1981 *The Collected Poems*, one of the final typescripts of "Mary's Song" shows the phrase "the cicatrix of Poland" crossed out and replaced in Plath's handwriting by "scoured Poland." Even if the revision does represent the poet's final preference, it is hard to say whether the latter phrase should be read as interchangeable with the typed phrase that Hughes preserved. Notice, however, that according to the handwritten phrase "scoured Poland," the adjectival quality of "scoured"—while strictly referring to the sense in which Poland has been scoured for its

Jews—still makes it seem as though the adjective offered a qualitative estimation of Poland itself. See Sylvia Plath, *The Collected Poems*, 294.

23. Indeed, as Richard Allen Blessing has remarked, Plath is deeply implicated in the language of commercial advertising, having served the poems up at times as parodic renderings of advertising techniques and promoted herself as poet-product. Blessing, "The Shape of the Psyche: Vision and Technique in the Late Poems of Sylvia Plath," in *Sylvia Plath: New Views on the Poetry*, ed. Gary Lane (Baltimore: Johns Hopkins University Press, 1979), 57–73, esp. 68.

24. I have in mind here especially the hermeneutic elaborated by René Girard. See esp. *Violence and the Sacred*, trans. Patrick Gregory (Baltimore: Johns Hopkins University Press, [1972] 1977), according to which the genealogy of sacred myth traces—even as it simultaneously veils—foundational socially constructive acts of collective violence.

25. T. S. Eliot, "The Wasteland," in *The Complete Poems and Plays*, 1909–1950 (New York: Harcourt, Brace, & World, 1971).

26. Cp. again Britzolakis, who reads Plath's allusion to the famous battle of the Hellenic world as a revision of modernist topoi employed by Yeats and Eliot alike (in "The Statues" and "Geronition," respectively). According to Britzolakis, Yeats and Eliot each read the battle as symbolic of the European defeat of "Asiatic formlessness," a formlessness that is figuratively and mythically feminine, so that Plath's revision would imply what Julia Kristeva calls "women's time" as a resistance to heroic, masculine chronologies most typically marked by battles (*Sylvia Plath and the Theatre of Mourning*, 211–12).

27. The "grave in the air" *(ein Grab in den Lüften)* is quickly answered in Celan's poem by the "grave in the ground" *(ein Grab in der Erde)* that the prisoners are ordered to dig, not only as if this antiphonal fulfillment were an inevitability emptying their transcendent hopes but as if history were emptying the elegy of its ordinary devices such as the consolatory apotheosization. In much the same vein, when Plath characterizes the incandescent flames of the crematoria as having "glowed like heavens," she refuses to grant transcendence the separation between secular reference and greater meaning upon which it depends.

28. The Eichmann trial is commonly credited with bringing the term *Holocaust* into broader public consciousness as the name for Nazi genocide. See, for instance, Jeffrey Shandler, *While America Watches: Televising the Holocaust* (New York: Oxford University Press, 1999), 83–132; Peter Novick, *The Holocaust in American Life* (Boston, MA: Houghton Mifflin, 1999), 127–45. Among Plath's more severe critics, there is an unstated consensus based itself on a loosely anachronistic supposition—that the cultural memory of the Holocaust had already been defined in terms that were susceptible to violation. As the earliest of the critical voices, Steiner is perhaps the most forgiving, in part because he saw from his place in history that Plath was one of the writers "in no way implicated in the actual holocaust, who have done most to counter the general inclination to forget the death camps" (301). By the time Leon Wieseltier, echoing aspects of both Steiner's and Howe's argument, offered in a 1976 book review of a Holocaust work by Dorothy Rabinowicz yet another condemnation of Plath's imaginative trespasses, the parameters of Holocaust memory had been more clearly defined. With the historical study and cultural memory of the Holocaust on the rise in America, Wieseltier stood on firmer cultural ground when he accused Plath of having failed to recognize the incommensurability of these events with her personal experience and

asserted that "[f]amiliarity with the hellish subject must be earned, not presupposed." See Wieseltier, "In a Universe of Ghosts," *New York Review of Books*, Nov. 25, 1976, 20–23, esp. 20.

29. In previous poems such as "Song for a Revolutionary Love" and "Insolent Storm Strikes at the Skull," Plath had employed *holocaust* without any intended reference to the Nazi genocide, exploiting the term as a reference to a consuming violence in which the sacrificial object and intent have become so confused as to bewilder the original biblical redemptive meaning. As Jacqueline Rose observes, Plath's prior uses of *holocaust* along the lines of its biblical connotation reveal an ambivalence of identification—pertaining specifically to the subject-positions of victim versus aggressor—that also characterizes Plath's broader use of Holocaust imagery (*The Haunting of Sylvia Plath*, 210). In this instance just cited from "Mary's Song," however, there seems to be little of the ambivalence of which Rose speaks.

30. Citing Marjorie Perloff's lament that Plath's poetry lacks the Eliotic aesthetic virtue of the "objective correlative," Rose suggests that what most critics of Plath's Holocaust language hold in common is a preference for a testimonial, non-metaphoric mode of speech and, according to Rose's psychoanalytic hermeneutic, a facile and impossibly literal rendering of the human psyche. Perloff, "The Two Ariels: The (Re)Making of the Sylvia Plath Canon," in *Poems in Their Place: The Intertextuality and Order of Poetic Collections*, ed. Neil Fraistat (Chapel Hill: University of North Carolina Press, 1986), 308–33; Rose, *The Haunting of Sylvia Plath*, esp. 205–7.

31. Presumably, psychoanalysis must argue—although Rose herself avoids this treacherous ground—that the criminal self-rationalizations of the Nazis exemplify a collective performance, reified by an entire cultural system, of the elaborate veiling of personal motivation and a self's constitutively aggressive instincts. Yet this is not Rose's interest: she is concerned with the contemporary memory of history and the attitude a subject assumes—be she the child of the survivor, the child of a Nazi, or an ordinary citizen imaginatively implicated in each of these imaginative positions—in taking up the difficult past. Among those who employ the psychoanalytic method in studying the Holocaust, from Saul Friedländer to Dominick LaCapra, there is a like concern with what history means as an act of transmission, sometimes outweighing what it means as a complex of actions and motivations internal to a moment in time. See LaCapra, *Representing the Holocaust: History, Theory, Trauma* (Ithaca, NY: Cornell University Press, 1994); Friedländer, *Memory, History, and the Extermination of the Jews of Europe* (Bloomington: Indiana University Press, 1993).

32. See Betty Friedan, *The Feminine Mystique* (New York: W. W. Norton, 1963).

33. The letter is from Oct. 21, 1962. See Sylvia Plath, *Letters Home: Correspondence, 1950–1963*, ed. Aurelia Schober Plath (New York: Harper & Row, 1975), 473.

34. See Èlie Cohen, *Human Behavior in the Concentration Camp*, trans. M. H. Braaksma (New York: W. W. Norton, 1953); Bruno Bettelheim, *The Informed Heart* (Glencoe, IL: Free Press, 1960).

35. Hungerford, *The Holocaust of Texts*, esp. 30–39.

36. Jahan Ramazani suggests that although her language for grief is crudely and frankly aggressive, Plath is not at all an atypical mourner, but perhaps a prototypically modern mourner. Jahan Ramazani, *Poetry of Mourning: The Modern Elegy From Hardy to Heaney* (Chicago: University of Chicago Press, 1994), 263–85.

37. See section 2:14–20 in Nietzsche, *On the Genealogy of Morals*, 81–91.

38. Again, Jacqueline Rose's reading of "Daddy" partly anticipates my own. When Rose contextualizes Plath's troubled imaginative relation to the Holocaust by citing a character from a Jean Stafford novel who speculates about a German father who might have "gone back to Würzburg" and "become a Nazi," she comes close to the ethical core of the problem, but then shies away from it by making Plath's similar use of the father as an imaginary Nazi a figure for the ambivalences governing ordinary identification with the father and paternal law. Rose, *The Haunting of Sylvia Plath*, 229.

39. Jean Améry, *At the Mind's Limits: Contemplations by a Survivor on Auschwitz and Its Realities*, trans. Sidney Rosenfeld and Stella P. Rosenfeld (Bloomington: Indiana University Press, 1980), 68.

40. Améry is troubled by a letter to the editor in a 1948 newspaper warning Americans not to "act so big around here" because "Germany will become great and powerful again" and by the rapid fulfillment of that prophecy, as also by an encounter with an ordinary German who, after inquiring whether Améry is an "Israelite," suggests that the "German people bear no grudge against the Jewish people" (66–67).

41. Sylvia Plath, *The Bell Jar* (New York: Harper & Row, 1971), 36.

42. At the very least, Plath suggests, a speaker of German would want to be vigilant about de-Nazifying the German tongue, making sure to avoid any idiom traceable to the Nazi language rules. Her imaginative abhorrence of German—or at least the abhorrence she attributes to her stand-in speakers—suggests the nexus between language and history articulated by Berel Lang. Arguing against poststructuralist views of language that conceive of language as an ahistorical or transhistorical medium separate from its objects, Lang has insisted upon reading the history of language as reflective of its social and political context and therefore implicated in the uses to which language is put. As soon as one conceives of discourse as a means of agency, Lang contends, some understanding of origin and purpose must be associated with meaning. Thus the linguistic developments coinciding with and presiding over the Nazi genocide "would disclose features resembling those of the process of genocide itself" (Beryl Lang, *Act and Idea in the Nazi Genocide* [Chicago: University of Chicago Press, 1990], 81–102, 83). If for Plath the German tongue seems forever "barbed" by atrocity, for Lang the Nazi language rules reveal something of the historical intentions of the agents and come to characterize language itself in a new figurative capacity—what Lang chooses to call the figure of the lie. For the newly coined German words of Nazism (Lang concentrates especially on the term *Endlösung*) seem more insidious than ordinary euphemisms, more deliberately irreferential in relation to the history of which they spoke without speaking, and they demand of us that we call language itself to account for its historical function.

Index